# American Civilization

*American Civilization* is a comprehensive introduction to contemporary American life. It covers the key dimensions of American society including geography and the environment, immigration and minorities, government and politics, foreign policy, the legal system, the economy, social services, education, religion, the media and the arts.

This fourth edition has been thoroughly revised and includes many updated diagrams, tables, figures and illustrations, as well as coverage of the George W. Bush presidency, the 2004 elections, the manifold effects of the 9/11 terrorist attacks, the Iraq Gulf War, and the war on terrorism. *American Civilization*:

- covers all core American Studies topics at introductory level
- contains essential historical background for American Studies students at the start of the twenty-first century
- analyzes gender, class and race, and America's cosmopolitan population
- has useful photographs, diagrams, questions, terms for discussion and suggestions for websites for further research.

*American Civilization* is a vital introduction to the crucial and complex identities of America.

**Daivd Mauk** is Senior Lecturer in North American Area Studies at the University of Oslo and is also the author of *The Colony that Rose from the Sea: Norwegian Maritime Migration and Community in Brooklyn*.

**John Oakland** is Senior Lecturer in English at the Norwegian University of Science and Technology and the author of *British Civilization* (now in its 5th edition), *Contemporary Britain* and *British Civilization: A Student's Dictionary* (now in its 2nd edition).

For supplementary exercises, questions and tutor guidance, go to www.routledge. com/textbooks/0415358310.

# American Civilization

## An introduction

Fourth edition

**David Mauk and John Oakland**

Routledge
Taylor & Francis Group

LONDON AND NEW YORK

First published in 1995
by Routledge
2 Park Square, Milton Park, Abingdon, Oxon OX14 4RN

Simultaneously published in the USA and Canada
by Routledge
270 Madison Ave, New York, NY 10016

Second edition published in 1997
Third edition published in 2002
Reprinted 2004
Fourth edition published in 2005

*Routledge is an imprint of the Taylor & Francis Group*

© 1995, 1997, 2002, 2005 David Mauk and John Oakland

Typeset in Berling and Futura by Keystroke, Jacaranda Lodge, Wolverhampton
Printed and bound in Great Britain by TJ International Ltd, Padstow, Cornwall

*British Library Cataloguing in Publication Data*
A catalogue record for this book is available from the British Library

*Library of Congress Cataloging in Publication Data*
Mauk, David, 1945–
    American civilization : an introduction / David Mauk and John Oakland.— 4th ed.
        p. cm.
    Includes bibliographical references and index.
    1. United States—Civilization. 2. United States—Civilization—
    Study and teaching—Foreign countries. I. Oakland, John. II. Title.
    E169.1.M45 2005
    973.931—dc22

                                                                    2005000589

ISBN 0–415–35830–2 (hbk)
ISBN 0–415–35831–0 (pbk)

# Contents

# Plates

# Figures

# Tables

# Preface and acknowledgements

This book deals mainly with central structural features of American (US) society, such as politics and government, the law, the economy, social services, the media, education and religion. Chapters on the country and the people are also included in order to emphasize the geographical and human diversity of US civilization. Each chapter attempts to assess the attitudes of Americans to the social and cultural structures in which they live and operate.

Methodologically, the book combines descriptive and analytical approaches within a historical context. Each chapter has its own historical perspectives and provides information on debates and recent developments in the USA. The book is intended to allow students to organize their own responses to American society and to encourage discussion. Essay and term exercises at the end of each chapter can be adequately approached from material contained in the text. Further information may be found in relevant web sites and a recommended dictionary for terms is Alicia Duchak (1999) *A–Z of Modern America*, London: Routledge.

A book of this type is indebted for many of its ideas, facts and statistics to a range of reference sources, which cannot all be mentioned here, but to which general acknowledgement is made (see also 'Further reading' in each chapter). Particular thanks are due to public-opinion poll sources, such as Gallup, Harris, Polling Report, the Roper Center, CNN, *USA Today*, *Fox News*, CBS, NBC, ABC, *Newsweek*, *Time*, the *New York Times*, *Los Angeles Times* and the *Washington Post*.

# Chronology of significant dates in American history

| | |
|---|---|
| 20,000–12,000 BC | Asians and Mediterranean peoples migrate to the Americas |
| c.3000–2600 | Mayan civilization flourishes in Central America |
| c.AD 350–1250 | Anasazi build pueblo 'apartment' complexes in the American south-west |
| 1001 | Vikings establish 'Vinland' settlement in Newfoundland |
| 1050–1250 | Mississippian culture dominates the mid-western and south-eastern United States |
| 1300s | Aztec civilization rises in Mexico |
| 1492 | Columbus comes ashore in the Bahama Islands |
| 1492–1542 | European explorers visit and map parts of the Americas |
| 1497 | Europeans begin fishing in the Great Banks off the east coast of North America |
| 1519–21 | Hernán Cortéz invades and conquers Mexico |
| 1518–1620 | Smallpox and other European diseases decimate Native Americans |
| 1607 | Jameston, Virginia settlement established |
| 1619 | First African workers arrive in Virginia |
| 1622 | Native Americans and Virginians wage war |
| 1620–30 | Pilgrims and then Puritans found New England colonies |
| 1637 | Native Americans and Puritans wage war |
| 1624–81 | New Amsterdam (New York), Maryland, New Sweden, Carolina, New Jersey and Pennsylvania are founded |
| 1636, 1647 | Harvard College and then public schools start in Massachusetts |
| 1680–1776 | The first wave of non-English immigrants arrive in the North American colonies |
| 1732 | Georgia, the last of the thirteen English colonies, is founded |

| | |
|---|---|
| 1730s–1740s | Religious ferment reaches a peak during the first Great Awakening |
| 1757 | New Yorkers riot against British policies |
| 1770 | British troops fire on Boston protestors |
| 1775, 1776 | The American Revolution begins; the Declaration of Independence |
| 1783 | The Treaty of Paris recognizes the independence of the United States and grants it the territory south of Canada to the Mississippi River |
| 1787 | A strong federal government under the US Constitution replaces the loose league of states under the Articles of Confederation |
| 1789 | George Washington takes office as President; federalists and anti-federalists compete in Congress |
| 1792 | The New York Stock Exchange opens |
| 1803 | The Louisiana Purchase from France adds a huge slice of the continent's mid-section to the USA; the US Supreme Court claims the power to declare laws unconstitutional |
| 1808 | Congress outlaws the import of African slaves |
| 1810 | New York passes Philadelphia in population at third US census |
| 1808–13 | Shawnee leaders Tecumseh and the Prophet organize the eastern tribes to resist US expansion beyond the Appalachians |
| 1812–15 | The USA wins no major battle in the war with Britain on American soil |
| 1815–25 | Industrialization starts in the New England and mid-Atlantic states |
| 1820s–1840s | A religious revival sweeps across the frontier in the second Great Awakening; social and utopian reform movements spread |
| 1820s–1880s | About 16 million Europeans and smaller numbers of Asians and Latinos immigrate in the second wave |
| 1825 | Opening the Erie Canal secures the economic power of the east |
| 1831–8 | Native Americans removed from the south along the Trail of Tears to 'Indian Territory' in Oklahoma |
| 1830s | The Democratic Party emerges and competes with the Whigs |
| 1845–8 | Conflict and war with Mexico; annexation of Texas, California and the south-west |
| 1848 | The first women's rights convention at Seneca Falls, New York |
| 1850s | Anti-foreign 'nativist', abolitionist and pro-slavery movements dominate US politics; the Republican Party emerges |
| 1861–5 | Civil War rages over slavery and states' rights |
| 1862 | The Homestead Act grants land to people who live on and farm it for five years, spurring massive settlement of the inland west |
| 1865–75 | Constitutional amendments and a civil-rights act are passed to secure the citizenship and rights of former slaves |
| 1877 | Reconstruction of the south ends; southern race laws progressively deny African Americans rights in the 1880s and 1890s |
| 1869, 1882–3 | Trans-continental railroads completed |

| | |
|---|---|
| 1890 | The 'battle' of Wounded Knee ends centuries of open warfare against Native Americans; the US census bureau announces the 'closing of the frontier' |
| 1890–1930 | About 45 million 'third-wave' immigrants arrive, mostly from southern and eastern Europe but also from Asia, Canada, Latin America and 'old' immigrant countries |
| 1898 | Anti-imperialist debate in Congress; the Spanish–American–Cuban–Filipino War |
| 1890–1920 | Progressive Era reforms in social institutions, politics and government |
| 1917–18 | America fights with the Allies in the First World War |
| 1919 | The first tabloid newspaper, the New York *Daily News*, appears |
| 1919–33 | Prohibition of alcoholic beverages is the law under the Eighteenth Amendment to the Constitution (repealed by the Twenty-First Amendment) |
| 1920 | Women win the right to vote through the Nineteenth Amendment |
| 1921 | The Red Scare and general restriction of immigration start |
| 1929 | The Wall Street Crash signals the start of the Great Depression; the size of the House of Representatives is set at 435 |
| 1920s–1940s | Hollywood's classic period of film production |
| 1920s–1970s | Progressively more of the Bill of Rights applies to state law and cases |
| 1932 | Franklin D. Roosevelt is elected President and implements the New Deal to bring the USA out of the Great Depression |
| 1937 | The Supreme Court accepts New Deal powers of federal government |
| 1939 | Commercial television introduced at the World's Fair in New York City |
| 1941 | On 7 December Japan bombs the Pearl Harbor naval base in Hawaii, and the USA enters the Second World War |
| 1946 | The post-war baby boom begins |
| 1947 | The National Security Act transforms American government for the Cold War; the Truman Doctrine sets path of US foreign policy |
| 1950–3 | McCarthy era 'Red scare' and Korean War |
| 1954 | Racial desegregation begins with the US Supreme Court *Brown* decision |
| 1955 | The American Federation of Labor (AFL) and the Congress of Industrial Organizations (CIO) combine |
| 1958 | The National Defense Education Act funds scientific competition with the USSR |
| 1953–74 | US involvement and war in Vietnam; massive protests at home and abroad against the war in the 1960s; African Americans, Native Americans, Latinos, women and gay Americans fight for civil rights |
| 1963 | President John F. Kennedy is assassinated; Lyndon B. Johnson assumes the presidency |
| 1960s | Great Society and War on Poverty social reforms; the high point of the youth 'counter culture' and of religious ecumenism in the USA |
| 1964 | The Civil Rights Act outlaws discrimination in housing and jobs |

| | |
|---|---|
| 1965 | The Voting Rights Act protects voter registration, especially in the south; the Elementary and Secondary Education Act provides massive funding for education reform |
| 1966–2004 | In the continuing fourth wave of immigration, over 33 million people arrive, most from Latin America and Asia, but also from the former USSR, Africa and the Middle East |
| 1968 | Martin Luther King, Jr. and Robert Kennedy assassinated; 168 cities erupt in race riots |
| 1970 | More Americans live in suburbs than in cities or rural areas |
| 1972 | Nixon's 'new federalism' begins the return of power to the states |
| 1973 | *Roe* v. *Wade* decision legalizes limited abortion rights for women |
| 1974 | President Nixon resigns as a result of the Watergate scandal |
| 1981 | AIDS first identified in the USA |
| 1970s–1980s | The rise of Christian fundamentalism and conservative religious political activity |
| 1986–8 | Mikhail Gorbachev and Ronald Reagan cooperate to bring the end of the Cold War; the Iran–Contras scandal casts a shadow over the second Reagan administration; George H. W. Bush wins the presidency |
| 1991 | The USA leads the Persian Gulf War to drive Iraq out of Kuwait |
| 1993–2001 | President Clinton presides over the longest economic boom in US history |
| 1996 | Devolution of policy-making power to the states occurs through the Welfare Reform Act |
| 1999 | Congress impeaches but does not convict President Clinton |
| 2000 | George W. Bush wins the presidential election after a five to four divided decision of the US Supreme Court stops Florida vote recounts and calls for uniform vote-counting procedures |
| 2001 | The No Child Left Behind Act sets in action the most far-reaching national educational reform since the 1960s; the World Trade Center is destroyed and the Pentagon is attacked by terrorists; the USA initiates a war on terrorism in Afghanistan and globally |
| 2002 | The Help America Vote Act passed to standardize voting procedures within states; USA Patriot Act and the authorization of the Department of Homeland Security transform American government for the War on Terrorism |
| 2003 | The US-led coalition of the willing invades and occupies Iraq |
| 2004 | No weapons of mass destruction found in Iraq; George W. Bush wins a second term as President and the Republicans secure larger majorities in both houses of Congress. |

# Chapter 1

# The American context

- Ethnic culture
- Political-legal culture
- Economic culture
- Americanness and national identity
- Social and institutional change
- American attitudes to US society
- *Exercises*
- *Further reading*
- *Web sites*

Many images have been, and are, associated with the USA. People inside and outside the country have varied, and often conflicting, views about it. Some of these perspectives are based on observable and quantifiable facts. Others may be conditioned by ideology and rhetoric.

American self-images sometimes betray an exalted and isolationist view of the nation's claimed 'exceptionalism' (a unique mission in the world, difference from other countries, idealistic values, high aspirations and belief in its own destiny). But, historically and at present, there have been divided opinions in the USA itself about the country's ideals, values, institutions, political policies, sense of purpose and national identity. American society remains split politically, economically and socially to varying degrees, although there are also substantial unifying forces at work. Opinion polls suggest that, under the impetus of national and international events, Americans, like other peoples, swing between periods of idealism/positivism and cynicism/dissatisfaction about their country. However, periods of doubt and conflict, such as those during the two world wars (1914–18 and 1939–45), the 1930s Great Depression, the 1945–89 Cold War, the 1950s–1960s civil-rights campaigns, the 1960s–1975 Vietnam War and the 2003–4 Iraq War, have often resulted in adaptation and renewal.

Some non-American (but traditionally pro-US) opinion laments what is seen as a recent decline in historic American values and the great republican ideals of the USA, which acted as a beacon to the rest of the world. Other more extreme views are frequently driven by anger, prejudice, envy, ignorance or bias towards other systems. For example, some current US foreign policies, stemming from America's position as the world's only superpower, are forcefully criticized by both its enemies and some of its supposed allies. This has been evident since the 11 September 2001 attacks on New York and Washington (9/11) after which the US Administration sought to protect its domestic and global interests, declared its opposition to terrorism and initiated coalition military action in Afghanistan and Iraq.

In order to understand the contemporary USA and appreciate how it has developed historically, some conditioning factors need to be emphasized. Among these are:

■ the treatment of Native Americans and other minority ethnic groups over time;

■ the early colonial settlement of the country by Europeans from the late fifteenth century and the establishment of specific social values and structures;

**PLATE 1.1** Terrorist attack on World Trade Center, New York, 11 September 2001. The South Tower, attacked by the first plane, is burning; the second plane heads for the North Tower. (*Rex Features*)

- the War for Independence from Britain (1775–83);
- the westward expansion of the new nation;
- the effects of large-scale immigration into the country, especially in the nineteenth and twentieth centuries;
- the Civil War to end slavery and southern-state secession from the Union (1861–5);
- the vaunted principles of the nation (like human dignity and rights to freedom, justice and opportunity) contained in the Declaration of Independence (1776) and the US Constitution (1787);
- associated ideologies of egalitarianism, individualism and utopianism;
- the later development of corporate capitalism with its management and business philosophies;
- increasing government regulation and the growth of an overarching bureaucracy that have arguably undermined individual autonomy;
- American attitudes towards the rest of the world, particularly during the two world wars and the Cold War period;
- the development of the USA as a dominant economic, military and cultural force since the nineteenth century;

■ current arguments as to whether the USA is the prime driver of contemporary globalization (interdependent economic, political and cultural forces) or whether America itself is also subject to globalizing forces beyond its control.

These historical features have created three major cultures in the USA, which may conflict with each other and operate on levels of idealism and pragmatism. The first is an ethnic culture centred on Native-American civilizations, European colonial settlement, African-American slavery and immigration movements, which reflects the society's human diversity. The second is a political-legal culture based on individualism, constitutionalism and respect for the law. It tries to unite the people under ideal versions of 'Americanness', such as egalitarianism, morality and patriotism, which should be reflected in political and legal institutions. The third is an economic and consumer culture driven by corporate and individual competition which encourages profit and the consumption of goods and services. Most aspects of US society are directly or indirectly conditioned by these major cultures. However, a considerable number of people (such as youth groupings, political extremists, radical fringes and an underclass of disadvantaged, unequal individuals) may be alienated from them.

Since American independence in 1776, these elements have created what has been seen as a unique, 300-year-old national and cultural identity in the USA. The difficulty lies in determining what this may actually be in practice. Some critics argue that, at a time of profound transformation, the nation is in danger of losing its traditional foundations and is suffering from a crisis of self-image. Others maintain that, on the basis of information in the 2000 census, a sense of American nationalism and unity is in fact growing and becoming stronger.

## Ethnic culture

In terms of ethnic culture (see Chapters 2, 3 and 4), US colonial settlement was largely composed of British arrivals, who shared the land with existing Native-American communities and other Europeans. Until 1776, over half of the population came from the British Isles. These people assimilated other early European settlers into a white, mainly Anglo-American, Protestant dominant culture. They were responsible for promoting many of the new nation's political, social, constitutional and religious institutions, which produced a mainstream American identity and set of values whose impact is still felt. Their political principles were based on democracy, grass-roots sovereignty (independence of the people) and scepticism about government. Their social values were conditioned by a belief in individualism, the work ethic (working hard in this life to be rewarded here and in the next) and the rule of law (respect for and acceptance of legal rules applicable to all individuals).

After the colonial settler period and American independence from Britain, north-western Europe supplied over two-thirds of episodic US immigration for most of the nineteenth century. There were also many Asian immigrants (particularly Chinese) during this time. At the end of that century there was a shift towards newcomers from southern and eastern Europe. Much of this later immigration was neither Anglo nor Protestant, and it significantly altered the demographic composition of the USA. Despite increasing immigration restrictions, the twentieth century saw a great variety of other nationalities from all over the world immigrating to the USA. In the 1980s, 1990s and early twenty-first century, the largest groups of immigrants have come from Asia, South and Central America and the Caribbean. Today, the largest minority immigrant population is Latino. Its increasing presence is found in southern states such as Florida, Texas, New Mexico and California, as well as in the big cities of New York and Los Angeles and in smaller towns throughout the country, for example, in the mid-west. In total, some 60 million immigrants have entered the USA between 1820 and 2000.

The effects of early colonial settlement, the importation of African slaves and later immigration on US culture have been substantial, in terms of both the figures involved and the high number of very different groups with origins worldwide. This background of colonial settlement, large-scale immigration, slavery and Native-American experiences is different in size and scope from that of other nations, arguably defines American history as special and provides the USA with a distinct, ethnically based identity. There is therefore some truth in the frequent assertion that America is a nation of immigrants (and the descendants of immigrants). Other critics argue, however, that the heart of the USA lies in the original European settlers, that Anglo-Protestant culture is still central to American national identity, and that the country remains a fundamentally Protestant society with its large number of mainstream and evangelical Protestant churches. These features continue to influence social, economic and political life.

Immigrants have considerably affected public life at different times in US history. But they have also experienced difficulties of integration into the existing society due to language problems or differences in cultural practices. There have been conflicts and racial tensions between settled groups and successive waves of immigrants which have sometimes erupted into violence. These factors reveal an intolerant nativism (discrimination towards newcomers by the existing population) and racism in many areas of American life, frequently in institutionalized form, which have continued to the present. Ethnic diversity has brought advantages and disadvantages, but it has also reduced the dominance of the original Anglo-American Protestant culture, which had to take account of a growing social pluralism. However, it is argued that the USA has historically managed to integrate its immigrants successfully into the existing society, and newcomers have generally adapted to American life.

On the other hand, many diverse ethnic groups have had to both coexist and struggle for individual expression. Today, they must somehow live together in spite of tensions between them, and there is always the possibility of serious political and social instability. In some cases, this may amount to rejection of immigrants by indigenous Americans, or rejection of Americanization by some immigrant groups. Critics continue to debate whether these conflicts (arising out of social pluralism) and the problems of assimilation or integration by new groups should be seen as distinctively American or whether they are also applicable in varying degrees to other nations that have diverse populations.

## Political-legal culture

The second major American culture lies in the political-legal arena (see Chapters 5, 6 and 8). Its nature has been largely shaped by

- the central place of law and the Constitution in American life;
- the restrictions that the Constitution places upon politics;
- the fact that many Americans believe in minimal government, especially at the federal level;
- the need to produce consensual (widely agreed) national politics.

The Constitution has to be interpreted by the judiciary (particularly the US Supreme Court in Washington, DC), and the governmental system of checks and balances sometimes results in stalemate. But these features do help to solidify the society, and idealized versions of 'America' constructed through its political institutions (both federal and state) and a general respect for the law can minimize conflict.

These features of political-legal culture also illustrate the degree of abstraction that is involved in defining 'the USA' and 'Americanness'. The notion of what constitutes 'America' has had to be revised over time and reflects the tension between a materialistic practical reality, with its restrictions, and an idealistic abstract hope. Racial or ethnic differences have demonstrably presented the greatest barriers to national unity, and race and immigration continue to be concerns. Consequently, it is often argued that the American political-legal system consists of both hard-nosed manipulation of group and ideological interests and exaggerated rhetoric to promote a common ideal.

US society has had to deal with the tensions resulting from ethnic diversity following centuries of immigration. Responses to pluralism have often resulted in consensus politics based on political and judicial compromise. US politics are not normally therefore considered to be as polarized or radical as in other nations, although public-opinion polls have historically suggested an underlying 60 per cent support for Democrat Party policies and 40 per cent for the Republican

Party. In 2004, this became more polarized on many issues, including 50 per cent support for both political parties. Differences between them for dealing with majority and minority rights, the economy, education, religion and social issues continue to play a central, and sometimes divisive, role in American society. Polarization includes support and opposition across party lines on issues such as abortion.

American politics often tend to be more concerned with local, special and regional or state interests than national matters, reflecting the federal nature of US government. Politicians in Washington, DC promote their own constituency legislation as a response to local and regional pressures (including ethnic and minority matters). Such concerns, as well as national issues, often persuade American voters to vote simultaneously for political representatives from different political parties. A drawback to political participation has been the low turnout of voters for many types of recent elections in the USA (except for the 2004 presidential election). Some critics argue that this suggests a significant alienation from the political process and a feeling that power is in the hands of an elite political establishment that does not consider the concerns of ordinary voters (see 'American Attitudes to US society', pp. 14–17).

## Economic culture

The third major culture comprises the economic system and its associated consumerism (see Chapter 9). The US economic and social cultures are both materialistic/practical and idealistic/abstract. A competitive economic philo-sophy, which is supposed to deliver a range of consumer goods and services demanded by the market, is connected to a belief in individualism. Americans historically have had to fight for their own personal economic and social survival, a process which can also give rise to exploitation of others, excesses and a Darwinian 'survival of the fittest' mentality. The competitive nature of American life arguably contributes to disparities of wealth, social inequalities and varying life opportunities. But this model disguises the structures of economic co-operation, charitable organizations and volunteerism, which have also always been present in American society.

The corporate domination of economic life can also militate against the individual consumer, resulting in inferior products, bad service and little variety or real choice. Americans have historically been very sceptical of Big Business as well as Big Government. Corporate behaviour can be corrupt and fraudulent, as witnessed by successful prosecutions of business leaders and the collapse of corporations such as Enron (2003), WorldCom and Tyco.

**PLATE 1.2** Shopping mall in Orlando, Florida, 1991. Malls have become a consumer and cultural institution in American life and a symbol of economic capitalism, which appeal to many social groups, particularly teenagers. They consist of, usually under one roof, a wide variety of shops, cafes, restaurants, banks and car parks, and may often be located outside city or town centres.
(*Paul Brown/Rex Features*)

## Americanness and national identity

The ethnic, political-legal and economic cultures influence and are reflected in other aspects of American life, such as education (see Chapter 11), the health-care system and social services (Chapter 10), the media (Chapter 12), religious groups (Chapter 13) and the worlds of the arts, sports and leisure (Chapter 14). They also condition questions of what it means to be American ('Americanness') and what constitutes national identity.

A significant historical dilemma for the USA has been how to balance the need for national unity with the existence of ethnic diversity and, thus, how to avoid the dangers of fragmentation. An emphasis was initially placed on 'Americanization', the assimilation of different ethnic groups into a shared, mainly Anglo-American-based identity. The familiar metaphor of the 'melting pot', to indicate ethnic blending, was frequently seen instead as pressure to totally integrate into this dominant culture, with a resulting loss of ethnic identity.

In recent decades, debates on national identity have centred on questions of unity (or Americanization) as against diversity (or ethnic pluralism and multiculturalism). These reflect a pattern which has shifted between reform/ liberal and consolidation/conservative periods. In the 1950s, ethnic differences and issues seemed to be declining, but have revived since the 1960s, particularly with the growth of Latino ethnic groups in the 1990s. Arguments have vacillated between the adequacy of old values of Americanism (often represented by conservatives) and ethnic- or minority-group interests (supported by liberals). It is suggested that the American ideal of *e pluribus unum* (out of many one) is an abstract concept which does not reflect reality. On the other hand, emphases on ethnicity and difference have arguably weakened the possibility of achieving a set of values that could represent a distinctive 'American Way of Life'. Some critics feel that American society is at risk because of the diversity of competing cultures and interest groups, with each claiming special treatment. They maintain that the sense of an overarching American identity has weakened in the past thirty-five years.

From the late 1970s through the 1990s, there has been a reaction against liberal policies and affirmative-action programmes for minority groups, which allegedly discriminate in the latter's favour in areas such as education and employment. Conservatives assert what they consider to be traditional American values, and many are opposed to liberal policies on abortion, gun control, school education, same-sex marriage, religion, the death penalty and immigration. These debates have further increased anxieties about national identity and where the country is headed. The conflicts over supposed fundamental American values continue at present in many areas of national life.

Such concerns have led critics to argue that the USA should be regarded ethnically, culturally and ideologically as a 'mosaic', 'salad bowl', 'pizza' or 'stew mix', rather than a 'melting-pot'. The old 'melting pot' model of America, which implied ultimate cultural unity, has been rejected in some quarters. But the metaphors of salads and stews nevertheless suggest that variety and difference should somehow be incorporated into a larger 'American' whole.

The metaphors do indicate a certain acceptance of cultural and ethnic pluralism. Hetereogeneity (difference) and an adherence to roots have continued despite pressures and arguments in support of homogenization (sameness). It is argued that degrees of separateness and assimilation vary between ethnic groups, and that absolute social integration is both undesirable and impossible. But this can lead to hybrid cultural identities on the one hand and the breakdown of strong national links on the other.

Critics of 'diversity' and 'ethnic pluralism' maintain that the USA is in danger of splitting apart under the strain of identity politics, political ideologies, ethnic division, cultural differences, gender wars and economic inequality. However, it is also argued that while there are extremes of opinion, unfairness, diversity and vested interests in the society, strong underlying moral and political commitments to freedom, justice, tolerance and equality under the law limit divisions and promote unity, homogeneity and stability. American ideologies were historically formed from violent struggles as well as Enlightenment reason, and the USA still has to live resiliently with conflict and anxiety.

Arguably, the tension is between absolute pluralism (referred to in some models as multiculturalism where the interests of an ethnic group are equally valid to any other and should be supported) on the one hand and an acceptance of pluralism under a prevailing umbrella American identity on the other. The latter solution has to be achieved within defining national structures which allow the facts of pluralism and identity with roots to exist. Degrees of assimilation (such as citizenship for immigrants, education, home-ownership, language acquisition, intermarriage, economic opportunities and upward mobility) could then be achieved, while differences would be seen as valid. The 2000 US Census seems to indicate that natural forces of assimilation have been growing and that a sense of civic commonality or a distinctive American nationalism have increased (see 'American Attitudes to US society', pp. 14–17). Nevertheless, a liberal, intellectual ideology maintains that all ethnic cultures are equally valid and that a multicultural, multi-ethnic society should be the ultimate national goal.

Opposed critics argue that the arrival of large numbers of Latinos (including Mexicans) in the USA since the 1980s has created a substantial community that allegedly rejects Americanization and American traditional values. Official bilingualism (English and Spanish), especially in California and the south-west (together with Spanish-speakers in Florida, Texas and elsewhere) and an alleged Latino reluctance to renounce old national identities seem to suggest a model composed of one nation with two cultures. But many Latinos do in fact integrate into the American whole. Historically, Irish, Jewish, Chinese and Italian immigrants, among others, have been subjected to suspicion and hostility before achieving integration. The sense of a current crisis and fear of a growing decline in national unity may therefore seem exaggerated and may overlook the US ability to Americanize immigrants.

Whatever the degree of attempted social incorporation, Americans have historically tried to construct a sense of an overarching national identity and unity by binding the ethnically diverse population to central images or symbols of 'Americanness', such as the national flag (also known as the Stars and Stripes, Old Glory or the Star-Spangled Banner), the pledge of allegiance to the flag, the Declaration of Independence, the Liberty Bell, Abraham Lincoln's Emancipation Proclamation and Gettysburg Address, the 'Star-Spangled Banner' (the US national anthem) and the Constitution. These are meant to provide common cultural signs which promote loyalty to shared notions of what American citizenship, 'America' and 'Americanness' might be. Their representative qualities attempt to avoid the potentially divisive elements of economic, social, class or ethnic differences.

Certain social and individual values have also been traditionally associated with these symbols, particularly those rights stemming from the Declaration of

**PLATE 1.3** A girl in Cedarburg, Wisconsin celebrates Independence Day, 4 July. This official US holiday commemorates the day in 1776 when the Continental Congress sitting in Independence Hall, Philadelphia gave its approval to the Declaration of Independence from Britain, and is now celebrated with processions, speeches, flags and fireworks.
(*Stewart Cook/Rex Features*)

Independence, the Constitution and the Bill of Rights. In the frequent attempts to define 'Americanness', elements such as self-reliance, individualism or sturdy independence, utopianism, egalitarianism, freedom, opportunity, democracy, liberty, anti-statism (distrust of government), populism (grass-roots activism), a sense of destiny and respect for the law are stressed. They stem from the ideas of Puritan religion and the European Enlightenment, which influenced the framers of the Declaration of Independence and the US Constitution. Thus, there are layers of idealism and abstraction in American life that coexist, and may often clash, with reality. Yet this situation is not unique. It echoes the experience of other countries, particularly those that are unions, federations or collections of different peoples with contrasting roots and traditions, who need to erect new national identities while preserving some aspects of their original identities.

The degree to which these values are accepted and propagated in US society is significant, irrespective of whether they are individually or nationally achieved. They are attractive and valid for many people and are revealed both in times of normality and crisis. A key feature of American life, therefore, is how individuals manage to combine traditional ideals of the nation with the actual realities of society and how they cope with the resulting oppositions. There is an essential pragmatism beneath the surface idealism, a need to apply ideas or values to real situations and a 'can-do' respect for practical solutions to problems.

Traditionally, some critics have tried to explain the USA and its national identity by 'American traits'. Features like restlessness, escape from restraints, change, action, mobility, quests for new experiences, self-improvement and a belief in potential supposedly constitute typical American behaviour. They are often attributed to the legacy of immigrant and frontier experiences and an American belief in progress, both for the individual and for the larger society. Americans allegedly refuse to accept a fixed fate or settled location, but seek new jobs, new horizons and new beginnings in a hunt for self-fulfilment and self-definition. The huge sales of self-improvement books based on popular psychology suggest that such attitudes (or the desire to attain them) are widespread.

Many Americans, on the other hand, seek roots and stability in their lives, their institutions and in their search for a national identity. Similarly, while the alleged informality of American life is supposedly founded on individualism, egalitarianism and a historical rejection of European habits, many Americans respect and desire formalities, order and hierarchy.

Americans may stress their individualism, distrust of Big Business and Big Government and their desire to be free. But communalism, voluntary activities, charitable organizations and group endeavours are also a feature of US life. Individuals additionally have to cope with corporate, political and social bureaucracy, employment environments and economic and social hierarchies with their associated power bases. Indeed, American literature is full of characters' romantic attempts to be free and their frequent failures when faced with the realities of society and their individual conditions. Public-opinion polls also reflect the tension between ideal aspirations and everyday facts of life (see 'American Attitudes to US society', pp. 14–17).

One cannot therefore define a single and simple set of traits which are shared by all Americans. Diversity, individual differences and departures from consensual norms, whether from personal, social, religious or economic circumstances/values, limit possibilities and can result in contradictions or tensions rather than unified beliefs. Arguably, the supposedly American traits are universal characteristics and are neither exceptional in themselves nor distinctively American.

Nevertheless, the three major cultures and various subcultures have produced a composite Americanness and distinctive US image, which have influenced an international or globalized culture. They are expressed through Hollywood films, television and radio, music and art, newspapers and magazines, professional and amateur sport, consumption patterns, well-known chain stores and brand names, corporate and financial institutions, business and management philosophies, political activity, ethnic concerns, religion and popular culture.

## Social and institutional change

The major US cultures are not static. On the one hand, they may influence and refashion other nations' cultures. On the other hand, international pressures for change can similarly modify the major cultures themselves. Even though these are driven and considerably conditioned by increasingly multinational or global forces, they must also remain responsive to specific American political, minority and consumer pressures. A national mass culture and economic system are inevitably integrationist forces as they cater for the American market.

Social organizations have been gradually constructed over time and reflect a variety of values and practices. Some of these structures are particular to the USA and others are similar to those of other nations. All have developed over the past 300 years to cope with, and adapt to, an increasingly complex, diverse and dynamic society. They take many different forms and sizes, operate on national, state and local levels, and may be public or private in character.

The larger elements, such as federal and state governments, are involved with public business, but there is also a range of smaller social activities, such as sports, local communities, neighbourhoods, religion, the theatre and various expressions of ethnic identity. These may take on more individualistic forms than the larger public institutions.

For some critics, it is the localized life and behaviour of people in small-town America which typically defines their society, rather than centralized federal institutions. However, the larger frameworks do serve as a cement which holds local activities and people together. They also contribute to an umbrella sense of American identity and 'Americanness'. The USA, like other countries, gains its identity from a mixture of the local and the national, which inform and influence each other.

The American 'way of life' is partly defined by how citizens function within and respond to local and national institutions, whether positively or negatively. The large number and variety of such institutions means that there are many different 'ways of life' and all contribute to the diversity and particular characteristics of American society.

The following chapters stress the historical context of US growth and suggest that the contemporary still owes much to the past. Social structures are adaptable, provide frameworks for new situations and their present roles may be different from their original functions. They have changed and evolved over time as they have been influenced not only by elite and government policies, but also by grass-roots impulses and reactions. This process of change and adaptation continues and reflects current anxieties and concerns in American life.

Social structures at various levels contribute to a culture of varied and often conflicting habits and ideals, as well as being practical organizations for realizing them. The following chapters therefore attempt to present a range of critical viewpoints on the society and its institutions in an attempt to describe what may, or may not, be regarded as distinctively American. They first consider the physical geography of the USA and its cultural regions, indigenous peoples, settler and immigration experiences, and women and minorities. They then examine the central social structures within which Americans have to operate, analyse their historical growth and modern roles, and consider their underlying values.

## American attitudes to US society

Social structures are not remote abstractions. They affect individuals directly in their daily lives. Despite their diversity of origins and values, Americans do have shared concerns. They can identify in public-opinion polls what are for them the major problems facing the country and which affect most people in varying degrees. Although there is some scepticism about the accuracy of polls, they are now regarded as significant guides. They valuably reflect how respondents are sensitive to changing conditions over time. Such concerns can determine people's judgements on political and other issues at any one time, including elections.

In the first half of 2004, all American polls (according to PollingReport in May 2004) showed that the economy (including taxes and the federal budget deficit), unemployment, jobs and foreign competition were primary concerns for people, together with education (see Table 1.1). But as the country approached the presidential election in November 2004, the campaign against terrorism, domestic (homeland) security, foreign policy and Iraq became increasingly important, although the economy and jobs were still prioritized; education slipped in the ratings. Social questions about health care, Medicare (medical programme for people over sixty-five years of age), Medicaid (medical care for low-income people under sixty-five), the cost of prescription drugs, social security (federal

**TABLE 1.1** Top fourteen problems facing the USA, 2004.

| Problem | Extremely/very important (%) |
|---|---|
| Education | 86 |
| The economy | 86 |
| Terrorism | 85 |
| Health care | 82 |
| The situation in Iraq | 80 |
| Taxes | 74 |
| The federal budget deficit | 72 |
| Foreign affairs | 65 |
| The environment | 62 |
| Corporate corruption | 60 |
| Immigration | 55 |
| Gun policy | 53 |
| Abortion | 52 |
| Same-sex marriage | 44 |

*Source:* Gallup, February 2004

payments to people who are unemployed, poor, old or disabled), abortion and same-sex marriage were also prominent. Concerns about corporate corruption and immigration had climbed up the poll ratings, whereas worries about gun control, drugs, the death penalty and crime (long significant topics in the polls) had declined. This finding corresponds with an overall decreasing US crime rate in recent years.

In terms of more general attitudes to the state of the nation, a variety of polls in 2004, according to PollingReport, showed that a majority (between 61 and 62 per cent) of Americans reported dissatisfaction with the way things were going in the USA. Most polls also reported that many respondents (between 42 and 58 per cent) felt the country was on the wrong track. Only a minority of polls (such as *Time*/CNN) showed that a majority of respondents were either satisfied with the country's progress or thought that it was on the right track.

A Harris Feel Good Index in 2003 had also shown relatively small approval ratings, with 50 per cent of respondents feeling good about the state of the nation, 47 per cent feeling good about the morals and values of Americans in general, and 35 per cent feeling good about the nation's economy. Given the alleged optimism of Americans, their faith in their society and belief in an ability to achieve the American Dream, it is instructive to consider the results of polls which report on alienation in US society (see Table 1.2) between 2000 and 2003. These

**TABLE 1.2** Alienation in the USA, 2000–3.

| Americans tend to feel that . . . | 2003 | 2002 | 2001 | 2000 |
|---|---|---|---|---|
| . . . the rich get richer and the poor get poorer | 69 | 72 | 69 | 69 |
| . . . what you think doesn't count very much any more | 56 | 55 | 49 | 56 |
| . . . most people with power try to take advantage of people like yourself | 60 | 61 | 48 | 59 |
| . . . the people running the country don't really care what happens to you | 46 | 44 | 36 | 53 |
| . . . you're left out of things going on around you | 40 | 30 | 33 | 39 |
| Percentage mean of responses to questions | 54 | 52 | 47 | 55 |

Source: adapted from Harris Alienation Index, the Harris Poll, December 2003

findings suggest a degree of powerlessness felt by ordinary Americans in the face of economic, political, bureaucratic, corporate and institutional forces.

In terms of the ethnic composition of the country, and given the considerable significance of original settlement and later immigration in US history over the centuries, attitudes to national identity and immigration appear to be shifting somewhat. The US Census 2000 Supplemental Survey found that when asked to describe their ancestry, more Americans trace their roots to Europe than anywhere else in the world (17 per cent German, 12 per cent Irish and 10 per cent British/English). But these three largest ancestral groups in fact saw their numbers decline by 20–5 per cent between the 1990 and 2000 censuses.

'American' or 'US' was the fourth largest ancestral identity. This finding from the census suggests that more people now identify themselves and their ethnic background as simply 'American' or 'US', without the need for a qualifying hyphen such as Irish-American. According to the *Christian Science Monitor* in June 2002, this does not represent a denial of roots but rather an increased sense of commonality, patriotism and American nationalism. But it is also argued that natural forces of assimilation, such as intermarriage, education and upward mobility, have weakened many Americans' bonds with their immigrant roots, particularly in the later generations. Newer immigrants retain stronger ancestral ties, while other groups, such as many African Americans, now seem more willing to employ both a hyphenated identity and an 'American' label, or even only the latter.

Nevertheless, tensions concerning ethnicity and immigration were shown in a *CBS News/New York Times* poll in January 2004 which found that 45 per cent of respondents believe legal immigration numbers should be reduced and only 16 per cent thought that they should be increased. This finding has been reflected in other polls and suggests that many Americans see legal immigration as a problem and believe that illegal immigration should be stopped. This might indicate that there is still a nativist current in American society which is at odds with the values of much of the country's political and economic leadership. The government, for example, accepts that skilled and unskilled immigration is necessary to support the economy and an ageing population.

Some critics argue that the meaning and definition of a more unified national and civic US identity remain elusive. They maintain that a candid debate about the essence of American identity is needed in the very fluid present situation. Opposed and partisan positions between the unifiers and the pluralists/ multiculturalists still operate.

Many Americans may generally appear to believe in the inherent validity of American values, but they continue to question what is meant by these values, how consensual they are and, consequently, what it means to be American.

## Exercises

Explain and examine the significance of the following names and terms.

| | | |
|---|---|---|
| slavery | individualism | rhetoric |
| populism | ethnic | anti-statism |
| diversity | consensus | corporate |
| grass roots | culture(s) | consumerism |
| America | frontier | salad bowl |
| utopianism | pluralism | assimilation |
| nativism | egalitarianism | Americanization |
| ideology | brand names | multiculturalism |

Write short essays on the following questions:

1.  What are some of the characteristics that you would associate with the American people and their society? Why?

2.  Try to define the term 'social structure' and examine its possible usages.

3.  Is the study of the major cultures an adequate way to approach American society?

4.  Do you find that the public opinion poll findings in this chapter give a valid picture of American society? Give your reasons after carefully examining the poll results.

# Further reading

Campbell, N. and A. Kean (1997) *American Cultural Studies: an introduction to American Culture* London: Routledge.

Ferguson, N. (2004) *The Rise and Fall of the American Empire* London: Allen Lane.

Hall, J. A. and C. Lindholm (1999) *Is America Breaking Apart?* Princeton, NJ: Princeton University Press.

Huntington, S. P. (2004) *Who Are We? America's great debate* New York: Simon & Schuster.

Leach, E. E. (2004) *Interpreting the American Dream* London: Palgrave/Macmillan.

Lipset, S. M. (1996) *American Exceptionalism: a double-edged sword* New York: W. W. Norton & Company.

Micklethwait, J. and A. Wooldridge (2004) *The Right Nation: why America is different* London: Allen Lane.

Moen, P., D. Dempster-McClain and H. A. Walker, (eds) (1999) *A Nation Divided: diversity, inequality and community in American society* Ithaca, NY: Cornell University Press.

Pope, D. (ed.) (2001) *American Radicalism* Oxford: Blackwell.

Sandel, M. J. (1996) *Democracy's Discontent: America in search of a public philosophy* Cambridge, Mass: Belknap Press of Harvard University Press.

Sargent, L. T. (ed.) (1995) *Extremism in America* New York: New York University Press.

Woods, R. B. and W. B. Gatewood (2000) *The American Experience: a concise history* New York: Harcourt Brace.

Zinn, H. (2003) *A People's History of the United States: from 1492 to present* London: Longman/Pearson.

# Web sites

<http://usinfo.state.gov/usa/infousa/>
<http://usinfo.state.gov/journals/journala.htm>
<http://usinfo.state.gov>
<http://www.census.gov>
<http://www.firstgov.gov>

**American Studies Crossroads Project:**
<http://www.georgetown.edu/crossroads/index.html>

**Public opinion polls:**
<http://www.csmonitor.com>
<http://www.gallup.com/poll>
<http://www.lib.duke.edu/reference/polls.htm>
<http://www.roper center.uconn.edu>
<http://libweb.sonoma.edu/web/statistics.html>
<http://www.harrispollonline.com>
<http://www.pollingreport.com/prioriti.htm

# The country

With an area of 3,615,122 square miles (9,363,123 square kilometres) the United States is exceeded in size only by Russia, Canada and China. Of the fifty states, forty-eight lie between the Atlantic and Pacific Oceans, and between Canada and Mexico, while two, Alaska and Hawaii, lie in the north-west corner of the continent and the Pacific Ocean, respectively. Island possessions in the Caribbean and the Pacific add another 11,000 square miles (17,600 kilometres) to American territory.

The most pronounced feature of the country is its variety. Its natural environment varies from the arctic to the tropical, from rainforest to desert, from vast plains to rugged mountains. Exploiting its natural resources has depleted reserves, caused extensive pollution and shown a wastefulness that has led to dependence on resources from other nations, although the country's own natural riches remain the main support of its economic life. Strong environmentalist movements and public concern since the mid-1800s have successfully lobbied for a national system of nature preserves and government monitoring and regulation of the environment. The use of natural resources has become a matter of balancing economic and environmental priorities.

## Natural resources, economic development and environmental concerns

Approached from the Atlantic Ocean or the Gulf of Mexico, the country's first land formation is the Atlantic Plain, a coastal lowland stretching from New England to the middle of Texas. A narrow coastal strip in the north, the plain gradually widens to include large parts of the southern states. Its soil is mostly poor but includes a fertile citrus-growing region and the Cotton Belt in the south, which have both been intensively developed for commercial farming. The Plain's most important natural wealth is found along and in the Gulf, where much of the nation's crude-oil and natural-gas reserves are located. Water pollution from industrial development in the north and commercial fertilizers and oil-drilling in the south have posed the most serious threats to the Plain's environment.

Inland from the Atlantic Plain, the land rises to the Piedmont, a gently rolling fertile plateau. Along the eastern edge of the Piedmont is the fall line, where rivers running down to the Atlantic form waterfalls. When water power was used for grain and textile mills, America's first industrial cities grew up along the northern fall line near the coast. The Piedmont rises to the Appalachians, much-eroded

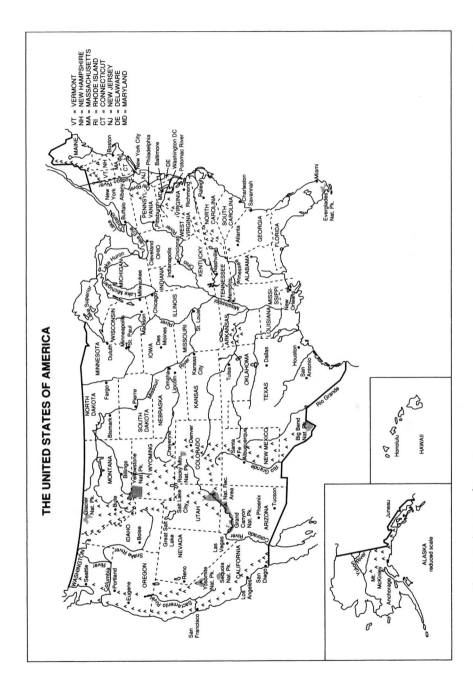

**FIGURE 2.1** The United States of America.

**PLATE 2.1** The skyline of Dallas, Texas. The Dallas–Fort Worth metropolitan area is part of the state's moister, more densely populated eastern third.
(*Popperfoto/Samantha Chamberlain*)

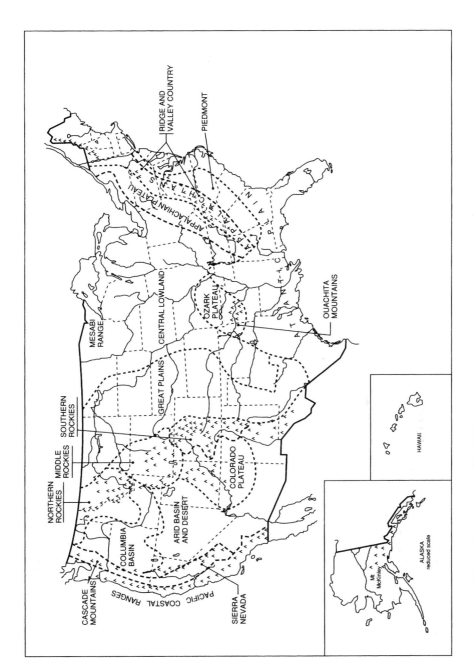

**FIGURE 2.2** Physical geography of the USA.

mountains from Canada to Alabama that separate the eastern seaboard from the interior. These mountains, the Appalachian Plateau, and the rugged ridge and valley country to their west delayed European invasion and settlement (see Figure 2.2).

Although the Appalachians and the upland sub-regions contain minerals, only iron, building stone and coal are found in large quantities. The coal deposits in Pennsylvania and West Virginia, in the area called Appalachia, are among the world's largest and once provided fuel for developing industry in the north-east and the Great Lakes regions as well as for heating homes across the nation. Today, Appalachia is among the nation's most depressed areas because 'cleaner' gas, oil and atomic energy have mostly replaced coal. Producing and using these newer energy sources, however, have also been identified as the main sources of air pollution and acid rain.

West of the Appalachian highlands lies the Central Lowland, a vast area stretching from New York state to central Texas and north to Canada, which resembles a huge, irregular bowl rimmed by the Great Lakes and highlands. The iron ore in one of these, the Mesabi Range at the western edge of the lakes, with the coal of Appalachia, made the development of America's industrial core possible. The Central Lowland is not entirely flat. The glacial moraine, an area of rocky territory with many lakes, runs along a line just north of the Ohio and Missouri rivers. On both sides of the moraine, the lowland has a table-like flatness except near rivers that have dug gorges. The lowland also varies in rainfall and temperature. Rainfall decreases towards the west, resulting first in a change from forests mixed with fields to the prairies, where trees are rare. Farther west, the high prairie grass changes to short grass at the 20-inch (50-centimetres) annual rainfall line where the Great Plains begin (see Figure 2.2). From north to south, the long winters of the upper mid-west change to the snowless winters of the gulf states.

The natural resources of the Central Lowland, which is often called the nation's breadbasket, are its soil and fossil fuels. The fields of oil and gas in Texas, Oklahoma and Kansas were the nation's most important domestic supply until reserves in Alaska were tapped. Across the lowland the increase in large-scale agribusinesses in recent years has produced intense efforts to deal with unwanted side effects, including polluted water supplies from plant fertilizers and insecticides and the leakage of concentrated animal feed and sewage from industrial pig, chicken and freshwater fish farming.

The Great Plains is a band of semi-arid territory almost 500 miles (800 kilometres) wide between Canada and Mexico. The plains rise so gradually towards the west that large parts of the region appear to be utterly flat. Most of the plains, however, are broadly rolling, and parts of the northern plains are cut up into spectacular gorge and ridge country called 'badlands'. The buffalo grass of the plains makes them excellent for ranching, but some areas, watered by automated artesian wells or irrigation, are now high-yield farm country. The

**PLATE 2.2** Crop spraying in Idaho.
(*Sipa Press/Rex Features*)

plains' mineral wealth, mainly low-grade brown coal, is extracted through environmentally damaging strip-mining.

From the western edge of the Great Plains to the Pacific coast, a third of the continental United States consists of the Cordillera mountain chains (the Rockies and the Pacific ranges) and the basins and plateaux between them. Near the Southern Rockies' western slopes is the Colorado Plateau, a maze of canyons and mesas, the most famous of which is the Grand Canyon. Surrounding the Plateau is the desert south-west. Valleys and plains rather than mountains occupy much of the Middle Rockies. The Wyoming Basin has provided a route through the mountains, from the Oregon Trail that pioneers followed to the inter-state highways of today. In the northern Rockies are vast wilderness areas and the Columbia Basin, which is etched by the remarkable canyons of the Snake and Columbia rivers.

The western arm of the Cordillera consists of two lines of mountains with a series of valleys between them. In from the coast are the highest peaks, including active volcanoes. The inland valleys contain much of the west coast's population and economic activity, from Washington's Puget Sound to the Willamette Valley of Oregon and California's Central Valley. All these valleys are blessed with rich soils, and the more southerly were relatively easy to irrigate. Since the invention of refrigeration, these valleys have supplied the nation with fruit and vegetables. The mountains between the valleys and the coast include major earthquake zones, such as the San Andreas Fault, which caused the 1906 quake that levelled San Francisco. A chronic water shortage, however, rather than earthquakes, seems to be the most serious environmental problem to a majority of westerners.

In Alaska, the Cordillera divide into three parts that include North America's highest peak, Mount McKinley at 20,320 feet (6,194 metres). Largely fragile tundra, Alaska's interior is comprised of mountains, broken plateaux and fairly flat valleys with a cold inland climate. Much of coastal and island Alaska has a temperate climate because of warm ocean currents. The building of the trans-Alaska pipeline, coastal oil spills and, since 2000, the debate over plans to open the Arctic National Wildlife Refuge to oil exploration have tested the nation's will to protect Alaska's nature.

The American Cordillera are world famous for fabulous veins of precious metals, such as the gold of the Sierra and Yukon and the Comstock silver lode of Nevada. More recently, industrial metals like copper and lead and more unusual metals, for alloys, have been mined. Large occurrences of oil and gas are found in California and Wyoming, and the Colorado Plateau contains uranium, oil shale and soft coal. To extract the oil and coal, say mining companies, open-pit and strip-mining are necessary. Conservationists, on the other hand, argue that this mining devastates parts of the plateau as thoroughly as it destroyed areas of the Great Plains and Appalachia.

The natural riches of Hawaii are vegetable rather than mineral. The state contains almost a million acres (200,000 hectares) of commercial forest and twice as much land suitable for tropical farming. Trade winds give the islands a temperate climate. The volcanic mountains catch much rain on the windward side of the islands so that the leeward side has only moderate rainfall.

## Coastlines and river systems

Among the most important physical features and resources of the country are its coastlines, harbours, ocean currents and network of lakes and rivers. The shallow waters of the Continental Shelf off the North Atlantic coast known as the Great Banks contain many kinds of fish and attracted fishermen from Europe even before European settlers established their first colonies in the New World. The east coast has a warmer climate because of the Florida Current. Fine harbours and estuaries made the sites of New York city, Philadelphia and Baltimore excellent locations for trade.

The great eastern water systems are those that drain the Central Lowland: the Mississippi with its major tributaries and the Great Lakes–St Lawrence system. One of the world's great inland water networks, the Mississippi system carries freight from New Orleans north to Minneapolis and east to Pittsburgh. Western tributaries of the Mississippi are mostly unfit for navigation, but since the 1950s the Missouri has carried heavy barge traffic as a result of dams, locks and dredging. Because canals connect it to the Mississippi, the Great Lakes–St Lawrence system functions as the second half of one vast network of inland waterways. The biggest group of freshwater lakes in the world, the Great Lakes carry more shipping than any other inland lake group. The fertile farmland surrounding the lakes and the iron, lumber and fossil fuels near their shores supported the rapid urbanization and industrialization of the mid-west in the 1800s. The opening of the St Lawrence Seaway in 1959 made the lake cities international seaports by bypassing the obstacles to ocean-going freighters in the St Lawrence with huge locks.

On the west coast, limited rainfall and scant mountain run-off dry up all but three river systems, the Columbia, the Colorado and the San Joaquin–Sacramento, before they reach the sea. They do not support shipping, but the west's largest rivers have brought prosperity by providing hydroelectric power and irrigation. The Columbia, once a wild white river, now runs down through dams and calm lakes, turning the arid plateaux of Washington state into vegetable gardens and supplying electrical power to several states. The Colorado serves the same purposes on a smaller scale. Proposals for its further development have met opposition because more dams would destroy the beauty of the Grand Canyon and other canyon lands.

## Conservation, recreational areas and environmental protection

Although the country's population is now over 280 million, most of these people live in relatively small areas. Some parts of the country are not suitable for urbanization because of climate or difficult topography. Others have been set aside as recreation areas or wildlife preserves. These and other factors give the USA a great variety of national, state and local parks and open spaces. In the USA, conservation of natural beauty and resources through national parks gained acceptance in the late 1800s, with vocal support from President Theodore Roosevelt, among others. Yellowstone National Park, the first nature preserve created by Congress, was put under federal control in 1872. Congress established the National Park Service in 1916 and gave it the difficult double duty of making the areas entrusted to it accessible for industry and public enjoyment, and of preserving them for future generations. The Park Service now administers over 200 different sites, whose combined territory exceeds 40,000 square miles (104,000 square kilometres) of land and water. There are national parks in all parts of the nation, but the largest and most famous are located between the Rockies and the Pacific.

Government protection of the parks means controlled development. The federal Department of the Interior and its Land Management Bureau have long granted licences or leases allowing private economic interests to use the parks' resources at low cost. According to federal law, the government must balance the interests of developers, holiday-makers, environmentalists and Native Americans. Some say this ideal of 'multiple use' may have worked when the west was underpopulated, but that today it satisfies no one and could lead to the loss of irreplaceable resources.

In the 1960s, a remarkable period of protest and reform in the USA, conservationist and environmentalist organizations grew in strength in response to exposés of pollution, such as Rachel Carson's best-selling book *Silent Spring*, and a series of environmental disasters, including a gigantic oil spill off the California coast and the chemical explosion and burning of the Cuyahoga river in downtown Cleveland, Ohio. The high level of public concern became obvious in 1970 when 20 million people took part in the first Earth Day, a nationwide 'teach-in', focused on the dangers of pollution. Concerted lobbying of Congress by grass-roots groups and highly organized environmental organizations like the Sierra Club and National Audubon Society soon resulted in a series of landmark federal laws. In the same year an independent regulatory body, the Environmental Protection Agency (EPA) took on the national government's responsibility for monitoring and protecting America's natural environment, and the Clean Air Act gave the EPA the duty of identifying and reducing airborne pollutants. By the end of the 1970s the Clean Water Act, Safe Drinking Water Act and the Superfund statute, which provides emergency federal funding for eliminating

**PLATE 2.3** The skyline of downtown Seattle with its famous 'space needle' tower. (*Novastock/Rex Features*)

the health hazards of toxic-waste sites across the nation, were in effect. These laws have been repeatedly strengthened and extended in the decades since their enactment due to the environmental damage caused largely by sprawling urban development, new and outmoded industrial sites, and innovative commercial forms of farming and food processing.

# Climate

Arctic and tropical climates are limited to high mountain-tops, inland Alaska, Hawaii and the southern tip of Florida. The middle latitudes are, however, known for wide variations in temperature and rainfall, and the great size of North America reinforces these differences. In general, the more distant a place is from an ocean, the more it has temperature extremes in the summer and winter. Near the inland centre of the continent in North Dakota temperatures have varied from a summer high of 121 °F (49 °C) to a winter low of –60 °F (–51 °C). Most climates in America are distinctly inland because, with the general eastward movement of air across the country, the Cordillera mountain system limits the moderating influence of the Pacific to a narrow strip along the west coast. Thus, San Francisco experiences only a small differential between winter and summer temperatures, but coastal cities in the north-east have the same range of temperatures that extend from the Rockies to the east coast. The easterly direction of weather systems across the country also means the Atlantic Ocean has only a weak moderating influence.

### Rainfall

Rainfall from the Pacific Ocean is so confined to the coastal strip by the Cordillera that the areas between the mountains and the Great Plains are arid or semi-arid. Farther east, rainfall increases because warm, moist air moves up over the nation's middle from the Gulf of Mexico, producing rainfall. This rain often comes in cloudbursts, hailstorms, tornadoes and blizzards, with rapid temperature changes as cold Canadian air collides with warm, humid air from the Gulf of Mexico.

### The seasons

In winter, dry frigid Canadian air moves south, spreading cold weather to the plains and lowlands and causing storms at its southern edge. In summer, that stormy edge moves north as gulf air brings hot weather that eliminates much of the temperature difference between the north and south.

Along the Pacific, seasonal changes follow another pattern. Winter in the Pacific north-west is overcast and drizzly as a result of warm, moist air from the Alaskan coast. Southern California is a climatic refuge in winter because of its mild temperatures and long periods of sunny weather. In summer, the Pacific north-west has mild air from the Pacific, and, except in the mountains, is nearly rainless. Farther south, summer means dry, hot air and high temperatures. Autumn in the north-east and upper mid-west is marked by mild days, frosty nights and crystal-clear skies. Spring here brings temperate weather, but autumn and spring are also the seasons when the gulf and Canadian air masses lurch most violently together, spawning hurricanes along the gulf and Atlantic coasts in the fall and tornadoes in the Mississippi valley in the spring.

## The regions: cultural geography

The definitions and boundaries of American regions vary according to the uses they are put to and according to the people making the divisions. More than one meaningful division of the country into regions is possible, and cultural regions defined as groups of states give only approximate borders because cultural boundaries rarely coincide with political units. Individual Native-American cultures, geographic areas and states, moreover, often show a unique mixture of traits that makes their inclusion in regional cultures inaccurate at best.

**PLATE 2.4** Waits River, Vermont, with autumn foliage.
*(Rex Features)*

## Native-American cultural regions

Many distinctive Native-American cultures existed when Europeans arrived in the mid-1500s. An estimated 10 million Native-Americans then lived in cultures with several hundred mutually incomprehensible languages and widely varying social structures. Any survey of cultural regions in such a diversity of groups must focus on broad similarities. (See Figure 2.3.)

In the woodland eastern half of the country were areas now known as the north-eastern and south-eastern maize regions, where a variety of native cultures depended on hunting, fishing, farming and gathering. These are called maize cultures because maize, or corn as it is called in the USA, was the most important staple of the Native-Americans' diet. The longer growing season in the south-eastern maize region resulted in more extensive and highly developed agriculture. In the east as a whole, most housing was constructed of wood, bark and thatch. Women and children usually farmed while men hunted and fished. Well-known cultural groups here were the Iroquois, Huron, Mohican, Delaware and Shawnee in the north, and the Powhatan, Creek, Cherokee, Seminole and Natchez in the south.

The Native-American cultural area in the prairies and Great Plains is known as the plains or bison region. For thousands of years the population of this area was sparse compared with other parts of the continent. People lived along waterways and depended on river-bank farming, small-game hunting and gathering. Lacking any other means of transportation, they went on a communal buffalo (bison) hunt once a year on foot. Then, between 1700 and 1750, they discovered how to use the horses that reached them from Spanish-controlled areas to the south, and plains cultures were transformed. The population grew because the food supply increased dramatically when bison were hunted on horseback. Learning of this, some tribes, such as the Dakota, migrated from nearby woodlands to the open steppes farther west. Plains peoples exchanged their settled farming customs for the nomadic culture of year-round buffalo hunters, discarding sod lodges for the portable *tipi* and evolving a society dominated by a warrior hunting class. The groups transformed by the arrival of the horse (the Blackfoot, Crow, Cheyenne, and Dakota) are among the best-known of Native-Americans, largely because of their fierce resistance to white settlement on their hunting grounds.

The Native-American cultural region called the south-west once encompassed a diversity of native cultures, nomadic hunters and gatherers as well as farmers, but most of its people relied on advanced forms of irrigated agriculture. Hopi, Zuni, and Acoma people, among others, lived in the two- to three-floor adobe, or stone buildings called puebloes, and farmed nearby land. These cultures all traced ancestry through the female line, and men did the farming while women owned the fields. The Navajo and Apache were latecomers to the region, hunters and gatherers who migrated south from the Canadian plains between AD 1000

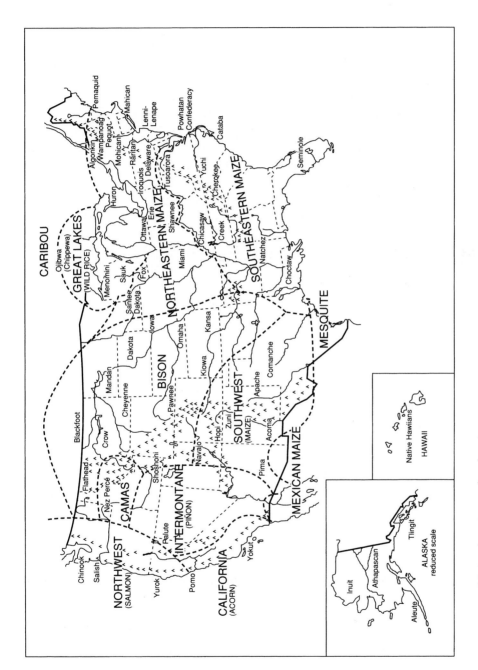

**FIGURE 2.3** Native-American cultural regions.

**PLATE 2.5**  The Navajo Indian Nation Reservation, Monument Valley, New Mexico. Today both men and women among the Navajo practise the sheep-herding learned long ago from the Spanish.
(*Sipa Press/Rex Features*)

and 1500 and who adopted farming from the pueblo-dwelling peoples. The Navajo later learned sheep-raising, peach-growing and silver-working from the Spanish, while some Apache groups took up aspects of nomadic plains cultures, such as the *tipi* and hunting buffalo on horseback, and copied cattle-raising from Spaniards and Americans.

The California-intermontane cultural area included the barren territory around the Colorado plateau and most of California. The nomadic hunters and gatherers that lived here are often considered materially the poorest of the continent's native cultures. On the other hand, their loosely organized family bands are often praised for their democratic political traditions and peaceful way of life.

The plentiful nature available to the coastal cultures from northern California to southern Alaska made them a stark contrast to highland cultures of the nearby inland areas. Among the most advanced groups of related cultures north of Mexico, the north-west peoples lived in coastal villages similar to independent city states. Well supplied with wild plants and game, the Chinook, Tsimshian, Kwakiutl, Haida and Tlingit did not need to farm. Fishing for salmon represented their primary economic activity, but saltwater fishing and whaling were also important. They made long seagoing canoes and massive wooden lodges, decorating these, household items, and totem poles with symbolic carving. These peoples of plenty are well known for the *potlatch*, several days of feasting during which a leading family gave its guests extravagant gifts. The family's wealth was demonstrated by the richness of its generosity, and the guests' degree of satisfaction determined their hosts' prestige in the community. The north-west coastal peoples were among the few non-agricultural societies to practise slavery, which was common in Native-American farming cultures.

The various Inuit groups (including the Aleuts) are the native peoples of Alaska and the Aleutian Islands. The Inuit arrived relatively late and wanted to distinguish themselves racially from Native Americans living farther south. The coastal peoples are skilled sea-hunters, while the inland cultures are based on hunting big game. The stereotype of the 'Eskimo' as a nomadic sea-hunter living in an igloo comes from the Inuit culture of far north Canada. The Inuit of Alaska are settled villagers who build underground sod-walled houses. Fast and efficient dog sledges and kayaks made it possible for them to live in one place and supply themselves with food.

Indigenous Hawaiians gathered food from the tropical forests, terraced mountain-sides and irrigated their fields to grow crops. Expert open-sea fishermen from outrigger canoes, they also built semicircular fish ponds along the seashore. The priesthood, aristocracy and royal family owned most of the land, which was divided into strips that extended from a mountain-top to a distance under coastal waters to meet all the owners' needs. The common people lived in small areas where they had limited rights to fish, water, wood, wild foods and farming.

## Attitudes toward the land

Attitudes toward land and land-ownership in Native American cultures varied. Group possession and communal use of land were most common. Almost all native groups had a concept of their own territory that was theirs by long residence and whose boundaries they defended or extended as circumstances demanded. Picturing native cultures as idealized societies in which land had only spiritual value is invariably wrong because it romanticizes and oversimplifies the realities of life in North America before European settlement. The Indians were aware of their dependence on the land, which led most native cultures to deify or revere nature. On the other hand, some cultures exploited their environment until it became depleted. Others over-hunted until some animals became extinct. If resources became scarce, groups moved to meet their needs, and conflict with other cultures resulted.

# Cultural regions in the contemporary USA

Today's cultural regions result from varying mixtures of European antecedents, with Native-American elements, at their most noticeable, representing one of several ethnic ingredients. The main American regions are much-used concepts for understanding subdivisions of American culture and society. Still, US regions tend to be less distinct than those in older, more demographically stable countries. The European settlement of North America is relatively recent and the high mobility of the American population adds to the homogenizing effects of popular mass culture, modern transportation, urbanization and the centralization of the economy and government. America also shows an opposing trend towards decentralization and heterogeneity. Among the factors that reveal the nation's increasing regional diversity are differing attitudes towards environmental protection, energy use, sexual orientation and abortion.

## *The north-east*

The north-east often seems to be one unit when viewed from other sections of the country. Stretching from Maine, south through Maryland and west to the border of Ohio, the whole region is known as densely populated, highly urban and suffering from becoming post-industrial (changing from older heavy industry to a high-tech service economy). In fact, the north-east is arguably still the nation's economic and cultural centre, and is two regions (New England and the mid-Atlantic) rather than one.

New England itself is often divided into two parts. Southern New England (Massachusetts, Connecticut and Rhode Island) has long had a cultural importance out of proportion to its size, natural resources and population. Massachusetts received the largest number of early colonists from Britain and rapidly developed stable institutions, cohesive communities and an expanding population that strongly influenced the rest of New England and the northern half of the country during the eighteenth and nineteenth centuries.

Americans trace several aspects of the nation's traditional core culture to southern New England. The original settlers' goal of founding a model religious community that would inspire reform in England was generalized to 'American exceptionalism', a belief that the nation has a special mission and ability to set a good example for the rest of the world. The region supposedly also bequeathed the country belief in the so-called Puritan work ethic, the faith that hard work and good morals are rewarded in this world and the next. In the mid-nineteenth century, New England authors such as Ralph Waldo Emerson expressed central values that for over a hundred years were taught in US schools as the foundation of the entire nation's culture. In the schools' popularized version, the American creed was an optimistic individualism expressed in introspective self-reliance and self-improvement, thrift, hard work and a belief in progress.

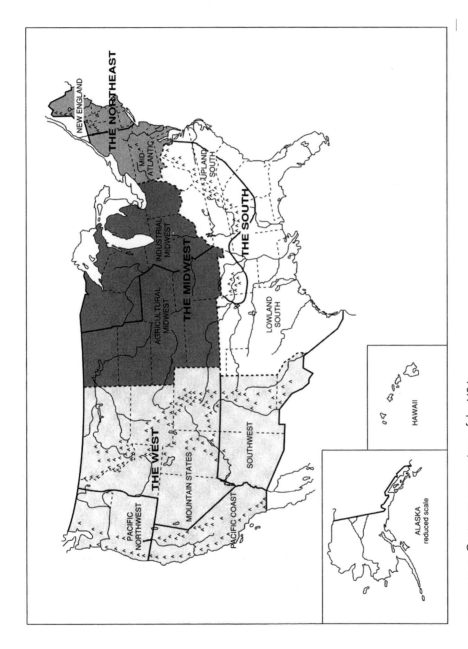

**FIGURE 2.4** Contemporary regions of the USA.

In the 1800s, New England Yankees became famous first as fishermen and travelling pedlars, then as clipper-ship builders and sailors, and finally as mill-owners and factory-workers. The fall line near the coast, by providing cheap water power close to trade routes, made the region the cradle of American industry. When industry converted to steam and electricity, the region lost manufacturing jobs to parts of the country richer in the natural resources essential to modern industry. One of New England's greatest strengths in its economic competition with other regions today is its concentration of quality institutions of higher education and research. New England is now a leader in innovative business methods, publishing and high-technology industries. The region's tourist industry flourishes because of its scenic qualities and status as a repository of the nation's history. The northern zone of the region (Maine, Vermont and most of New Hampshire), with its woodland mountain areas, has developed a lucrative industry providing summer cottages and second homes for people who want to escape east-coast cities.

Early New England was devoted to preserving a homogeneous society based on a shared religion. On the other hand, from its founding, the mid-Atlantic region accepted a Euro-American diversity. The original vision of America as a pluralistic mix of religions, ethnic groups and races developed here. With a larger, more varied population, better soil, and a greater share of natural resources, the mid-Atlantic region surpassed New England in trade and manufactures during the 1700s. During the next century, these advantages helped the mid-Atlantic region grow into the nation's commercial-industrial hub. Its harbours became the nation's premier port cities, and here too the fall line provided cheap water power. The mid-Atlantic region also has passages through the Appalachian Mountains. First roads, then canals and later railroads followed these east–west routes as they opened western New York, Pennsylvania and the Great Lakes states to settlement and carried farm products to the coastal cities of the mid-Atlantic region. The Erie Canal, joining Lake Erie with New York City, made the cost of shipping a ton of freight from the lake to the city nearly twenty-four times cheaper. In the decade after the canal's opening, the pattern of transportation down the inland rivers to New Orleans shifted towards New York, which became the nation's largest and wealthiest city.

By the later 1800s, transportation and trade welded together New England, the mid-Atlantic region and the big cities of the Great Lakes and inland rivers. This was the urban industrial core that attracted people to jobs in a variety of 'smokestack' industries. Although it includes agricultural areas, the distinguishing aspect of the core is still the size and closeness of its racially and ethnically mixed industrial cities. They contain many groups now, but in popular opinion Boston seems Irish, Buffalo is Polish, and New York City mostly Jewish, Italian, African, Asian and Caribbean. By the 1970s, the migration of heavy industries to foreign nations and 'high-tech' companies to the south and south-west resulted in the core being rechristened the 'Rust Belt'. Like New England, this region has had to develop new jobs, diversify its economy and recruit employers with tax breaks and social services. But the economic tug of war between the regions continues, and the south and west still attract more jobs and people than the urban core.

## The south

Traditionally, this region includes the eleven states from Virginia to Texas that formed the Confederacy during the Civil War. In addition, the 'border states' from West Virginia to Oklahoma are arguably southern. Far from homogeneous, the south has two subregions, the lowland south on the Coastal Plain and the upland south in the Piedmont, southern Appalachians and Ozarks. The lowland south's diversity includes the Creole and Cajun areas of Louisiana and the Caribbean-African influenced Sea Islands off the Atlantic Coast. The urban south, Florida and Texas have lost much of their traditional character because of economic transformation and migration from other parts of the nation as well as large-scale immigration. Starting in the 1990s, the massive settlement of Latinos brought a similar transformation to much of the rural and small-town south.

The distinctiveness of the southern lowland developed with the earliest settlement along the Atlantic coast. The first colonists, Englishmen who came for economic rather than religious or political reasons, did not find the gold and silver that Spanish discoveries made them dream about, but the climate and soil proved suitable for growing and exporting cash crops such as tobacco and cotton, that required much manual labour but offered huge profits. Soon estates larger than the family farm (called plantations) became common and resulted in dispersed settlement with a few small urban centres. To meet the need for fieldworkers, plantation-owners imported indentured servants (people who sold themselves into virtual slavery for four to seven years to pay for their passage to North America). By the late 1600s, however, planters turned to Africans sold into permanent slavery for labour. African slavery existed in all the American colonies, but became the main source of workers only in the plantation south.

As late as the 1830s, a proposal to end slavery failed by only one vote in the Virginia legislature. The cheap fertile lowlands to the west, improved machinery for harvesting cotton and high prices for the crop from the northern and British textile mills that were the backbone of the early Industrial Revolution made cotton 'king', as people then said. This confirmed the contrasts between the industrializing north and the slave-dependent south that led to the Civil War. The need to justify slavery and the shared memories of secession, war, defeat and occupation by Union armies reinforced southerners' regional ties. Although slavery ended with the Civil War, cotton remained the region's main cash crop into the 1930s, and most African Americans remained dependent on their former masters for work and a place to live. The migration of African Americans to northern cities, the Civil Rights Movement, the mechanization of cotton-growing and industrialized food-processing plants manned by recent Latino immigrants are typical of the progressive reorganization of the southern economy. Agriculture is still important, but today its products are much more varied. Industry has also moved south because of low energy and labour costs and natural resources such as iron ore, bauxite, oil, gas and vast pine forests.

An increasingly urban-industrial south forms the eastern arm of the so-called 'Sunbelt', a swathe of the southern and south-western USA that attracts financial, high-tech and media industries to growing population centres from Atlanta, Georgia to Dallas, Texas. Since late 1960s Civil Rights laws and voter-registration drives, the important roles of African Americans in public life and their support for the Democratic Party have driven most conservative white Americans to the Republicans, making the south a two-party region for the first time in a century. In response to these changes, African Americans' migration out of the region reversed in the late 1900s. The rapidly growing Latino population further complicates the picture by voting largely as Democrats. Still, surveys indicate that southerners as a whole remain less educated, more religious, more conservative and more predominantly old-stock American than the population of the other regions.

## The mid-west

The mid-west includes the states bordering the Great Lakes and two tiers of states west of the Mississippi river from Missouri and Kansas north to Canada. The Great Lakes states with their many manufacturing centres are called the industrial mid-west, although they are also important farm states. In similar fashion the two western tiers of states are called the agricultural mid-west, in spite of industrial cities such as St Louis and Minneapolis. In the national consciousness, the mid-west is one region: the American heartland of family farms and small towns, perhaps naïvely provincial and optimistic, but still the moral and social centre that mediates between the other regions.

The early routes of western migration through the Appalachians met in the Great Lakes states, making them the first place where the cultures of New England, the mid-Atlantic and the south combined. By 1860 the Great Lakes mid-west was well integrated into the markets of the north-east, and during the Civil War it gained a proud sense of its identity from having sacrificed men and wealth for the preservation of the Union. After the war, the settlement of the trans-Mississippi agricultural mid-west was completed as steel-plated ploughs tore up the deep-rooted buffalo grass of the prairies and Great Plains and turned them into farmland. In the 1900s, machinery and new strains of winter wheat made these areas some of the most productive farmland in the world. Eventually this same technology rendered the American ideal of the independent small farmer obsolete, as 'agribusinesses' replace the family farm.

In recent decades mid-western industrial cities have made great strides towards economic and environmental recovery, despite persistent problems with the loss of manufacturing jobs, slums and urban blight that follow in the wake of de-industrialization. Today Indianapolis, Detroit and Cleveland, for example, can boast of glamorous downtown convention centres, museums and resurgent industries that no longer pollute the air and water. Chicago, the national hub of the commodities market, an important international seaport, and the home of widely diversified industry and cultural institutions, remains the region's premier city.

Mid-western political traditions show a mixture of pragmatic caution and organized protest. While the region has the reputation of being conservative, it was the birthplace of the Republican Party, which opposed the spread of slavery and nominated Lincoln for the presidency. Later, the agricultural mid-west was home to the Populist and Farmer-Labour parties, which protested the economic domination of the north-east, and a centre of the Progressive Movement, which strove to make American governments more honest, efficient and democratic. Mid-western states, such as Minnesota and Wisconsin, have since then been leaders in social and environmental reform. Though mid-western farmers were reluctant to become involved in the First and Second World Wars, they became internationalist in outlook once mid-western agriculture became dependent on exports in the 1950s. Mid-western cities and universities were especially prominent in the opposition to the Vietnam War.

## The west

'The west' is a myth, a popular set of values and a region of the country. It represents possibility, freedom, self-reliance, the future. As a region, it is made up of three parts: the south-west, the mountain states, and the Pacific coast.

The south-west consists of New Mexico, Arizona and parts of surrounding states with a similar climate and culture. Seized during the Mexican–American War of 1848, this area now has a mixture of old, unusually strong Spanish-Mexican and Native-American communities – and a blend of people from many parts of the country who came in large numbers after 1945. Today cattle- and sheep-ranching are important for the economy, but dams on the major rivers and wells have transformed deserts into irrigated farmlands and metropolitan areas, such as Phoenix and Albuquerque. The warm, dry climate has proven attractive to people with respiratory ailments as well as electronics and aerospace companies. Mining, the petroleum industry and tourism, in the south-west's stunning national parks, are also important economic supports.

The federal government is the largest landowner in the south-west and even more clearly dominates the economy of the mountain states. The importance of its decisions about the leasing of federal lands becomes obvious when one learns that the government owns over four fifths of Nevada, two thirds of Utah and vast areas of the subregion's other states. The traditional independence of long-time residents is increasingly frustrated by their lack of control over local resources. Newcomers from other regions, environmentalists, business people, Native-American groups and government officials debate how resources should be used. The population density is low but appears to be growing so rapidly that some westerners think in-migration and development are nearing their acceptable limits.

Mining the mountains' mineral riches provided the basis for migration to the subregion and continues to be an economic mainstay. The mines brought the outside investment, transportation infrastructure and business that laid the financial foundation for urban areas such as Denver and Butte. Agriculture depends on ranching and forestry because other forms of farming require irrigation, and water rights have become as precious as rare metals. Las Vegas and Reno found wealth through the gambling and entertainment industries. Salt Lake City is the heart of the Great Basin Mormon centre that is more homogeneous than any other cultural area in the USA. Today it prospers by expertise in computer software and technology as well as by mining and irrigated agriculture.

European settlement of the Pacific coast began with the establishment of Spanish missions in California in the 1700s and included Russian and British domination of the Pacific north-west before the USA gained sovereignty over the area in the 1840s. The coastal territories attracted sizeable populations and qualified as states before the interior west because of the 1849 Gold Rush and reports of the lush greenness of the Oregon and Washington valleys. The San Francisco area was the first to experience rapid development because it was the port of entry for the Gold Rush 'Forty-Niners'. By the 1870s it was an industrializing metropolis that produced finished goods which successfully competed with imports from the east.

Today the city is the hub of a larger area that includes Berkeley and its famous university, Oakland with its many industries, the Silicon Valley complex of computer firms, Stanford University and the Napa Valley wine district. Los Angeles has experienced rapid population growth ever since it became the terminus of a transcontinental railroad in 1885. The LA metropolis, a group of cities connected by a maze of highways, is home to the Hollywood film and media conglomerates as well as major energy, defence and aerospace companies. California's two largest urban areas contain every major racial and ethnic group in the nation, with especially large Asian and Latino elements. Politically, southern California has the reputation of being conservative while the northern part of the state is considered liberal.

In the Pacific north-west the population and culture show less Latino and more New England and north-west European influence, while Asian-American groups are as well established as farther south. During the past thirty years, so many people and businesses have relocated to Washington and Oregon that state

**PLATE 2.6** Vineyard in Napa Valley, California, one of the inland agricultural areas between the western arms of the Cordillera.
(*Sipa Press/Rex Features*)

authorities have attempted to limit growth. Their avowed goal is to preserve the environment and quality of life through a mixed economy based on agriculture, forestry and tourism, as well as on heavy and high-technology industries.

Resource and land-management are major issues in Hawaii and Alaska, as they are in the continental west. Hawaii's government instituted a detailed land-use system soon after it became a state in 1959. The law not only provided areas for commercial, industrial and residential building, but also protected farm-land, nature reserves and tourist attractions. In the nineteenth century, settlers from the mainland recruited large numbers of Asians to work on plantations. But after 1900, when the islands became a US territory, these contract labour arrangements became illegal, and high immigration has resulted from better knowledge of the islands' attractions and easier transportation in the age of aviation. Today, the people are highly urban and have a make-up that is unique in the nation. The majority is Asian American, with people of Japanese extraction comprising the largest nationality group. Whites make up the largest minority, followed by smaller groups of Latinos, African Americans and native Polynesians.

The federal, state and Native-American tribal governments own over 99 per cent of Alaska. Much of its history has involved struggles between resource-hungry developers, who lease land from government and create jobs for local residents, and conservationists, who lobby public authorities to restrict land-use because they view Alaska as the last chance to preserve an American wilderness. Until Alaska won statehood in 1959, settlers and natives there subsisted primarily through fishing, hunting and logging. Except for the short-lived Klondike Gold Rush of 1898, the area seemed destined to prove right the sceptics who said the country had, in 1867, bought a ridiculously expensive Russian icebox containing only sealskins and salmon.

During the 1950s and 1960s, Alaska received a wave of immigrants who wanted to escape the congestion and pollution in the forty-eight contiguous states. At the end of the 1960s, oil strikes off the state's northern coast increased interest in developing this 'empty' land. The negotiations over how the environment should be preserved and the profits from the oil shared were the most critical in Alaska's history. The huge amounts of land and money Native Americans received in compensation gave them an entirely new status. The state profited so much that it replaced its income taxes with an annual oil dividend of about $1,000 per resident. To safeguard wildlife and the tundra, the trans-Alaska pipeline was insulated and lifted several feet above ground.

The results of oil development have been mixed. The population grew rapidly, reaching over half a million by 1990, but, though the per-capita income for Alaskans is the highest in the nation, so is the state's unemployment rate. Much of Alaska's employment boom was temporary. In 1989 the supertanker *Exxon Valdez* went aground and spilled millions of gallons of oil on Alaska's coasts. The demands for a clean-up united environmentalists, the fishing and tourist industries, Native-American organizations and ordinary citizens.

## Changing public attitudes: where do we go from here?

Few Americans would consider giving up modern lifestyles and technology, but many have understood that the quality of life in the future means reconciling environmental and pro-development interests to manage the nation's natural resources wisely. Still, polls in early 2001 showed that only four out of ten Americans worried about environmental problems a great deal, and just 13 per cent expected newly elected President George W. Bush to strengthen US polices to protect the environment. The public was evenly divided over the President's withdrawal of US support for the global-warming treaty adopted in Kyoto, Japan in 1997. Americans gave a relatively low priority to the country's pollution problems, ranking crime, health care, drug abuse, energy shortage and hunger and homelessness as more serious worries. On the other hand, over half believed the quality of the environment was worsening and two-thirds thought 'only some progress' had been made in correcting this negative trend during the previous thirty years. The same large majority blamed the federal government, US corporations and the American people, about equally, for doing too little to protect the environment. Yet half or more of those interviewed said they were 'sympathetic but not active' in the environmental movement, and only one in six claimed to participate actively.

**TABLE 2.1** Ranking of proposals to improve the environment, 2001.

|  | Favour (%) | Oppose (%) |
|---|---|---|
| Setting higher emissions and pollution standards for business and industry | 81 | 17 |
| Spending more government money on developing solar and wind power | 79 | 19 |
| More strongly enforcing federal environmental regulations | 77 | 20 |
| Setting higher auto-omissions standards for automobiles | 75 | 23 |
| Giving tax breaks to provide incentives for drilling for more oil and gas in the USA | 53 | 43 |
| Expanding use of nuclear energy | 44 | 51 |
| Opening up the Alaskan Arctic Wildlife Refuge for oil exploration | 40 | 56 |
| Setting legal limits on the amount of energy that average consumers can use | 35 | 62 |

*Source*: Gallup Poll Topics: Environment, Complete Review of Gallup Poll Analyses on Environment, 30 July 2001.

# Exercises

Explain and examine the significance of the following terms:

| | |
|---|---|
| Atlantic Plain | eastern maize regions |
| Piedmont | south-west |
| fall line | plains or bison region |
| Appalachians | north-west coastal cultures |
| Appalachia | Environmental Protection Agency |
| Central Lowland | Hawaiians |
| glacial moraine | attitudes toward land |
| Great Plains | north-east |
| Cordillera | urban industrial core |

continued

Colorado Plateau                        south
California's Central Valley             mid-west
Mississippi system                      west
Great Lakes–St Lawrence                 land-use system
trans-Alaska pipeline                   National Park Service
                                        'continental' climate

Write short essays on the following questions.

1.  Outline the main physical features of the USA, describing the country's most important natural resources and commenting on the environmental cost of their use.

2.  Discuss the causes of differences between Native-American and contemporary American cultural geography.

3.  Describe US pollution problems and conservation efforts with the attitudes shown in the text and Table 2.1 in mind.

## Further reading

*Statistical Abstract of the United States*, US Printing Office, annual.
The World Almanac and Book of Facts: 2000 (2001) Mahwah, NJ: Funk and Wagnalls Corporation.
*Time*, weekly magazine.
US Bureau of the Census, occasional series and reports.

## Web sites

<http://www.gallup.com/poll/indicators/indenvironment.asp>

**The United States Geological Survey:**
<http://www.usgs.gov/education/index/html>

**Maps, historical and geographical:**
<http://www.usgs.gov/fact-sheets/maps-us/index.html>

**Study materials:**
<http://intractive2.usgs.gov/learningweb/homework_geography.asp>

**The United States Environmental Protection Agency:**
<http://www.epa.gov/epahome>

**American environmental laws and regulations:**
<http://www.epa.gov/epahome/lawregs.htm>

**Geographical and environmental information from the federal government:**
<http://www.firstgov.gov>

# Chapter 3

# The people
## Settlement and immigration

## Mother of exiles

Immigration is a central aspect of US history. Believing in the American Dream of creating a better life for themselves, many tens of millions of people have come to live in the USA. They thus changed their homelands, America and their family histories forever. They strengthened the nation's commitment to 'the dream' and to its ideal of being a refuge for the poor and oppressed, a nation of nations. Gradually, over the centuries of massive immigration and the struggles of newcomers to adjust to American conditions, the view that the nature of the nation was and *should be* a composite of many national backgrounds, races and cultures gained popular acceptance. This view continues to face the enduring opposition of those who believe newcomers should leave their homeland cultures behind and 'Americanize', as well as the dilemma of deciding what is necessary to hold the country and its increasingly diverse population together.

Americans' (and the immigrants') core idealism, pride, and naïvety are embodied in Emma Lazarus's sonnet 'The New Colossus', which is displayed inside the base of the Statue of Liberty (see Plate 3.1). There is some truth to the dream. Settled peoples have been able to climb a 'ladder of ethnic succession' as new waves of immigrants arrive. For most of the foreign-born, life in the USA has meant an improvement over their situation in the 'old country', the realization of modest hopes for land- or home-ownership, for example. Later generations have enjoyed more significant socio-economic progress, though 'rags to riches' careers are rare indeed.

**PLATE 3.1** The Statue of Liberty.
(*Henry T. Kaiser/Rex Features*)

# 'The New Colossus'

Not like the brazen giant of Greek fame,
With conquering limbs astride from land to land;
Here at our sea-washed, sunset gates shall stand
A mighty woman with a torch, whose flame
Is the imprisoned lightning, and her name
Mother of exiles. From her beacon hand
Glows world-wide welcome: her mild eyes command
The air-bridged harbor that twin cities frame.
'Keep ancient lands, your storied pomp!' cries she
With silent lips. 'Give me your tired, your poor,
Your huddled masses yearning to breathe free,
The wretched refuse of your teeming shore.
Send these, the homeless, tempest-tost, to me,
I lift my lamp beside the golden door!'

However, the newcomers have also contributed to America's history of social disorder. The meeting, conflict and mixing of cultures has fuelled widespread discrimination, economic exploitation, anti-foreign movements and debates over equality, opportunity and national identity. In a country whose history began with the meeting of Native Americans and European colonists and continued through the importation of African slaves and several waves of immigrants, there has never been a single national culture.

The search continues for a metaphor that captures the character of American society. Is it best understood as an Anglo-American core culture to which newcomers sooner or later merge into as they assimilate? Or should it be some form of cultural pluralism as suggested by, among other images, the metaphors of 'a melting pot', 'a salad with clearly identifiable ingredients', or 'a stew' with those ingredients mixed in the sauce of a common civic culture's habits and ideals? Some commentators reject both the claims of a unitary culture and of cultural pluralism, preferring instead forms of multiculturalism, in which multiple traditions are the ideal, and no cultural group, however old or influential historically, receives priority. Americans disagree over the nature of the process and what the ultimate goal should be: the assimilation, even homogenization, of newcomers or the acceptance of a permanently pluralistic society.

## Early encounters between Europeans and Native Americans

When European explorers and settlers encountered Native Americans in the late 1400s, a long history of mutual incomprehension and conflict began. These encounters amounted to a collision of worlds. Contacts between the Americas and other continents had been so rare that plants, animals, diseases, and human societies evolved into different forms in the 'new' and the 'old' worlds. Europeans and Native Americans caught diseases from each other. Europeans survived the first contacts better, but for most of the seventeenth century well over half of them died from difficulties in adjusting to the new environment. The Native Americans fared far worse: epidemics annihilated entire native cultures. North America's pre-Columbian population of 10 million shrank to between 2 and 3 million. The exchange of plants and animals had effects that were just as far reaching. Horses, donkeys, sheep, pigs and cows were alien creatures to Native Americans. Potatoes, maize and tobacco were discoveries to Europeans. The potato played a key role in the great population growth that brought millions of European immigrants to the USA in the 1800s.

European societies were so diverse that Spaniards and the English could hardly imagine living in the same place in peace. Some Native-American cultures viewed other indigenous peoples with a dislike no less intense. Yet, each continent's diversity of cultures were related, even quite similar in broad outline, when compared with cultures from the other continent. Thus, all Europeans tended to look alike to Native Americans, and most Europeans seemed incapable of seeing Native Americans as anything but a single people.

Native Americans were pantheists. They believed that the divine was in all things and that human beings were no more important than any other part of the world. Europeans viewed human beings as the highest creation of a God who made all things fit a system called the Great Chain of Being. In it only angels and human beings had souls and rational intelligence; white people were more highly favoured by God than brown, red or black people; men ranked higher than women; and every person had a place in a social class. The vast differences in these two visions led to equally contrasting attitudes toward nature, society and the individual. To the European, changing nature from a wilderness to a garden was one of society's chief aims. Man did God's work by revealing the divine order in the world and exploiting the good things God had given him. It was natural that time and land were viewed as commodities to be measured, bought and sold as part of the individual's pursuit of success. Native Americans saw nature as sacred, as something to be revered or accepted rather than changed. Theirs was a communal life in which material goods as well as individual talents belonged to the group and were valued for its preservation.

To Europeans, Native Americans seemed lazy and wasteful of nature's potential. Viewing time as fluid, they had only vague concepts of the past and the future, and so seemed utterly unreliable. Because they viewed nature as a great mother, they could not comprehend how pieces of her could be sold and owned by individuals. From the first European settlement until today, the main focus in conflicts between these continental culture systems has been land-ownership.

# The founders

The people who established the colonies are considered founders rather than immigrants because they created the customs, laws and institutions to which later arrivals (the first immigrants) had to adjust. The Spanish occupied coastal Florida, the south-west and California in the 1500s and 1600s. After trying to enslave the natives, they worked to convert them to Christianity, farming and sheep-herding. As many natives rejected this way of life, the Spanish colonies faced border attacks for over 200 years.

The English established their first permanent settlement at Jamestown, Virginia in 1607. Their monarch had no desire to rule distant colonies, so instead the Crown legalized companies that undertook the colonization of America as private commercial enterprises. Virginia's early residents were so preoccupied with a vain search for gold and a sea passage to Asian markets that the colony floundered until tobacco provided a profitable export. Settlers were difficult to recruit until the company offered them free land. Then the colony expanded rapidly, although most newcomers wanted to be tobacco plantation owners, not fieldworkers. Because of the scarcity of plantation labour, in 1619 the first African slaves were imported. Supported by tobacco profits, Virginia imported 1,500 free labourers a year by the 1680s and had a population of about 75,000 white Americans and 10,000 African slaves by 1700.

In the 1630s, Lord Baltimore established Maryland as a haven for Catholics, England's most persecuted minority. Maryland's leadership remained Catholic for some time, but its economy and population soon resembled Virginia's. In the 1660s, other English aristocrats financed Georgia and the Carolinas as commercial investments and experiments in social organization. Within a generation, these colonies too resembled Virginia, but their cash crops were rice and indigo. The southern settlers warred with the natives within a few years of their arrival and by the 1830s drove the Native Americans from today's south.

To escape religious oppression in England, the Pilgrims, a small group of radical separatists from the Church of England, founded the first of the northern English colonies in 1620 at Plymouth, Massachusetts. The Puritans, who established the much larger Massachusetts Bay colony in 1630, wanted to purify the Church of England, not separate from it. Mostly well-educated middle-class people, they emigrated for religious, political and economic reasons. In America they believed they could create a 'city on a hill' to show how English society could be reformed. To that end, over 20,000 Puritans migrated to Massachusetts by the early 1640s. By the latter 1600s, the bay colony expanded to the coast of present-day Maine, swallowed up Plymouth, and spawned the colony of Connecticut. Flourishing through agriculture and forestry, the New England colonies also became the shippers and merchants for all British America. Because of their intolerance towards dissenters, the Puritans' New England became the most homogeneous region in the colonies.

King Powhatan comands C.Smith to be flayne his daughter Pokahontas beggs his life his thankfullness and how he Subiecled 39 of their kings riade$ histo.

**PLATE 3.2**  King Powhatan ordering English adventurer John Smith (1580–1630) to be executed while the King's daughter Pocahontas begs for his life to be spared.
(*Mansell/Time Pix/Rex Features*)

The founding of the middle colonies (New York, New Jersey and Pennsylvania) was different. The earliest European communities here were Dutch and Swedish outposts of the fur trade that almost accidentally grew into colonies. New Netherlands, along the Hudson River and New York Bay, and New Sweden, along the Delaware River, recruited soldiers, farmers, crafts-men, clergymen and their families to meet the needs of the fur traders who bought pelts from the natives. New Sweden lasted only from 1638 to 1655, when the

Dutch annexed it. New Netherlands itself fell to the English fleet in 1664. The Dutch maintained their culture in rural New York and New Jersey for over 200 years. They also set the precedent of toleration for many ethnic, racial and religious groups in New Amsterdam. Before it became New York, the city had white, red, brown and black inhabitants; institutions for Catholics, Jews and Protestants; and a diversity that resulted in eighteen different languages being spoken. Although the dominant culture in colonial New York and New Jersey became English by the end of the 1600s, the English authorities continued the tolerant traditions of the Dutch in the city.

Pennsylvania's founders were Quakers who flocked to the colony after Charles II granted the area to William Penn in 1681 as a religious refuge. As with the Pilgrims and Puritans, official English tolerance took the form of allowing persecuted minorities to emigrate. Penn's publicizing of cheap land and religious freedom brought some 12,000 people to the colony before 1690. His toleration attracted a population whose diversity was matched only by New York's.

# The first wave: colonial immigration, 1680–1776

The founders had come for economic gain and religious freedom, but their descendants gave the first large wave of European newcomers a warm welcome only if they were willing to conform to Anglo-American culture and supply needed labour. The reception that immigrants received varied according to location and the individual's qualities, from the extremes of largely hostile New England, to the more tolerant, diverse middle colonies. It was with mixed rural New York settlements of north-west Europeans in mind that St Jean de Crévecoeur, an immigrant farmer from France, first stated in 1782 the idea that in America 'individuals of all nations are melted into a new race of man'. He insisted, however, that the people in this first version of the melting pot had to turn their backs on their homeland cultures and included only the Europeans in the settlements he knew. Like the colonists everywhere at the time, he thought that the white people along the wilderness frontier, like the Native Americans, soon descended into savage barbarism, and he tolerated them primarily because they provided a protective buffer against the natives.

Although conditions in their homelands also played a decisive role, this first wave was possible only because after 1660 the Crown opposed emigration from England and Wales but encouraged it from other nations. In 1662, King Charles II licensed the Royal African Slave Company as the supplier of slaves to English colonies, and during the next century about 140,000 Africans arrived after surviving the appalling conditions and brutal treatment on slave ships.

The largest group of immigrants (voluntary newcomers) were the Scots-Irish. With encouragement from the English, their ancestors left Scotland for northern Ireland in the 1500s. Yet, roughly a quarter of a million of them left northern Ireland after 1680 because of economic discrimination by the English. Most paid their passage across the Atlantic by becoming indentured servants (contracting to labour without wages for four to seven years in the colonies). When their term of service was finished, they usually took their 'freedom dues' (a small sum of money and tools) and settled on the frontier where land was cheapest. Constantly looking for better land, the Scots-Irish are the source of the stereotype of frontier folk, who feel it is time to move if they can see the smoke from a neighbour's chimney. This moving scattered their settlements from western New England to the hill country of Georgia and made it difficult to preserve their cultural heritage.

The period's 200,000 German immigrants aroused more opposition than the Scots-Irish. The largest non-English speaking group in the colonies, they believed their descendants had to learn German if their religion and culture were to survive in North America. For mutual support, they concentrated their settlements. In the middle colonies, German families lived so closely together in some areas that others found it hard to settle among them. Like the Scots-Irish, the Germans lived on the frontier, but they usually stayed behind when settlement moved farther west. Developing German-speaking towns, they kept to themselves and showed little interest in colonial politics. For some, the final straw was the Germans' prosperity. Renowned for their hard work, caution, farming methods and concern for their property, they were too successful, according to their envious neighbours. Benjamin Franklin expressed what many feared when he said they might 'Germanize us instead of us Anglicizing them'. In a period so near the religious wars of the Reformation, the reception Germans met also varied according to whether they were non-conformists, reformed Lutherans or Catholics.

Other smaller groups in the first wave showed contrasting ways that immigrants could adjust to new and varied conditions. England sent some 50,000 convicts and perhaps 30,000 poor people as indentured servants to ease problems at home while supplying the labour-starved colonial economy, and these people formed an underclass that quickly Americanized. Immigration from Ireland included thousands of single, male Irish Catholic indentured servants, who assimilated even more rapidly than the Scots-Irish, because of religious discrimination and the difficulty of finding Catholic wives. The Scots, perhaps because of their hatred of English attempts to suppress their culture at home, followed a pattern more like that of the Germans, using compact settlement, religion, schooling and family networks to preserve their culture for generations in rural areas. A French enclave persisted in South Carolina, but the French Huguenots and Jews, who settled in port towns, illustrated a contrasting tendency. English colonists severely limited their civil rights and sometimes attacked their churches or synagogues, but accepted marriage with them as long as they changed their religion. As a result, their communities nearly vanished.

This first wave of immigration transformed the demography of the colonies. By 1776 English dominance had decreased from four fifths to a bare majority (52 per cent) of the population. The great diversity of the peoples in the country led Thomas Paine, the colonies' most famous political agitator, to call the USA a 'nation of nations' at its founding. African-American slaves composed 20 per cent of this population and were a majority in large parts of the southern colonies. Most Native-American cultures had been forced inland to or beyond the Appalachians. Non-English peoples were a majority in the coastal towns, Pennsylvania, the south and parts of all the other colonies. However, the cultural, political and economic dominance of Anglo-Americans was clear.

## The second wave: the 'old' immigrants, 1820–90

Between 1776 and the late 1820s, immigration slowed to a trickle. The struggle for independence and the founding of the nation welded the colonies' diverse peoples together as Americans. The dominant Anglo-American culture and the passage of time weakened the old ethnic communities. Although Dutch and German areas of influence remained locally strong, most ethnic groups assimilated. In the 1820s most Americans and immigrants therefore thought the situation was unprecedented when the second wave gathered strength. Few newcomers were aware of the colonial enclaves, and Americans reacted as if the new ethnic districts that formed were completely novel.

The changes occurring in Europe and the USA also made the situation seem different. A range of factors pushed Europeans from their homelands. Religious persecution drove many German Jews to emigrate, and political unrest forced out a few thousand European intellectuals and political activists, but economic push factors were decisive for most of the northern and western Europeans who are commonly called the 'old' immigrants. Europe's population doubled between 1750 and 1850. In Ireland and parts of Germany rural people depended on the potato, which yielded more food per acre than grain. The rapid growth of cities encouraged farmers to switch to large-scale production based on farm machinery, the elimination of smallholdings and enclosure of common lands. With these changes, such a large population could not make a living in the countryside.

The industrial revolution and an international trade boom spread from Britain to the Continent and the USA during this period, but reached different regions at different times. If nearby cities offered industrial work or jobs in shipping, emigration rates were lower. But the population surplus from the countryside was so large that huge numbers of people left anyway. Stage migration (moving first to the city and, after some years, from there to a foreign country) became common. Following changes in the Atlantic labour market, people moved to where the jobs were. Steam ships and trains made migration abroad safer, faster and cheaper, and 'America letters' from family and friends in the USA gave a remarkably accurate picture of changing economic conditions there. Of the 60 million people who left their homelands between 1820 and 1930, two thirds settled in the USA. During the 'old' immigration, 15.5 million people made America their home.

The largest immigrant groups, in order of size, were Germans, Irish, Britons and Scandinavians, but many other peoples, including French Canadians, Chinese, Swiss and Dutch also came in large numbers. The factor that pulled most people to the USA was an apparently unlimited supply of land. Few seriously considered the claims of Native Americans. Another pull factor was work. The USA needed both skilled and unskilled labour. American railroad companies as well as state and territorial governments sent immigration agents to Europe to recruit people with promises of cheap fertile farms or jobs with wages much higher than they could earn at home. News of boom times in the USA, land giveaways such as the Homestead Act of 1862, and the discovery of gold in California brought peaks in the rising immigration.

## Settlement patterns and nativism

While the newcomers settled everywhere, they were most numerous in the urban manufacturing centres of the north-east and the recently settled farm-lands and frontier cities of the mid-west and Pacific coast. The 'old' immigrants found many economic niches, supplying much of the market for domestic servants, mill and factory workers, miners, loggers, sailors, fishermen and con-struction workers. Most came with enough funds to travel to places where fellow countrymen could help them adjust to American society, but after potato rot ruined the crop that supported Ireland's rural population, huge numbers of Irish immigrants arrived in the 1840s and 1850s with so little money that they stayed where they landed.

British immigrants seemed nearly invisible because they spoke English and Anglo-Americans' culture was much like theirs. They also won the gratitude of American businessmen up to the 1850s because they brought knowledge of Britain's most recent machines and industrial organization in their heads. White and Protestant, Scandinavians had language problems that made them seem slow to comprehend and at times they were ridiculed for their homeland ways, but they experienced less discrimination than some other groups. Nativism (the dislike of people and things foreign) plagued many 'old' immigrants in spite of their apparent similarity to native-born Americans. Germans were welcomed for their technical knowledge and industry, and admired for a culture that was Europe's most respected at that time. But they were also stereotyped as Prussian marionettes or Bavarian louts, criticized for clannishness, and were targets of temperance movements that attacked their habit of drinking in beer halls after church on Sundays. German Jews were excluded from education, the professions and shunned in many social circles.

The Irish suffered many forms of discrimination and were often stereotyped as dirty, lazy and drunken. The most serious opposition they faced, however, came from anti-Catholic bigots, who burned convents and churches as early as the 1830s. All the large immigrant groups found themselves involved in controversies over the control and content of the public schools, but none were so critical of the schools' attempts to Americanize immigrant children as the Irish (usually through the reactions of Irish-American priests).

Anti-foreign agitation reached its first peak in the 1850s. Along with anti-Catholicism, this nativism focused on popular versions of ideas made famous by Alexis de Tocqueville's *American Democracy*, which claimed that the basic social and political character of the USA was transplanted to New England from the mother country. The Know Nothing or American Party believed that not only the Irish, with their alleged loyalty to the Pope in Rome, but also all non-British immigrants, threatened this precious heritage, and so proposed tripling the time needed to gain US citizenship and restricting immigrants' voting rights. On that platform, Know Nothings won dozens of seats in Congress and numerous state and local offices, especially in the north-east. Internal divisions and the coming of the Civil War defused this nativist movement. Another arose in the 1860s in the west and achieved its goal, the Chinese Exclusion Act, which ended Chinese immigration in 1882. Racism and the fear of unemployment and depressed wages motivated the labour organizations that spearheaded the campaign.

## The third wave: the 'new' immigrants, 1890–1930

The 'new' immigration marked a change in the origin of most immigrants. Around 1890 immigration from north-west Europe declined sharply (but did not stop), while arrivals from southern and eastern Europe rose. By 1907, four out of five newcomers were 'new' immigrants. Between 1890 and 1914, the volume of immigration also soared, topping a million annually several times and equalling the 15.5 million of the old immigration in just twenty-four years. In numerical order, the largest 'new' groups were Italians, Jews, Poles and Hungarians, but many Mexicans, Russians, Czechs, Greeks, Portuguese, Syrians, Japanese, Filipinos and others also immigrated.

To most Americans, the change mostly involved the feeling that the typical immigrant had become much less like them. The religions, languages, manners and costumes of the Slavic peoples seemed exotic or incomprehensible. Eastern Orthodox Jews, the Mediterranean nationalities and Asians appeared to belong to other races. But this tidal wave of people was in several ways similar to its predecessors. The basic economic push and pull factors had not changed. The commercialization of farming, urbanization and industrialization had simply spread east and south. The new immigrants had the same dream of bettering their own and their children's future. Like the Puritans, eastern European Jews emigrated because of religious persecution, chiefly the bloody Russian pogroms.

Transportation improvements continued, increasing the flow of migrants. Falling train and steam-ship ticket prices (often prepaid by relatives in America) made migration affordable even for the very poor and the young. Cheap travel also permitted people to see immigration as a short-term strategy, instead of a lifelong decision. Many new immigrants were sojourners, 'birds of passage', who stayed only long enough to save money to buy land or a small business in the old country. In general, the new immigrants were younger, more often unmarried, and more likely to travel as individuals rather than in family groups. The opportunities in America had changed somewhat too. The closing of the frontier around 1890 signalled the end of the era of government land-giveaways. Less than a quarter of the newcomers found employment in agriculture. The Japanese in California are the best example of those who succeeded by buying unwanted land and making it productive. Four fifths of immigrants went where the jobs were: to the industries in the big cities of the north-east and Great Lakes mid-west. America had an enormous need for factory workers, but due to mechanization, most jobs were unskilled and poorly paid.

## A renewed immigration debate and immigration restriction

The size of the new immigration and the altered job market resulted in larger urban immigrant quarters than Americans had ever seen. Crime, overcrowding, insanitary conditions and epidemics in immigrant ghettos caused alarm and reform before the Civil War. Now these problems seemed insurmountable, and many Americans doubted that the more 'exotic' foreigners could be assimilated into society. Reactions to the situation in the cities were various. Reformers established 'settlement houses' and charities to help immigrants adjust, worked to Americanize them and fought for better housing and parks. Some saw that the ghettos were important buffer zones where immigrants could use their mother tongues and follow old-country traditions while gradually adjusting to the USA. Others concluded that the ghettos proved that restrictive immigration laws were needed.

In 1909, Israel Zangwill's play *The Melting Pot* popularized the idea that the diverse groups in the USA would eventually fuse many races and cultures through intermarriage and become a new people. To many a native-born reformer, that was a more radical version of the melting pot than they could accept, and to them the metaphor meant that the immigrants should conform to Anglo-American culture, for their own good. Nativists of the time could not imagine a greater calamity than such a melting-pot 'mongrelization' of the white race. An opposing, traditional view was that the USA should be an example of what Horace Kallen called 'cultural pluralism', the belief in a collection of cultures united by loyalty to the same political and civic ideals. But pluralists had long split over the issue of race. The founding fathers, for example, made the national motto '*e pluribus unum*' (out of many one), but in the Naturalization Act of 1790, they permitted foreigners to become American citizens only if they were white.

Restriction, even regulation of immigration, was slow to develop in the USA, which encouraged immigration and, until 1875, only asked local authorities to count immigrants. Foreigners could become citizens in five years and vote as soon as they applied for citizenship. Finally, in 1891, the federal government took responsibility for regulating immigration and the next year opened Ellis Island, the famous screening depot for immigrants in New York Bay. In the 1920s, however, those who believed the USA could not successfully integrate so many immigrants won the passage of severely restrictive, racist immigration laws. The National Quota Acts represented the climax of a campaign for restriction that achieved its first result in 1875, when the federal government began a piecemeal listing of banned groups that, in time, included convicts, prostitutes, the Chinese, lunatics, idiots, paupers, contract labourers, polygamists, political radicals, the Japanese and illiterates.

**PLATE 3.3** The registration room at Ellis Island in New York Bay in 1912, where government officials decided on the eligibility of most new immigrants to enter the USA. (*Corbis*)

The influence of eugenics, the pseudo-scientific racism of the early 1900s, which purported to prove experimentally the superiority of Anglo-Saxons over all other 'races', was evident in the list and later legislation. So was the combination of First World War super-patriotism that demanded 100 per cent Americanism, and the ideological insecurity that grew after the Russian Revolution of 1917. Finally in 1921, Congress passed the first general limitation on immigration, the Emergency Quota Act, that drastically reduced the annual number of European newcomers to 358,000 (less than a third of pre-war levels), and introduced *nationality quotas*. Each European nation's allotment of immigrant visas per year equalled 3 per cent of the foreign-born in the USA from that country at the federal census of 1910.

The dissatisfaction of restrictionists with this law revealed the groups they feared most, Asians and the new immigrants from Europe. In 1924 the Asian Exclusion Act ended all immigration from Asian nations, and a National Origins Quota Act reduced European nationality quotas to 2 per cent. More important, it moved the census for counting the foreign-born of each group back to 1890, when only small numbers of 'new' immigrants were in the USA, so that their quotas became much smaller. The 1924 Act also introduced a new concept, national *origins* quotas, based on the accumulated part of the American population of each European national background between 1790 and 1920, which cut the quotas for all European nations but the United Kingdom by one half to two thirds. In 1929, when the national origins quotas went into effect, Britain's was 65,361, while Italy's, for example, was 5,802 and Syria received the minimum of 100 visas. This narrow, specifically Anglo-American definition of the national identity remained the legal framework for immigration to the USA until 1965.

## Wartime policies and the search for principle in immigration policy

Writing immigration law that functions as intended has proved difficult. The Quota Acts did end the new immigration, and arrivals from northern and western Europe did fall sharply, but immigration from the United Kingdom also declined. Even the western European nations with much reduced quotas left those unfilled. Nor did Congress guess that arrivals from 'non-quota' nations, such as Mexico, and US territories, such as the Philippines and Puerto Rico, would soar into the millions by 1960. Events during these years defied governmental plans. The depression of the 1930s put a stop to mass immigration. Local authorities and 'vigilantes' forcibly deported about half a million Mexican Americans, many of them US citizens, during that decade. Nazi and fascist regimes caused an enormous flow of refugees, 250,000 of whom Congress admitted as non-quota immigrants under special laws. Many more, including 20,000 Jewish children, were turned away because the USA was unwilling to put aside national origins quotas during a time of high unemployment and rising anti-Semitism.

The Second World War and the Cold War caused several contrasting shifts in policy. The government imported temporary farm labour from Mexico under the '*bracero* program' due to wartime labour shortages and lifted the ban on Chinese immigration because of foreign-policy considerations. Yet it also bowed to panicky racists on the west coast, who feared foreign spies, and confined 115,000 Japanese Americans in 'internment camps', confiscating most of their property. After the war, federal law provided for the entry of families formed by US service people abroad, and several hundred thousand displaced persons (those so uprooted by the war that they had no homes to return to) were admitted by Acts of Congress. Between 1948 and 1959, Cold War refugees from communist countries, like Hungary and Cuba, also came.

The total of non-quota immigrants for those years reached 750,000, and made a mockery of the idea of regulating immigration according to national origins quotas. Moreover, during the Cold War, when the USA competed with the USSR for the allegiance of non-aligned nations, the racist principles underlying the quotas were a foreign-policy embarrassment. In 1952, the McCarran–Walter Act stated that race was no longer a reason for refusing someone an immigrant visa. Instead it started the so-called 'brain-drain' to the USA by reserving the first 50 per cent of visas for each country for people with needed skills. But the law kept the national origins principle, gave many Third World countries tiny quotas, and made communist or socialist associations a bar to immigration. Pressure for an entirely new approach grew.

The Immigration Act of 1965 provided this new approach, but also had unforeseen consequences. It replaced national origins quotas with hemispheric limits to annual immigration. To emphasize equal treatment, all nations in the eastern hemisphere had the same limit of 20,000 immigrants annually. A system of preferences set principles for selecting immigrants. Reunifying families, the most important principle, reserved nearly three quarters of immigrant visas for relatives of American citizens or resident aliens. Spouses, minor children and parents were admitted outside the limits. Grown children, brothers and sisters were given special preferences. The second principle continued the 'brain-drain' by reserving 20 per cent of visas for skilled people. Refugees received the remaining visas. Legislation made the national limit and preference system global in the 1970s.

Congress intended to make up for past injustices to southern and eastern Europeans through 'family reunification' visas for siblings and grown children, which it hoped would lead to the reappearance of 'new' immigrants. For ten years the plan worked, but by 1980 it became clear that the family preferences benefited people from other nations much more. In 1965 Europe and Canada provided the majority of immigrants to the USA, but by 1980 less than a sixth came from those places and four fifths were almost equally divided between Asia and Latin

America. Expecting western nuclear families, American lawmakers did not anticipate how Third World peoples would use the family reunification clauses to bring in extended families.

# The fourth wave: 1965 to the present

The 1965 law ushered in the fourth major wave of immigration, which rose to a peak in the late 1990s and produced the highest immigration totals in American history by the end of the decade. In addition to the many immigrants allowed by the hemispheric limits (changed to a global total of 320,000 in 1980), the wave has included hundreds of thousands of immediate relatives and refugees outside those limits. It has also contained millions of illegal aliens, who cross borders without (or with false) papers or arrive at airports on student or tourist visas and then overstay.

Between 1960 and 2002 nearly 35 million people settled legally in America. The list of the ten largest nationality groups in Table 3.1 for 1960 shows only two Latino and no Asian immigrant groups but many European nationalities. The prominence of Mexicans, however, foreshadowed future trends. At the peak of the fourth wave in the 1990s, some 9.5 million more newcomers arrived. The second list of groups, in 2002, *after* the peak brought by the 1965 Act, reveals the law's unexpected benefits for the Third World immigrants of the fourth wave. In 2002 three quarters of the legally resident foreign-born in the US were Latino (51 per cent) or Asian (24 per cent).

**TABLE 3.1** The effects of the fourth wave on the ten largest immigrant groups, 1960 contrasted with 2002.

| *1960* | | *2002* | |
|---|---|---|---|
| 1 | Mexicans | 1 | Mexicans |
| 2 | Germans | 2 | Filipinos |
| 3 | Canadians | 3 | Indians |
| 4 | British | 4 | Chinese |
| 5 | Italians | 5 | Dominicans |
| 6 | Cubans | 6 | Vietnamese |
| 7 | Poles | 7 | Canadians |
| 8 | Irish | 8 | Koreans |
| 9 | Hungarians | 9 | Cubans |
| 10 | Portuguese | 10 | Salvadoreans |

*Source*: Office of Immigration Statistics, US Department of Homeland Security, 2004

**PLATE 3.4** Mexican illegal immigrants crossing the border fence, Tijuana, Mexico, 1999.
(*Dave Gatley/MAI/Time Pix/Rex Features*)

Like the earlier waves of newcomers, the fourth includes a broad range of socio-economic groups. One result of saving visas for needed occupations is that a very noticeable minority are highly skilled workers, professionals (especially engineers, doctors and nurses), and entrepreneurs with capital. The large majority of *both* legal and illegal immigrants are similar to those who have arrived since the 1820s. They are above average educationally and economically at home, but below average in these areas in the USA. They have come because commercialization and industrialization (now revolutionizing the Third World) have disrupted their traditional economies.

At the socio-economic bottom of this wave are people who obtain visas because they are near relatives of recent, more skilled immigrants or who take jobs Americans do not want. Among the latter are Latino women recruited by agencies as live-in domestic servants and nannies. Spreading the word about these jobs and moving into better-paid work once they have acquired more English, they bring their families and forge the links in 'chain migration' based on a network of female contacts.

The nationalities and skin colours of most people in this wave are different and more various, however, and they arrive in different ways and settle in different places. There are colonies of Hmong in Minneapolis, Vietnamese on the Mississippi Delta, east Indian hotel-owners across the Sunbelt, Middle-Eastern

Muslims in Detroit and New Jersey and large concentrations of Latinos – not only in the south-west but also in the rural south and mid-west as well as the nation's big cities. These large foreign-born settlements have given rise to contemporary forms of racism and nativism. Groping for ways to adjust to the changes in their country's population, some Americans are again resorting to broad stereotypes.

## Attitudes to immigrants: the contemporary debate

In 1982, when the Gallup Organization asked Americans whether specific ethnic groups had been good or bad for the USA, on the whole, the longer the group had been the country, the more favourable was the public response. Thus, by then large majorities thought Irish Catholics and Jews, who earlier suffered from widespread discrimination, had been good influences on the country. Racial attitudes, however, appeared to be decisive in creating long-term low opinions of non-white ethnic groups. Less than half of the Americans questioned in 1982 thought Japanese, Chinese and African Americans had favourably affected the country, and only one in five or less approved of having recent non-white groups, such as Puerto Ricans, Vietnamese and Haitians in the USA.

PLATE 3.5 A crowd enjoying a recent Macy's Thanksgiving Day Parade in New York City. (*Corbis*)

Large numbers of Asian immigrants in the fourth wave arrive with more capital and a higher level of education than most Latinos. Those facts and popular attitudes towards some Asian cultures' emphasis on respect for parents, education and hard work have led some media commentators to lump all Asian Americans together under the label of the 'model minority'. This ignores the large majority of Asian immigrants who come with little money and education; the problems of Asian refugees who have experienced wartime traumas; and job discrimination and violence against Asian Americans. For its own convenience, the federal government invented the word 'Hispanics' to put in a single category all the Central and South American Spanish-speaking cultures arriving in the USA in the fourth wave. A handy label for official statistics, the word became identified with illegal immigrants in the popular mind because of the large number of immigrants unlawfully crossing the border with Mexico. It thus contributed to prejudice against hugely diverse Latino populations, even though 'illegals' come from countries as diverse as Ireland and Iran.

Illegal immigration causes heated debate over government policy to control entry to the USA. One segment of public opinion stresses that tolerating illegal immigration encourages a general disregard for the law, lowers wages for other workers, and undermines the 1965 law that gives all nationalities an equal chance for immigrant visas. Other Americans emphasize that illegal immigrants take jobs that US citizens do not want, are paid less than the legal minimum wage, work in substandard conditions, and, while needing the benefits of social-welfare programmes, dare not reveal the facts of their situation for fear of being deported.

The federal government responded to this ongoing debate in 1986 by passing the Immigration Reform and Control Act (IRCA). The law attempted to minimize illegal immigration while expressing acceptance and giving rights to people already inside the USA. It sets fines and penalties for employers who hire illegal aliens and also attempts to prevent employment discrimination through rules that outlaw firing or refusing to hire people because they look foreign. The law offered 'amnesty' (legal immigrant status) for illegals who had stayed in the USA for four years, and for some temporarily resident farmworkers. Almost 3 million people became legal immigrants through IRCA. Their improved situation was the one great success of the legislation. It proved difficult to document evidence that employers had broken the law, and the number of illegals, which declined at first, rose again to between 9 and 11 million in a few years.

In spite of rising reactions against immigration in the 1980s, national policy became more liberal through the Immigration Act of 1990. It raised the annual total of immigrant visas, the limit for individual nations and the number of asylum seekers who could remain in the USA. It also removed restrictions on the entry of many groups, including homosexuals and communists, people from nations adversely affected by the 1965 law, and additional family members, including the spouses and children of illegals given amnesty. During the economic boom

**PLATE 3.6** After 9/11, finger-printing and biometric identification techniques became routine for immigrants and all others entering the USA.
(*Corbis*)

of the 1990s, the shortage of unskilled labour made most Americans willing to overlook the problem of illegal immigration.

Since 1990, sharp differences in public attitudes to immigration have been evident. The backlash against the level of immigration grew strong by the mid-1990s, especially in some groups in the seven states (California, New York, New Jersey, Florida, Texas, Illinois and Arizona) where over three quarters of newcomers settled. In California, a referendum that denied illegal immigrants educational and social services passed easily but was blocked by court challenges initiated by opponents of the measure. More restrictive attitudes also found expression in the federal immigration and welfare reform laws of 1996. These strengthened border controls against illegal immigration, made it easier to deport 'suspicious' visitors and immigrants, required family in the USA to take more responsibility for keeping newcomers off the welfare roles, and denied *legal* immigrants federal welfare benefits (illegal immigrants never received them). Court cases and action by the Clinton administration prevented this last provision from having much impact.

President George W. Bush expressed generous attitudes towards some foreign workers in early 2001, when he welcomed a proposal from the President of Mexico for a new *bracero* worker programme and amnesty law. During the recession and the War on Terror that followed, however, he did not implement the proposal. After the 9/11 terrorist attacks, polls showed that large majorities of the public favoured further strengthening border controls against illegal immigration and a decrease in legal immigration. In response, the government more energetically used the provisions of the 1996 law, and through the USA Patriot Act of 2002 developed new biometric identity checks to regulate entry to the country, conducted intensified surveillance of the foreign-born and called in immigrants, especially Arab Americans, for questioning and possible detention or deportation.

Five years into the twenty-first century, US law still allowed the world's highest level of legal immigration, nearly a million annually, most of it non-white and non-Western (culturally). An inability or unwillingness to enforce existing law resulted in the continued tolerance of additional millions of illegal immigrants, most of them Latinos. This situation suggested that in the forty years since the 1965 immigration-reform law, Americans' self-image had become extraordinarily inclusive when compared with the narrow Anglo-American national identity enshrined in US law until that time.

Sharp differences, nonetheless, continued to mark American public opinion about immigration after 2001. Most of the country's economic, political and cultural elites accepted high levels of legal and illegal immigration. The general public, on the other hand, increasingly linked immigration to concerns about national security, population growth, environmental problems and cultural differences. Majorities of those polled therefore favoured more effectively restricting entrance to the country. A dramatic example of this chasm in attitudes about immigration occurred in 2004. Having implemented a variety of national security measures in response to the 9/11 attacks, President Bush announced his support for a revised guest-worker-amnesty plan, similar to the one proposed by Mexico three years earlier. The public rejected the idea by large margins in a series of polls, and it quietly disappeared from the presidential agenda. In this divided climate of opinion, it was uncertain whether the public's concerns would in time bring a less generous American immigration policy.

## Exercises

Examine and explain the significance the following names and terms.

| | | |
|---|---|---|
| indigenous peoples | middle colonies | pluralism |
| pantheists | first wave | national origins quotas |
| Great Chain of Being | old immigrants | 1965 Immigration Act |
| immigrant (*contra* founder) | stage migration | fourth wave |
| Virginia | nativism | IRCA |

continued

| | | |
|---|---|---|
| northern colonies | new immigrants | 1990 and 1996 Immigration Acts |
| push and pull factors | melting pot | The 2002 USA Patriot Act |

Write short essays on the following topics.

1. Explain why the encounters between Native Americans and Europeans were so disastrous.

2. Describe one or more of the four major waves of immigration and discuss causes for the kind of reception the newcomers received.

3. Debate which of the metaphors for understanding the nature of American society is most accurate and enlightening.

4. Critically discuss the evolution of American immigration law and the social forces that produced it.

## Further reading

Barkan, E. R. (1996) *And Still They Come: immigrants and American society, 1920 to the 1990s* Wheeling, Ill.: Harland Davidson.

Barkan, E. R. (ed.) (1999) *A Nation of Peoples: a sourcebook on America's multicultural heritage* Westport, Conn.: Greenwood Press.

Gjerde, J. (ed.) (1998) *Major Problems in American Immigration and Ethnic History: documents and essays* New York: Houghton Mifflin Company.

King, Desmond (2000) *Making Americans: immigration, race and the origins of the diverse democracy* Cambridge, Mass.: Harvard University Press.

Kraut, A. M. (1982) *The Huddled Masses: the immigrant in American society, 1880–1921* Wheeling, Ill.: Harland Davidson.

Lieberson, S. and M. C. Waters (1988) *From Many Strands: ethnic and racial groups in contemporary America* New York: Russell Sage Foundation.

Office of Immigration Statistics, US Department of Homeland Security (DHS), 2003–2004.

US Bureau of the Census, decadal series and current population reports (CPR).

US Bureau of the Census, Special Study (May 2001) Why People Move: Exploring the March 2000 CPR.

US Bureau of Labour Statistics, annual reports.

## Web sites

<http://www.gallup.com/poll/indicators/indimmigration.asp>
<http://www.census.gov/main/www/cprs.html>

**DHS, US Citizenship and Immigration Services:**
<http://uscis.gov>
<http://www.census.gov/Press-Release/www/2001/cb01-04.html>
<http://factfinder.census.gov>
<http://washingtonpost.com> (archives, search and special reports)

# Chapter 4

# The people
## Women and minorities

- The reason for American women's and minority history
- Women in America
- Native Americans
- African Americans
- Asian Americans
- Latinos
- *Exercises*
- *Further reading*
- *Web sites*

# The reason for American women's and minority history

Discrimination has given women and some minorities a special status in American society. For much of American history, male-dominated society in the USA has forced women, Native Americans, African Americans, Asian Americans and Latinos into inferior categories. As a result, these groups have their own histories as subjects of changing opinion and government policy even though their experiences are integral parts of the nation's history. They have moulded American history through their struggles for equality and resistance against discrimination. Inequality has led to group differences in attitudes, class, occupation, income, health, housing and crime. The gap between national ideals and the realities of prejudice has agitated the nation's conscience and prompted a very uneven but persistent progress toward greater equality.

There has been constant debate over the proper means of creating a more just society. Neither policy-makers nor the subjects of policy have agreed on the course to follow. Over a century of federal civil rights laws has proved that changes in the law often do not function as intended, nor do they assure changes in attitudes. Defining what equality means has proved difficult. Most Americans have supported equality of opportunity (an equal chance to develop one's abilities and to be rewarded for them) but not equality of results (an evening-out of economic, social and political power). Thus, most attempts to redistribute wealth have failed or have been short-lived. Affirmative-action programmes and election districts that arrange for preferential treatment of women and minorities, in order to correct the effects of past discrimination, face strong opposition. Although Americans favour equality, they are at odds about what it is and about the degree to which government can or should provide it.

## Women in America

Numerically a majority, women today experience unequal treatment in significant ways. They are assigned prescribed roles and do not work in the most prestigious occupations, earn as much money or enjoy positions of equal social status as often as do men. Popular attitudes continue to keep women in their traditional place. Mostly working in poorly paid service jobs, they are severely under-represented in politics and the highest levels of business management. Nevertheless, great changes in their position have occurred.

Historically, women's legal status in America was determined by English common law. Until the mid-1800s, a woman experienced a 'civil death' upon marriage, which meant she ceased to exist legally except through her spouse. She had no right to own property, control her wages or sign contracts. Divorce, granted only in extreme cases, was easier to obtain for men than for women. A single woman was expected to submit to her father's or brother's will until she married. Claiming they were by nature physically frail and mentally limited, men kept women economically dependent.

There were historical circumstances and attitudes that worked against or contradicted this conventional view of women. On the western frontier, women's skills were as essential as men's and the scarcity of women meant they could not be pampered. 'Back East' the shortage of men meant widows and single women were often needed to fill the occupational roles of men. From the earliest colonial days, most American women have worked. The churches proclaimed idleness to be a sin for both sexes. Before the industrial revolution, most necessities of life were made at home, and women were expected to be as proficient at handicrafts as men. Women were a majority among the first factory workers when the industrial revolution began in New England textile mills. Before the Civil War they worked in over 100 industrial occupations. However, they were concentrated mostly in the less skilled jobs and earned on average about one quarter of men's wages. Women were among the first workers involved in strikes and demonstrations for higher pay and better working conditions. From its beginning they joined the labour movement and formed their own unions when men showed little interest in organizing them.

## The nineteenth century

Some middle and upper-class white women were leisured or had no paid work at home. Among these were the founders of girls' schools between 1800 and 1850 and of famous women's colleges, such as Vassar and Mount Holyoke, in the latter 1800s. These social classes also produced most of the century's female reformers, who were prominent in the crusade against alcohol abuse and in movements to improve conditions in prisons, insane asylums, hospitals, schools and immigrant ghettos.

The first movement for women's rights was closely related to female reformers' experiences in abolitionist (anti-slavery) campaigns. Women abolitionists publicized parallels between discrimination against African Americans and women after they were attacked as 'unwomanly' for speaking to mixed audiences of men and women. In 1848 two abolitionists, Lucretia Mott and Elizabeth Cady Stanton, led the first women's rights convention in Seneca Falls, New York. In language taken from the Declaration of Independence, the convention's 'Declaration of Sentiments' called for property and divorce rights, educational and employment opportunities and the vote.

Thereafter, the women's movement held regular conventions and, with mixed results, worked to realize their stated goals. Before the Civil War Susan B. Anthony led successful efforts to improve women's status in marriage and divorce as well as their economic rights under New York state law. A few years later, however, these liberal provisions were repealed. Women were increasingly accepted as teachers and moved into nursing and government-office work during the war. Feminists joined the successful campaign for the constitutional abolition of slavery through the Thirteenth Amendment, but the movement split in two when it became clear that only African-American men were offered the vote in the Fourteenth and Fifteenth Amendments.

One faction opposed all proposals for broadening the franchise that excluded women, championed a wide range of women's rights and pursued the vote through a federal women's suffrage amendment. Another group thought the best plan was to present women's voting rights as a separate issue from suffrage for African-American men, avoid involvement in other causes that would alienate influential groups and concentrate on winning the vote on a state-by-state basis.

The latter group first tasted victory when Wyoming Territory granted female suffrage in 1869, but of seventeen states that considered women's suffrage between 1870 and 1910, only three approved it. Several other states gave women voting rights limited to municipal or school issues and elections. Although men continued to deny women membership in unions for skilled workers, female activists assisted unskilled women's unionization and mounted successful campaigns against child labour. On the other hand, their fight for abortion rights, birth control and membership on juries met with failure until after the Second World War.

## The twentieth century

The movement united behind efforts for ratification of the Nineteenth Amendment, which granted women the right to vote in all elections in 1920. Women strongly supported campaigns to deal with political corruption and urban social problems at the turn of the century. Therefore, many male politicians thought women would vote for a broad range of social reforms or form a women's party to defeat conservative male candidates.

These fears proved to be unfounded as women voters divided over issues in much the same way as men. Many women's rights organizations disbanded soon after suffrage was won, and women's economic position improved slowly in part because of disagreement within the movement about whether there should be any legal differences between the sexes. Female social reformers who demanded protective measures that treated women as a special category successfully lobbied for laws limiting women's working hours and occupational choices to protect their safety and health. Until the 1970s civil rights legislation for women and court decisions affecting their rights were generally based on such a protectionist approach.

Other feminists insisted that this approach kept women in poorly paid jobs and prevented equality with men because it assumes that women are the weaker sex. These activists proposed another constitutional change as early as 1923, the Equal Rights Amendment (ERA), to eliminate the remaining legal inequalities between men and women. Some opponents of the ERA feared it would overturn protective legislation for women. Such dissension and the generally conservative mood of the country contributed to the relative dormancy of the women's movement between the late 1920s and the early 1960s.

The turning point in women's employment came after the Second World War. Many married women who went to work during the war continued to work in peacetime, and many more joined them in the following decades. While 15 per cent of married women were employed in 1940, by 1970 almost 50 per cent had jobs. Many more married women were working and the majority in 1970 were middle-aged and middle class. Husbands accepted the change with little protest because most wives did not take jobs until the children entered school and then earned wages that kept the family in the middle class. Not only were larger numbers of women of all classes, married and single, working, but a larger percentage of them were getting a higher education.

Thus, when a new women's movement blossomed in the 1960s and 1970s, challenging the view that women's place was keeping house, many Americans agreed. The reality they lived no longer squared with conventions of the past. Again stimulated by African Americans' demands for civil rights, the women's movement lobbied effectively for the 1964 Civil Rights Act, which was the first such legislation to explicitly ban discrimination based on sex as well as on race. The more radical feminists of the 1970s rejected conventional gender roles and family life as stifling, patriarchal and frequently dysfunctional. By mid-decade, women's lobbying had helped pass laws that promised women equal treatment in the job market and admission to higher education, equal pay for equal work and equal availability of loans and credit. Advocates of women's rights also pursued their goals through litigation (court cases). In 1973 the Supreme Court legalized abortion through the *Roe* v. *Wade* case brought by women lawyers; since then the court has limited abortion rights only marginally. In a series of rulings during the 1970s and 1980s, it also supported affirmative action programmes which aimed to increase the number of women and minorities among employees or students until it equalled their proportion in the local population. In the 1978 *Regents* v. *Bakke* case, the court struck down a policy of using numerical quotas for affirmative action, but it still supports flexible programmes that encourage companies and institutions to actively recruit women and minorities. In the 1990s, however, rising public opposition to affirmative action was evident in a referendum in California and a federal district court decision in a Texas case that ended 'positive discrimination' in favour of women and minorities in those states.

**PLATE 4.1** National Organization for Women (NOW) protestors hold a pro-choice demonstration in Virginia, 1995.
(*William F. Campbell/Time Pix/Rex Features*)

A major initiative for women's rights in the twentieth century, that ultimately failed, was the Equal Rights Amendment to the US Constitution (ERA). Its text stated that neither the states nor the federal government could limit a person's rights on the basis of sex. In 1972 Congress passed the ERA with little opposition. To become a part of the Constitution, it then had to be approved by three-quarters of the state legislatures. However, after many states passed it in the early 1970s, support lagged and the ERA fell three states short of ratification in 1982.

Explanations for its failure differ. Some believe the conservative swing in public opinion that elected Ronald Reagan worked against ratification. Opposition among women who felt their accepted role would be undermined also weakened the chances for success. Others note that national opinion polls throughout the period showed majorities for ratification, but emphasize the difficulty in winning the three-quarters majority of states required. The National Organization for Women (NOW, founded by a group of older, moderate women in 1966) asserted that the struggle for ratification was well worth the effort because it raised women's awareness of their social position, involved them in the political process on their own behalf, and helped pass equal-rights provisions to many state constitutions. Yet others comment that the ERA was not necessary by the 1980s because civil-rights laws and court decisions had accomplished the same goal.

**PLATE 4.2**  African American women outside a hairdressers in Harlem, 2001.
(*Sipa Press/Rex Features*)

## Evaluating the contemporary situation for women

Today, court action has reduced the legal hindrances to equality between the sexes. 'Protective' laws based on sexual stereotypes have been repeatedly overturned. Employment ads cannot ask for applicants of only one sex. Most large private organizations that prohibit female members are banned. Federal Courts support strict laws against sexual harassment (unwanted sexual advances). Polls indicate that since law professor Anita Hill accused Supreme Court nominee Clarence Thomas of sexual harassment during televised Senate hearings in 1991, more women are prepared to take men to court over sexual offences, and more men expect them to do so. Judicial approval of state laws granting unpaid maternity leaves in the late 1980s led more private employers and public authorities to institute maternity leave programmes. In 1993 Congress mandated unpaid leave after the birth of a child for some 42 million workers. By the early twenty-first century, many employers also offered child day-care centres for working mothers, but women in low-wage jobs were seldom offered these facilities and could not afford to take unpaid maternity leave.

Women's groups and public surveys continued to indicate that in these and other ways, the progress made since the 1970s was limited. The incidence of rape and other forms of sexual harassment rose while other crime rates fell between

1995 and 2005, which some attributed to women's increased willingness to complain and others thought was part of a 'backlash' against the women's movement. Women's groups who focused on the easy availability of pornography and media violence as causes of child and wife abuse won few policy changes. On the other hand, in the 1990s, over half of all bachelor's degrees were awarded to women, who now earn higher degrees more often as well. These are mostly in fields traditional for women that offer lower earnings (such as the fine arts, foreign languages and nursing), but today women are making unprecedented inroads in highly paid 'male' professions (such as engineering, medicine and the law). Women ran for, and were elected to, high public office in record numbers during the past decade and a half but were still far outnumbered by men in government and management in 2005.

Perhaps most worrying, women's economic position still seemed to illustrate in exaggerated form the distance between the rich and the poor in the 1980s and 1990s. The 'feminization of poverty' continued to increase, especially after the economic boom of the 1990s ended. Women's earnings were still only two thirds of men's in 2003, and they remained largely segregated in the semi-skilled service sector. The income of working single mothers increased at a slower rate to that of other families during the boom and fell more rapidly after it. While the 1996 Welfare Reform Act helped many people find work in good times, by 2004 increased numbers of single mothers found themselves without work or without day care for their children, or both. Women were several times as likely to be living in poverty as men, and female-headed families made up nearly half of all poor families.

## Native Americans

Viewing Native Americans as a minority amounts to discussing their relationships to the European Americans that became the dominant population group in the USA. A story of invasion, prolonged military conflict and pressure to adjust to the demands of white hegemony, Native-American history is complex but has two primary aspects: the behaviour and governmental policy of white people towards 'first Americans' and the responses these actions provoked. The conflict was always an uneven one. In early days, Native Americans were outnumbered at the point of contact. Sicknesses reduced their population drastically while the influx of Europeans became enormous. Europeans' metal goods, textiles, written languages and books gave them a decisive technological advantage. European cultures were also more aggressively expansive and acquisitive.

## *Patterns formed in the colonial period*

British settlers came in much greater numbers than other Europeans and primarily sought land, rather than trading partners or mineral riches. They presented Native Americans with a threatening front of compact settlement, brought their own women and segregated themselves from the natives. Thus, no large mixed race of 'mestizos' appeared in British America.

Relations between the natives and the English were marked by distrust, resentment and disastrous wars. A predictable sequence of events set the pattern for almost three hundred years of contact. First was a short period of relative peace when the settlers exchanged technology for land, furs and knowledge of the Native Americans' survival techniques. Then conflicts caused by trade disagreements, expanded white settlement and cultural misunderstanding escalated into full-scale war. In the 1620s and 1630s the natives tried, by war, to expel the intruders and threatened the existence of the Virginia and New England colonies. During the third phase of massive retaliation, the natives were defeated militarily. Often the colonists received help from tribes that were traditional enemies of those that attacked the settlements. During the final phase, Anglo-American policies aimed at easing the expansion of settlement while minimizing the 'Indian threat'.

For the most part, colonists were left to devise their own solutions to this threat until the 1750s. In victory they usually tried to exterminate native opponents, drive them farther inland or enslave and deport them. Often, the settlers negotiated treaties based on a policy of forced separation to free territory for colonial settlement and to end violence. The natives were moved to distant lands that (the colonists promised) would be reserved for them permanently. In short, the 'Indian reservation' system dates back to the 1630s and 1640s.

Colonial authorities promised to protect the rights of reservation natives. Some colonists also encouraged them to adopt European ways and Christianity. In New England, villages of Christianized natives were known as 'praying towns', for example. But assimilation on distant reservations failed. Native peoples further west attacked the reservations because they objected to intrusions into their territory. Colonists squatted on reservation land when it was no longer distant from colonial settlement, and colonial authorities rarely acted to limit settlement. Native Americans resented and resisted attempts to assimilate them. Thus one cycle of violent conflict followed another, and Native Americans were continually pushed further west. In outline, with the substitution of US for British authorities, this general sequence of developments continued into the early 1900s.

In the eighteenth century, Britain and France competed for power in North America. Both vied for native allies, which led Native American groups to offer their allegiance to the highest bidder. The Iroquois Confederacy in western New York and Pennsylvania, for instance, was especially successful in playing one

European power against the other and, for a long time, was able to channel white settlement to the south of its territory. The French generally won support from more tribes because their trading activities seemed far less threatening.

To change this, the British government established a new policy during the French and Indian War (1754–63). It gave gifts to native leaders, bypassed the colonists through direct negotiations with the Indians and, most importantly, set a western limit to colonial settlement. The proclamation of 1763 made a line west of the Appalachian Mountains the official boundary of British America. To the west of the line was 'Indian Country', which settlers had to leave. Parliament had applied the colonists' policy of separation to both settlers and natives and had created a huge reservation. Its action brought enough tribes to Britain's side to defeat the French, who gave up much of their land claims in North America. The line infuriated the colonists, who ignored the proclamation but cited the limit on western settlement as a reason for rebelling against the mother country. When the American Revolution came, most tribes remained loyal to Britain. The USA therefore treated several tribes as conquered nations after the war and demanded their lands without payment.

## Conquest and removal, 1783–1860

Through the treaty of 1783, Britain ceded to the USA all the land between Canada and Florida to the Mississippi River and asked no protection for Native American rights. With the coming of peace, tens of thousands of settlers moved into the area, but over 100,000 Native Americans blocked their way. In the Great Lakes region a powerful native confederacy would not permit settlers north of the Ohio River. On the southern frontier, several tribes refused to give up lands, despite pressure from southern states. First the USA sent armies against the northern confederacy to take its land by conquest. When American forces suffered repeated defeats, however, the USA negotiated a treaty after its first major victory. The confederacy ceded huge amounts of land but won annual payments of goods and cash in return. Thus the US government set an important precedent that recognized Native-American land claims and the need to pay for lands taken by settlers.

Abandoning reliance on military conquest, many American leaders promoted a new version of the assimilation policy. Congress sent teachers and missionaries to the natives to transform them into farmers who could live in American society. The Native Americans were not asked if they wanted to be 'civilized', and those who favoured harsher policies said their resistance was proof that assimilation was impossible.

Meanwhile, observing the rapid growth of the white population west of the Appalachians between 1800 and 1810, the Shawnee leaders Tecumseh and The Prophet worked to form a grand alliance of tribes east of the Mississippi to limit US expansion. Tecumseh applied to the British for help when he heard that the two nations might go to war. The difficulty of unifying warring tribes defeated

**PLATE 4.3** Tecumseh, leader of the Shawnees, who was killed in the battle of the Thames in Canada, 5 October 1813, is shown here wearing a British medal and tunic.
(*Peter Newark's American Pictures*)

Native Americans' last attempt to control the land east of the river. While Tecumseh was lobbying for support among southern tribes, Americans defeated his forces in the north and British guns were discovered at his headquarters. A year later Tecumseh and his allies joined the British against the USA in the war of 1812, and Tecumseh was killed. The loss of both leadership and British support led many tribes to move further west after the war.

Tribes who remained found themselves forced to accept a revival of the old separation policy, now called removal, defined as moving Native Americans west of the Mississippi. Thomas Jefferson supported the idea as early as 1803, when he argued for buying the area from the Mississippi to the Rocky Mountains (the Louisiana Purchase) from France. Removal gained popularity even with so-called friends of the Native American who said removal would give the natives a chance to acquire social and political skills for assimilation away from squatters, disease, alcohol and poverty.

In 1830 President Andrew Jackson, famous as a combatant against the Native Americans in the war of 1812, signed the Indian Removal Act. Many tribes north of the Ohio River had signed individual removal treaties before that time and had moved to parts of present-day Kansas. Now, federal policy required the removal of all remaining tribes to a permanent 'Indian Territory', in today's Oklahoma. State authorities so terrorized southern tribes that all but two (the Seminoles and the Cherokees) accepted removal as the only alternative to extermination.

The Seminoles held out for seven years through guerrilla warfare in the Florida Everglades. The Cherokees had adopted many American institutions including industries, schools, a newspaper and an American-style government and constitution during the earlier period of federal assimilation programmes. Influenced by the society around them, some Cherokees (mostly those who had intermarried with Americans) were slaveholders. The Cherokee appealed to the US federal courts to fight removal plans and the state of Georgia's seizure of their lands. The Supreme Court ruling in this case set a precedent for later decisions concerning Native Americans' rights and status, even though it had little immediate effect. The court said a Native American tribe was neither an independent nation nor a state but a 'domestic dependent nation'. Within US borders, tribal lands were still outside American political structures. By right of first residence, Native Americans had sovereignty over their lands and could lose them only voluntarily and with just compensation. The federal government alone could negotiate with a tribe. State laws did not apply on Native-American lands or reservations, where native laws took priority. American citizens could not enter Native-American lands except by permission or treaty right. By implication, the Removal Act and Georgia's actions were declared illegal.

President Jackson and Georgia ignored the court's rulings. Federal troops and state militia in the winter of 1838 'escorted' the Cherokee to Indian Territory. Because of the weather, harassment by Americans, and poor government planning for food and shelter, a quarter of the Cherokees died during the march along the path called 'The Trail of Tears'.

By 1840 nearly 100,000 Native Americans had been forcibly removed to Indian Territory. Here, the great differences in the terrain and climate required painful adjustments for eastern woodlands peoples. Put on much smaller parcels of land than they were used to, groups with long traditions of mutual hostility were forced to live side by side. Western Indians resented the newcomers' intrusion into their lands and raided the territory for food and livestock. Unable to cope with the situation and often not given the protection and material aid promised by the federal government, many Native Americans in the territory sank into dependence, alcoholism and poverty.

## *War, concentration and forced assimilation, 1860–1934*

During the Civil War, several southern tribes in Indian Territory supported the south by supplying Confederate armies with food, and so, after the war, were asked to give up even more land by the north. At the war's end, removal was replaced with a policy of concentration as Americans occupied the prairies and plains once considered the 'Great American Desert' and rushed in to profit from gold and silver strikes in the west. US government support for trans-continental railroads increased settlement and quickened the slaughter of the buffalo on which the plains natives depended. Native Americans were to be concentrated on reservations to free as much land as possible for development.

Between 1850 and 1890 the Native Americans in the west struggled unsuccessfully to keep their land. The familiar pattern of settlement, conflict escalating to war, treaty-making and treaty violation leading to new wars was repeated. At the famous battle of the Little Big Horn, for example, Dakota warriors led by Sitting Bull and Crazy Horse killed Lieutenant Colonel Custer and his men when they attempted to punish the Native Americans for attacking gold prospectors who broke the treaty with the Dakotas by entering their sacred Black Hills.

The era of open warfare ended with the so-called battle of Wounded Knee. This bloodbath resulted from clumsy attempts by American authorities to suppress the Ghost Dance religion that promised believers a return to the happy conditions before the appearance of the Europeans. Accused of promoting the religion, Sitting Bull was arrested and killed by Native American police while in custody. When US soldiers tried to disarm a nearby group of Dakotas at Wounded Knee Creek, they fought back in anger over reservation conditions and the death of Sitting Bull. The panicked troops sprayed the men, women and children with machine-gun fire until all 300 were dead.

From the 1870s to the 1930s the US tried to assimilate the Native Americans quickly. The motives for this ranged from an unselfish wish to free natives from dependence and poverty to a barely disguised aim to acquire reservation lands cheaply. Assimilation programmes also caused dissension within native groups. Native Americans who had white relatives or who were already rather Americanized tended to favour adoption of US institutions. Racially unmixed natives were often cultural traditionalists who resisted all forms of assimilation.

The efforts at Americanization took three main forms. The first was the deliberate eroding of tribes' legal authority. On reservations, agents from the US

Bureau of Indian Affairs (BIA) made all final decisions. In the 1870s and 1880s Congress removed any appearance of local control by declaring the end of tribal sovereignty and treaty-making and replacing tribal rule with the application of US or state laws. In the same years Congress gave private companies rights to use Native Americans' land without their consent. Granting US citizenship was another way of weakening tribal authority, because it gave Native Americans individual rights they could defend in court and made them responsible as individuals to state and federal law. By 1905 over half of all Native Americans had US citizenship, and in 1924 Congress extended citizenship to the rest.

Americans who believed assimilation could be achieved in a single generation put their faith in the second major plan for assimilation: educating Native American children at boarding schools far away from their reservations. To break all ties with tribal culture, the pupils were forbidden to wear native clothing, practise native customs or religions or speak native languages. Both academic and vocational, the curriculum stressed American history and government. In the 1880s and 1890s the BIA founded some two dozen of these schools, as well as day and boarding schools on reservations, where the discipline and curriculum were similar.

Allotment programmes (dissolving reservations into small farms owned by Native American families) was the keystone of the third method of assimilation. Tried out before the Civil War, allotment became US policy for all but a few tribes under the Dawes Act of 1887. Typically, allotment plans gave a Native American family 160 acres and single adults half as much. This nearly always left a huge amount of 'surplus' reservation land available for sale to non-Native Americans.

Supporters of the Dawes Act believed that Native Americans would experience the American dream of becoming economically self-reliant and politically independent farmers through allotment. The process would as effectively Americanize them as it had millions of European immigrants, in the opinion of many. But critics pointed out that Native-American farming was communal, not a collection of individual holdings. Without time to develop an American sense of land-ownership and farming methods, the results of allotment might be the cheap sale of 'Indian family farms' to white Americans and starvation among huge numbers of landless Native Americans. To prevent this, the Dawes Act forbade the sale or leasing of allotted land for twenty-five years. But when Congress removed these restrictions after just four years, Native Americans' lands changed hands rapidly. By 1934, some 4 million acres of reservation land had been declared surplus and sold to white Americans or sold by failed Indian farmers to white Americans. Allotment had provided a bonanza for speculators and land-hungry settlers.

## Tribal restoration and termination, 1934–70

By the 1930s studies had repeatedly blamed allotment for the extreme poor health, poverty and low educational levels of Native Americans. Franklin D. Roosevelt's 'Indian New Deal' attempted to correct the mistakes of the past. The relief and employment programmes available for other Americans suffering from the depression were extended to Native Americans. New better-staffed hospitals for Native Americans were built. Most boarding schools were replaced with local schools offering religious freedom, bilingual education and programmes to nurture native culture.

The Indian Reorganization Act of 1934 was the centrepiece of the reversal of public policy known as tribal restoration. It repealed allotment, supported the return of considerable 'surplus' land and allotment farms to communal ownership and provided federal funds for further adding to tribal lands. The BIA was now required to help develop self-government on reservations. Money was provided for founding these governments, which were offered federal credit for the conservation and economic development of local resources. Each tribe could accept or reject the Act through a referendum. The Indian New Deal made effective progress towards providing social services, an economic base and self-government on reservations, until funding ended at the start of the Second World War.

By 1953 advocates of rapid assimilation again constituted a congressional majority, however, and pushed through three new programmes. The first aimed to settle Native-American claims against the USA by offering financial compensation for lost lands and treaty violations. Once claims were resolved, the BIA proposed termination (dissolving the tribe/reservation as a legal entity and making Native Americans ordinary citizens of local and state governments). Then the BIA could complete the process of assimilation, the argument went, by helping former members of the tribe find work in cities. Instead of making natives 'regular' Americans by transforming them into farmers, this new policy (called relocation) was designed to accomplish the same end by turning them into industrial workers.

By the 1960s most of the progress of the New Deal years was reversed, and the policy of assimilation again seemed bankrupt. Termination and relocation had increased welfare dependency and social alienation rather than producing self-sufficiency and social integration. Native-American interest groups formed to seek change through lobbying and court cases. Protest organizations, such as the American Indian Movement (AIM) employed direct action to capture media attention. AIM activists occupied Alcatraz Island in San Francisco Bay as Native American territory, marched on Washington along 'The Trail of Broken Treaties', and barricaded themselves against federal authorities for weeks at Wounded Knee to publicize the need to review the history of US treaty violations.

## The situation of Native Americans in recent history

The activism of the 1960s and 1970s bore fruit in many ways by the early twenty-first century. Native-American law firms won important victories in US courts. Native American lawyers convinced judges to view tribes according to their early nineteenth-century status as dependent domestic nations, which helped them successfully champion traditional religious practices, tribal independence, mineral and water rights and the return of ancient artefacts and skeletons. Court actions also returned or brought payment for vast tracts of land to honour old treaties.

An important goal of the intertribal 'self-determination' movement was to lobby the federal government for equal treatment and self-government. The movement's initial success was confirmed in 1968, when the passage of the Indian Civil Rights Act guaranteed individuals living on reservations all the rights included in the US constitution. That at once protected them from rights violations by American or tribal governments and allowed tribes to qualify for the welfare and poverty benefits available to other citizens. From then to the present, federal laws building on this Act have made US funding and other assistance available for improving the health services, child care, housing and education of Native Americans, on and off reservations.

In 1975, Congress confirmed this legal status in the Indian Self-Determination Act, which gave tribal councils most powers exercised by state governments. The councils develop both an economy and social institutions that are tailored to their own natural resources and values. At the tribes' request the BIA may offer assistance, but its role is phased out as tribes become autonomous. In response, councils have developed industries (including hundreds of food-processing, oil, gas and mining firms), irrigation systems, tourist resorts, thirty-one colleges (some of them offering both BA and MA degrees), and over a hundred tribal gambling casinos that earn Native Americans around a billion dollars a year. A few tribes have grown rich from mineral deposits. For example, about 20 per cent of US oil and two thirds of the country's uranium are on reservation land.

As life on the reservation has improved, the flight of Native Americans to US cities has been reversed, but as early as the 1990 census, only one out of four Native Americans was a 'reservation Indian'. The other three lived in urban areas where jobs were more plentiful and varied. The adjustment to the city has not been very successful for Native Americans. About 20 per cent live below the poverty line, unemployment is high and those with jobs frequently earn low wages. A small well-educated elite enjoys a much higher standard of living and frequently is well integrated in American society.

In 2000 most 'reservation Indians' still lived in appalling conditions. Of all American ethnic groups, they had the highest unemployment, alcoholism, school drop-out and suicide rates. Many cases of malnutrition and mental illness as well as an exceptionally short life expectancy indicate that much remains to be done to improve the situation. Yet, at the 2000 census, 4.1 million Americans identified themselves as wholly or partly native. That is more than double the 1990 figure and far more than the birth rate alone can explain. One answer is that people could mark more than one race on census forms for the first time in 2000, but tribal leaders and experts point to a wish to share in gambling revenue and affirmative action programmes, widespread interest in family history and, most important, to the decline in the social stigma attached to being Native American.

# African Americans

The 36 million African Americans today who comprise the county's second-largest minority group are mostly old-stock Americans, but include growing populations from Caribbean and African countries. When Africans first arrived in the American south in 1619, they did not come as slaves. By the late 1600s, however, hereditary slavery had become the rule and African Americans were degraded to the status of property. Some owners treated their slaves better than others, but all had ultimate power over what was theirs. For black people, slavery meant hard work, poor living conditions and humiliation. Slave labour was especially important on large tobacco and rice plantations in Virginia and Maryland. When the US became independent, slaves made up about 20 per cent of the population.

Dependence on slaves diminished as tobacco and rice grew less profitable in the early 1800s. At the same time, moral indignation over the slave trade grew so strong that in 1808 the importation of slaves was banned. New technology, however, then made slave labour more important than ever before. Eli Whitney's cotton gin, which cleaned cotton many times faster than was possible manually, meant greatly increased profits if plantation owners had more slave cotton-pickers to keep their cotton gins in full operation. By 1860 the slave population had grown to just under 4 million. With a booming cotton economy (and cheap land available from 'removing' the Native Americans), the cotton south expanded westward. This often meant that slave children had to move away from their parents to serve their masters, who were often the younger sons of slave-owners, on newly developed plantations.

Between 1820 and the Civil War, several compromises were reached in Congress to keep the number of slave and free states equal. Anti-slavery supporters felt this policy condoned slavery, while slave-owners thought each state should be able to decide whether it wished to be 'slave' or 'free'. Compromise finally failed, and the Civil War began in 1861. Lincoln freed the slaves in the undefeated parts of the south in early 1863 through the Emancipation Proclamation and, after Union victory, Amendments to the Constitution ended slavery, granted the former slaves citizenship and gave black men the right to vote. Congress repealed the black codes the southern states had passed to limit the rights of former slaves. However, with no land or education, most black people had to work as sharecroppers or had to lease land and equipment from their former masters. Rents were so high that they had to give most of their crop in payment and had little to sell to get out of debt.

The new constitutional amendments were enforced in the south by the presence of the Union army during the period of reconstruction. In 1876, however, the troops were withdrawn and the north abandoned the cause of the former slaves. For eighty years the federal government let the south alone. Southerners did not accept black people as equals; they passed laws which denied them social, economic and political rights and they segregated almost every aspect of public life. These 'Jim Crow laws' remained in effect in most southern states until the 1960s. On the Supreme Court a southern majority interpreted the Fourteenth Amendment to mean no *government* should deny equal protection, but private persons could. The *Plessy* v. *Ferguson* case in 1896 established the court's separate-but-equal doctrine approving segregation.

In 1909 a group of black and white people founded the National Association for the Advancement of Coloured People (NAACP) to fight for African Americans' civil rights in general and to win repeal of the separate-but-equal doctrine in particular. At the time, Jim Crow laws affected most African Americans because about 90 per cent of black people lived in the south. In 1915 the NAACP persuaded the Supreme Court to annul the grandfather clause, which denied the vote to persons whose grandfathers had not voted in the 1860s, but violent intimidation and discriminatory local laws still kept southern black people from voting. In 1935 the NAACP won the invalidation of some residential segregation laws, but again with little practical effect.

The much smaller black population in the north grew rapidly and developed vibrant urban communities around the time of the First World War. *De jure* segregation (separation of the races by law) was the rule in the south. In the North, de-facto segregation (racial separation through informal means) was almost universal and forced black people to live in ghettos, such as such Harlem in New York City, the country's most famous black community. By the 1920s, black people's bitter disappointment over their limited freedom in northern centres resulted in protest movements, some demanding integration (like the NAACP) and others, such as Marcus Garvey's, promoting self-help in preparation for a return to Africa. In 1935 the NAACP won the invalidation of some residential segregation laws, but to little practical effect. In spite of these developments, the mass migration from the south continued. The rush for jobs in munitions and weapons industries during the Second World War accelerated the move to the north and also brought black settlement in west-coast cities. By the 1950s almost half the nation's African Americans lived in restive ghettos outside the south.

From 1938 the African-American lawyer, Thurgood Marshall, who later became the first black Supreme Court justice, led the NAACP legal defence group; and more liberals took seats on the Supreme Court during the following twenty years. These developments helped the NAACP achieve more success in the courts, where it attacked the separate-but-equal doctrine by showing the inequalities forced on black students by school segregation. The Supreme Court did not overturn the doctrine, but during the following decades its decisions made segregation almost impossible to implement in graduate and high schools. Not until 1954, however, in the *Brown* v. *Board of Education* case, was the separate-but-equal doctrine reversed. The court followed up this historic ruling with the annulment of *de jure* segregation in public places, and thus sent black people a message that the time was right to fight for their cause.

Implementing these changes was difficult. The south offered massive resistance, and the court got no help from the other branches of government. President Eisenhower had publicly supported segregation, and a conservative coalition of southern Democrats and Republicans dominated Congress. Not until violence broke out in Little Rock, Arkansas, when nine black students tried to attend a white school in 1957, did the President send the national guard to enforce the court's ruling. The next President, John F. Kennedy, used the guard or federal marshals several times in other southern districts to desegregate the schools. Defiant southerners therefore avoided desegregation in other ways. White people who could sent their children to private schools that were not bound by federal law. By 1964 only 2 per cent of black children in the south attended desegregated schools. In 1969 the Supreme Court ordered the desegregation of all public schools, and later approved measures to force integration, such as racial quotas, the grouping of non-contiguous school districts, and bussing in order to achieve racial balance in the schools.

Since segregation still determined residential patterns (most black people lived in the inner cities while white people lived in the suburbs), there was strong opposition to bussing. After the court ruled against bussing plans between cities and suburbs, unless discriminatory districting could be proved, in 1974, few new attempts to bus pupils were made. Fifty years after the *Brown* decision around 70 per cent of America's schools were racially mixed, but those in inner cities were still mostly black, Latino and Asian American.

Other forms of *de jure* racial discrimination existed in the south in the 1950s. Black people then were also prevented from voting and were kept out of jobs and white facilities. In 1955, Rosa Parks, a black woman from Montgomery, Alabama, was arrested and fined for taking a seat in the white section at the front of a bus. This incident sparked a black boycott against the city's bus system led by the young Baptist minister Martin Luther King, Jr. One year later the federal courts ruled that segregated transportation violated the Fourteenth Amendment. The African-American civil rights movement of the 1950s and 1960s was under way. King was one of the organizers of the Southern Christian Leadership Conference (SCLC), which coordinated civil-rights activities. His 'I Have a Dream' speech to more than 250,000 people at the Lincoln Memorial in 1963 is regarded as one of the most inspiring calls for racial equality in American history.

White officials' brutal suppression of civil-rights protests in the south, newly visible on nationwide television, made Americans more conscious of racial injustice. President Kennedy addressed the problem for the first time from the White House and called fighting racism a moral issue. The Civil Rights Act of 1964 outlawed discrimination in jobs and public accommodations, and the following year the Voting Rights Act led to black-voter registration drives that transformed politics in the south.

This has been called the non-violent revolution. However, peaceful protestors, both black and white, were killed and, while Martin Luther King, Jr. was advocating non-violence, other black people felt changes were too slow in coming. Disappointed with how little change civil-rights laws brought to their daily lives, residents of the black ghetto in Los Angeles exploded in riots in 1965. Detroit and Newark witnessed massive property destruction and dozens of deaths from race riots in 1967.

Black radicals wanted to establish an alternate African-American culture inside the USA. Some of these formed the Black Power and Black Panther movements. Malcolm X became one of the most famous black Muslims, the Nation of Islam, who created their own variant of Islam and rejected America's lifestyle and politics. These movements became involved in violent conflicts with the police. For many black people, non-violence seemed defunct as a means of winning civil rights. Malcolm X was killed in 1965 and three years later when Martin Luther King was assassinated, 168 American cities erupted in the flames of racial conflict.

## The contemporary situation for African Americans

In retrospect, it is clear that passing laws was the easy part. The nation has still not found a way to enforce civil rights laws. Malcolm X hoped that violent revolution would not be necessary, that warning of the violence that would result from not listening to Martin Luther King would be enough. But it was not. How can one quarter of black people be brought out of poverty? The issue of violent protest born of prolonged frustration and poverty was the chief question that fractured the black civil rights movement.

To make use of equal opportunity, African Americans need higher education and the skills to obtain better-paid jobs. That, in turn, should enable them to afford better housing and improved living standards. In 2002, however, their wages remained depressed and their unemployment and poverty rates were twice those of white people, even though they graduated from high school and attended college about as often as white people did. For, despite the Fair Housing Act of 1968, most black people still face discrimination when they buy or rent housing. Residential desegregation has been minimal and equal standards in the schools have therefore not been achieved. Only half as many black people *completed* a college degree as white people in 2002. And even when they did have equal

**PLATE 4.4** Malcolm X, who advocated a self-sufficient Black Muslim culture within the United States, speaking at a rally in New York City in 1964.
(*Burt Shavitz/Pix Inc./Time Pix/Rex Features*)

qualifications on paper, the appearance of being better qualified often had limited effects if employers doubted the quality of their credentials, assumed that participants in affirmative-action programmes get special treatment, or felt alienated from black people because the races continued to have little contact with each other.

In 2000 there were over 7,000 elected black officials in the USA (including 300 mayors), while there had been less than 100 in 1964. However, continued socio-economic inequality and the unkept promises of public policy and ideals continue to make mainstream black leaders, such as Jesse Jackson, urge personal responsibility and self-reliance on their community and increase the appeal of more radical, racist black figures, such as Louis Farrakhan. Ironically, the 2000 census showed that the most progress in residential desegregation in the 1990s occurred in the south, where black people leave cities for suburbs at the same time as white people, instead of decades later as in the other regions. Between 1990 and 2005 black people migrated into the south in record numbers, reversing their century-long flight from the region.

## Asian Americans

'Asian American' is a convenient term that lumps together a diverse collection of immigrant and American-born populations. It includes, for example, both Hmong tribespeople who came as refugees after the Vietnam War and the descendants of the Chinese who settled before the Civil War. The principle of continental origins is used to justify putting in one category people with different religions, skin colours, socio-economic backgrounds and historical experiences. The US census compiles information on this diverse composite group together with another such group, 'Pacific Islanders', which includes native Hawaiians, Guamanians and Samoans, among others. In 2002 Asian Americans numbered 12.5 million people (4.4 per cent of the US population) and were the nation's second-fastest growing minority.

In the 1990s the Asian-born population exploded in size, increasing on average by nearly 49 per cent and by 200 per cent or more in some cities in every region of the country. At the same time both their prominence in the fourth wave of immigrants and their diversity increased. The six largest Asian ancestry groups (Chinese, Filipino, Asian Indian, Vietnamese, Korean and Japanese) have been joined by hundreds of thousands of people from some twenty other Asian nations in the past decade. It is only the old-stock American perception that all these people *look* Asian (and the different treatment that this perception has caused) which has given them related experiences in the USA.

The first large group of Chinese, some 370,000 people, came with the second-wave 'old' immigrants between the late 1840s and 1882. One fifth settled in Hawaii and the rest on the west coast, mostly in California. About 400,000 Japanese immigrated between the 1880s and 1908 and settled in roughly equal numbers on the west coast and in Hawaii, where they composed the largest Asian immigrant group. Small groups of Koreans and East Indians (about 7,000 each) came to the islands and west-coast states from 1900 to 1930. During the same period, approximately 180,000 Filipinos immigrated, about three in five of them first arriving in Hawaii.

**PLATE 4.5** Chinatown in downtown Chicago with the Sears Tower, the city's tallest skyscraper, in the near background.
(*Sten Rosenlund/Rex Features*)

The situation of Asian immigrants varied greatly between Hawaii and the mainland. In the islands, most were recruited as contract workers on sugar plantations, where they performed back-breaking labour under military-style discipline and the supervision of abusive overseers. Nationality groups were segregated in different camps and pitted against each other to keep wages low and prevent a unified labour movement. But plantation owners were dependent on these workers and so provided food, housing and medical care. To get workers to stay when their contracts ended, they helped women immigrate, encouraged family life, supported religious and ethnic customs and built schools and community centres.

The discrimination Asian Americans suffered in Hawaii was much milder than that on the mainland because they made up a large majority of the islands' workforce. In 1920, when they worked in every part of Hawaii's economy, Asian Americans comprised over half of the islands' population, and about two in every five people there were Japanese Americans. Thus, most Japanese Americans on the mainland, but less than 1 per cent of those on the islands, were put in concentration camps during the Second World War. In the 1930s, Asian Americans began to assume prominent positions in Hawaiian politics. Since 1959, Hawaii has been the only state in which they have both played major roles in state politics and represented the state in Congress.

On the mainland the situation of Asian Americans was fundamentally different until the mid-1940s. Always a tiny minority compared to European Americans, they could much more easily be made victims of systematic discrimination. Anti-Asian campaigns in the Pacific west were designed to segregate Asians from white people, prevent them from competing economically and end their immigration entirely. Anti-miscegenation laws against racial-mixing forbade marriages between Asians and white people. Many businesses refused them products and services. The only housing they could find was often in Asian-American ghettos. A series of Supreme Court decisions decided that they were non-whites and therefore ineligible for citizenship. Many western states also passed alien land laws, which prohibited non-citizens from leasing or owning land. In 1882 the Chinese were excluded from immigrating. The 1908 Gentlemen's Agreement, prohibiting the entry of Japanese labourers, was followed in 1921 by the 'Ladies' Agreement' that banned Japanese women's immigration. Three years later all Asians were barred from immigrating.

With assistance from sympathetic white people, Asian Americans fought these forms of oppression. They found loopholes in the land laws, circumvented immigration exclusion laws, created their own job opportunities by starting businesses, formed union and protest organizations and, through these, stood up for their rights through strikes and lawsuits. For all Asian American groups apart from Japanese Americans, the Second World War brought decisive social and economic improvements.

Public attitudes became positive to the Chinese, Koreans, Filipinos and East Indians, whose homelands were American allies. Members of these groups joined the US armed forces or intelligence networks. Tens of thousands of Japanese-American youths left the concentration camps to serve in the American military and prove their loyalty! War industries gave Asian Americans professional and skilled work that previously had been denied them. By the war's end, all four groups could immigrate and all but Koreans had won citizenship rights. Between 1945 and 1965, discriminatory laws against Asian Americans were repealed or struck down by the courts.

Refugee laws permitted the entry of Asians who had married American military personnel, and in 1965 a new immigration law opened the way for the huge wave of Asian immigration that is still continuing. As a result of the Vietnam War, hundreds of thousands of Vietnamese, Laotian and Cambodian refugees have settled in the USA. Today's Asian newcomers are quite different from the earlier immigrants in some ways. A significant minority consists of well-educated professionals, and many more come from urban areas, where they worked in modern industries. More of the recent immigrants also arrive as families rather than as single men and plan to settle permanently. On the other hand, recent refugees are often destitute, poorly educated and unprepared for city life. Numbers of Japanese newcomers are now small while the totals from other Asian nations have set new records.

## Asian Americans today

Since the mid-1960s, the popular media have often depicted Asian Americans as the country's most successful ethnic groups, its 'model minority'. Their high median family incomes, unusually high level of academic achievement and low rates of unemployment, crime, mental illness and dependence on welfare have been held up as examples to other minority groups. A closer look at the situation, however, shows that significant numbers of Asian Americans have serious socio-economic problems and face considerable discrimination.

Asian Americans are twice as urbanized as white people. One reason for this is that their high family incomes are more dependent than white people's on living in central cities with large, diverse job markets. Only these places can provide work for the number of family members who work long hours and contribute their wages to one household income, which, taken together, is higher than the family incomes of white households. In *personal* incomes Asian Americans have not caught up with white Americans. One reason for this is that they are more concentrated in semi-skilled service trades and low-level professional and management positions. Still, despite the large number of refugees from Asia, about half as many people in these ethnic groups lived in poverty in 2002 than was the case among Latin Americans, the other large body of recent immigrants. Asian Americans' educational attainments, moreover, were closest to those of white people at the last census, but a so-called 'glass ceiling' of prejudice still kept them out of the higher management levels of industries and professional firms. The slums of major American cities that have a high incidence of poverty, health problems, drug abuse and teenage gangs often overlap with parts of Asian-American communities.

The media image of Asian Americans' success, moreover, caused resentment that fed a rising wave of anti-Asian activity in the 1980s, when the US Civil Rights Commission reported dozens of cases of racial slurs, violent assaults, vandalism and harassment against Asian Americans. Across the nation, conflicts occurred between Korean store-owners and residents of the Latino or African-American communities where many of these shops are located. In the 1992 Los Angeles riots, their shops became the special target of looters and some 1,800 Korean businesses were destroyed. After reactions to the rapid progress of Asian immigrants and economic competition from Asian nations cooled during the boom years of the later 1990s, however, Asian–African relations in the USA improved.

## Latinos

A Spanish language and cultural background is the inexact basis for calling people with ethnic origins in the Caribbean, Central and South America 'Latinos' or 'Hispanics'. Thus the term does not apply to people from countries in the Americas that have been influenced by other European cultures, such as Brazil, Haiti or the Bahamas.

Those commonly called Latinos include the Central or South American descendants of Native American peoples, African slaves, immigrants from other European nations and Asia and mixtures of these groups. In 2000 somewhat more than half of Latinos identified themselves as white. The majority are Catholics, but significant numbers are Protestant or members of other religions. Most are relatively recent immigrants, but Mexican Americans have been coming in large numbers since the late 1800s and include the descendants of the early Spanish settlers from the 1500s.

Over 37 million people (13.3 per cent of the population) were counted as 'Hispanic or Latino' in the 2002 Current Population Survey. Those figures represented somewhat more than a 60 per cent increase in just ten years and made the Latino population the fastest growing in the nation. Today Latinos are a larger minority group than African Americans, and the significance of that fact is even clearer when one remembers that the largest part of the 9 million or so undocumented immigrants in the USA are Latinos.

Two thirds of Latinos are Mexican Americans and live in the south-western states or in large mid-western cities such as Chicago. The other groups are small by comparison. Puerto Ricans, the third largest group, make up 9 per cent of

Latinos and have concentrated their settlement in New York city and other northern urban areas. The two next largest groups, Cuban and Dominican Americans, comprise 3.7 and 2.4 per cent and have their largest communities in Florida and New York city. The remaining Latinos come from about thirty national origins, the largest of which are Salvadoran, Guatemalan and Colombian. At the 2000 census the striking change was that a huge number of Latinos, the second largest group, did not identify a national origin, which might mean they view themselves as Latino Americans or Americans and suggests a growing integration of Latinos into society in the USA.

Like Native Americans, African Americans, and Asian Americans, Latinos have faced race prejudice and economic discrimination in jobs, housing, education and politics. The high number of Latino newcomers, especially illegal immigrants, has led to rising hostility or worry about Latinos. In the south-west, border patrols and local police often stop Latinos on the assumption that they might be illegal aliens. The 'racial profiling' that has led police departments to single out African Americans as suspects has also affected Latino Americans.

For decades, Latino children were sent to segregated 'Mexican' schools in the south-west. When federal courts declared them to be white in the 1940s, the situation improved somewhat, but a decade later local officials used these rulings to 'integrate' schools by creating districts where most pupils were Latino or African American, while non-Latino white pupils attended school elsewhere. Today the great majority of Latinos still go to school in segregated districts. In the past they were often punished for speaking Spanish and met pressure to Anglicize their culture at school. In the late 1960s and 1970s court cases established their right to instruction in Spanish but most bilingual programmes (education offered in both the pupils' mother tongue and English) ease the transition to English rather than maintain the pupils' Spanish heritage.

In the south-west, Florida and the New York City area Latinos achieved political influence decades ago by being elected to office on all levels of government. In the 1960s and 1970s, they organized 'brown power' protest movements that fought for civil rights on the streets and in the courts, enhancing Latinos' pride and stimulating a variety of cultural institutions. Latinos have long been actively involved in union movements of many kinds despite the prejudice of some white labour leaders. The largest occupational group of Latinos was for many years migratory farm workers. César Chávez became the first nationally well-known Latino leader in the 1960s through his successful strike negotiations as head of the United Farm Workers Union of California.

## Attitudes to Latino America: the nation's largest immigrant subculture

Public opinion regarding Latinos, always mixed, grew increasingly negative as the immigration of Spanish-origin groups skyrocketed in the 1990s. Reactions

EN TEXAS...SI SE PUEDE

**PLATE 4.6** César Chávez, leader of the United Farm Workers, speaking to union members in California in 1979.
(*Michael Salas/Time Pix/Rex Features*)

were particularly strong from Texas to California but noticeable across the nation. Over twenty states declared English their official language in reaction against the use of Spanish by Latinos. Polls in 1993–4 showed that President Clinton and Florida's governor had widespread public support for intercepting Cuban boat people at sea and preventing their entry as refugees. In the Elian Gonzales case at the end of the 1990s, Cuban Americans again found that most Americans did not share their view when the opinion polls supported returning the boy to Cuba.

Latinos won an important victory in 1982 when the Supreme Court decided that the children of illegal immigrants were entitled to public education. In 1994, however, California's voters passed Proposition 187, which challenged the ruling and would have denied the state's illegal immigrants all social services except emergency medical attention but for court actions brought by civil rights groups. In 1996 a clear majority of California and Texas voters ended all state affirmative action programmes in the knowledge that many of these helped many Latinos secure better education and jobs. In 2003–4 polls in California showed that large majorities opposed allowing illegal immigrants to receive state driving licences, without which this largely Latino group would finding making a living increasingly difficult.

The census in 2000 showed that Latinos were the least likely of foreign-born groups to complete high school or college. Almost one in every five Latinos remained illiterate. Unemployment and poverty rates among Latinos were also the highest among the foreign-born, which commentators blamed chiefly on their educational situation, the enormous increase in Latino immigration in past years and rising anti-Latino feeling in the regions of their greatest concentration.

On the other hand, in 2000 and 2004 there were also signs of Latinos' growing political influence, which ought to help secure policy changes to improve their opportunities and status. During the presidential election campaigns in these years the candidates paid extraordinary attention to the 'big' states where most Latinos live, and the close vote in one of these, Florida, decided the outcome in 2000. Moreover, census bureau analyses indicated a year later that Latinos had become a large minority that politicians would have to reckon with in 122 of the 435 districts for congressional elections in 2002. In the 2004 presidential election both candidates visited Latino communities and attempted to communicate with voters in Spanish. Unprecedented numbers of Latino Americans were elected to office, including two new members of the US Senate, one from Colorado and the other from Florida. In the last elections record numbers of Latinos registered and voted, demonstrating their new political clout.

As the 2000s began, some spoke resentfully of the 'browning' or 'Latinization' of America. Others relished signs of growing Latin visibility in the nation's culture from Spanish-language signs and businesses to new foods, popular music and fashion.

# Exercises

Explain and examine the significance of the following names and terms.

| | | |
|---|---|---|
| equality of opportunity | English common law (regarding women) | abolitionists |
| Seneca Falls Convention | women's suffrage | protectionist legislation |
| ERA | affirmative action programmes | Roe v. Wade |
| forced separation | 'domestic dependent nation' | forced assimilation |
| Indian New Deal | Self-Determination Act | Asian contract workers |
| anti-miscegenation laws | urban ghettos | model minority |
| hereditary slavery | black codes | Jim Crow laws |
| Plessy v. Ferguson | NAACP | de jure segregation |
| non-violent revolution | illegal immigrants | minority school district |
| bilingual education | César Chávez | |

continued

Write short essays on the following questions.

1.  Discuss the factors that have contributed to the improved status of American women since the colonial period.

2.  Evaluate the motives and effects of US policy toward Native Americans.

3.  Give a critical review of the aspects of African Americans' struggle for equality that you find distinctive from that of other minority groups.

4.  Compare and contrast early and recent Asian-American immigrants and the treatment they have received in the USA.

5.  Describe the make-up of America's Latino population and discuss the kinds of discrimination it has faced.

## Further reading

Acuña, R. (1988) *Occupied America: a history of Chicanos* New York: Harper & Row.

Berry M. F. and J. W. Blassingame (1982) *Long Memory: the black experience in America* Oxford: Oxford University Press.

Cordova, C. B. and J. del Pinal (1996) *Hispanics-Latinos: diverse people in a multicultural society* Washington, DC: National Association of Hispanic Publications.

Franklin, J. H. and A. A. Moss (1987) *From Slavery to Freedom: a history of Negro Americans* New York: Alfred A. Knopf.

Hurtado, A. L. and P. Iverson (eds) (1994) *Major Problems in American Indian History* Lexington, Mass.: D. C. Heath.

McWilliams, C. (1990) *North from Mexico: the Spanish speaking people of the United States* Westport, Conn.: Greenwood.

Norton, M. B. and R. M. Alexander (1996) *Major Problems in American Women's History* Lexington, Mass.: D. C. Heath.

Oswalt, W. O. and S. Neeley (1996) *This Land Was Theirs: a study of North American Indians* Mountain View, Calif.: Mayfield.

Ruiz, V. L. and E. C. DuBois (eds) (1994) *Unequal Sisters: a multicultural reader in U.S. women's history* London: Routledge.

Takaki, Ronald (1998) *Strangers from a Different Shore: a history of Asian Americans* 2nd edn Boston, Mass.: Little, Brown.

## Web sites

<http://usinfo.state.gov/usa/race/ethnicity/divlinks.htm>

<http://www.lib.msu.edu/foxre/currpop.html>

<http://www.gallup.com>

<http://www.washingtonpost.com> Special reports, The 2000 Census (2001)

<http://www.census/gov> 'The Foreign-Born Population of the United States, March 2000, Population Characteristics' (2001); 'Overview of Race and Hispanic Origin, Census 2000 Brief' (2001); 'Mapping Census 2000: The Geography of U.S. Diversity' (2001)
<http://www.census.gov/cps> (cps =current population surveys)
<http://www.census.gov/geo/www/mapGallery/images/hispanic.ipg>

# Chapter 5

# Political institutions
## The federal government

- ■ Historical origins
- ■ The constitutional framework
- ■ The political parties
- ■ The legislative branch
- ■ The executive branch
- ■ The judicial branch
- ■ Attitudes to branches of the federal government
- ■ *Exercises*
- ■ *Further reading*
- ■ *Web sites*

Stable political institutions have been particularly important in a nation of immigrants. Many commentators feel that loyalty to the basic structures and principles of government has acted as the cement that has held together so large and diverse a nation. Today, the USA holds several records for political stability and longevity. Arguably the oldest functioning democracy, the country also has the world's oldest written constitution and political party (the Democratic Party). Much has changed in American government and politics since the nation declared its independence in 1776. The Constitution of 1787 has endured not least because it has proven amenable to changing interpretations and open enough to assimilate important extra-constitutional elements. Even so, political institutions in the USA have been, and continue to be, the subject of heated debate.

## Historical origins

The English authorities allowed the American colonists to evolve political institutions (governors, assemblies and courts) with little outside interference. Partially based on local control and the consent of the inhabitants, these traditions of self-government later inspired the independence movement, formed the foundation for the constitutions of the independent states after 1776 and served as the model for the federal government erected through the Constitution of 1787.

At first most Americans opposed a strong central government, which they identified with British oppression. The first US constitution, the Articles of Confederation (1781–8), established a loose league of independent states under a very weak central government. With no executive or judicial branch, the national government consisted only of a one-house legislature that lacked financial, diplomatic and military power. Much like the United Nations, the confederation had to ask the member states for everything, from military forces to money for operating expenses.

Soon chaos in the nation's economy and international relations made members of the merchant classes support stronger central government. These 'federalists' argued for the adoption of the new constitution drafted in Philadelphia in 1787. The anti-federalists, who pictured the country's future as largely agricultural, opposed the new constitution because it endangered the sovereignty of the states and lacked a list of protections for individuals. Only when agreement was reached that ten amendments to satisfy these objections (later called

**PLATE 5.1** The Capitol, Washington, DC.
(*John Hartman/Rex Features*)

the Bill of Rights) would be added was the constitution ratified. Thus, the new framework of national government reflected ideas from both sides of the debate.

This constitution returned to the colonial tradition of a government with three branches (the legislative, executive and judicial). Unlike revolutionary-era state governments, however, it did not make the legislature paramount. Instead, it provided for branches that had to cooperate to perform the functions of government. It also changed the nature of the union. The loose confederacy became a federation whose national government had powers that remedied the weaknesses of the Articles. Federal law became supreme in the areas covered by those powers. But the states' territorial integrity and their sovereignty in all other areas were guaranteed.

Three compromises secured the states' approval for the new government. The first balanced the representation of small and large states in Congress. In the House of Representatives the number of seats per state was made proportional to population to please the states with large populations. In the Senate every state was given two seats, regardless of population, to please the small states. The second compromise patched over conflicts between the north and south over slavery. Once representation in one chamber of Congress was made dependent on population, the issue was how to count the large number of slaves in the

**PLATE 5.2**   The first cabinet of the USA in 1789: President George Washington, Thomas Jefferson, Alexander Hamilton, Henry Knox and Edmond Randolph.
(*Mansell/Time Pix/Rex Features*)

south, who were not citizens and who were legally property rather than people. In the north, the states had abolished slavery or contained very few slaves. The compromise stated that three fifths of the slaves would count for representation in the House, but that importing of slaves could be outlawed by 1808. In the early years of the nation this compromise gave the slave states additional power in the House of Representatives and the Electoral College that chose the President. The drafters also compromised on economic disagreements by permitting Congress to tax imports but not exports, which simultaneously kept the prices of southern agricultural exports low and opened the door for tariffs to protect northern manufactures from cheap imported goods. Critics, then and since, have pointed out that two of these compromises tacitly approved slavery by giving it advantages in the framework of the federal government.(See the Appendix for the three compromises in Article I of the Constitution.)

# The constitutional framework

Four fifths of the original text of the Constitution remains unchanged, and only seventeen amendments have been added after the Bill of Rights. Yet its thought and language have remained flexible enough to be interpreted differently by succeeding generations. The changes in US constitutionalism have been significant but few. They have come through amendments and judicial review rather than revolutionary upheavals. The enduring principles in the Constitution are republicanism, federalism, the separation of powers and the system of checks and balances.

## *A republican form of government*

Republicanism is the belief in a government without any classes of people privileged by birth (thus excluding a royal family and an aristocracy) or by occupational class (prohibiting, for example, a privileged class of priests or the clergy). The Constitution of 1787 specifically prohibits inherited titles and the establishment of a state religion in the USA. Article 4, Section 4 of the document, moreover, guarantees each state in the union a republican form of government.

## *Federalism*

The Constitution establishes the principle of federalism through the concepts of 'reserved' and 'delegated' powers in the Tenth Amendment. It reserves to the states or people those powers not specified or reasonably inferred as federal from the wording in the Constitution. American federalism is a political system in which the governing power (sovereignty) is shared between the national government and the states. The states delegated some powers to the national government in 1787 but reserved most powers to themselves. The powers of both are limited by the rights preserved for the people in the Preamble of the Constitution and the Bill of Rights. The preamble stresses popular sovereignty (the idea that 'the people' are the power behind government). The people's representatives created the government and can alter or totally replace it.

The USA has a hierarchy of law. The US Constitution is the country's supreme law. Acts of Congress signed by the President as well as state and local laws must conform to it. State and local laws must in addition conform to the state constitution. This legal hierarchy led the federal Supreme Court to assume the role of final interpreter of the US constitution through 'judicial review'. Connecting state and national law, the court decides what government activity is permissible on any level under the Constitution. The US Constitution limits the court's work and thus judicial review to 'cases and controversies'. This means the court cannot interpret the constitutionality of a law unless someone brings legal charges against that law to a lower court and appeals the case to the US Supreme Court.

The Constitution's broad language has allowed the Supreme Court to expand federal power into areas originally left to the states. Congress, for example, has extended its activities through clauses giving it broad power to regulate commerce, provide for the general welfare and create all laws that are 'necessary and proper' to carry out the other powers granted to the federal government in the Constitution. In practice, therefore, government activity in the USA today falls into three categories: that allowed the states alone, that permitted only to the national government and that shared by both levels of government.

## *The separation of powers*

The third basic principle in the Constitution is the separation of powers between the legislative (Congress and support agencies), executive (the President and executive bureaucracy) and judicial (the US Supreme Court and other federal courts) branches. In this non-parliamentary system, no person may serve in more than one branch at the same time. Thus the President and the heads of the executive departments, as well as federal judges, may not sit in Congress. The separation of powers is also institutionalized in other ways. The President, senators and representatives are selected through independent elections that do not all occur at the same time. The areas that elect them (the nation, states and congressional districts) are different and so are the lengths of their terms of office. Thus they each feel responsible to different voters and develop quite dissimilar political loyalties and priorities. As a result, one or both of the houses of Congress are often controlled by one major party while the presidency is held by the other.

The Constitution further separates the branches by listing the powers of each one. It thus outlines the limits of legislative, executive and judicial action. As intended by the drafters of the Constitution, separating the branches prevents the concentration of power in any one and creates both cooperation and tension between them.

## *Checks and balances*

The branches must share power through a system of checks and balances. The President nominates federal judges, including justices of the Supreme Court, but the Senate must confirm their appointment. Senatorial approval is also needed for treaties negotiated by the executive and the President's candidates for other high federal offices. The President can veto legislation passed by Congress, but a veto can be overridden by two thirds majorities of both houses. One house of Congress balances and checks the other in that Bills must pass both. Congress can remove members of the other branches from office through impeachment but the President can pardon people accused of federal crimes and Supreme Court justices are appointed for life terms, dependent on 'good behaviour'.

In the period 1999–2001 presidential impeachment and pardons dominated American politics. The Republican-controlled House of Representatives impeached President Clinton; that is, a majority of its members supported charges that he had committed 'high crimes and misdemeanours' in his attempt to conceal an affair with White House intern Monica Lewinsky and therefore should be removed from office. Only once before in the nation's history had a President been impeached (after the Civil War when the House supported charges against President Andrew Johnson). Then, as at the end of the 1990s, the House vote seemed highly partisan, and when the Senate sat as a court and tried the President on the House charges, the President was acquitted. Remarkably, Clinton's popularity and effectiveness in office was little impaired by the disgrace of impeachment. In early 2001, during his last days in office, Clinton granted pardons to friends and supporters, as most Presidents do, and again earned the anger of opponents without losing popularity.

Congress can raise money through taxes and spend it on government programmes. When implementing laws, though, the President and executive departments control the way funds are used by setting rules that interpret the language of federal law. Congress can create, regulate or eliminate elements of the executive branch below the Vice-President and of the judicial branch below the Supreme Court. It can thus respond to the other branches' attempts to frustrate its intentions. Finally, as noted, if someone challenges a law, the Supreme Court can declare it unconstitutional and can thus force the other branches to revise their actions. In all these ways the Constitution checks each branch's exercise of power and balances power between the branches.

### Constitutional change

The provisions for amending the federal constitution stress the federal principle by involving both the national and the state governments. Amendments can be proposed by two thirds majorities in Congress or by a constitutional convention called by two thirds of the states. Any changes must be ratified by the legislatures of or conventions in three quarters of the states.

Important changes in the constitutional framework have come through both formal and informal means, that is, through the amendment process as well as through evolving customs and changing historical circumstances. Amendments have generally enhanced federal power at the expense of the states, and have democratized participation in government. The three Civil War Amendments written by the victorious north contributed to both these general trends. They abolished slavery (the Thirteenth), gave all the former slaves citizenship (the Fourteenth), and allowed former male slaves the right to vote (the Fifteenth). In the twentieth century, the Fourteenth Amendment, which requires states to respect the rights of US citizens by extending to them 'due process of law' and the 'equal protection of the laws', has proven essential to protect the civil rights of individuals.

Other amendments democratizing American politics are the Seventeenth (1913), which provided for the selection of US senators by a popular vote rather than by the state legislature, the Nineteenth (1920), which granted women the vote, and the Twenty-sixth (1971), which lowered the voting age to eighteen. The Sixteenth Amendment (1913) gave the federal government much greater financial power than the states have by granting Congress the right to tax incomes, whatever their source.

So-called 'extra constitutional' changes in the political system (those that occur without the amendment process) have been even more important. Among these are political parties, primary elections, the congressional committee and subcommittee system, the Executive Office of the President and the Supreme Court's power of judicial review. The federal government has greatly increased its power at the expense of the states, but political power in the USA is still split among the branches and decentralized due to the powers reserved to the states.

## The political parties

The founding fathers viewed political parties as factions (interest groups that pursue narrow private interests rather than the common good). They designed a constitutional system that, together with the size and diversity of the country, was meant to keep factions so divided that no one of them could gain significant power. Yet parties emerged quickly and the Constitution was one cause of their appearance.

The separate and staggered elections required for senators, representatives, and the President, as well as the republican form of government guaranteed the states, create many fragmented electoral interests. However, they also ensure many and frequent elections. Parties arose in part because organizations were needed to recruit, screen and nominate candidates for these elections. The separation of powers also helped create parties because a tool was needed to coordinate the policy initiatives of the separated branches. The founders set up a system that encourages two parties, rather than no parties. Only one person is elected from each electoral district and that person needs only a plurality (more votes than any other candidate) to win the election. Thus coalitions form *before* elections. Political parties are few in number and are coalitions of interests with middle-of-the-road programmes whose vagueness results from compromises made to unify dissimilar elements. Since 1856 there have been two major national parties: the Democrats and the Republicans.

Two other factors have been important for the development of a two-party system in the USA. First, winning the presidency is so important that it has inspired two broadly based national coalitions, one consisting of the party in the White House and the other of everybody else. Second, there has usually been a division of voters into two camps on the important issues, such as slavery or government regulation of the economy.

## Differences between the parties

Despite their broad diversity and the diffuseness of their ideologies, the two major parties represent different political orientations. Their differences are seen in the view the voters and activists for each have of themselves. For example, Republicans much more frequently identify themselves as conservatives. Until recently, the major parties could also be distinguished by their strength in different regions of the nation. In the decades after the Civil War, both parties were competitive in only a few states. The south blamed the party of Lincoln for the war and so voted almost exclusively for the Democrats. The rest of the nation tended to be heavily Republican. From the 1890s to 1930s this regional division deepened as discriminatory state election laws disenfranchised African Americans in the South, and as the Republican party became more associated with big business.

Franklin D. Roosevelt's New Deal Coalition complicated the picture. He forged a national majority by appealing to both the white supremacist south and the urban multi-ethnic, multiracial north-east and mid-west. From 1932, when Roosevelt was first elected President, until 1968, Democrats were conservative in the south but often liberal in other regions of the nation. Republicans were conservative in the rural mid-west and the west as a whole, but frequently moderate or liberal in the north-east. During the thirty-seven years since then, regional differences have become less important. In 1968, southern Democrats left the party to support Alabaman segregationist governor George Wallace as an independent candidate in the presidential election because of the party's support for the African-American civil rights movement. Since then white conservative southerners have increasingly voted Republican, first in presidential elections, but since the late 1980s also in congressional and state contests. Meanwhile, the growth of African-American voting, the influx of people from other regions and the economic modernization and urbanization of the south have made it a two-party region, where the weight of white opinion is conservative Republican but Latinos, the elderly and people from other regions are potentially decisive political 'swing' groups. In the 2004 presidential election the Democrats were stronger on both coasts, in big cities, their inner suburbs, the urban industrial mid-west and the north-east, while Republicans did best in rural areas, small towns, outer 'white' suburbs, the south and the mountain states.

Across the nation today the Democratic party label tends to represent a moderate-to-liberal political orientation. During the same period, the Republican party has become more uniformly conservative as its moderate-to-liberal wing in the north-east, upper mid-west and Pacific north-west has shrunk and lost influence to conservative activists. The ideological centre of the Republican party supports small government, minimal regulation of business, low taxes and private solutions to poverty and social problems. Since the 'Reagan revolution' in the 1980s, party allegiance to these policies has become more pronounced as its centre shifts to the right. In 1996, Presidential Candidate Bob Dole seemed moderate compared to most delegates at the Republican convention, but in 2000 and again in 2004 George W. Bush moved further right.

Democrats are more in favour of government management of the economy, a public social safety net and unions. Bill Clinton, who moved the party to the political centre in the 1990s, had a party majority behind his moderate democrat label but nearly alienated his party's liberal wing in 1996. For thirty-five years, opinion in the parties has also divided over a number of social issues. More Democrats have favoured civil rights and affirmative action programmes for minorities, gun control and abortion rights. More Republicans have favoured reducing government spending and balancing the federal budget, but President Clinton adopted both of these positions and milder forms of Republican stances on welfare reform, taxes and small government.

By the late 1990s both parties seemed further to the right, but in the next two presidential elections, differing views on these issues marked the party platforms and split the voters into almost equal camps. In 2000 Al Gore edged the Democratic party back towards its historic base, and in 2004 John Kerry attempted to balance traditional Democratic positions on domestic issues while charting an equally tough but 'smarter' course in the wars in Iraq and Afghanistan and the global war on terror. Meanwhile, George W. Bush appealed to and mobilized the conservative wing of the Republican party with increasing success.

**PLATE 5.3** Democratic nominee John Kerry speaking during the first presidential debate, which focused on national-security and foreign-policy issues, in 2004 at the University of Florida, Miami.
(*Ron Sachs/Rex Features*)

A range of economic and social indicators also showed differences between the parties in 2004. Democrats had, on average, lower incomes, less education and less prestigious occupations. They were also more often female, Jewish, urban and members of racial minority groups. Until the 1980s, most white Catholic ethnics were also Democrats, but now they more often split their allegiance.

## Party organization

The federal system results in parties that organize and function on three distinct levels. State and local party organizations vary a great deal. They are affiliated with, but not controlled by, the national parties, which usually do not interfere in their activities except to offer funds or services. The parties have organizing committees on every level with the Republican and Democratic national committees and their chairs at the top. Some critics say cooperation between the party levels is growing stronger. Others note an advantage in the current separated levels. The state and local parties are active on a continuous basis, while the national organizations lie mostly dormant between presidential elections. The party which loses presidential elections (as the Democrats did most of the time between 1969 and 1988) can sustain its strength in Congress and state governments. Both parties seem weak compared with European parties. Nearly all candidates label themselves as Democrat or Republican, but the party does not control their election campaigns or the policies they advocate.

### Independent candidates and 'third' parties

Independent candidates and minor or splinter parties (so-called 'third' parties) have a long history in America. They seldom win federal elections because of election rules and the public's loyalty to one of the major parties, which about half the voters inherit from their parents. Independents' victories nearly always occur in state or local contests in which exceptional circumstances play a larger role.

There are several types of third parties. In national elections, independents like Ralph Nader (in 2000 and 2004) and some third parties attract votes from people who are dissatisfied with the major parties and the government in general. Other third parties, such as the Socialist and Libertarian parties, represent ideologies that have only small followings in the USA. Others are single-issue organizations, such as the Prohibition, Women's, Right to Life and 'Green' Parties. The most important third parties have been those that result from splits in the major parties. One of these was the 'Bull Moose' Progressive Party formed from the Republican party's liberal wing by Theodore Roosevelt. It won over 27 per cent of the vote in the presidential election of 1912, which helped put Democrat Woodrow Wilson in office. In the 1990s and 2000 third parties perhaps also decided who became President. The impact of third parties, however, is most evident in the adoption of their policy suggestions, such as primary elections, direct election of senators, women's suffrage, income tax and a balanced budget by the major parties.

## The legislative branch

In addition to the staffs of individual members and congressional committees, Congress draws expertise from its own library, research service, and accounting, budget and technology-assessment offices.

During the crisis decades of the Cold War, the President seemed more important than Congress because of the executive's capacity for quick and decisive action. But since the 1970s, Congress has attempted, with limited success, to reassert authority over the nation's legislative agenda, military involvements and international commerce. A very powerful institution, it is no longer the dominant branch of the federal government, as the founders intended. Its main functions are law-making (mostly dealing with the President's legislative agenda), forming structures and programmes to implement policy, overseeing the resulting

**PLATE 5.4** A female suffragist stands alone before a crowd of men in New York City in 1910 to lobby publicly for help in winning the vote. She would have to wait another ten years to be heard constitutionally.

(*Time Pix/Rex Features*)

bureaucracy, raising and allocating government funds and advising the President on foreign affairs and appointments.

## Differences between the chambers

While the chambers of Congress are in theory equally powerful, there are several significant differences in their membership, organization and practices. As originally intended, the House continues to respond more quickly than the Senate to the electorate's mood. Elections every two years in smaller geographical units allow representatives to more closely reflect the current views of local voters than do senators, who serve six-year terms and represent whole states. The large majority of both chambers has always consisted of middle-aged white men, many of whom are usually lawyers. The House contains the more diverse membership. For example, when record numbers of women and members of minority groups ran for seats in 1996, it had fifty-two women, thirty-seven African Americans, nineteen Latinos and three Asian Americans, while the Senate had nine women (including the chamber's one black member), two Asian Americans, one Native American and no Latinos. Since then the number of women and people from minority groups in Congress has continued to rise slowly. After the 2000 elections, there were sixty-two women in the House and thirteen in the Senate and four years later that chamber included two Latino members.

There are constitutional differences between the chambers as well. To qualify for a seat in the Senate, a person must be thirty years old, a citizen for nine years and a resident of the state where elected. Representatives must be twenty-five, seven years a citizen and (by custom) a resident of their district. Financial bills must begin in the House, although the Senate can amend them. Treaties and presidential appointments must be approved by the Senate. Size, however, is the constitutional difference that has the most important effect on the chambers.

Because of its much greater size, the House must regulate its business carefully. The speaker of the House and the Rules Committee are given considerable power to schedule the work of the chamber, limit debate and restrict amendments to a Bill from the floor. The speaker also influences the assignment of members and Bills to committees, decides which Bills are brought up for a vote and has total power over who speaks during debate. The speaker is chosen by the majority party and in turn chooses his party's members on the Rules Committee. The majority party also elects a majority leader as the speaker's next in command and a whip to help round up votes. The other party selects a minority leader and whip.

The smaller Senate has much more relaxed procedures and no officer with power comparable to those of the speaker. Bills can be considered in any order and at any time a majority of the chamber wishes. There are majority and minority leaders, and both parties use the whip system to get out the vote. The Constitution appoints the Vice-President presiding officer of the Senate and requires the senators to elect a President *pro tempore* to chair the chamber in the Vice-President's absence. Most members usually find the position so powerless that it is turned over to a junior senator.

The real leader of the chamber is the majority leader, but even he has no formal power to limit debate or amendments. Members can therefore engage in a filibuster (an attempt to defeat a Bill by talking until its supporters withdraw it so that other business can be finished). Only if sixty members of the chamber vote for closure, which limits speeches to one hour, can a filibuster be stopped. In practice filibusters seldom occur. When they do, it signals an issue (or presidential appointment) considered so important that senators are unable to compromise, and therefore filibusters receive considerable notice. Amendments to a Bill during Senate debates can be irrelevant to its subject or purpose. Some of these 'riders' are attached in an attempt to ensure the Bill's defeat. Others are added to secure the passage of proposals that would have great difficulty in winning a majority if forwarded separately.

## *Congressional organization*

Members of Congress organize themselves in several ways. The most important of these is by party. Members divide along party lines on between a third and a half of the votes that take place in Congress. Special party groups pick the officers of each chamber and decide which committees members will work on. Each party gets a number of committee members equal to the percentage of seats it won in the last elections. The majority party wins the leadership positions and the most committee staffing.

Members also act on the basis of other loyalties. In the House, state delegations are important, especially since the members from states with large populations represent big, potentially unified voting blocks on some issues. Congress has well over 100 caucuses (interest groups formed to lobby other members) that allow members to gather in groups that are increasingly important rivals to the parties as the source of policy proposals. There are conservative, moderate and liberal caucuses for each party, as well as caucuses formed to promote regional, economic, ethnic, racial, and women's issues that cross both party and chamber divisions. Three decades ago Congress had only four caucuses. Today some commentators claim they cause the fragmentation of Congressional planning.

## *Powers and functions of Congress*

The Constitution grants Congress 'all legislative powers' in the federal government. Only Congress can make laws. The President, interest groups and private citizens may want laws passed by Congress, but only if they can convince a member of *each* chamber to introduce their proposals is there a chance that these will become federal law.

Law-making is only the best known of the legislative branch's duties. Members are truly representatives, so much of their work involves 'casework' (handling pressure groups' and voters' complaints and requests). The national legislature alone can make the federal budget. No federal funds can be raised, allocated or spent without its direction. Congress also has the constitutional authority to regulate foreign and inter-state commerce. Only it has the power to raise, finance and regulate military forces and to declare war. The legislative branch has great power over the other arms of the national government. It created all the federal courts below the Supreme Court, can (and has) changed the number of Supreme Court justices and decides which cases the federal courts can hear by defining jurisdictions. Congress, not the President, established the departments and the executive bureaucracy.

## The committee system

Congress does most of its work in committees in which members gain the expertise and power to make their mark on public policy. The volume and complexity of legislation introduced each year became so huge that committees became an indispensable tool for the division of labour. The committee system assigns members to specific legislative work, the supervision of executive departments and agencies, hearings on public issues and (in Senate committees) on presidential appointments.

Members strive for assignments on committees of the greatest concern to their states or congressional districts. As government became involved in wider areas of life, the two dozen or so standing (permanent) committees in each chamber have spawned many subcommittees. Thus, for example, one is not surprised to see a House member from Mississippi as the chairman of the agricultural subcommittee dealing with cotton. The most senior member of the majority party traditionally becomes chair of a committee and through this position exercises control over its power to 'kill' or promote a proposal. Since the early 1970s, however, subcommittees have multiplied in number and have won greater independence, and chairmen have been chosen by secret ballot, which has not always resulted in election by seniority.

## How a bill becomes an Act of Congress

The steps in the law-making process are similar in both chambers. Bills can be introduced in one chamber first or in both simultaneously. After that, the Bill is referred to a committee, which usually refers it to a subcommittee. There members air their views, gather reports from experts and lobbyists and hold hearings to get opinions on the proposal. The next step is a 'mark-up session' during which the subcommittee agrees on changes in the Bill. It is then returned to the committee for another mark-up session before it goes to the whole chamber for debate and a vote on passage.

Most Bills 'die' in committee or subcommittee because they were introduced only to publicize a member's willingness to 'do something' about an issue or because they are too flawed or controversial for passage. If Bills pass both chambers, in a few cases amendments added in one or both result in different texts. Then a conference committee from both chambers produces a compromise text for final votes in the House and Senate. If the compromise Bill passes, it is sent to the President, who may sign or veto it.

## Congressional elections

Elections for Congress take place in two different subdivisions of the nation: congressional districts, each of which chooses one member of the House of Representatives, and states, each of which selects two members of the Senate. Congressional elections take place every two years, when all members of the House of Representatives and one third of the Senate face re-election.

The House expanded as new states entered the union and their populations grew. But in 1929 its size was fixed at 435 (with three additional non-voting delegates from the District of Columbia). Since then the seats are divided among the states according to their population by a process called reapportionment (reassignment of the number of House seats to each state) after every ten-year federal census. The Constitution guarantees each state a minimum of one representative. The number any state has above this minimum depends on how large its population is compared to that of the other states. Since the size of the House is constant, states with declining or slowly growing populations lose seats, and those with more rapidly growing populations gain seats. From 1950 to 2000, the political power of the north-eastern and Great Lakes states in the House has declined while that of parts of the south, south-west and Pacific coast has risen.

The 1962 Supreme Court ruling in *Baker* v. *Carr* required redistricting (the redrawing of the geographical lines between districts) to follow the one-person-one-vote principle by creating congressional districts with equal populations. Each district contains about 550,000 people. The 1982 amendments to the federal Voting Rights Act required that a state's plan for redrawn district lines must make it likely that minority-group members will be elected to the House in numbers equivalent to the group's portion of the population of the state. In the 1990s court challenges to the constitutionality of 'minority majority' districts reduced their number, but there were few protests, since record numbers of minorities are getting elected to Congress. Today, moreover, the use of sophisticated statistical computer models make it possible for the majority in state legislatures to design a legal redistricting plan that satisfies virtually any political priorities it has. After 2000 the Texas legislature, according to most commentators, created five more 'safe' districts for Republicans by just such a process.

The two-member constituencies for the Senate are a major exception to the principle of single-member election districts in the USA. Even these, however, function as one-member districts because only one of a state's senators is elected in any election year.

One key to understanding the nature of Congress lies in remembering that the USA does not have a parliamentary form of government. In a parliament, the prime minister is usually the leader of the majority party in the legislature after a general election. Members of a parliament keep in line with party policies because voting independently can cause the fall of the government. In that kind of system, members owe their seats to political parties, and voters choose between parties rather than individual candidates. Voting independently in office can lead to deselection by the party at the next election.

Congress does not choose the chief executive. Its members can vote without fear that the government will fall if they do not support their party. This means that they can give their first allegiance to their state or congressional district, rather than to their party or to the chief executive. Members of Congress owe their seats to elections in which their personalities and individual positions on issues matter more than party labels. The parties cannot control who enters congressional elections or directs these campaigns. And most candidates organize their own campaign staff and cover the cost of running for office through their own fund-raising. The party is but one of several sources of support.

To run for a seat in Congress, a person must usually win a primary election first. Two or more candidates from the same party compete in a primary for the right to represent the party in the general election campaign. They may put themselves forward or be recruited by the party. State laws require people to document the seriousness of their bid for the party label by collecting a certain number of signatures supporting their candidacy before their names are put on the primary ballot. Victory in a primary is often achieved with a plurality rather than a majority of the votes because the field of candidates is frequently between three and five. In some states, a run-off primary is held between the two front-runners when no candidate wins a majority. In the general election there are usually two candidates, a Democrat and a Republican, although independent or third-party candidates sometimes run.

Being a member of Congress has become a career. Between 1946 and 2004 more than 90 per cent of House members and about 75 per cent of senators won re-election. Most observers agree that incumbents (sitting members) have advantages over challengers. They use their office for media attention, their names and faces are consequently better known, and they can take credit for helping to pass government programmes that benefit the state or district. Voter dissatisfaction with Congress reached a peak in the 1990s according to opinion polls, but incumbents won re-election at only slightly lower rates in 1998 and 2000. On the other hand, more incumbents retired in the 1990s to avoid electoral defeat.

The Democrats had majorities in both Houses of Congress for almost the entire time from 1954 to 1994, losing control only of the Senate between 1980 and 1986. The advantages of incumbency helped the party stay in power so long, but backfired in 1994–6 as voters made Democrats the target of their discontent with government. The mid-term elections (those between presidential election years) usually result in losses for the majority party, and in 1994 cost the Democrats the control of both chambers. The Republican party won majorities in both houses for the first time in forty years and, on taking office, made a major shift in the leadership, committee composition and staffing of Congress. The Republicans have kept a majority in both houses since then, except for a short period when they lost control of the evenly divided Senate early in George W. Bush's first term. They consolidated their control over Congress after 2000, gaining increasing majorities in the 2002 and 2004 elections.

# The executive branch

Some 2.7 million civilians and 1.4 million active-duty military employees work in this largest branch of the federal government. The degree of control the President has over the departments, independent agencies, branches of the military and government corporations in the federal bureaucracy depends on the rules set up by Congress. Over 99 per cent of civilian federal bureaucrats, for example, are hired through competitive examinations required by the Civil Service Act, rather than by presidential appointment.

The President nominates the highest officials in the executive branch: the secretaries and assistant secretaries who lead the departments, the chief administrators of agencies and commissions and the ranking officers of American embassies. These appointments must be approved by the Senate. Only the roughly 2,000 high-level positions in the Executive Office of the President (EOP) are filled without congressional approval.

## The Executive Office of the President

The main components of the EOP that operate outside the White House are the Council of Economic Advisers, the National Security Council, the Office of Management and Budget and the Central Intelligence Agency (CIA). Inside the White House are the first lady's staff and the President's own staff, which includes his personal advisors (some of whom are carried over from his election staff), his press secretary, congressional liaison officer and chief of staff. The structure and operation of the EOP and the upper levels of the executive branch vary, depending on the style and character of the President. For instance, the cabinet, though it is composed of department secretaries and other key officials, has played a smaller role in the policy development of recent administrations.

## Qualifications for and powers of the presidency

The President's powers and qualifications reflect the Constitutional clauses intended to prevent the development of presidential government while providing for strong national leadership. The President must be a natural-born citizen, at least thirty-five years old, and have been a resident of the USA for at least fourteen years. He is more independent of the legislature than the chief executives of most democratic governments because he is elected separately from Congress and cannot be removed from office by a vote of no-confidence.

The price of his independence is having no guarantee of majorities in the Houses of Congress, the difficulties of lobbying for support in an institution of which he is not a member and the limits put on his powers by the system of checks and balances. But the chief executive is the only official elected by voters in all the states and on that basis can claim to be the sole politician who rises above the self-seeking goals of party politics in the national interest.

**PLATE 5.5** President George W. Bush delivering the State of the Union Address, 1 March 2003. (*Corbis*)

Presidential duties are stated in the Constitution, delegated by Congress or are the result of circumstances. The most important extra-constitutional duties are acting as chief of state and party leader. The President became the nation's ceremonial head of state by default, because the Constitution provides no other office for that purpose. He became the national leader of his party as parties developed into the organizers of the nation's political life and the presidency became increasingly powerful. The President's popularity with voters can often affect the success of his party's candidates for other offices. After the 1994 congressional elections, for example, polls showed that most voters used their votes to express displeasure with President Clinton's policies. In 2002 President George W. Bush energetically used the prestige of his office to help his party win majorities in Congress.

The office's constitutional powers are the result of interpreting rather vague phrases in the document. The President is the administrative head of the nation because the Constitution states that 'the executive power shall be vested in the President'. What that and other constitutional phrases mean in practice has evolved from the claims that Presidents have made without provoking Congress or the courts to effectively oppose them. As chief administrator, the President is required to see that the laws are carried out. This is understood to mean managing the bureaucracy and enforcing existing policies, but, interpreted broadly it has enabled Presidents to break a strike or send troops to integrate a public school.

## The President and foreign policy

The Constitution names the President as commander-in-chief, making him the highest ranking officer in the armed services, but gives Congress the power to declare war. The founders' attempt to give the legislature control over the executive's military power proved so limited that in 1973 Congress passed the War Powers Act to restrain the President by requiring congressional approval for deployment of American troops abroad within specified time limits. Presidents have unanimously called the Act unconstitutional and have followed its notification procedure only when it suited them. Since the Second World War most wars the USA has engaged in have never been declared. Congress has instead passed joint resolutions giving the chief executive nearly carte blanche to conduct these 'armed conflicts' as he sees fit.

The President's military power is one of several factors that strengthen his position as foreign-policy leader. This is the arena where the executive branch has most clearly developed a dominance. Presidents have learned to circumvent the constitutional clauses that require approval by two thirds of the Senate for ratification of a treaty and a simple majority for confirmation of diplomatic appointments. The National Security Advisor, who owes his position solely to the President's choice, has become most Presidents' main advisor in formulating foreign policy. And decisions are most often carried out through executive agreements, which do not have to be approved by the Senate.

The President has at his disposal four major organizations to support his conduct of foreign affairs: the Departments of State and Defense, the CIA and the National Security Council. Faced with these facts, Congress continues to assert its role in foreign policy but recognizes presidential leadership. In addition, since 2002 the chief executive has a new permanent division of the executive branch, the Department of Homeland Security (DHS), to assist him in mobilizing and disciplining the public for national defence during the global war on terrorism, an open-ended period of national crisis that some commentators have christened the 'second cold war'. (See Chapter 7.)

## Chief law-maker

The President's role as legislative leader developed in part from constitutional clauses requiring him to inform Congress about the 'state of the nation' and to suggest the 'measures' he considers 'necessary or expedient'. Another clause allows him to convene a special session of Congress if he deems it necessary. However, the President did not usually set the legislative agenda until the twentieth century.

In 1921 Congress weakened its monopoly on the 'power of the purse' by the Budget and Accounting Act, which delegated to the President the power to screen the budget proposals of executive-branch departments and agencies. As a result, the White House routinely sets policy priorities by proposing how much money shall be given to government programmes. But not until the Great Depression of the 1930s did the President become heavily involved in drafting a coordinated 'package' of bills for congressional action. The New Deal proposals of Franklin D. Roosevelt marked a new era in presidential legislative activity, but then the President sent bills to Congress and let it decide what to do with them. Today, Presidents follow their progress through Congress closely and use legislative aides to lobby hard for their passage.

A President who is an effective legislative initiator and lobbyist has less need of his veto power. Vetoes can take place in two ways: with a veto message giving presidential objections or by no action being taken within ten days of the adjournment of Congress on bills that come to the White House (the so-called pocket veto). The President's veto power is limited. Congress may override it, and only from 1995 to 1997 did the executive have a line-item veto on financial bills. Thus members of Congress can press unwanted proposals on the President as 'riders' to bills the executive wants passed.

## *Presidential elections: money, caucuses and primaries*

Electing the President is a long, complicated and costly affair. After conferring with political advisors, individuals hold press conferences between eighteen months and a year before the election to announce that they are running for President. Several serious candidates from each party commonly propose themselves. Over the following months these candidates 'test the water' to see if support for their candidacy in different parts of the nation is warm enough to raise the tens of millions of dollars necessary to pay for the upcoming primary-caucus campaign. Most would-be candidates drop out of the contest during this demanding 'invisible primary', which seemed to strongly favour those with support among the nation's most wealthy until 2004, when Democrat Howard Dean raised more than sufficient funds through small donations made over the Internet. Since the election-campaign finance reforms of the 1970s, candidates can win matching public funds to pay for this part of the election campaign on the condition that they accept a spending cap and that they demonstrate that they have broad-based citizen support by getting many small donations in twenty different states. Even though the spending cap was about $50 million for the nomination campaign in 2004, both candidates refused public funding so they could spend more.

From February to June of the presidential election year the states conduct the process of narrowing the field of candidates to one from each party through two electoral procedures, caucuses or primaries. Both procedures are indirect: party voters choose delegates to the party's national convention and give these delegates the authority to make its official nomination of a candidate. Most states use presidential primaries to narrow the field of candidates, but fifteen held party meetings called presidential caucuses in 2004. Because they result in the choice of roughly 80 per cent of convention delegates, presidential primaries attract much more attention than the caucuses. Many are closed, that is, they are elections in which only registered members of the party holding the primary can vote. Thus one state can have two presidential primaries, a closed primary for each of the major parties. Some are open primaries, voters from either party can participate, and a few are semi-open, allowing both independents and voters from one party to vote.

In the past several elections, through so-called 'front-loading', growing numbers of states have moved their primaries to dates earlier in the season. As a result, the winner of the Democratic Party's nomination in 2004 was clear at the beginning of March, months before he was officially chosen by his party's convention in July. Thus John Kerry's and President Bush's campaign organizations began confronting each other while they raised money for the post-convention campaign, which costs much more than the funding needed for winning the party nomination.

The government provides some financing for party conventions and supplies full public funding for the post-convention campaigns of major party's nominees up to a spending cap (in 2004 $75 million for each candidate), if they opt for government funding. Because they raised and spent far in excess of that limit, neither major candidate accepted these government moneys in 2004. Central provisions of the Bipartisan Campaign Reform Act of 2002 established rules controlling the ways public or private money can be used during the election process. Most important, the Act banned the use of 'soft money' raised in a party's name and limited funding by independent political action committees (PACs), because these sources of money no longer mostly paid for grass-roots political participation but instead funded 'issue ads' in the print and broadcast media close to election day that attack the opponent's position while seeming to educate the public.

## Media politics: the conventions, ads and presidential debates

During the 'primary season' the media keep a running count of the delegates pledged to each candidate and track the front-runners' progress towards a majority of delegate votes at the party conventions in July and August. As a result, in recent decades each party's choice has been clear before the convention. The party 'in the White House' has re-nominated the incumbent (the person in the office), and a single 'out party' candidate has accumulated a delegate majority at his convention by the end of the primaries and caucuses.

Still, the proportional representation from primaries that the Democrats and some states now require sends more divided blocks of delegates to the conventions. Caucuses and primaries bind delegates only on the first roll-call vote of the states. If no candidate wins a majority, delegates are free to switch loyalties on later votes, and the final choice of the convention, theoretically at least, could be unexpected.

If present trends continue, however, the interest in the convention will lie elsewhere. Because the convention is televised, both parties present a 'packaged media show' of unity designed to demonstrate that the internal disagreements of the primary season are forgotten. In the 1990s, however, George H.W. Bush and Bob Dole distanced themselves from some parts of the platform agreed on at the convention because the more extreme elements in the party had successfully used majorities on convention committees to promote their views.

Most national party meetings between the early 1990s and 2004 have been the well-orchestrated media events that are typical of today's party conventions, with factions such as Jesse Jackson's Rainbow Coalition and Republican John McCain's supporters accepting subordinate roles. In the 1990s and early 2000s presidential candidates announced their vice-presidential 'running mates' weeks in advance, denying television viewers that convention suspense. Today the party conventions offer competing media presentations of the parties and their candidates. The key question is which of these mass appeals is the more successful at convincing the voting public to identify with its candidate and view of the country's choices.

The parties and their candidates eventually face each other in the post-convention campaign that runs from late August until the voters go to the polls at the beginning of November. Candidates still criss-cross the country to make themselves and their stands on the issues known, but now stay in a city only long enough to arrange for the media to take them into the public's living rooms. More than in earlier phases of the campaign, hugely expensive short television 'spots' are used by all the major parties and candidates, as much to portray the faults of their opponents (negative campaigning) as to put themselves in the best possible light. Because of the high cost of television campaigning, candidates also depend on getting free coverage by making the evening news with their regular campaign activities.

Since 1988, television advertisements sponsored and funded by independent partisan groups have played an increasingly visible (some would say decisive) role in the media battles of presidential elections. In that year Republican partisans used a television ad featuring a close-up of Willie Horton, an African-American convict in Massachusetts (who had committed a violent crime while on a weekend furlough from prison) to label Democratic candidate Michael Dukakis 'soft' on crime, even though, as Governor of the state, Dukakis had opposed the furlough plan. In a similar fashion, groups outside candidates' and parties' official organizations have since then looked for and given media coverage to scandalous behaviour allegedly involving opponents. In 2004 both Republicans and Democrats attempted to gain electoral advantage by attacking the military record of the opposing candidate. The 'Swift-boat Veterans for Truth' who impugned Kerry's service in the Vietnam War continued their television attacks long after Republican Senator John McCain and then President Bush decried the ads and defended Kerry's record.

In the closing months of the campaign, public debates that are televised live nationwide offer the candidates the best chance to exploit the mass-media audience for a campaign boost. In recent years, there have been three presidential debates and one vice-presidential debate. Since the first televised debate in 1960, when Senator John F. Kennedy bested President Richard Nixon in visual appearance and style, the debates have seemed to favour the challenger over the incumbent. A larger audience watches the debates than any other single event in the campaign (over 50 million viewers for the first debate in 2004), and a large segment of voters say the debates are likely to influence their choice. Both candidates are wary of making mistakes in front of this enormous audience and so eagerly prepare to meet any question with a well-informed answer. Yet, more often than not, the debates are an unreliable predictor of who will be elected. In 2004, for example, opinion surveys indicated that the public viewed Kerry as the winner of all three debates, but Bush won re-election by a clear margin. Other factors, such as the public's division over key issues and the candidates' performance in untelevised campaign activities are often decisive.

## Election day

On election day the television networks display huge maps of the country to track two different tallies of the results. One is the 'popular vote' (a count of how many voters across the country have supported the candidates). At first these figures are estimates compiled by polling organizations who ask people how they voted as they exit the polling stations. By late evening, the count for eastern states may be official. But because of the difference in time zones, the popular vote in the Pacific west will not be known until very late.

The popular vote, however, does not determine who wins. Not only are the candidates chosen in an indirect fashion through the primaries, but the final election is also decided indirectly. In accordance with rules in the Constitution, the popular vote is not counted nationally, but by state. The second tally on election-day television screens is the electoral-college vote. Each state has a number of votes in the college equal to its members in Congress (two senators plus its number of representatives in the House). The District of Columbia has three votes, making a total of 538 'electors' in the college. After the ten-year census, the number of electors per state is adjusted to reflect the changing size of their populations and so, congressional delegations (see Figure 5.1).

The members of the electoral college travel to their respective state capitals in mid-December and cast the ballots which officially decide the election when they are counted in the Senate in January. The media make the electoral result clear long before then because, except for the electors from Maine and Nebraska, members of the college are pledged to vote together for the winning candidate in each state. The Supreme Court has determined that states cannot *require* electors to vote for that candidate, but few electors have not. The plurality system has its most dramatic effect in the electoral-college vote.

The candidate who wins a state (even with a minority of its popular vote) receives *all* the votes in the college. The system is supposed to reward 'small states' which get three electoral votes no matter how small their population. Today, however, most people are concentrated in a dozen or so 'big states' and only a few of these are 'competitive' (divided in their support for the candidates). Thus most time and money in the campaign is spent in states like Florida and Ohio to win large blocks of highly contested electoral-college votes. On the other hand, when an election is exceptionally close, as in 2000, even the three electoral votes of the smallest states could be decisive.

In such a system, most voters are unwilling to 'waste' their votes on third-party candidates, who almost never win whole states and votes in the college, as Table 5.1 documents.

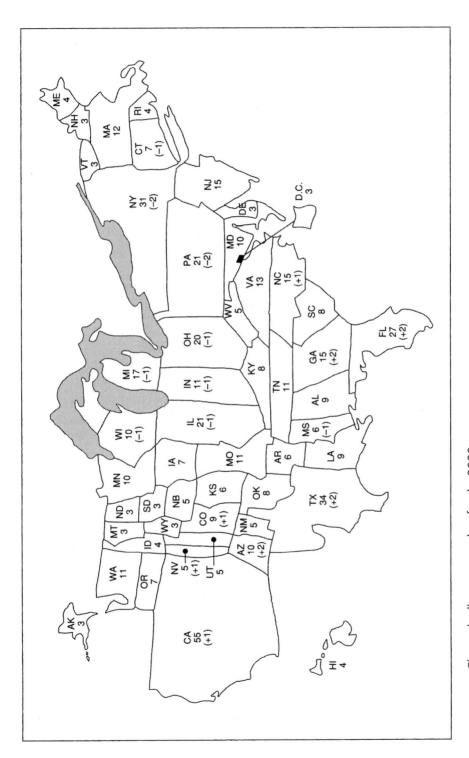

**FIGURE 5.1**   Electoral-college geography after the 2000 census.

*Note:* Changes in states' electoral votes because of the 2000 census are shown in parenthesis

**TABLE 5.1** US presidential elections, 1932–2004.

| Year | Candidates[a] | Parties | % of popular electoral vote | Vote[b] |
|---|---|---|---|---|
| 1932 | Franklin D. Roosevelt | Democratic | 57.4 | 472 |
| | Herbert C. Hoover | Republican | 39.7 | 59 |
| | Norman Thomas | Socialist | 2.2 | |
| 1936 | Franklin D. Roosevelt | Democratic | 60.8 | 523 |
| | Alfred M. Landon | Republican | 36.5 | 8 |
| | William Lemke | Union | 1.9 | |
| 1940 | Franklin D. Roosevelt | Democratic | 54.8 | 449 |
| | Wendell L. Wilkie | Republican | 44.8 | 82 |
| 1944 | Franklin D. Roosevelt | Democratic | 53.5 | 432 |
| | Thomas E. Dewey | Republican | 46.0 | 99 |
| 1948 | Harry S. Truman | Democratic | 49.6 | 303 |
| | Thomas E. Dewey | Republican | 45.1 | 189 |
| | J. Strong Thurmond | States Rights | 2.4 | |
| | Henry A. Wallace | Progressive | 2.4 | |
| 1952 | Dwight D. Eisenhower | Republican | 55.1 | 442 |
| | Adlai E. Stevenson | Democratic | 44.4 | 89 |
| 1956 | Dwight D. Eisenhower | Republican | 57.6 | 457 |
| | Adlai E. Stevenson | Democratic | 42.1 | 73 |
| 1960 | John F. Kennedy | Democratic | 49.7 | 303 |
| | Richard M. Nixon | Republican | 49.5 | 219 |
| 1964 | Lyndon B. Johnson | Democratic | 61.1 | 486 |
| | Barry M. Goldwater | Republican | 38.5 | 52 |
| 1968 | Richard M. Nixon | Republican | 43.3 | 301 |
| | Hubert H. Humphrey | Democratic | 42.7 | 191 |
| | George C. Wallace | American Independent | 13.5 | 46 |

| Year | Candidate | Party | Popular vote (%) | Electoral vote |
|------|-----------|-------|------------------|----------------|
| 1972 | *Richard M. Nixon* | *Republican* | *60.7* | *520* |
| | George S. McGovern | Democratic | 37.5 | 17 |
| | John G. Schmitz | American Independent | 1.4 | |
| 1976 | *Jimmy Carter* | *Democratic* | *50.1* | *297* |
| | Gerald R. Ford | Republican | 48.0 | 240 |
| 1980 | *Ronald Reagan* | *Republican* | *50.8* | *489* |
| | Jimmy Carter | Democratic | 41.0 | 49 |
| | John B. Anderson | Independent | 6.6 | |
| | Ed Clark | Libertarian | 1.1 | |
| 1984 | *Ronald Reagan* | *Republican* | *58.8* | *525* |
| | Walter Mondale | Democratic | 40.6 | 13 |
| 1988 | *George Bush* | *Republican* | *53.4* | *426* |
| | Michael Dukakis | Democratic | 45.6 | 111 |
| 1992 | *Bill Clinton* | *Democratic* | *43.0* | *370* |
| | George Bush | Republican | 38.0 | 168 |
| | H. Ross Perot | Independent | 19.0 | |
| 1996 | *Bill Clinton* | *Democratic* | *49.4* | *379* |
| | Bob Dole | Republican | 41.0 | 159 |
| | H. Ross Perot | Reform | 9.6 | |
| 2000 | *George W. Bush* | *Republican* | *47.9* | *271* |
| | Albert Gore, Jr. | Democratic | 48.4 | 266 |
| | Ralph Nader | Green | 2.7 | |
| | Patrick Buchanan | Reform | 0.4 | |
| | Harry Browne | Libertarian | 0.4 | |
| 2004 | *George W. Bush* | *Republican* | *51.0* | *286* |
| | John Kerry | Democrat | 48.0 | 249 |
| | Ralph Nader | Independent | 1.0 | |

Notes: [a] Victor in italics. [b] In some elections a few electoral votes went to candidates whose percentage of the popular vote was insignificant.

Still, the 2000 presidential election showed how the small number of votes that third-party candidates win *within* states can determine the outcome of the entire national contest. In ten states (a total of 105 electors in the college) the race was so close that the winner's margin of success was less than the vote taken by Nader's Green Party, Buchanan's reform ticket or these minor parties together. (Again, look at Table 5.1.)

In 2000 the election was closest in Florida, where Bush won by 0.01 per cent of the vote. In 2004 Ohio was the state that, by a thin popular vote margin, provided Bush with the margin of victory in the electoral college to become President. In 2000 victory was clear only after court challenges over election recounts in Florida counties ended with the US Supreme Court decision that these recounts did not apply uniform standards to all votes and so were un-constitutional. The state's election arrangements became globally infamous because of the differences exposed in the voting machines and counting procedures, which not only decided the election result (by a margin of 537 votes!) but undercounted or wrongly counted the votes of the elderly and minorities. In 2004 Bush's victory was clearer, in these decisive 'swing' states and in the nation as a whole.

## Reform the system?

Two larger realities were exposed in 2000: first, Americans had divided with a fine evenness between the views represented by the major candidates and, second, the presidential election system, in theory and practice, had undemocratic elements. There has long been debate about whether election of the President through the electoral college should be continued, but no concerted effort for change has emerged. Critics remind the public that a close election can be thrown into the House of Representatives to be decided by an undemocratic one-vote-per state ballot there, as the Constitution requires, if no candidate wins a majority in the electoral college. (Only because of the unprecedented Supreme Court decision was that avoided in 2000.) A candidate can win the popular vote but lose in the college, political scientists note, as occurred three times in the 1800s and again in 2000, when Gore won half a million more votes but lost in the election. Supporters of the status quo note that, in the American federal system, the college properly gives weight to states and also produces a clearer result. (Those effects were also evident in 2000, but hardly in a satisfying way.)

The flaws in the *practice* of the system seemed as least as grave in 2000. Former President Jimmy Carter, who had inspected and critiqued elections in many parts of the world, reported a 5 per cent error rate in Florida, one which fell below international election commission standards. Since the results were nearly as close in nine or more other states and similar variations in machinery and counting appeared in these places, the need for reform of these arrangements across the nation seemed clear. In 2002 Congress passed the Help America Vote

Act that required each state to submit a plan for uniform voting procedures and standards and which provided federal funds for implementing changes. Although the process of reform was still incomplete, the 2004 election revealed a fairer, more smoothly operating system.

# The judicial branch

The only court specifically mentioned by the Constitution is the US Supreme Court. However, Congress has established lesser federal courts in a three-tier system, as well as courts for tax, customs, patent and military law. District courts have original jurisdiction in most federal cases. Only about one-sixth of the decisions of these courts are appealed to the next tier, the US courts of appeals.

Most of the US Supreme Court's work consists of hearing cases from US courts of appeals or state supreme courts. These cases raise federal questions (controversies arising under the Constitution, federal law or treaties). In addition it has original jurisdiction in cases which involve a state or officials of the federal government. In 1990, a typical year, it heard ten cases under its original jurisdiction and handed down decisions on 130 cases that it selected from 4,500 appeals for review. The decisions of lower federal courts become final in cases it refuses to hear, which means those judges also exercise judicial review, though usually that means following earlier decisions set by the US Supreme Court.

The Constitution creates a separate judicial branch with a single Supreme Court that has an unspecified number of justices with terms of office dependent only on their 'good behaviour'. In practice, the number of justices has varied between five and ten, according to the will of Congress, but in recent history has been eight, plus a chief justice. Terms of office have, by tradition, been for life or until voluntary retirement. As no justice has ever been impeached, life terms have given justices an impressive degree of independence. Of the 144 men and two women nominated to the Court, about four in five have been confirmed by the Senate. In 1987 Richard Bork became the last presidential nominee to be rejected.

## *Judicial review*

Today, the fame and influence of the Supreme Court result from its power of judicial review, the right to decide in cases determining whether congressional, presidential and states' acts are in accordance with the Constitution and to declare them void if it deems they are not.(See 'The constitutional framework' on pp. 107–10.) The court claimed the right of judicial review by stages and won gradual acceptance for its practice between 1796 and 1865. In the first year the court asserted its right to invalidate state laws that it considered unconstitutional. In *Marbury* v. *Madison* (1803), it claimed the power to invalidate an

**PLATE 5.6** The US Supreme Court in session.
(*Priscilla Coleman*)

unconstitutional federal law. Later decisions extended judicial review to cover executive acts. The court's review power maintains the supremacy of federal law and a uniform interpretation of the Constitution from state to state. As a practical fact, only the Union victory in the Civil War established the supremacy of federal law, the US Constitution and the Supreme Court as their interpreter.

Once that pattern of authority was accepted, Supreme Court decisions became a powerful force shaping public policy because they became precedents that all other state and federal courts followed in similar cases. But there remain two views on how the court should exercise the power of judicial review. One, called judicial restraint, holds that the justices should limit their review to applying the rules explicitly stated or clearly implied in the Constitution or Acts of Congress. If cases raise questions not clearly answered by existing law, the court should leave those questions for the elected politicians to decide. The other view, termed judicial activism, maintains that justices ought to let the general intent or principles underlying the text of the Constitution and federal statutes be their guide in applying often vague legal language to a changing society. In the activist view, the court should not hesitate to intervene in political questions to protect the Constitution and prevent infringements on individual rights.

In the course of US history, there have been cycles of judicial activism and restraint. The activist period before the Civil War was followed by a cycle of restraint that lasted until 1937. During these years the court generally held that the government's right to regulate the economy was not clearly implied in the Constitution. Instead it asserted that private business and property were protected from federal regulation by the Fourteenth Amendment, even though the Amendment was originally intended to guarantee the rights of former slaves.

In the 1890s the court handed down a series of decisions that legalized racial segregation and the disenfranchisement of African Americans in the south by ruling that the regulation of public facilities and elections exceeded the constitutional powers of the national government. In the 1930s the court invalidated so many of the economic programmes in Franklin D. Roosevelt's New Deal that he proposed 'packing' the court with more amenable justices until one member of the court provided a majority for the President by adopting new views in 1937.

A new period of judicial activism began in that year, extending to the end of the 1980s, during which the court rarely invalidated economic legislation but overturned dozens of laws that it believed infringed individuals' rights. It reversed its earlier stand on segregation in the *Brown* decision (1954) and since then has protected minority voting rights, affirmative action programmes to increase educational opportunities for racial minorities, abortion rights and the right to unrestricted political expression, even if that means burning the American flag.

Republicans Reagan and George H.W. Bush appointed five justices who they hoped would move the Court into another period of judicial restraint. Once on the bench, however, justices have frequently surprised and disappointed their sponsors. Moreover, in his first term, moderately liberal President Clinton has appointed a second woman, Ruth Bader Ginsburg, whose views have generally not coincided with those of the alleged conservatives. For the present, however, the court is allowing more government discretion in limiting abortion rights and affirmative-action programmes and is showing a willingness to reconsider earlier decisions in voting rights and segregation cases. In 2003, however, this supposed 'conservative' court declared unconstitutional a state law that prohibited consensual sex among adult homosexuals in *Lawrence and Garner* v. *Texas*. During his second term George W. Bush is likely to appoint justices who favour a restrictionist approach.

Some commentators criticize a system in which an appointed judicial body can overrule the democratically elected branches of government. Others point out that in over 200 years the court has invalidated only around 120 sections of federal law but nearly ten times as many provisions of state law. These rulings, it must be remembered, were all in response to disagreements between specific parties and limited to the particular points of law raised by those parties. Nevertheless, the court's judicial review can be overridden, since Congress and the President (and state governments) can revise their acts and constitutional amendments can be passed.

# Attitudes to branches of the federal government

The Supreme Court's decisions relieve the other branches of taking positions on politically sensitive questions. The court has reversed itself when older decisions no longer seem valid and, according to a study covering its rulings from the mid-1930s to the mid-1980s, it was in line with public opinion at least as often as the other branches. Evidence from Gallup and Roper opinion surveys from the mid-1980s through to 2004 show that the American public trusts only the military, organized religion, the police and banks more than the court. In those years, people in the USA had more confidence in the court than the President, and two to three times more confidence in it than in Congress.

This suggests that the question of whether judicial review by the Supreme Court is a democratic process is more complicated than it at first appears. Though the justices are not elected, they are responsive to and receive support from popular opinion. It is notable that public confidence in the court did not fall after its controversial decision that resolved the disputed presidential election of 2000.

Public attitudes to the President are less stable than those regarding the Supreme Court. Whether the chief executive deserves it or not, the public lays the blame or credit for the nation's current situation and how it is handled at his door. As President Harry Truman famously said, 'The buck stops here', referring to his desk. Thus, the first President Bush got the blame for the economic recession at the start of the 1990s and Clinton the credit for the boom that followed. On the other hand, the public always unites behind the President in times of military crisis. Its confidence in the President during the Gulf War in 1991, and after the terrorist attacks on the World Trade Center and the Pentagon in 2001 was much higher than it was for the Supreme Court or Congress.

The public had little confidence in Congress in the 1990s, when the institution had support from only a quarter or fifth of the people polled. In 2001 only health-maintenance organizations were held in lower esteem by the public, among the sixteen major institutions included in a Gallup poll. The legislative branch won no boost for its response to international crises and got the blame for the budget crisis in 1995–6 and the impeachment of the President. By tradition, and especially since 1945, the public expects the President to conduct foreign policy and Congress to handle the allocation of financial resources. The legislators won no moral battle with the public during the impeachment process and the trial in the Senate, when support for Clinton fell significantly but not nearly as much as it did for Congress. Some commentators note the irony that the branch the founders of the US government intended to be the most democratic (Congress) is the one least popular with the public, while others say the public treats it precisely as the founders intended by reacting most critically to the part of government they require to be most responsive to people's needs and changing attitudes.

# Exercises

Explain and examine the following names and terms.

| | | |
|---|---|---|
| Articles of Confederation | 'third' parties | incumbents |
| popular sovereignty | Speaker of the House | presidential appointments |
| 'reserved' powers | Majority Leader | line-item veto |
| 'necessary and proper' clause | filibuster | presidential caucuses |
| the separation of powers | congressional caucuses | electoral college |
| winner-take-all system | reapportionment | original jurisdiction |
| a two-party region | primary elections | judicial review |

Write short essays on the following questions.

1. How are the principles of federalism and limited government protected by the Constitution of 1787 and its amendments?

2. Compare and contrast the chambers of Congress, giving particular attention to the effects of their different size, membership and terms of office.

3. Discuss the powers of the President and contrast his position with that of a prime minister in a parliamentary government.

4. Describe American parties and elections and discuss the causes and effects of their most distinctive elements.

5. Critically discuss the stages in the presidential election system, defending in a balanced fashion how democratic you think the process is.

6. What are some of the arguments for and against the Supreme Court's power of judicial review?

# Further reading

Barone, M. and G. Ujifusa (annual) *The Almanac of American Politics* Washington, DC: National Journal.

Ceaser, James W. and A. Busch (2001) *The Perfect Tie: the true story of the 2000 presidential election* Lanham, Md.: Rowman & Littlefield.

Fisher, L. (1995) *Presidential War Power* Lawrence, Kans.: University Press of Kansas.

Freeman, J. (2002) *A Room at a Time: how women entered party politics* Lanham, Md.: Rowman & Littlefield.

Hudson, William E. (2004) *American Democracy in Peril: eight challenges to America's future* 4th edn Washington, DC: Congressional Quarterly Press.

Lowi, T. J. and B. Ginsberg (2004) *American Government: freedom and power* 8th edn New York: W. W. Norton.
McKeever, R., J. Zvesper and M. Maidment (1999) *Politics USA* London: Prentice Hall.

## Web sites

<http://usdoj.gov>
<http://gallup.com/poll/indicators>
<http://thomas.loc.gov>
<http://fpc.state.gov>
<http://lcweb.loc.gov/global/executive/fed/html>
<http://www.politics1.com>
<http://en.wikipedia.org>
<http://cnn.com>
<http://c-span.org>
<http://www.nytimes.com/politics>
<http://www.latimes.com>
<http://washingtonpost.com/wp-dyn/politics>

# Chapter 6

# Political institutions
## State and local government

- The place of state government in American federalism
- The evolution of state government and federalism in the USA
- The structure of state government
- Local government
- *Exercises*
- *Further reading*
- *Web sites*

Both advocates and critics of the European Union have compared it to a 'United States of Europe'. Europeans are presently grappling with dilemmas of constitutionality and government structure similar to those weighed by the drafters of the Constitution of 1787. The vastly different historical situation of European nations today makes comparison dubious. Nonetheless, political leaders in both times and places have considered the similar issues of how much power should be centralized and how much left to national ('state' in the USA) or local government.

The answers the founding fathers gave to these and related questions defined the particular brand of federalism originally established in the USA. But such issues are not decided once and for all. They are part of an ongoing debate about the nature and purposes of government. The answers given at different times provide a map of the evolving character of American federalism and state and local government in the USA.

## The place of state government in American federalism

A whole article of the Constitution is devoted to the states. Article 4 recognizes the limited sovereignty of the states by denying the federal authorities the power to alter the boundaries of existing states without their permission. The federal capital, Washington, could be founded only because the states of Maryland and Virginia agreed to give up some of their territory to create the District of Columbia. Constitutional procedures for the admission of new states on an equal footing (having 'full faith and credit') with the original thirteen and a clause guaranteeing them a republican form of government recognize *states* as the main building blocks of the American system. The importance of the states is also woven into other provisions of the Constitution, such as the rule that membership in both chambers of Congress and the election of the President are determined by state. In addition, amendments to the US Constitution can only be made with the approval of three-quarters of the states. The above protections and privileges alone go a long way towards explaining the current movements for statehood in Puerto Rico and the District of Columbia.

At the time, it was thought that the Constitution provided for an appropriate division of powers between the national authorities, the states and the people. As one of the founding fathers, James Madison, explained, 'the great and aggregate interests' were 'referred to the national, and the local and particular to state governments'. Thus some powers are prohibited the states by the Constitution. They can neither coin money, nor conduct their own foreign policy, keep their own military services, make war or set their own customs duties.

All these were recognized as 'delegated powers', aggregate interests that had to be exclusively the national government's to prevent conflicts among the states and between them and the federal government. In addition, the Constitution specifically gives the national authorities the responsibility for protecting the states from foreign invasion and internal rebellion. To protect the rights of the people from both levels of government, clauses such as the right to a jury trial were included in the main document and many more rights were secured through the Bill of Rights.

A considerable list of powers remained that were 'reserved', considered to be local and particular interests inappropriate for the federal government. To the states was reserved the establishment of local governments and protecting public safety and morals, which came to mean providing police, fire and sanitation departments, among other institutions. States also took responsibility for furnishing educational and health facilities as well as for levying taxes and borrowing to fund all these activities.

States wrote their own codes of civil and criminal law. The maintenance of internal transportation networks, issuing of licences for activities within the state (marriage licences and certification for the professions, for example), and incorporation of businesses were taken to be parts of their regulation of state commerce. Not least, state legislatures determined voting qualifications and conducted elections for all levels of government. Moreover, the Tenth Amendment, which reserves to the states or people those powers not granted the federal government, was then thought to be an important constitutional guarantee of the states' sovereignty.

Some government activities were commonly understood to be *concurrent powers*, ones shared by the states and national authorities, because the Constitution does not designate one level of government as primarily responsible. These functions included law-making, establishing courts, taxing, borrowing and providing for the general welfare. A basic principle of federalism is that two levels of government exercise authority and powers over the same territory. That apparent overlapping has not usually been problematic because the national government applies these powers to relations between the states, while each state exercises them only within its borders.

## The growth of federal power

Over time, however, the existence of concurrent powers and disputes concerning them have worked to the advantage of the federal authorities. Despite the kind of federalism the Constitution defines, power has shifted dramatically from the states to the federal government for those and several other reasons. Briefly put, historical circumstances and practical politics have determined the balance of power between the states and the nation more than has constitutional theory.

Not only the defeat of states' rights advocates in the Civil War but also a series of historical crises (such as the world wars, the Depression, the problems of urbanization and industrialization, the Cold War, common standards in education nationally and, today, the war on terrorism) have proved to be beyond the capacities of the states and so have strengthened the national government. In these crises, whether they were domestic or international, the then accepted limits of national power were also judged too confining for the solution of the problems at hand. Therefore, at these times, the federal government has interpreted its constitutional powers quite broadly, and the states (and usually the federal courts) have accepted the transfer of power to the national authorities.

A number of changes that increased national power resulted from constitutional amendments. For example, until after the Civil War, the Bill of Rights was assumed to apply only to relations between citizens and the national government. But two general phrases in the Fourteenth Amendment (1868) require *states* to offer citizens 'due process of law' and 'equal protection of the laws'. The US Supreme Court has interpreted these phrases to mean that states too must meet the standards set in the Bill of Rights. The Court has therefore upheld federal civil-rights legislation as well as the demands of individuals for protection from state actions. Other amendments have limited states' power over tax revenues, voting rights and elections.

Most of the growth in federal power, however, has come through law-making and political pressure. Congress has used the so-called 'elastic clause' of the Constitution to set precedents for federal legislation in almost every area of life. That clause gives Congress the right to make any laws that are 'necessary and proper' to carry out its other powers. Frequently the President has lobbied Congress to invoke this and other broad constitutional phrases because the public expects the Chief Executive to lead the nation out of troubled times. Both these federal branches have cited their concurrent power of promoting the 'general welfare' as a reason for encroaching on state authority.

Federal laws have often included grants-in-aid (funding earmarked for specific purposes) as a means of persuading states to give the national government a say in their internal affairs. Grants-in-aid hold out the possibility of gaining resources to solve pressing problems, but usually require states to accept federal regulations determining how the money will be used. Many grants are offered as 'matching funds', which means a state receives no more support from Washington for a project than it contributes itself. Just such an arrangement was used for the No Child Left Behind Act education reform in 2001 and the Help American Vote Act election reform in 2002.

The promise of funding operates as a powerful incentive. The threat to *deny* funds is as powerful a pressure for getting states to give up their own standards for federal standards. Simply by choosing to fund some kinds of activities and not others, the federal government has often been able to set states' policy agenda. The combined effects of concurrent powers, national crises, constitutional amendments, Supreme Court decisions, congressional legislation and grants-in-aid has been a strong trend toward centralized government over the past two centuries.

## The evolution of state government and federalism in the USA

The foundation for the expansion of federal powers was laid between 1803 and 1865, when the Supreme Court established its power of judicial review and the tradition of broadly interpreting the federal government's constitutional powers. Even so, both the national and the state governments exercised their powers in a small way for most of the nineteenth century. Until the 1930s the main way the federal government affected most citizens was through its help in promoting the economy by developing the frontier. Its armies fought Native Americans and forced them farther west. It gave new states federal land for schools and joined states and private entrepreneurs to build roads and canals. From the 1860s on, Congress wrote legislation providing free or cheap land on the frontier for settlers homesteading in the wilderness and companies engaged in building trans-continental railroads.

When the federal government attempted to legislate in the areas of public health, safety and order in the 1800s, the Supreme Court ruled that these were *solely* the concern of the states. Likewise it decided that the regulation of business was purely a matter for the states. On the whole, the Court acted in accordance with the theory known as 'dual federalism'. The court asserted that state and federal governments have clearly separated spheres in which each is sovereign. It interpreted the Constitution narrowly, limiting government activity on any level to explicitly granted powers. Thus, it commonly approved neither federal nor state laws regulating industry and labour. Strongly influenced by laissez-faire economic theory, from the 1880s through to the 1920s the court refused to accept laws to regulate child labour, minimum wages and working hours, safety or working conditions.

At the start of the Great Depression, the states were still the sole provider of most services understood to be reserved to them by the drafters of the Constitution. Washington, DC did not regulate citizens' behaviour and provided them with very few services beyond the post office. The combination of the economic crisis, Franklin D. Roosevelt's New Deal legislation and the court's advocacy of a new theory of federalism transformed the governmental landscape by 1939.

By then the national authorities' regulation of the economy and creation of a social-security safety net ushered in the era of cooperative federalism. The court interpreted the Tenth Amendment and elastic clause broadly. It viewed the division of powers between state and federal governments as less distinct and less important than the ways they might work together. Many of the most vital activities of the authorities were now assumed to be among the concurrent powers of government. Sweeping expansions of both state and federal powers resulted from the change in the court's philosophy, but Washington's share of all money spent on domestic needs nearly tripled while the states' expenditures on these problems remained the same.

Grants-in-aid programmes began with the New Deal laws and grew rapidly in number for almost forty years. In the 1950s such grants resulted in heavy federal involvement in secondary and higher education as part of the effort to compete with the Soviet Union's technological progress. They also supplied states with funds for the massive inter-state highway system built at the time. In the 1960s grants helped pay for efforts to enforce civil- and voting-rights legislation as well as the ambitious goals of Lyndon B. Johnson's Great Society and War on Poverty programmes. Johnson aimed at nothing less than the realization of equal opportunity and a better quality of life for all Americans.

Grants-in-aid mushroomed in kind, number and expense. The federal government became active in local law enforcement, low-rent housing projects, urban mass-transit, health services and job training. It shared responsibility for virtually all the services that had been functions of the states. For the first time, moreover, it encouraged applications for aid directly from local governments and private community groups, frequently bypassing the state authorities in its decisions on financing.

By the early 1970s, a counter reaction set in. State and local governments complained of over-regulation, wasteful bureaucratic red tape and the tendency of the national government to place new duties on them without supplying sufficient funding. Conservatives in both parties called for a return to dual federalism, and President Nixon's proposals in 1972 amounted to just that, although he called them the 'New Federalism'. His revenue-sharing cut most strings attached to federal grants so that the lower levels of government could gain more power in setting priorities and standards. Combining many grant programmes into large block grants for sectors such as health or education services aimed to accomplish the same purposes.

The New Federalism had little success in stopping the shift of power from the states to the national government. Members of Congress were unwilling to give up taking credit for and exercising control over the distribution of federal money to their districts or states. Revenue-sharing was ended in 1986, and most grant programmes returned to their former pattern even earlier.

President Reagan promised to revive New Federalism, but the main effect of his administration was to reverse the trend of increasing federal aid to state and local government. Such aid dropped by 25 per cent in the early 1980s, and to date has grown only slightly, in spite of the federal-budget surpluses of the 1990s (which turned into record deficits by 2004). Federal grant programmes grew in that decade, but state and local governments had to bear more of the cost of new programmes. In exchange, congressional leaders and all Presidents since Nixon have agreed to set fewer binding federal regulations on grant programmes.

In fact, during the past decade or so the federal government has left the solution of growing numbers of national problems to the states through an American form of devolution. That decentralization of policy-making inevitably means that inequalities among the states grow, because cuts in federal grants hurt poor states most. During the 1990s boom, the wealthier states made up for the loss of federal funds through increased state incomes, while the poorer states cut services and hovered near bankruptcy. Since 2001 rich and poor states alike have cut services to the bone as they made the drastic reductions required to satisfy the balanced-budget clauses of their constitutions.

Most political commentators interpreted the Republican triumph in the 1994 mid-term elections as a sign that the national mood favoured the devolution of power and responsibility away from the national government. In 1996 federal aid for needy families was devolved to the states with Democratic President Clinton's approval. From then to 2000, Clinton agreed with Congress on the removal or relaxation of federal regulation of telecommunications, agriculture, civil rights, pollution prevention and environmental protection. In the same years Supreme Court decisions disallowed Acts of Congress that would have enforced national regulations through clauses permitting citizens to sue the government.

During his first term, George W. Bush, a self-proclaimed 'compassionate conservative', met some conventional expectations of conservatives in the debate over federalism but not others. By 2005 he had pressed through two large tax-reduction packages and promised wholesale tax reform in his second term. Thus he apparently aimed both to reduce the size of the national government by starving it of funds and to free the public (especially those with capital) of the burden of federal taxation. On the other hand, some called him America's first 'big-government conservative' because he intruded into policy areas traditionally belonging to the states and enlarged federal spending by some 29 per cent (triple the growth rate during the 1990s). He implemented an agenda for national standards for better schools, faith-based federal social services, sex-education programmes from the national Department of Education promoting abstinence and a Medicare prescription-drug plan for the elderly. He pursued these goals simultaneously with initiatives in foreign policy and national security that required the funding of a military build-up, wars in Afghanistan and Iraq and the astronomically higher costs and number of federal regulations of homeland security arrangements since the attacks of 11 September, 2001 (9/11). At the end of George W. Bush's first term, the imbalance between federal and state power had arguably never been greater, but receiving a much greater election victory in 2004, the President advanced a large agenda for his second term.

# The structure of state government

As the fundamental principles of all American governments were first developed by the original states, it is hardly surprising that the structure of state and federal governments are similar. Each of the fifty states has a written constitution. Each also has a separation of powers among three branches that share power through a system of checks and balances.

All of the state legislatures, except Nebraska's, have the same format as Congress with two houses, usually called the state senate and state assembly. State legislatures also work through committees and pass laws through a process very like that used in Congress. Like the President, the chief executive of a state, the governor, enjoys the powers of administration, appointment and veto. The structure of a state judiciary is also broadly parallel to the federal court system. In most states there is a state supreme court and under it appeals courts and (parallel to the US district courts) county or municipal courts.

There are, however, some important differences in the structure of state governments. State constitutions are typically several times longer than the US Constitution because they contain many more detailed provisions and much more specific language. Instead of reserving whatever powers are left undefined to a lower level of government or the people, the drafters of state constitutions attempt to be as explicit as possible. Such detailed documents less easily adapt themselves to broad interpretation and consequently are much more frequently amended. New York state's constitution has been amended over 200 times in the past century, for example, while only twenty-seven amendments have been added to the US Constitution since 1787. Most states have written entirely new constitutions or extensively rewritten their old ones not once but several times.

The branches of government also have distinctive elements at the state level. Most state legislators are part-time law-makers. They often divide their time between the legislature and a law practice or business in their home districts. State legislators have fixed terms of office like members of Congress, but they do not choose to run for re-election as often. Instead, they go back to full-time work in their current private jobs or use their government experience to enter a new line of work. Thus, well over a third of all members in state legislatures are newcomers at any time and as many are relatively inexperienced.

State legislators' interest in careers in government is low for several reasons. Compared to what they can earn in the private sector, the annual salary is low. Travelling between the capital and the member's district as well as maintaining an office in both places requires considerable time and expense. Sitting in the state legislature does not bring much prestige, even though it disrupts family life and leads to the forced neglect of members' other part-time profession or business.

Some experts on American government argue that the states should change to full-time, professional, well-paid legislatures. But tradition and the enormous cost of converting to full-time law-makers make the present situation likely to persist. The traditional view is that having part-time legislators is an advantage. Their businesses or jobs in local districts keep them concerned about the well-being of the community they represent. As one political scientist explained, 'Part-time legislators really have something at home, unlike congressmen who don't have anything to come home for except trying to get votes'.

In practice, the debate may be moot, however, because the federal government's increasing withdrawal from grants-in-aid programmes has forced state governments to assume more responsibility. The increased workload of state law-makers has already produced a strong movement towards full-time legislatures in the more populous states.

There are also important differences between a governor's situation and that of the President. On the one hand, most governors have two powers the President lacks. They usually have more complete control over the state budget. Most also have the line-item veto, which allows them to accept some parts of a bill passed by the legislature while vetoing other parts.

On the other hand, in many states the governor's power is weaker than the President's in four important ways. First, many are not free to make as many appointments as the President does. More state officials are elected than at the federal level of government. Second, many states have a tradition of electing several of a governor's department heads. For example, the State Treasurer, Attorney General and Commissioner of Education are often elected.

These other state executives are popularly considered part of the governor's 'team' at election time. But each must get elected separately and that makes them more independent of the governor. Many times, these department heads do not even belong to the governor's party. State parties often seem less important to voters than selecting a team of state executives that represent a range of different races, ethnic groups and economic interests.

Third, governors have less control over suggestions for new laws. Starting early in this century, many states developed two procedures for taking suggestions for new laws (or changes in old laws) directly to the voters, bypassing the governor and usually the legislature. The 'initiative' allows citizens to call for a vote on a state law or constitutional amendment, either in the legislature or by the public at the next election. Those proposing the initiative must petition the state for this vote by collecting signatures from somewhere between 5 to 10 per cent of the state's registered voters. A little under half of the states currently permit some form of voter initiative.

The referendum, a direct vote of the public on an issue, may be the result of a successful initiative, a requirement for amending the state constitution, or an item put on the ballot by the state legislature. Known as 'propositions', referenda are allowed in half the states. Referenda on constitutional changes are required in all but one state.

It is politically dangerous for governors to oppose procedures that make state government more democratic by giving ordinary voters a say in state law-making, even though some propositions may have harmful effects. Thus state executives have found it difficult to speak out against proposals similar to Proposition 13, passed in California in 1978, which so reduce taxes that state and local governments must cut back on basic services. In the 1970s the use of referenda grew rapidly and in the 1980s numbered nearly 250 in every congressional election year, leading some critics to doubt whether the public could be informed enough to vote intelligently on so many issues. In the 1990s the trend continued and politicians made little protest, even though the most common and successful proposal put limits on the number of terms they could run for office. By 2000, however, term limits had been found unconstitutional for federal offices, and the tide of propositions at election time had started to abate somewhat.

The fourth important way governors have lost power is through special-district governments, authorities designed to deal with a specific problem that crosses governmental boundaries. Some special districts have become so powerful that they are popularly called regional governments. Most special districts have been established since the First World War. Some have been suggested by federal authorities but, like all forms of local government, special districts are created by the states.

State legislatures do not aim to weaken the governor's position by founding special districts; rather, legislatures simply recognize that growing problems, such as air pollution, land and water shortages, refuse disposal and regional traffic jams, cannot be efficiently handled within one legal jurisdiction. Several states and often many local governments share the responsibility for dealing with these problems.

Coordination between so many separate authorities becomes difficult if not impossible. Many of America's big cities are merely the centres of much larger metropolitan areas that include many suburbs, several satellite cites and even 'pockets' of rural territory. Most special districts have been established in just these areas, where the need for coordinated public services is greatest.

Special districts are governed by official representatives from the various local and state governments in the area where regional problems exist. But special districts also have their own staffs and budgets. Usually both are funded mostly by grants from the federal government and are therefore outside the governor's control. Presidents Ronald Reagan and George H.W. Bush said they intended to reduce the role and importance of special districts. Though the number of special districts reached nearly 30,000 by the beginning of the 1990s, however, neither President took any significant action in the matter, because the problems the districts are set up to solve have only become more serious. Thus, it is instead likely that special districts will gradually take more planning initiative from state governors and state governments generally.

The judiciary branch of state government is different from the federal judiciary in two important ways. First, many state and local judges are elected, rather than appointed, to terms of office that vary from four to fifteen years. In

**PLATE 6.1**   Florida's Supreme Court Justices.
(*Phil Sears/Rex Features*)

many states, even the state supreme court justices are elected. Generally, the election of judges is meant to make the judicial branch more responsive to changes in public opinion. It is also meant to make the removal of unpopular or incompetent judges easier. Of course, as a result of their election, state and local judges are more frequently accused of being swayed by political pressures. Once on the bench, judges are required by law to be impartial. Therefore, it is not considered unusual that both major parties will endorse the same person for judge, if that candidate is known as a fair and competent jurist.

Second, the state supreme court cannot be sure of handing down the final decision in the most important cases that come to it. Of course, that is because the federal constitution takes precedence over all other law and the US Supreme Court therefore, has the power to review the constitutionality of both federal and state laws. The importance of this fact became abundantly clear in 2000, when the US Supreme Court reversed the decision of the supreme court of Florida to allow manual recounts of the presidential election in the state, and thus determined the outcome of the presidential election as a whole.

# Local government

The fifty states are divided into some 83,000 units of local government. In addition to the special districts, there are counties, towns, cities, boroughs and school districts. The states create these (and other) kinds of local governments and determine their powers.

No local government in the USA has sovereignty, power in its own right. Units of local government are not even mentioned in the federal constitution. They exist because they have been created by the states as instruments, tools to help the state carry out its responsibilities. Some local governments have been established by state constitutions while others came into being through acts of state legislatures. Special districts often result from agreements among two or more states.

Local governments vary tremendously across the country, because each state has developed its own system of local authority. Most states are divided into counties, although in Louisiana, the parallel unit of government is called a 'parish' and in Alaska a 'borough'. Counties also vary greatly in population, size and function. Still, most counties share several general responsibilities. They are usually the main units of government in rural areas. Counties rarely have any law-making power, but instead act as agents of the state. They serve as administrative units that carry out some state-wide programmes in local areas, such as keeping records and issuing different kinds of licences.

All the powers of local government are really powers of the state. The state just delegates the work of providing local facilities and services to smaller units of government. Thus the states often set general standards and guide-lines, but ask counties to carry out the functions that are delegated. Typically, these functions include providing local transportation systems, schools, fire and police protection, water and sanitation systems and medical programmes and buildings. Counties also collect the local property taxes to pay for these services.

County government usually consists of a board of somewhere between three and twelve members, a county court and the chief officers of county departments. Board members, or commissioners as they are often called in more populous counties, are elected and serve on a part-time basis. Their powers usually include deciding how local taxes should be raised and spent for county programmes, as well as the authority to establish zoning codes that regulate the purpose for which land may be used.

The boards have no influence over the county court, but their power of the purse and zoning gives them significant control over local department heads. The county superintendent of schools, for example, must have the board's support to raise more money for local schools or to have a site for a new school approved. Other administrative officers commonly found in a county include the county sheriff, the medical examiner or coroner, commissioner of health, the recorder or registrar of property deeds and the clerk (who issues licences and keeps population records). Because they carry out state law on a daily basis, all these officers of county government usually determine what the law means in practice for most residents.

**PLATE 6.2** A street sign outside Los Angeles City Hall shows its sister cities.
(*Varley/Sipa*)

In built-up, heavily populated areas, the states have usually created substitutes for county government. In urban areas, most tasks that used to be performed by counties have been taken over by municipal governments: cities, towns, villages, boroughs or special districts. The meaning of these common terms varies widely, according to the legal definitions established by each state. For example, 'city' usually indicates an urban unit of local government with a population of at least several tens of thousands.

Most states define smaller built-up areas as villages, towns or boroughs. There are, however, many exceptions to this rule of thumb. In Kansas, a 'city' may have a population of only 200 people. In Illinois, the 'village' of Oak Park has a population of over 60,000. The term 'town' also has various meanings in different parts of the country. In New England, much of the land had been divided into towns *before* state governments were established. Counties were only later mapped out and never became as important as towns in providing the main services of local government in the New England states.

The confusion of terms is not made easier by the US Census Bureau, which has developed its own vocabulary for analysing units of population. Documents from the federal government often discuss 'metropolitan statistical areas' (MSAs) and 'consolidated metropolitan statistical areas' (CMSAs). These terms are very useful for mapping the population concentrations that cross the boundaries of state and local governments. They have often helped demonstrate the need for special districts, but they have no legal status as units of government.

Most states have granted urban units of government some form of home rule, a legal status amounting to limited local autonomy. This gives them a degree of legislative power to establish local law and usually a municipal charter that functions as a kind of local constitution. Ordinarily this charter of incorporation cannot be altered without the approval of local residents. However, if there is disagreement with the state over the limits of the powers granted in the charter, state and federal courts almost always interpret the municipal government's powers narrowly.

The structure of municipal governments varies widely. In most a mayor is the chief executive, and the mayor decides policy together with a city council. The amount of power allowed the office under the city charter may make the mayor merely a figurehead or the primary decision-maker in local affairs. Since the early 1900s, a large number of cities have experimented with or adopted 'city-manager government', in which the city council is the chief political organ of government and a professional administrator, the city manager, carries out its decisions.

The council writes local laws, called 'ordinances', in the policy areas granted it by the state charter. The mayor may or may not have the veto power over such council legislation. As in counties, a range of officials carry out local policy in specific sectors of local-government activity. The mayor or city manager usually prepares an annual budget proposal based of these officials' requests for money and available sources of income, and submits it to the council for approval.

Until recently, the financing of both county and municipal government came primarily from real-estate taxes, but by 1990 property taxes supplied only about a third of funding. Another third came from state governments, and a tenth came from the federal government. Both state and federal financing was generally tied to grants-in-aid programmes that gave these other authorities an important role in local decision-making and often aimed to alleviate the effects of local poverty or socio-economic inequality. The remainder of local funding generally came from a variety of fees and charges. To make ends meet and launch new programmes, large cities have increasingly raised additional revenue through sales and income taxes.

The meanings and powers of local governments vary so much for three main reasons. First, local authorities developed in several different historical periods. Second, these governments reflect the effects of local conditions, such as climate, natural resources and the various population groups that have settled there over time, bringing with them a variety of traditions for handling local affairs. Third and most important, each state is free to give local governments whatever powers and functions it chooses.

To citizens, the state's definition of local government is very significant. In practice, local governments are delegated the job of providing most of the vital services citizens expect today. And the territory of local governments often

**FIGURE 6.1** Local governments and cities in the Great Lakes region.

overlaps. Towns, villages and cities often have authority inside parts of a county. Therefore, citizens must learn which local government is responsible for each necessary service. Otherwise, it becomes impossible to apply for the local services state law gives people a right to expect. A citizen cannot even complain effectively about problems with the water supply, refuse removal, school system and so on without knowing what unit of local government to contact.

There are arguments for and against the great number, variety and overlapping authority of governments in the USA. Some observers maintain that the situation is quite democratic in that it gives many citizens opportunities to participate in government and to affect the making of policy. Critics, however, note that voter participation is highest in national elections and lowest in local elections. Some suggest that US voters participate less in *all* elections than people in other developed countries because there are more opportunities for participation than the public has the capacity to focus on.

Another disadvantage often cited is that the complex sharing of powers and functions by all levels of government has become too difficult to disentangle for many people, so that they have great difficulties securing the very services government is instituted to offer. The same complexity makes individuals turn to organized lobbies that have the time and resources to influence policy. Thus, instead of bringing government to the people, some pundits complain, the current situation encourages the growth and power of special-interest groups.

Benefits of multiple governments are emphasized by other commentators. Some believe state and local governments with significant powers allow the nation to experiment with alternate solutions to problems on a small scale. That is why the states have long been termed 'fifty laboratories for democracy'. In recent years both states and cities have pioneered new plans for health-service management, pollution control and welfare reform, to name just a few examples. Many if not most governmental reforms since late in the twentieth century have been tested out at lower levels of government before being adopted nationally.

Other observers insist that only such varied and overlapping governments can respond to the sharply contrasting conditions that exist in a country as diverse as the USA. Smaller units of government can respond more quickly and appropriately to such differences. But local solutions are bound to generate inequality as well, in this view of the situation, and that is why the federal government must step in to protect minority rights and to even out economic disparities.

# Exercises

Explain and examine the significance of the following terms.

| | | |
|---|---|---|
| delegated powers | dual federalism | propositions |
| concurrent powers | cooperative federalism | special districts |
| elastic clause | New Federalism | ordinances |
| grants-in-aid | state constitutions | local governments |
| | full faith and credit | |

Write short essays on the following questions.

1.  Discuss the reasons for the changes in American federalism since 1787.

2. Compare and contrast the structure of the state and federal governments.

3. Give a critical evaluation of the use of the initiative and referendum in state government.

4. What are some arguments for and against the election of judges?

5. In your opinion, does the variety of overlapping governments in the USA represent a factor for increased democracy?

# Further reading

*Book of the States* (biennially published) Lexington, Ky.: Council of State Governments.

Bowman, A. O. and R. Kearny (1986) *The Resurgence of the States* Englewood Cliffs, NJ: Prentice-Hall.

*Census of Governments* (published every fifth year) Washington, DC: US Government Printing Office.

Dye, T. R. (1990) *American Federalism: competition among governments* Lexington, Mass.: Lexington Books.

# Web sites

<http://www.doi.gov/iga/statelocal.htm>
<http://lingo.ntnu.no/usakult> See government, state and local.
<http://www.access.wa.gov>
<http://www.state.ny.us>
<http://www.state.tx.us>
<http://www.state.ne.us>
<http://www.state.me.us>

# Chapter 7

# Foreign policy

# A nation apart? American attitudes to world affairs

On the one hand, the foreign policy of the USA is like that of all nations: it has always resulted from a mixture of self-interest and the attempt to act according to commonly held ideals. On the other hand, a factor that makes America's (and all nations') foreign policy distinctive is the size and strength of each relative to other nations at critical times in its history. In the beginning of its history the USA, then a weak and inconsequential actor on the world stage, emphasized 'soft power'(attracting support by example, ideals and diplomacy) to the near exclusion of other means of handling international affairs. Today, the nation is the world's only superpower, and in the view of some commentators, it too seldom uses soft power, especially since the terrorist attacks of 11 September 2001, and relies too frequently or hastily instead on 'hard power'(achieving support and goals through economic sanctions and military threats or force).

For the USA, the nation's vulnerability in relation to the European nations involved in the settlement of North America was decisive in its foreign relations until 1900 or, some argue, 1945. Only from the twentieth century on have other nations significantly challenged the Euro-centred character of American foreign relations. This situation, of course, also results from Europe's leadership in world affairs generally during much of American history and the predominance of Europeans among immigrants to the USA until recently.

Its history of settlement and immigration is another major influence on the character of US foreign policy. European colonists and later immigrants have usually had mixed feelings toward their homelands. They emigrated to escape aspects of their home societies but simultaneously harboured deep attachments to the old country. Consequently, immigration has produced both isolationism and internationalism in American foreign policy, as Americans expressed their wish to avoid or cultivate contacts with former homelands. Immigrants brought with them their homelands' history of international relations and often lobbied the American government to fight the old country's enemies and help its friends. Longer-settled Americans have periodically doubted the loyalty of recent immigrants. The USA has a history of perceiving threats to internal security from foreign agitators that has caused repression at home and strained its relations abroad.

Before Europeans founded lasting settlements on the east coast, 'promotional literature' written by European explorers established the idea that 'America' would evolve a new and better phase of civilization. Uncorrupted by the past, America would offer people a chance to start over and do better. From the earliest colonists, migrants to America have wanted to prove this 'promise of America' true to justify their decision to emigrate. Thus grew up the faith in American exceptionalism. This is the belief (rhetorical or sincere) that America's foreign affairs, unlike those of other nations, are not self-interested but based on a mission to offer the world a better form of society characterized by the ideals of 'the American creed': the US version of a republican form of government, economic and political freedom, egalitarian social relations and democracy.

When he spoke of a 'City on a Hill that the eyes of all people are upon' in 1630, the Puritan leader John Winthrop had in mind a religiously reformed community that would be a model for change in England. But later American leaders from George Washington to George W. Bush who have echoed Winthrop's words or sentiment were confirming Americans' sense that they had a unique mission to set an example for the rest of the world, to export American freedom and democracy and so conduct a foreign policy unlike that of any other nation. Whether real or imagined, American exceptionalism has had palpable effects on the history of US foreign relations.

In reality, the basic concerns that greatly influence the foreign relations of other nations have also played major roles in the formulation of American policy. Of necessity, the USA too has protected what it saw as its vital interests: economic success at home and abroad, access to important natural resources, support for its ideological views, respect for its military power and assistance in times of crisis. In practice, the USA has often seemed as concerned with realpolitik as other nations, in spite of both sincere and rhetorical devotion to ideals like those described above.

A third factor, the nation's geographical position, has also made its foreign relations unique. If one looks at the globe as Americans do, with the USA in the centre, two 'facts' that have coloured much of US foreign-policy history seem clear. First, broad oceans separate the Americas from the other continents. Second, most of the world's population and farmland, and *all* of the other great powers, are located in Europe and Asia.

For over 300 years the relative physical isolation created by the oceans encouraged those migrating to North America to believe they were leaving behind whatever they disliked in their home societies. Here was the basis for US isolationism, the belief that Americans could withdraw from involvement with the rest of the world and focus on domestic (internal) affairs. As the country expanded across the continent, its great size offered another excuse for believing the USA 'was world enough' for its inhabitants. Successive transportation, communication and weaponry revolutions, as well as the internationalization of the economy, eventually made isolationism founded on geographical separation an indefensible foreign-policy position. However, traditional attitudes continue to influence the views of many Americans.

Paradoxically, geographical separation has also contributed to a tradition of national insecurity. Looking outward and seeing the great powers of Europe and Asia on all sides, Americans have periodically felt surrounded. That anxiety resulted in a determination to create national security in the North American quarter of the globe. The USA has sought to be a quarter-sphere hegemon (the only great power on the continent), worked to drive European powers out, and striven to control the land, sea, air and, finally, the outer-space approaches to North America.

The *felt* need for continental security has been regularly advanced as a justification for territorial expansion through war, purchase or negotiation. The peoples who first bore the brunt of this preoccupation with security were Native Americans. Success in driving them westward fuelled Americans' ambitions and sense that they had a destiny to 'civilize' the continent.

Security was also the rationale for a ring of far-flung military bases and later, of radar stations beyond the country's borders. The USA, it should be remembered, entered both world wars primarily because of threats to its control of the continental sea approaches. President Reagan's strategic defence initiative (SDI) sought to extend this 200-year-old principle of quarter-sphere security to the space approaches to the USA. He envisioned using high-tech weaponry placed in space to shoot down missiles armed with nuclear warheads that might be sent to attack the USA. At first, supporters of the SDI viewed the likely attacker as the USSR, but with the end of the Cold War, so-called 'rogue nations' who ignored international law and supported terrorism appeared to be the most serious threat.

In the 1990s and early twenty-first century, therefore, American Presidents continued to support research and development for a 'national missile shield' against such threats. Shortly after taking office, George W. Bush announced a vastly bigger shield and offered America's allies protection behind it. Just months later terrorists used American passenger jets as fuel-laden bombs to destroy the Twin Towers of the World Trade Center in Manhattan and one side of the Pentagon in Washington, DC. Not since 1812 had a foreign force attacked the North American mainland, killed thousands 'at home', and wrecked symbols of US military and economic power.

The sudden vulnerability felt by the public seemed to make a mockery of the long search for security at the root of US foreign policy. Why had the FBI and CIA not uncovered the terrorists' plans, asked many. But their representatives and foreign-policy specialists in Congress, it appeared, had been warning of such 'low-tech' terrorism for years. The Twin Towers had been attacked with a car bomb some years earlier. In the immediate aftermath, some commentators reckoned that the tragedy proved that a missile shield could not make the nation safe, but the President and public polls showed increased determination to regain the nation's former sense of safety by all possible means, including SDI, whatever the cost. As the 'War on Terror' grew into wars in Afghanistan and Iraq and security

**PLATE 7.1** On the morning of 11 September 2001, terrorists piloted a commercial airliner, its crew and passengers into the Pentagon in Washington, DC.
(*Rex Features*)

measures that limited civil liberties and privacy at home, a small but growing number of voices asked what in the history of America's relations in the world had contributed to the catastrophic events, and weighed alternative foreign-policy futures. Meanwhile, many interpreted Bush's 2004 election victory as a mandate to stay the course in the prosecution of the multifaceted War on Terror that he had announced soon after 9/11.

## From neutrality to isolationism, 1776–1830

The first period in the history of American foreign affairs covers the years from 1776 until around 1830. During this time, it can be argued, US policy toward other countries (especially the European powers) resembled that of the newly established Third World nations in the twentieth century. Like those nations, the USA tried to steer clear of alliances with great powers and instead strove to keep its neutrality in foreign affairs and to act unilaterally. Fear of becoming a pawn of British or French schemes for expanded international power was the mainspring of American policy in this period.

Around 1800, the USA was a political and economic midget. It was hemmed in by British colonies to the north, French Louisiana in the west and, in the south, by the rich and powerful Spanish Empire that included Florida and today's south-west. During the colonial period, every war between the European powers had its American phase, and the new nation could not afford to have that pattern continue if it was to stabilize its political institutions and economy. Thus the USA for many years stayed aloof from the Napoleonic Wars and refused to become involved in the French Revolution, even though the French had been an indispensable ally in the War of Independence with Britain.

After serving as the nation's first President, George Washington stated the existing policy in general terms in his so-called Farewell Address (1796). Its main principle consisted of avoiding political and military alliances while cultivating trading relations with other countries. President Washington also advised the nation to remember its uniqueness and resulting need for unilateral action. When the USA strayed from these principles by entering the Napoleonic Wars on the side of France in 1812, the results were disastrous. British forces burned Washington, DC, the USA won not a single important victory, and the cost was enormous. After that object lesson, the core ideas of the Address remained a pillar of American foreign policy until after the Second World War.

The Alien and Sedition Acts (1798) were more evidence of the American fear of becoming a pawn of European powers. These laws were directed against foreign subversives who might undermine the nation from within. Fear of French sympathizers inspired the Acts, which allowed the President and courts to fine, imprison or deport any foreigner who seemed a danger to national security. The

Acts were an early sign of deep insecurities about the loyalties of newcomers in a nation of immigrants.

The foreign-policy statement from the early period that contributed most to the development of later policy was the Monroe Doctrine. Between 1800 and the 1820s, many Spanish colonies in Central and South America rebelled and declared their independence. The USA wanted to recognize these new nations but feared conflict with Spain and the possibility that Britain or France would intervene and return them to Spanish control. America was too weak to prevent European interference in Latin America, but it formally expressed its opposition to outside meddling in their affairs through the Monroe Doctrine.

The Doctrine can be reduced to three basic principles. The first (called non-colonization) is that the USA opposed any new colonies in the Americas. The second (non-intervention) demanded that the European powers remain uninvolved in the affairs of New World nations. In return for Europe's compliance with these rules, the USA would observe a third principle (non-interference) that amounted to accepting the presence of the remaining European colonies in the Americas and keeping aloof from European affairs. The USA could not enforce any of these principles until around 1900, when it had constructed a powerful navy. Until then, the British navy prevented other European nations from violating the Doctrine and opened Latin America for British economic influence.

The Monroe Doctrine transformed American neutrality into isolationism and combined it with the country's sense of having a special mission in the world. The Americas were declared the USA's exclusive sphere of interest. European-style kingdoms and Old-World politics were to have no place in the hemisphere, so that only the USA's brand of republican government would influence Latin America. In short, the Doctrine expressed the mixture of idealism and ideological domination that was to become typical of US relations with Latin America.

## From expansionism to imperialism, 1783–1914

The second period of American foreign policy overlaps with the first but extends into the early years of the twentieth century. During this time, the USA was preoccupied with developments that Americans often viewed as internal affairs: the settlement of a frontier that constantly moved further west, the struggle over whether slavery should be extended into new states or abolished, the effort to construct transportation systems to bind the continent together and ease the exploitation of its resources. Because all these processes consisted of, or were related to, territorial expansion, they were also central to the conduct of foreign affairs.

Early in the nineteenth century, the USA roughly tripled its territory through treaty and purchase. Agreements with Britain added the land between the Appalachians and the Mississippi River, the northern section of Maine and parts of Minnesota and the Dakotas. America bought Florida from Spain, and France offered the USA the land from the Mississippi to the Rocky Mountains in the Louisiana Purchase. Most Americans viewed these as legal and unaggressive ways to consolidate US territory and minimize the dangers of European interference. It was assumed that the European powers could legally transfer hegemony over the Native Americans with the right to their homelands. In reality, much of American foreign policy to about 1900 consisted of war and treaty negotiations with these native peoples.

Such enormous increases in the country's size inspired the growth of an intense national pride. The feats of frontier settlers evolved into myth and a set of idealized character traits. The farther west people and institutions were, the more truly American they appeared in the popular mind. Some advocates of expansion emphasized that only a nation spanning the continent could effectively isolate itself from external threats. Others told themselves that they were extending the benefits of democracy to less advanced peoples. Forthrightly racist expansionists said the 'red and brown' peoples were inferior and therefore had to be confined, conquered or at least dominated.

By the 1840s, the idea of America's expansion to the Pacific was being popularized as the nation's Manifest Destiny (its apparently inevitable, divinely determined fate). Since it was obviously meant to be, that expansion was also right, argued the expansionists. 'Oregon fever' sent thousands trekking across the plains and mountains. Facing threats of armed conflict, Britain gave up its claims to the present Pacific north-west and parts of the mountain states in border negotiations.

Americans were more militantly aggressive toward Mexico. American settlers seized power in Texas and asked that the area be annexed to the USA. When the Texas border with Mexico was disputed in 1846, the USA offered to buy the territory in question but took the first excuse to take it by war after Mexico refused to sell. Expansion in the south-west aroused strong opposition, especially in New England, where many argued against acquiring Texas (a slave-owning republic) and against endangering the lives of US troops to make more territory available for slavery. So Texans waited ten years for annexation and the Mexican War was the source of violent congressional debate. In 1848, however, the treaty at its end added the south-west, California and most of the southern mountain states to US territory.

In the decades after the Civil War, expansionists gained support from several sources. Businessmen and farmers demanded the opening of new markets abroad to prevent overproduction causing economic depressions at home. Military strategists pointed out that a strong navy and overseas bases were necessary to keep these markets open and protect US shipping. Religious leaders fused the ideas of Manifest Destiny and the 'white man's burden' to support overseas missions and the 'civilizing' of foreign peoples. Nationalists, now using the language of Social Darwinism, claimed Americans were surely the fittest to survive in the international competition for territory and influence. When the federal government declared the western frontier closed in 1890, some people feared that Americans would lose their strength and endurance if they did not find frontiers abroad.

Buoyed up on this wave of public opinion, US foreign policy became territorially and economically imperialist around the turn of the century. That is to say, America used hard power to impose its control on overseas peoples, both formally (through colonization, annexation and military occupation) and informally (through military threats, economic domination and political subversion). In 1898 the USA declared war on Spain as an imperialist power that was stifling Cuban freedom. Having won that 'splendid little war' (as the American Secretary of State called it), the USA acquired economic control over Cuba and the right to intervene in its affairs. It also acquired (as colonies) Puerto Rico, Guam Island and the Philippine Islands, where Filipino nationalists fought a bloody campaign for independence from the USA.

American trade expanded rapidly, especially in Asia and Latin America. Hawaii, Samoa and Wake Island were annexed and served as suitable bases for further economic expansion eastward. In an effort to protect its growing trade in China, the USA contributed troops to an alliance of European powers that put down a Chinese rebellion. It also announced the 'Open Door Policy', which demanded equal access to Chinese markets, to counter the Europeans' claim to exclusive trade rights in China. In Latin America, President Theodore Roosevelt instigated and ensured the success of a Panamanian revolt against Colombia in 1903 in order to secure the right to build and control the Panama Canal. A year later he announced the revision of the Monroe Doctrine known as the Roosevelt Corollary. According to the corollary, the USA was justified in intervening in the internal affairs of Latin American nations if their politics or economies became unstable. The European powers, however, were again warned that America would not passively permit their intervention in the western hemisphere. Between 1900 and 1917, the USA intervened in six different Latin American countries.

Critics known as the 'anti-imperialists' actively opposed overseas expansion. As a result of their efforts, for example, Cuba was not annexed and the Philippines were promised their freedom as early as 1916 (although the promise was not kept until 1934). Some anti-imperialists claimed that sending US military forces abroad for intervention or colonization upset the balance of power in foreign policy between the President and Congress by increasing his importance as commander-in-chief. Other opponents of imperialism stressed that America could gain access to foreign markets without oppressing other peoples. Prominent leaders of the progressive movement protested that America ought to clean up its political corruption and inequalities at home instead of exhausting its energies abroad. Both traditionalists and the progressives also asked Americans to remember their historic commitment to self-determination in the Declaration of Independence.

# Isolationism and internationalism, 1914–45

For nearly three years the USA maintained the fiction that the First World War was a European conflict that did not concern America. That was the neutral pose that President Woodrow Wilson held because it reflected the traditional isolationist views of the US electorate. But neutrality was impossible to preserve for three reasons. Wilson, along with many other US politicians, felt strong sympathies for the Allies. The majority of Americans shared his belief in loyalty to Anglo-American traditions, despite vocal German-American and Irish-American minorities opposed to an alliance with Britain. Finally, the US economy depended on trade with the warring nations, who each tried to prevent goods from reaching its enemy.

Most Americans had taken sides but were still reluctant to commit their fortunes and lives to intervention. Both Wilson and the public needed to believe they were entering the war for high moral reasons rather than the country's economic interests. Some two months before the USA declared war, Wilson provided that rationale through a new vision of collective security in his famous Fourteen Points, which appealed to the tradition of the American mission to create a new world order.

The essential elements of the Fourteen Points can be reduced to three major categories. The first was all nations' right to self-determination. National boundaries were to be redrawn after the war so that every 'people' could freely determine whether it wished to be an independent country. The principle of self-determination amounted to a plan for popular referenda on ethnic nationhood in Europe with no formula for determining how this would be implemented. The second category was a general set of principles for governing international conduct after the war. These were meant to prevent a return to the traditional European balance-of-power strategies that Wilson believed had caused the war. Among the main principles included were free trade, freedom of the seas, global disarmament and the outlawing of secret alliances. The remaining points described Wilson's proposal for collective security, a League of Nations that would put self-determination and the other principles into effect and defend them. The key provision here depended on the public commitment of each League member to defend the principles and each other by diplomatic and military means, when necessary. Except for the League, most of the points were cornerstones of America's traditional rhetoric if not of its practical policy.

The Fourteen Points constituted Wilson's public justification for participating in the war, and were but one set of conditions meant to limit US involvement. American troops remained separate from the Allied armies and fought under American commanders. Wilson called the USA an 'associate' rather than an ally to emphasize that it was in an emergency coalition, not a lasting alliance (and therefore remained true to the injunction against such alliances in Washington's Farewell Address).

When it finally came, American participation in the war was decisive but very limited. Significant numbers of American troops fought in Europe only during the last eight months of the war. About 110,000 US soldiers died in that time, compared to the 900,000 British, 1.4 million French and almost 2 million German troops that died in four years.

The conditions on American aid to the Allied war effort, combined with the Allies' very different experience with a long and destructive conflict, made the US position seem morally arrogant. Although America claimed to be materially disinterested, its call for freedom of the seas and free trade would benefit the USA most since its industrial plant was booming and its fleet the least damaged. The Allies wanted revenge and to make Germany pay for war damages. They rejected all the Fourteen Points but the League.

The US Senate failed to ratify the treaty Wilson brought home from the Paris peace conference. Many senators rejected the idea of the league because they were unwilling to bind the US to membership in a permanent international alliance. The foreign-policy-makers who took over after Wilson were not isolationists. Rather, they wanted to design safeguards for peace that would not limit America's traditional freedom to act unilaterally in world affairs. In 1921, the US negotiated separate treaties with the defeated central powers. The League was formed, but without US participation, it never became an effective international force.

During the rest of the 1920s, US foreign policy centred on eliminating obstacles to American trade. International peace and stability were essential largely so that, once established, US trade would remain free of interference. Many Americans also believed free trade fostered peace by making nations more open and familiar with each other. However, the US and European nations failed to agree on a plan to revive European economies by cancelling or easing their war debts to America, and in 1930 Congress passed the protectionist Smoot–Hawley Tariff, which effectively closed the US market to most European goods.

In the same years, the country advocated peace through disarmament and called for arms reductions and the destruction of some 2 million tons of navy ships. It reaffirmed and extended the Open Door Policy. Finally, it initiated the Kellogg–Briand Pact in 1928 under which sixty-two nations signed a pledge not to use war as an instrument of national policy. Critics called this pact and others the US entered at the time, a 'paper peace' since it depended on voluntary compliance alone.

In the 1930s, however, this limited internationalism was replaced by isolationism. As the German war machine marched into land after land and the rest of Europe rearmed, American voters made it clear that their last wish was to be dragged into another Old-World war. Over four-fifths of the people surveyed in a Gallup poll in March of 1941 were opposed to US intervention. At about that time, President Franklin D. Roosevelt had won congressional approval for the Lend-Lease Act, a disguised giveaway plan he invented because domestic opposition to open aid to the Allies was massive. Under Lend-Lease, the President could sell, but also let the Allies borrow or lease, war material, on the promise that it would be returned after the war.

The Japanese surprise attack on Pearl Harbor on 7 December 1941 accomplished overnight what Roosevelt could not in years of effort: it united the American people in a fervent commitment to war. In a few days Congress had declared war on all the axis powers and announced its support of the Allies. Almost as quickly, Roosevelt constructed a vision of a new world order for the post-war period. Determined to succeed where Wilson had failed, Roosevelt called the Allies the 'United Nations' almost from the start. He also ensured that American troops were integrated with those of Britain and France. Joint command and cooperation, he had decided, would prevent complaints about American arrogance.

Roosevelt's vision for world order after the war was expressed in his so-called Four Freedoms and proposal for the United Nations (UN). The Four Freedoms were cleansed of advantages to US business because they were rights contained

**PLATE 7.2** British Prime Minister Winston Churchill, US President Franklin D. Roosevelt and Soviet leader Josef Stalin at the Yalta Conference, February 1945.
(*Time Pix/Rex Features*)

in the American Bill of Rights (freedom of religion, speech and expression) or broad extensions of those, such as freedom from want and fear, that amount to a version of the American dream. The UN was to help make the Four Freedoms realities. A number of the UN's features were intended to make it a more effective organization than the League had been. Unlike its predecessor, the UN can take preventative action, ask members to contribute troops to an international 'peacekeeping' force, and act against aggressors (whether or not they are members) without approval from all its members.

At the Yalta Conference in February 1945, Roosevelt won Stalin's and Churchill's support for the UN. On other important issues, the results of the conference were much less clear. Roosevelt could not convince the other leaders to give up the concept of spheres of influence in Europe. However, he thought they had agreed to the establishment of democratic governments, under no other nation's direct control, in eastern Europe. All three leaders agreed that post-war Germany should not become a military power again quickly, but they could not resolve their differences on how to prevent that from happening. They therefore had to put off specific plans for dealing with post-war Germany.

## The Cold War era, 1946–92

As Soviet forces set up pro-Communist governments in eastern Europe in the weeks after the Yalta Conference, Roosevelt discovered how differently he and Stalin interpreted its results. Before he could establish a policy to deal with the new situation, Roosevelt died of a sudden heart attack. In August 1945, President Truman ordered the dropping of atomic bombs on Hiroshima and Nagasaki. He justified the mass slaughter of civilians by saying the attack would save many more lives (both American and Japanese) because it would bring the war to a rapid close without an invasion of the Japanese home islands. The chain of events dividing the globe into the opposing blocks of the Cold War was under way. A year later, Churchill said an 'iron curtain' existed between Soviet-controlled eastern Europe and western Europe with its American ally.

As the former allies struggled to influence the governments emerging on the borders of the Soviet Union after the war, American policy-makers became convinced that the Soviets were fanatically intent on establishing communist regimes around the world. In 1947 President Truman announced what became known as the Truman Doctrine in a speech to Congress during which he asked for funds to fight communist aggression in Turkey and Greece.

According to the Doctrine, the USA had to follow a policy of containment to prevent communist expansion anywhere in the world. The Soviet ideology, inherently a threat to the USA and to democratic institutions, was being spread through internal subversion as well as outside pressure. In a 'domino effect', as it was called, one nation after another would fall to Soviet domination unless the

USA led the 'free world' by actively intervening to prevent it. Thus the stage was set for direct American involvement in internal conflicts and wars, not only in Latin America (where the Roosevelt Corollary justified intervention) but also around the world. Containment became the cornerstone of American foreign policy throughout the Cold War. Pursuing containment protected and expanded US interests abroad and its implementation contributed to the formulation of other foreign-policy initiatives.

In the late 1940s the US took steps to meet the communist threat and in the process revolutionized its foreign policy. It kept its military forces near wartime levels, extending mandatory military service into peacetime and continuing its military build-up. When the Soviets rejected international inspection plans to enforce a ban on nuclear weapons, the USA reacted by expanding atomic research and giving nuclear weapons a central place in its arsenal. The National Security Act of 1947 reorganized the federal government to meet Cold War threats by centralizing control over all branches of the military in a new Department of Defense (the 'Pentagon') and creating the National Security Council (NSC) and the Central Intelligence Agency (CIA).

**PLATE 7.3** Mushroom cloud from a nuclear-weapons test, Nevada, 1951.
(*National Archives/Time Pix/Rex Features*)

In a sense, the Act put the country in a state of permanent military readiness by transferring enlarged powers over defence to the President and by making it easier for him to take aggressive action internationally without a declaration of war. By 1950 a NSC report known as NSC-68 defined the US stance: more than ever, America had an important mission in the world; on the USA lay the responsibility to lead the free world. To that end, the nation had to quadruple its military budget so that it could take the initiative in containing communism.

Meanwhile, Secretary of State Marshall became convinced that the USA ought to fund the economic revival of Europe. The motives for the so-called Marshall Plan were mixed. In general the hope was to learn from the mistakes of US policy after the First World War. Humanitarian concerns and ethnic ties played important roles in congressional and public approval of the plan. Economic concerns also inspired support. Assisting Europe could absorb surpluses that threatened to cause an economic recession in the USA, and a revitalized Europe would provide markets for American goods. Finally, it was believed that prosperous economies would strengthen European resistance to communism and thus contribute to the goal of containment. Approximately $15 billion were spent on this programme while it was in effect from 1948 to 1951.

The vision of one world united through the Four Freedoms faded and was replaced by the sense that the world consisted of two warring camps threatening each other with nuclear destruction. Therefore, the United States reversed its historic refusal to form permanent military alliances. The first of these, the Organization of American States (OAS), was founded in 1948, and was followed by the North Atlantic Treaty Organization (NATO) in 1950 and similar mutual defence pacts that eventually covered the globe. Commitment to internationalism had irreversibly replaced the country's traditional isolationism.

When Soviet troops entered Hungary in 1956 and crushed the revolt against Soviet domination, Hungarian Americans protested strongly. President Eisenhower announced that the United States would not intervene in their homeland because the Truman Doctrine did not extend to nations within the Warsaw Pact (the eastern-European–Soviet alliance organized as a counterforce to NATO). In 1968 when the Soviet Union and Warsaw Pact nations put down a popular revolt in Czechoslovakia, the USA followed the same policy of non-involvement.

In the early 1950s, the fear of communism set the stage for Senator Joseph McCarthy's hunt for Americans that were involved in 'un-American activities' as spies or tools of the Soviets. In a general sense, 'McCarthyism' was nothing new, although his blatant accusations against government officials were unprecedented. Fear of communist influence and Bolshevik immigrants appeared in the 'Red Scare' of the 1920s and was part of the old distrust of the foreign that stretched, in some form, all the way back to the Alien and Sedition Acts. McCarthy and his supporters did not create the wave of anti-communist hysteria. They merely exploited the public anxieties built up by the Cold War and the threat of nuclear destruction.

The CIA's covert involvement in the Bay of Pigs affair and the Cuban Missile Crisis raised Cold War tensions to new heights. Ironically, the superpowers' nuclear arsenals made mutual assured destruction (MAD), the basis for deterrence, the best chance of avoiding war. However, after the missile crisis, relations between the two superpowers began to improve. Developments furthering this trend included the Nuclear Test Ban Treaty of 1963 and the decision that neither superpower would intervene in the Israeli–Arab war. In the 1970s President Nixon initiated the policy known as détente (peaceful coexistence) and the gradual reduction of nuclear arsenals that later Presidents continued. Despite unstable periods in the superpowers' relationship in the decades to come, a similar understanding was reached during the Gulf War almost thirty years later in 1991, when both countries condemned the Iraqi occupation of Kuwait in the United Nations and joined in contributing forces to drive President Saddam Hussein's troops back into Iraq.

In Asia, the United States committed itself to containing communism in Korea, Vietnam, Cambodia and Laos. The Vietnam War, the first the USA had lost since the war of 1812, produced massive anti-war protests at home and anti-American demonstrations abroad. The conduct of the war demoralized the younger generation at home as well as US combat troops. The cost of the war drained funds from President Johnson's programmes to deal with domestic poverty and inequality. The frustrations of trying to win a 'limited war' led President Nixon to authorize the secret bombing of Laos and Cambodia without congressional approval.

The Vietnam War became a traumatic experience to the American people, and has therefore coloured later involvement in other countries. During the Gulf and Afghanistan Wars, the US chose to act in a multinational coalition after securing approval from the UN, even though Americans constituted the largest group of participants. Low-intensity warfare and short engagements executed with precision through technological weaponry, it was hoped, would replace the prolonged military engagement of the Korean and Vietnam Wars.

An important turning point in US foreign relations came when President Nixon opened talks with the leaders of mainland China, taking advantage of a split between China and the Soviet Union, and thus reduced the apparent threat of communism. In the following years American policy was less concerned with military control and, especially during the Carter presidency, more emphasis was put on supporting human rights in other countries. This angered the Soviets, as stories of dissidents confined in psychiatric 'hospitals' became well known through the work of Aleksandr Solzhenitsyn. In the later 1970s the relationship between the two powers grew more tense as a result.

The US–Soviet relationship went through several pendulum swings. American policy toward Latin America, for example, varied with the temperature of the Cold War. Still, the commitment to containment has generally led to US support to right-wing regimes in America's 'backyard', where apparent stability has often seemed more vital than human rights. In that frame of mind, in the 1980s the Reagan administration refused to stop giving the right-wing Contra rebels aid in their guerrilla war against the Sandinista government of Nicaragua when Congress cut off funding for the Contras. The Iran–Contras scandal revealed that Oliver North and other administration officials had secretly sold weapons to Iran and used the profits to aid the Contras, in direct contradiction of congressional policy and the administration's public statements. For some commentators, the lesson seemed to be that the Cold War produced an 'imperial presidency' that undermined the balance of power between the branches of government.

After proclaiming strong opposition to the communists' 'evil empire' and carrying out a massive military build-up, President Reagan also pursued peaceful coexistence. On the Asian scene, he extended the détente policy of previous Presidents when he signed a series of agreements with the People's Republic of China in 1984. He accepted friendly overtures from the General Secretary of the Communist Party in the USSR, Mikhail Gorbachev, which led to disarmament treaties in his second term and agreements on increasing trade and cultural relations under President George Bush, Snr.

In November 1989 the symbol of a divided Europe, the Berlin Wall, was torn down by cheering crowds from both sides, and in the following summer the two Germanies were reunited by a treaty signed by the four allies from the Second World War. In 1992 due to internal ethnic conflicts and economic strains, the Soviet Union split into a loose federation of republics.

## The sole superpower in the post-Cold War era

After over a decade of change, some main contours of the post-Cold War world and America's place in it became apparent. In Europe and the USA the elimination of the Iron Curtain and nuclear tension caused jubilation and optimistic attempts to fashion a better future. European leaders moved quickly to include ten of the recently independent eastern European countries in the European Union (EU). These countries thus grew less dependent on America for trade and military needs, although they continued to exhibit support for US foreign-policy views, partly perhaps in gratitude for America's long record of opposing their Soviet oppressors. Some of these nations (most notably Poland) became members of NATO, which reaffirmed their ties to the US even as that organization struggled to redefine its purpose and took on military duties outside the territory covered by the alliance.

Military conflicts and political unrest continued within the Russian federation and in newly independent neighbouring nations. The USA wanted to aid these nations with their reconstruction, just as the Marshall Plan had helped war-torn western Europe, but debated on how to do so without interfering too much in their internal affairs or provoking Russia. The initial attempt to do this came through the loose cooperation of the Partnership for Peace, but the USA largely left the handling of these problems to Russia. A more constructive result of the end of superpower rivalry appeared in US–Russian agreement during the Gulf War of 1991 that drove Saddam Hussein's invaders out of Kuwait.

In his first term, centrist Democrat President Bill Clinton made strengthening the domestic economy by increasing free trade his primary foreign-policy goal. By 1995 both the North American Free Trade Agreement (NAFTA), between Canada, Mexico and the USA, and the Uruguay General Agreement on Tariffs and Trade (GATT) had been ratified by the Senate.

George H.W. Bush and Clinton also attempted to define America's role in dealing with a major after-effect of the Cold War: the increasing disorder in Asia, Africa and Central America that involved former 'client states' of the super-powers. As the sole remaining superpower, the USA faced mounting pressure at home and abroad to act in these crises, but American policy-makers in the 1990s were at first reluctant to be on call as the world's police officer. In the hope that neighbouring countries would step in (the Europeans in the former Yugoslavia and other African nations in that continent's many 'trouble spots'), the USA delayed too long according to some critics. Then America initiated a series of multilateral strategic interventions in humanitarian crises (in Bosnia, Somalia and Haiti) and diplomatic efforts to bring peace in long-standing conflicts (in Northern Ireland, North Korea and Palestine).

The results of what some critics called the 'new interventionism' were mixed. American participation seemed effective in ending 'ethnic cleansing' in the Balkan conflict, for example, but the mission to feed starving civilians in Somalia changed into ill-executed efforts at 'nation-building' that ended in the death and humiliation of US soldiers followed by American withdrawal. Commentators debated over how often and how forcibly the superpower should act, those abroad generally wanting international leadership from America but expecting it to come in concert (most often through the UN) and in agreement with their policy aims. A prominent group of critics at home, supported by the Clinton administration, took this same view, but there was heated disagreement (most prominently from the so-called neo-conservatives) about how much the USA should allow its foreign policy to be influenced by the agendas of other nations and international organizations. A consensus appeared only about regret at America's not having intervened to end the genocide in Rwanda. While in Africa ex-President Clinton called that his administration's worst error, and in 2003 George W. Bush was prompt in asking for international action to stop the slaughter in Sudan's civil war.

After taking office in 2001, Bush formed a team of foreign-policy officials and advisors that included both moderates, such as Secretary of State Colin Powell, reported 'pragmatists', such as National Security Advisor Condoleezza Rice, and leaders often associated with neo-conservative views, such as Vice President Dick Cheney, Secretary of Defense Donald Rumsfeld and his chief assistant, Paul Wolfowitz. On the one hand, neo-conservative-policy commentators urged a new foreign policy realism. That approach dictated that the USA should review its international commitments, acting energetically to achieve key objectives and withdraw, while rejecting or scaling down involvements that did not serve the country's interests. Early in his first term, Bush's administration was involved with such a review, and its findings resulted in withdrawal from the Anti-Ballistic Missile Treaty and the Kyoto Protocol on global warming, rejection of the International Criminal Court, and disengagement from diplomatic efforts in Korea and the Middle East. In agreement with neo-conservative advisors, Bush also embarked on a major modernization and expansion of the country's military capabilities.

Until the terrorist attacks of 9/11, the Bush regime criticized the Clinton administration's willingness to engage US troops abroad. But from that day, other parts of the neo-conservative agenda marked the administration's handling of US foreign policy. The President announced a global war on terrorism, and within weeks the US military was engaged in destroying Osama bin Laden and the al-Qaeda terrorist-training camps in Afghanistan and replacing the Taliban regime that had sheltered them. The USA took note of its unchallenged status as the sole superpower and acted accordingly. It adopted a strongly interventionist stance to change the world according to American ideals and interests, rather than merely to manage the world's crises as a kind of global police officer. It used military force to bring regime change where it judged such action necessary.

In an age of global terrorism, President Bush announced, the USA could no longer wait for threats to materialize. Instead it had to use its intelligence-gathering capacities to discover threats and then strike enemies first, abroad, before they could attack the American homeland. The USA would take 'pre-emptive action', attacking an enemy as it prepared to strike, and 'preventative action', attacking even without evidence of an imminent enemy strike.

As early as the 1980s, neo-conservatives had identified 'rogue states' as the dispensers of terrorism and, therefore, as the prime candidates for US-led change. Bush identified some of these nations as an 'axis of evil' stretching from North Korea through Iran to Iraq. His administration convinced Congress of the imminent threat of Iraq's plans to use weapons of mass destruction and of its connections with al-Qaeda. Despite entrenched opposition, both at home and in the UN Security Council, the USA and its allies invaded and occupied that nation in early 2003. Although the President declared victory in major military operations in less than three months, the war wore on and American casualties rose as the US-led 'coalition of the willing' attempted to restore public order and put in place a stable democratic government.

Practising the neo-conservative principle that the USA should institute American-style democracy and market capitalism in the Middle East proved much

**PLATE 7.4** Coalition soldiers in central Baghdad during the Iraq War in 2003.
(*Sipa Press/Rex Features*)

more difficult than toppling Saddam Hussein's dictatorship. Meeting the challenge of continued global terrorism, much of it arising from radical Islamic groups, the war on terrorism could be credited with the destruction of many terrorist groups abroad and with preventing additional attacks on home soil. Its successes became controversial, however, due to the high financial burdens and serious limitations on individuals' civil liberties that resulted from the implementation of the administration's chief anti-terrorism law, the USA Patriot Act.

At election time in late 2004, a majority of the American public, while critical of some aspects of the war in Iraq and of efforts to counter terrorism, felt the Bush leadership deserved a second term to follow through on its foreign-policy goals. Shortly afterwards, the President announced plans to retain the more conservative members of his foreign-policy team and to promote Condoleezza Rice to Secretary of State, after Colin Powell resigned his post.

## The foreign-policy establishment debate

The governmental structures of the USA are yet another factor that make American foreign affairs distinctive. The Constitution's system of checks and balances requires the executive and legislative branches to share responsibility for the nation's relations with other countries. The nature of these branches, moreover, has resulted in opportunities for other institutions and groups to develop ways of influencing foreign policy decision-making. As a result, the official and unofficial groups that play a part in the foreign-policy establishment are many and varied. There are several competing centres of power whose importance changes over time and according to the situation.

During the nation's history, the balance of power between the two branches over foreign policy has shifted. Congress was the dominant partner for most of the nineteenth century, except for the Civil War years. The consensus of opinion is that the shift toward executive power during the 1900s resulted from the near constant international crises involving the USA. The President grew increasingly dominant until failures of executive policy involved with the Vietnam War provoked both congressional attempts to correct the balance between the branches and greater presidential caution in making foreign commitments. As a result of the success of the Reagan presidency's initiatives and the 9/11 crisis, however, a high degree of executive dominance in foreign policy has returned.

The President has several powers that make him the single most important figure in US foreign policy today. Each of these, however, is shared with other groups. He is the commander-in-chief but, with few exceptions, the President has been a civilian with very limited military experience. He therefore depends on the advice of the leaders of the armed forces and other military experts to meet his responsibility for national security. Even if the President is convinced that the vital interests or territory of the USA is seriously threatened, he cannot declare war. Only Congress can do that, and since the Second World War, it has been especially reluctant to do so. Consequently, Presidents have increasingly success-fully committed the nation to military action in other ways when they have perceived crises involving national security. The common pattern of events in recent decades is that the President commits US military personnel or otherwise responds to an attack on American interests or citizens, and soon after informs Congress, asking for a joint resolution of support from both of its houses if the 'military conflict' is likely to be of longer duration.

As the chief executive, one of the President's primary duties is to carry out foreign policy, but the Constitution requires the approval of both houses of Congress for the governmental expenditures that all foreign policy initiatives depend on. Not only must the President win majorities for his policies, there-fore, but he can also expect military leaders and bureaucrats to lobby Congress in favour of competing programmes. Further, congressional involvement does not stop there. The legislature often exercises its investigatory power to evaluate whether money is being spent as Acts of Congress stipulated and stops funding or repeals those Acts if it is dissatisfied.

The more specific foreign policy powers of the President are also limited, but chief executives have been released from the most important checks on these powers. No other official can nominate people to ambassadorial and other high-level positions in the American foreign service, but all such appointments must be approved by a majority in the Senate. Congress itself removed this limit in 1939, with the creation of the Executive Office of the President (EOP), which allows Presidents to rely on White House advisors, who do not need Senate approval. The EOP's National Security Council eclipsed the Departments of State and Defense as the centre of policy-making in foreign relations by the mid-1960s, and diminished congressional influence in foreign policy. The President alone can negotiate treaties with other governments, but all treaties must be ratified by an extraordinary majority (two thirds) in the Senate. Approval from so many senators has often seemed doubtful, especially since the First World War, however, and so Presidents have increasingly depended on more informal executive agreements, which do not require Senate approval.

Two important foreign-policy roles of the President, acting as both chief diplomat and ceremonial head of state, have grown greatly in importance since the beginning of high-speed air travel, electronic communication and supersonic weaponry. The possibility for extensive personal diplomacy between world leaders and the media attention it commands have made the President the visible maker of foreign policy more than ever before. During the Cold War with the threat of nuclear destruction in minutes and, since 2001, the possibility of a catastrophic terrorist attack, the greater speed of executive action is a convincing argument for presidential control of foreign affairs.

The organization of the congressional and executive institutions in the foreign-policy establishment create opportunities for many interest groups to exercise influence. Each chamber of Congress has a permanent committee that specializes in foreign policy with subcommittees to deal with all the major regions of the world and important international issues. Both chambers have, in addition, several other committees (with their subcommittees) that are involved in foreign policy decisions, such as the armed services, energy, commerce and intelligence committees.

The State Department and Department of Defense are, like Congress, organized into groups of specialists that focus on particular issues of international affairs or areas of the world. These groups formulate policy suggestions that they send through bureaucratic channels to the Secretary of State or the Secretary of Defense, who forward them to the EOP and Congress. Although the President usually decides on major policy concerns, department bureaucrats manage the daily implementation of policy. They can also hold investigative hearings. For these reasons, the full range of pressure groups and members of Congress try to catch the ear of influential officials in the State Department and Department of Defense.

There has long been debate about the foreign-policy establishment. According to some critics, deliberation and lobbying in roughly parallel structures in Congress and the departments produce wasteful redundancy, lost information and unnecessary confusion over policy alternatives. These observers emphasize that the foreign-policy establishment has yet another component, the personal advisors and agencies in the EOP. The President's national security advisor, the National Security Agency (NSA), the joint chiefs of staff of the military and the Central Intelligence Agency (CIA) often evolve a third set of priorities and policies.

Is it any wonder that over the half century of the Cold War some forty-five separate national security and intelligence gathering units grew up? This situation was partly to blame for the intelligence failures leading to the 9/11 terrorist attacks. One of the chief governmental changes in the wake of the tragedies consolidated those programmes into a single new structure, the Department of Homeland Security, in 2002.

# Exercises

Explain and examine the significance of the following names and terms.

| | | |
|---|---|---|
| isolationism | exceptionalism | Washington's Farewell |
| soft power | hard power | Address |
| Alien and Sedition Acts | Monroe Doctrine | expansionism |
| Manifest Destiny | imperialism | Roosevelt Corollary |
| anti-imperialists | Fourteen Points | limited internationalism |
| Four Freedoms | Yalta Conference | Truman Doctrine |
| National Security Act | Marshall Plan | McCarthyism |
| Vietnam War | détente | Gulf War |
| Iran–Contras scandal | post-Cold War era | 9/11 terrorist attacks |
| hegemony | USA Patriot Act | Department of Homeland |
| Iraq War | | Security |

Write short essays on the following questions.

1.  Critically evaluate the degree to which US foreign policy is (or has been) distinct from that of other nations.

2.  Summarize what you think are the important historical trends and turning points in the evolution of America's relations with the rest of the world.

3.  Critically evaluate the significant changes in US foreign policy from 1945 to the present.

4.  Describe the institutional structures in America's foreign-policy establishment and critically discuss how well they serve as a basis for the formulation of the nation's foreign policy.

## Further reading

Kennedy, P. M. (1987) *The Rise and Fall of the Great Powers: economic change and military conflict from 1500 to 2000* New York: Random House.
Lipset, S. M. (1996) *American exceptionalism: a double-edged sword* New York: W. W. Norton.
Magstadt, T. M. (2004) *An Empire if You Can Keep It: power and principle in American foreign policy* Washington, DC: Congressional Quarterly Press.
Merrill, Dennis and T. G. Paterson (2005) *Major Problems in American Foreign Relations, Vol. II: Since 1914*, 6th edn, Boston, Mass.: Houghton Mifflin.
Nye, J. S., Jr. (2004) *Soft Power: the means to success in world politics* New York: Public Affairs.
Paterson, T. G. (1995) *Major Problems in American Foreign Relations*, Vol. I, 4th edn Boston, Mass.: Houghton Mifflin.

## Web sites

<http://www.thomas.loc.gov>
<http://latimes.com>
<http://www.washingtonpost.com>
<http://www.cnn.com>
<http://www.nytimes.com>
<http://www.georgetown.edu/crossroads/index.html>
<http://usinfo.state.gov/journals/journala.htm>

# The legal system

The US legal system consists for practical purposes of independent courts, judges and lawyers who work within and service the state and federal law apparatus. This is concerned with two main types of law (civil law and criminal law). The individual cases which are dealt with by the courts and other institutions are accordingly classified as either civil or criminal.

Civil law involves claims for compensation (often financial) by individuals (or groups) who have allegedly suffered loss or damage through the acts of others. Domestic actions (divorce, children and custody), automobile accidents and personal injury cases are the largest civil matters. Civil law has a service role and tries to secure social harmony by settling disputes between individuals or organizations. This is achieved preferably by settlement during the course of litigation and negotiations. If no settlement is agreed, the case goes to a full trial.

Criminal law involves the trial and punishment of persons who have committed crimes against society, such as theft or murder. State, local and federal authorities prosecute groups or individuals in an attempt to establish guilt, which may result in a fine, imprisonment or (in some serious cases) execution. This is the control aspect of the legal system and the criminal law protects society by punishing those who have broken social codes embodied in the law. The trial and any punishment are also supposed to act as deterrents to potential offenders.

The legal system plays a central role on public and private levels of American society, to a greater extent perhaps than in other countries. The law is regarded very much as part of daily life and not as a remote abstraction. Legal issues and court decisions are matters of widespread interest and concern. They are also closely intertwined with the nation's political, social and economic life. Americans make active use of their legal system and are a litigious people. They are willing to take legal actions, are accustomed to seeking redress from the courts and have over 650,000 lawyers and judges to evaluate their cases.

There are several reasons for this cultural behaviour. First, active participation in the legal process derives from a colonial and frontier tradition of individualism in which Americans defended their own interests and rights. However, legal actions can also result from group causes. The War of Independence started from collective legal complaints by some (if not all) colonists against British rule and showed that law (if formulated correctly) could potentially protect individuals and communities against oppression by government and other authorities. However, there can also be a tension between individualistic and group values in US society.

Second, public and private life is influenced by, and stresses a constitutionalism which stems from the US Constitution (1776) and the later Bill of Rights (1789). These legal documents try to create a framework for the good society. They guarantee civil rights and freedoms for citizens and stipulate a separation of powers between an independent judiciary and the executive and legislative branches of government. Americans' expectations of social and political justice thus depend, ideally and practically, on the safeguards in these documents.

Third, such constitutional features are founded on a tradition of legalism (the belief that conflicts can in fact be legally resolved), which also stems from colonial times. Civil disputes between citizens, institutions, groups and branches of government, as well as criminal cases have to be legally decided by the federal and state court systems.

Issues of justice and rights are a fundamental concern in Americans' lives. They expect action from the criminal-justice apparatus and are prepared to go to the courts for satisfaction if they feel that their civil rights have been infringed by federal or state governments, doctors, hospitals, airlines, employers, the educational system, manufacturers, commercial companies or their neighbours. But, although an American 'civil-rights culture' has grown, this does not mean that all such cases succeed.

A very large number of civil and criminal cases are handled annually by the courts. Most are determined at state and local (rather than federal) levels. Americans have a constitutional right to have their cases quickly determined in a public trial by an impartial judge or jury (a selected number of citizens who decide the facts in many court cases).

Despite a concern with legal justice and claims that US society is humane and moral, law does not always imply justice, fair treatment and appropriate outcomes. The ideal frequently may not be matched by the reality, raising questions about delays and the quality of the legal system. The crucial question is one of access to both civil and criminal courts, and some individuals may not succeed. Access often depends upon the validity and nature of a case, wealth, social class and the level of court involved.

It is argued that the criminal and civil systems and some police forces must be reformed and corruption removed; that the disadvantaged and poor do not receive satisfaction despite the existence of legal aid (federal or state help to those unable to afford legal fees); that the legal system is biased towards the powerful and the wealthy; and that high legal costs are an obstacle to litigants seeking help.

The law can also be brought into disrepute by dubious or inadequate defence procedures by trial lawyers in criminal and civil cases; by prosecution conduct and incompetence; by plea-bargaining, which allows an accused person or defendant to avoid the heaviest criminal and civil penalties; by contingency fees, which specify a percentage payment to lawyers on the basis of positive results; by juries which may be biased on racial, social or political grounds; by tampering with or fabrication of evidence; by police procedures and conduct; and by lawyers who are accused of driving up costs. The question of victims' rights and compensation has increasingly become a contentious issue as has the behaviour of trial lawyers, particularly those who act for the defence in 'celebrity' cases.

## Legal history

The legal system is founded on customs brought to the USA by European colonists. Many forms were English, such as the common law (judge-made law), parliamentary/royal statutes or Acts and independent judges. Such elements have been adapted to distinctively American features like the US Constitution, the relationship between state and federal government and judicial review (the power of superior federal and state courts to invalidate laws and actions that violate the federal and state constitutions).

When the British colonized parts of North America in the seventeenth century, the common law, statute law and judges were adopted by some colonies. But other British and European settlers had left their homelands to avoid oppressive institutions and to create a fairer and freer society. They rejected the common law and created a code system of simple rules, which started in the Massachusetts Bay Colony in 1634.

However, as life stabilized in the colonies and as the population grew, such codes were insufficient to govern a more complex society. English legal structures were increasingly acceptable. Significantly, colonists in pre-Independence America protested strongly that the British Crown had denied them their traditional common-law rights and the Declaration of Independence (1776) contained many legal grievances.

After the War for Independence, the thirteen original states adopted the common law as the basis for their legal systems. But, as some states contained non-British settlers such as Dutch, Germans and Swedes, the common law had to accommodate other legal customs. The same process recurred later when the USA incorporated territories like California (1850). Each state thus interpreted and developed the common law in independent and individual ways. But when the USA purchased Louisiana (1803) with its existing French legal system, the common law was not adopted there.

The War for Independence also involved questions about the independent role of state governments. Federal government developed later, leading to a division of authority between states and federal institutions. This historical process means that most laws which directly and practically affect people today operate at the state and local level. The fifty states have their own legal systems, create their own laws in their own legislatures and have their own police forces and law courts. All (except Louisiana) apply their version of the common law, and most lawyers are qualified to practise in only one state.

Although anti-British feeling after independence led to criticism of the common law, lawyers and judges, this was reduced by new political factors. In 1787, delegates from the thirteen states at the Constitutional Convention in Philadelphia framed a Constitution for the USA, which became law in 1788. This stipulated that, while individual states remained as sovereign political entities in many areas, a new federal union of the states was also sovereign in its own sphere of competence.

Article 3 of the Constitution created a third branch of government, the independent federal judiciary: 'The judicial power of the United States shall be vested in one Supreme Court and in such inferior courts as the Congress may from time to time ordain and establish'. The founders of the USA considered the judiciary to be the weakest branch of government, restricted to applying the Constitution and the laws. But it later developed a central importance, particularly the Supreme Court in Washington, DC.

The Judiciary Act (1789) created new federal courts, which have two roles. They interpret the meaning of laws and administrative acts (statutory construction) and examine any law or administrative action by national or state authorities in the light of the US Constitution (judicial review). This latter

**PLATE 8.1** The US Supreme Court Justices. The Supreme Court consists of nine justices appointed by the President and confirmed by the Senate, who are led by a Chief Justice. They often represent different shades of legal and political opinion, ranging from liberal to conservative, and may come from specific ethnic backgrounds.
(*Sipa Press/Rex Features*)

important function of judicial review was initially contested by states' rights activists. But it was finally conceded and was an important factor in establishing a united nation.

The result of these historical developments was a legal organization for the whole country, and authority was divided between state and federal courts. The states still had their own courts, common law, constitutions and statutes and had jurisdiction over state law. But if a state-court decision violated federal laws or involved a federal question, the US Supreme Court could ultimately review and overturn it. Some federal and state matters may thus proceed from local courts to the Supreme Court and federal laws and the Constitution have (in theory) a uniform application throughout the country.

The independence and status of the judiciary were gradually strengthened. It is now regarded as an essential safeguard against potential abuse by the executive and legislative branches and fits into the American system of separation of powers and checks and balances. Some 846 federal judges are appointed by the President, subject to approval by the Senate. They serve until retirement and can only be removed for gross misconduct. All other judges at various levels are appointed by methods peculiar to individual states or are elected by voters.

A further historical factor increased the standing of the judiciary and courts. The initial Constitution contained few rights for individual citizens. Consequently, a Bill of Rights in the form of ten Amendments was voted by Congress in 1789 and ratified by the states in 1791. But such rights only applied at the federal level until the 1920s. The Bill of Rights (and later Amendments) gives protection to individual citizens against imprisonment without just cause, excessive fines or other forms of oppression. However, the courts still have to interpret these amendments in individual court cases.

Two other developments have added to the central place of law in US society. First, Congress (although given only limited power by the Constitution) has regulated American life in many ways through inter-state commerce Acts and other laws. The authority to 'regulate commerce among the several States' (the commerce clause) and to create laws 'necessary and proper' to carry out its powers has allowed Congress to pass social and economic legislation for the whole country. These laws may also be examined by the federal courts, although traditionally they have not interfered overmuch.

Second, US law has become increasingly complex due to increases in federal and state legislation. This means that business people, consumers and individuals are now more concerned with and directly affected by the law. They are very cautious about their legal transactions, contracts and court appearances and frequently need the assistance of professional lawyers.

Courts and judges in the USA at all levels, but especially the federal, make policy to varying degrees as they interpret and apply the law. It is argued that the courts are therefore political institutions and the judiciary is part of the political process. But judges do not make law or policy in the explicit way that politicians do. They function indirectly in the process of resolving disputes brought to their courts.

# The sources of US law

The two most important sources of contemporary US law are the common (or case) law and statutory law.

Versions of the English common law were accepted in all American states (except Louisiana) and much state law is now common law. It is administered and interpreted by the courts and is found in court decisions of judges, who generally adopt principles of law and decisions (precedents) from previous similar cases.

But the authority of precedent declined in the late-nineteenth and early-twentieth centuries. American judges now decide cases in terms of existing law and a sense of justice, so that the decision is fair and reasonable in the light of contemporary conditions. Generally, they follow the precedents unless there are good reasons for ignoring them.

Statutory law consists of laws which have been passed by state or federal legislatures. Such legislation is now very important. It grew considerably from the nineteenth century as state and federal government intruded increasingly into everyday affairs. The meaning and application of legislation is interpreted and determined by the courts.

Many social, economic and family matters are provided for by state statutes and are handled by state courts. At federal levels, statutory law is virtually the only type of law and includes the Constitution, treaties, Acts of Congress, presidential proclamations, executive orders and rules of federal departments.

# The court system

The courts play a central and influential role in American society. They directly affect the daily lives of citizens and their decisions are widely debated. Social and personal struggles are reflected in civil and criminal court battles.

US courts (see Figure 8.1) operate at both federal and state/local levels and have their own areas of authority or jurisdiction. State and local courts handle most of the legal work and are the most immediate for Americans. The federal courts only account for some 2 per cent of cases tried annually. But the existence of separate court systems makes some litigation more complicated than in many other countries.

Parties in a case may, in certain circumstances, appeal a court decision to a higher court. An appeal is an examination of procedures and legal principles on which the decision was based in the previous trial, as well as any new admissible evidence.

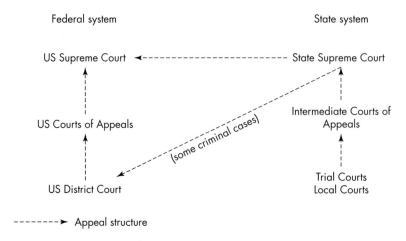

Federal system                                        State system

US Supreme Court ◄-------------------------- State Supreme Court

US Courts of Appeals                          Intermediate Courts of
                                              Appeals

                        (some criminal cases)

US District Court                             Trial Courts
                                              Local Courts

-------► Appeal structure

**FIGURE 8.1** The main US courts.


## The federal court system

Federal courts deal with cases which arise under the US Constitution or federal
law and any disputes involving the federal government. They also hear matters
involving governments or citizens of different states and thus play a part in state
law. If a case in the highest state court of appeal involves a federal question, it can
be appealed ultimately to the US Supreme Court.

The federal-court system forms a hierarchy. The three main levels of courts
are, in ascending order of appeal:

1.  US District Courts
2.  US Courts of Appeals
3.  the Supreme Court in Washington, DC.

A case involving federal jurisdiction is heard first before a federal district judge.
An appeal may be made to a US Court of Appeal and, in the last resort, to the
US Supreme Court.

Most federal cases begin and are settled in the lower US District Courts and
only a minority of cases are appealed. There are ninety-five district courts in the
USA (with states having at least one court). They are trial courts in which a judge
or a jury decides each case. Most citizens involved in federal litigation only have
dealings with the District Courts.

They try cases involving breaches of federal criminal law, such as bank
robbery, drug-dealing, kidnapping, mail fraud, inter-state crime, currency fraud
and assassination. Most of the work of the District Courts, however, is in areas of
civil law, such as taxation, civil rights, administrative regulations, disputes between

**PLATE 8.2** US Court House. This is a US District Court dealing with federal cases, situated in lower Manhattan, New York City.
(*Corbis*)

states and bankruptcy. Their caseload has increased since the mid-1960s in civil matters, due to more federal legislation.

The US Courts of Appeals system consists of fifteen courts sitting in each of the judicial circuits into which the USA is divided. These courts (with from three to five judges) mainly hear appeals from decisions of the US District Courts within the circuits. Most of their decisions are final and set a precedent for future similar cases. It is argued that these are the most important judicial-policy-makers in the USA. They are not, however, the ultimate authority because their decisions can be overturned by the US Supreme Court.

The US Supreme Court in Washington DC comprises a chief justice and eight associate justices, assisted by law clerks. It has jurisdiction in national and federal matters. But its main role is that of an appeal court, and it hears cases from lower federal and state courts. These appeals usually involve constitutional issues, questions of federal law and conflicts between two or more of the states.

The court has authority to review any executive and legislative action or law passed by any level of government (if challenged in a court case) and can declare it unconstitutional after judging its compatibility with the Constitution. Although not explicitly given this power of judicial review by the Constitution, the Supreme Court has developed such jurisdiction. It enables the court to profoundly influence many aspects of American life.

Its decisions have given protection and rights to African Americans and other minorities, produced influential decisions on education and religion and affected the death penalty and abortion issues. But, since 1790, it has ruled that only some 130 federal laws have been unconstitutional, although about ten times as many state and local laws have been invalidated. Supreme Court decisions can be overturned by the court itself, a constitutional amendment or an Act of Congress.

The court is obliged to rule on some 150 cases each year, but in a few instances can itself decide whether or not it will hear particular cases. It usually accepts cases which involve a basic constitutional principle, an important question of federal law or a conflict between state and federal law. It does not have the power to actually make laws. However, since its authority is independent of the other branches of government, its decisions may often have a legislative, policy-making (and arguably political) force.

In general the court plays a conservative role, following legal tradition and precedent. But it has had periods of controversial liberal 'activism' and has been criticized for exceeding its legal role of textual interpretation of statutory law and the Constitution, usurping the prerogatives of Congress, obstructing the popular will and preventing the passing of economic and social legislation. In recent years, it has chosen to rule on the 2000 presidential election (the Florida votes case) and declined to act in other matters that had seemed appropriate for review. Nevertheless, its caseload has expanded due to new legislation in civil-rights and federal regulations that has increased its 'political' profile.

## The state and local court system

State and local courts constitute a large, complicated and individualistic system. They have a wider jurisdiction than federal courts and much heavier workloads. They determine the guilt or innocence of persons accused of violating state criminal laws and decide civil disputes. Most criminal and civil cases, like assaults, theft (larceny), murder, divorce and property disputes are settled within the state system.

The Constitution stipulates that the states have areas of authority (or sovereignty) outside the federal judicial system. They have their own criminal and civil legal systems, laws, prisons, police forces, courts and associations of lawyers. Court systems and laws are similar in most states. But there are differences, such as court structures and names, sentences for murder and the minimum ages for marriage, possession of a driver's licence and purchase of alcohol. The states jealously guard their independence and are self-contained legal units whose courts deliver judgments from which there is often no appeal. But jurisdiction can be shared between federal and state bodies if an issue has federal implications.

Local courts are the lowest state courts and have a limited jurisdiction. They hear minor civil and criminal cases (misdemeanours) that often cannot be appealed and may not have a jury. Their names vary according to locality and the nature of the case. They may be known as police courts, town or city courts or justice of the peace courts.

**PLATE 8.3** Scene in a local court.
(*Priscilla Coleman*)

Trial courts are the next highest, have a more general jurisdiction and may consist of the following in different states:

- district, county or municipal courts, which hear civil suits and criminal cases,
- juvenile or family courts, which decide domestic, juvenile and delinquency cases,
- probate courts, which decide on wills and hear claims against estates and
- criminal courts, which determine criminal cases.

Most of the criminal, and some civil, cases will be heard by a jury.

Some three quarters of the states have intermediate appeal courts which hear appeals from lower courts. But the highest court is the State Supreme Court, which hears civil and criminal appeals from inferior state courts and can employ judicial review. Federal and constitutional matters may be appealed from this court to the US Supreme Court and some criminal cases can be appealed to the federal district courts.

# Federal and state court proceedings

American legal proceedings in both criminal and civil cases are based on due process (legal rights, fair procedures, trial and correct information) and the adversary system. The latter enables competing parties to present their views to an impartial third party, under procedural rules that allow the evidence to be given in a fair and orderly manner. A trial under the adversary process is designed to determine the facts under the appropriate law and to resolve cases by producing a judgment. It is the impartial third party (judge or jury) who decides the case based on the evidence presented to the court.

Some Americans may regard this technical process as game-playing or even corrupt. But the legal language and emphasis on correct procedure are supposed to safeguard the rights of citizens and to ensure equal protection under the law.

In practice, most civil disputes and some criminal cases are not resolved through court trials and many legal problems do not result in lawsuits. The legal profession generally attempts to avoid civil and (some) criminal contests in court by arranging settlements during the course of negotiation and litigation.

## *Criminal proceedings*

A range of rights and protections for citizens in criminal cases are provided by Amendments to the Bill of Rights, which have been added to by later judicial decisions.

These stipulate that individuals shall not be deprived of life, liberty or property without due process of law and should be given a speedy and public trial, usually by jury, in the location of the alleged crime. Accused persons have the right to question witnesses and compel most witnesses to appear on their behalf, the right to a lawyer for their defence (if necessary at public expense), the general right to remain silent and a right against self-incrimination.

There is protection against excessive bail (payment to secure freedom prior to trial); the police cannot force a confession from a prisoner or suspect by duress or threats and generally may not hold persons for more than two days without charging them with a criminal offence. Lengthy imprisonment in isolation prior to a trial is illegal and any confession obtained by the police in these circumstances is not acceptable to a court. It is argued, however, that such safeguards are not always observed by the criminal legal system and that individuals' rights may be abused.

Trial by jury is a fundamental tradition in America and is guaranteed in indictable (serious) criminal cases. It may also be employed in other criminal trials. Additionally, a defendant charged with a criminal offence may have been previously indicted by a grand jury or sometimes by a process of information at state level. The trial jury consists of between six and twelve ordinary citizens (depending on the level of the court), who make a decision based on the facts

## Pre-trial procedure

1. Arrest of suspect by police (Miranda rights must be read to suspect).
2. Custody (suspect may, if necessary, be held for up to forty-eight hours without formal charge).
3. Initial appearance of suspect before a judge. Judge determines whether there is sufficient evidence of a crime – probable cause – to charge the defendant, who is then informed of the charge details and his/her legal rights. If no charge is preferred, the defendant is released. If defendant is charged, the judge will set bail (the amount of money or conditions to release defendant from custody until trial) and determine legal representation.
4. Arraignment. Defendant appears in court for the reading of the indictment/information/charge. Their rights are explained and they enter a plea. On a not-guilty plea, a trial date is set. On a guilty plea, a date is set for sentencing.
5. Plea bargaining. Both sides come to an agreement on the charges without a full trial (for example, guilty to a lesser offence than murder with intent).
6. Discovery. If a case is set for trial, prosecution and defence disclose their witnesses and prosecution must generally produce all evidence against the defendant to the defence.

## Trial procedure in court

1. Trial held before a judge, who presides, and a jury that decides the facts of the case.
2. Selection of twelve jurors to form the jury.
3. Opening statements firstly by the state (prosecution) followed by the defence.
4. Evidence. Presentation and examination of oral (witness) and physical evidence by the prosecution. At close, the defence may seek a motion to dismiss. If unsuccessful, the defence presents its evidence. At close, rebuttal evidence may be called by the prosecution.
5. Objections may be made by either side to the nature of questioning. Questioning may consist of examination, cross-examination and additional questioning.
6. After all the evidence has been presented, there are final motions in the absence of the jury for a directed verdict from the judge. If this fails, the jury returns to listen to closing arguments first by the defence and then by the prosecution.
7. These are followed by the judge's instructions to the jury, the jury deliberation and the jury decision (verdict). Motions after verdict may be submitted (for example, for a new trial). If unsuccessful, the judge then enters a judgment on this decision and sets a date for sentencing.

*Source:* adapted from ABA *Law and the Courts: a handbook of courtroom procedures*

**FIGURE 8.2** Outline of procedure in criminal cases.

before them in court. A unanimous decision is needed in federal criminal cases and in most criminal cases in all states (although majority verdicts may sometimes be allowed).

After the trial, the Seventh Amendment guarantees that the accepted facts on which a trial was based cannot be re-examined in any appeal to a higher court and the appeal must therefore be based on other grounds. The Eighth Amendment states that there should be protection for the guilty from cruel and unusual punishment (see the death-penalty debate below, pp. 198–200).

District attorneys conduct criminal prosecutions under these rules at the local (county or city) levels. At the federal level, attorneys from the Department of Justice and from the offices of the attorney general and solicitor general represent the government in initiating and trying criminal cases and suggest cases to the courts.

It is estimated that some 90 per cent of serious criminal cases in the US are settled by a plea bargain. This is a system that allows courts to reduce the length and number of trials and allows defendants to reduce the severity of charges against them and their punishment. The argument for its use is to reduce courts' workloads, but it also puts those who cannot afford skilled lawyers at a disadvantage.

## Civil proceedings

Civil cases in federal and state courts are divided into categories. The majority deal with matters such as accident and personal-injury claims. The plaintiff serves documents on the defendant and, unless the case is settled out of court, it goes to trial before a judge and, sometimes, a jury. In more expensive cases, a jury trial must be held. A majority (rather than a unanimous) jury decision is permitted in civil cases in some states. A current concern is the amount of punitive damages being awarded in some cases by the civil courts.

# The legal profession

Hostility was shown towards judges after independence because of anti-British feeling, and in the nineteenth century attempts were made to democratize and de-professionalize the legal system. But generally judges have been given considerable respect in the USA, although it is argued that they can be too political or may bow to political pressure. However, lawyers (particularly corporate, divorce and 'celebrity' trial lawyers) tend to be treated with suspicion or even antagonism. Trial lawyers (usually for the defence) have attracted much negative comment for their alleged manipulation of evidence, the media and the jury.

## The judiciary

Federal judges are nominated by the President, confirmed by the Senate and appointed for life in what amounts to a political selection. They hold office during good behaviour and can be removed from office only by impeachment (trial by the Senate for gross misconduct). This process has been very rarely used and never successfully against a Supreme Court justice.

State judges may now be appointed, selected or elected (by the people) depending on the practices of individual states. They may also be investigated by state commissions which may recommend their disciplining or removal.

The judiciary has a range of functions and duties. It enforces the legitimate laws of the legislative and executive branches of government, but it also protects citizens against arbitrary acts by either executive or legislature. Judicial review gives the judiciary a crucial authority and judges' freedom from control by the other branches of government means that they are theoretically 'above politics'. This enables the courts and the judges to follow relatively independent courses of action within the law.

The authority of judges is generally supported by the public. The justices of the Supreme Court, for example, can be very influential (if not always trusted) and their decisions affect ordinary people's lives. Judges may, however, vary in their political inclinations from 'liberal' to 'conservative', and this may be reflected in their decisions.

## Lawyers

Americans tend to distrust lawyers although they do often need their services. This antagonism might be due to their courtroom behaviour, in some cases, to the perception that they drive up legal costs or to the large number of lawyers in society. In addition to their legal roles, they are very visible in business, politics and public life. It is estimated that one in 440 adult Americans is a lawyer and in Washington, DC the ratio is one in sixty-four.

Members of the legal profession, known as 'attorneys-at-law', 'counsellors' or simply 'lawyers', exercise broad functions, although some may specialize in one branch of the law. They give legal assistance such as the drafting of contracts, trusts or wills, settle conflicts outside court and also present criminal and civil cases in court.

Most lawyers today will have obtained a law degree from the law school of a university. The value of the degree varies greatly with the status of the school, although the best (such as Harvard and Yale) are world-famous. The degree gives the lawyer a general grounding in American law through academic lectures and practical casework. But lawyers also have to know the law of the state in which they will eventually practise and must pass the relevant state bar examination.

Lawyers may work for federal and state government or in industry and commerce, but the majority are in private practice and cater for individual and corporate clients. Some work on their own and serve a range of clients, however most lawyers practise in firms. Half work in two-partner firms consisting of an office attorney and a trial lawyer, who perform different functions. The other half work in bigger firms, which have a number of lawyers and may have offices worldwide. The three categories of lawyers in big firms are senior partners and junior partners, who receive a share of the profits, and associates, who are paid a fixed salary.

The lawyer's income is frequently a high one in the medium-to-big firms and is, on average, one of the highest in the country. The top students of the best law schools are normally able to join a prestigious law firm at a good salary and may quickly proceed to a partnership.

The financing of a law firm, in addition to ordinary commercial fees, may include other features. The contingency fee (payment upon results in personal-injury cases) can be charged at rates which may reach over 50 per cent of the damages awarded. But pro-bono legal help without fees may be provided for those who cannot afford to pay for legal services, and firms may participate in state and federal legal aid programmes for the poor. The provision of legal aid is an important and expensive federal programme, particularly since fees for legal services are generally very high. The public also seem to think that lawyers are overly concerned with money and that they drive up costs and their fees.

Lawyers have organized themselves at national and state levels into bar associations, which supervise the profession, protect professional interests and discipline their members. The American Bar Association (ABA) was created nationally in 1878. But only about half of all lawyers are ABA members. Most states require that lawyers must be members of the state bar association, which is affiliated to the ABA, in order to practise law in a state.

The ABA is a conservative organization and is often criticized. But its lobbying has improved the status of lawyers. It has fought for improvements in the law, legal education and the legal system. It also serves as a source of legal information to the public. The expert opinion and special status of the ABA are influential in the nomination of judges and in proposing changes in criminal and civil law.

# Crime and punishment

## *Crime*

Popular images, official statistics and personal experience surveys suggest that the USA has a high crime rate in real terms and in comparison with other western countries. Much of this is associated with professional crime organizations, local street gangs, drug-dealing and -usage and low-level offences. Yet crime is spread unevenly across the country and among victims. Furthermore, international comparisons suggest that US crime statistics are not exceptional in all cases and that rates for some crimes are in fact lower than in other countries.

Rates of serious violent crime (homicide, rape, robbery and assault) in the USA have declined since the mid-1990s. Property crime (burglary, theft (larceny) and motor-vehicle theft) and drug-abuse violations have also decreased. The majority of persistent overall offences continue to be property crimes and a smaller proportion are violent crimes against individuals. However, firearms are used in three-quarters of all these cases. Although murders had dropped dramatically in New York City by the late 1990s under a policy of 'zero tolerance' for crime, the national American murder rate continues to be the highest among industrialized nations, with Atlanta, Miami, Dallas, Fort Worth and St Louis having above-average rates.

The incidence of all crime is much higher in some (but by no means all) cities and in certain city areas, rather than in rural locations, many offences are un-reported and only 20 per cent of reported crimes are solved and their perpetrators convicted. Yet it is estimated that some 60 per cent of all crimes are committed by only 5 per cent of the population and that the majority of these persons have a prior criminal record.

Young people between fifteen and nineteen are the most criminally inclined age group. However, their numbers are declining and increased jobs, prosperity and tough police policies in the 1990s reduced the crime statistics. In some urban areas, murder is the main cause of death among non-white males between the ages of twenty-four and forty-five and non-white people have a much higher victimization rate than white people. For example, African Americans (12 per cent of the population) disproportionately account for 35 per cent of arrests for drug possession, 55 per cent of convictions and 74 per cent of prison sentences.

The reasons for crime are notoriously arguable and varied. Some critics maintain that the police and courts are too lenient in their treatment of criminal suspects and sentencing patterns, while the police criticize the courts and defence lawyers. Others blame urban slums, social deprivation, poverty, bad schools, lack of opportunities, unemployment, lack of discipline, unstable or dysfunctional families, inadequate parenting, drugs, organized crime, teenage gangs and the availability of guns and other weapons.

## Law enforcement

Some 553,000 officers and 212,000 civilians work in law enforcement. The implementation of state law is carried out by the police and detectives in the cities and by sheriffs or marshalls and constables (deputies) in rural areas. Federal crimes are the responsibility of the Federal Bureau of Investigation (FBI), which also provides technical assistance to state and local law-enforcement agencies.

However, there is sometimes tension over jurisdiction between the FBI and local or state authorities.

Crime prevention is a difficult job for law-enforcement officials and the courts. Public demands for stronger punishment for criminals and increased rights and compensation for crime victims and their families create added pressure and expense. Other factors influence the debate, such as overcrowded prisons, accessibility of guns, uncertain civil rights and the vexed question of the death penalty. Courts and law-enforcement officers thus have difficulties in coping with the legitimate needs and demands of society and the rights of suspects.

## Rights of criminal suspects

The Constitution ideally guarantees equal justice under the law for all citizens and the individual's right to freedom and security. Various amendments and later court decisions also protect the rights of criminal suspects.

The Fourth Amendment, for example, protects citizens against unreasonable search and seizure. It is generally illegal for the police to search people's homes, persons or papers unless they have a warrant. The Supreme Court has created exceptions so that the police can in some circumstances search and act without a warrant. However, any incriminating evidence that results from an illegal police search is controversially excluded from a criminal trial.

Another rule established by the Supreme Court in Miranda (1966) extended the protection of criminal suspects. The police must read suspects their legal rights before they are arrested or questioned. These include the right to remain silent, to have an attorney present during questioning, and to consult a lawyer before making a statement. If the police proceed incorrectly, any evidence obtained from questioning cannot be used in court. This may mean that persons who are actually guilty go free because of a technicality.

Many protections for criminal suspects stem from liberal Supreme Court decisions in the 1960s. Conservatives agitate for the reversal of these rulings and other provisions which arguably overprotect suspects. They maintain that such rules hinder law enforcement and the protection of society and shift the balance of doubt towards suspects. Liberals argue that any reduction in the rights of criminal suspects may affect innocent people and leaves too much power and control in the hands of the police and the criminal-justice system.

## The death penalty

In 1972, the Supreme Court ruled in *Furman* v. *Georgia* that the death penalty for homicide and other serious crimes amounted to 'cruel and unusual punishment' (Eighth Amendment) and was unconstitutional. This decision was reversed in 1976 in *Gregg* v. *Georgia*, which ruled that the death penalty was not unconstitutional in itself if it is applied in a fair and impartial manner.

Some critics argue that the Supreme Court decided the case in a narrow legal sense and ignored the moral and ethical implications of the 'cruel and unusual' clause. For them, the use of the death penalty illustrates the gap between law and justice in American society. Some thirty-eight states have the death penalty as punishment for murder. Given the uncertain state of the law and opposition to the death penalty, there were fewer executions between 1965 and 1983. However, the number of prisoners on 'death row' rose from 1976 resulting in an increased total of 666 executions between 1976 and 2000 (particularly in southern states). Of the people executed, 55 per cent were white, 36 per cent were African American, 7 per cent were Latino and 2 per cent were Asian or Native American. The total of eighty-five inmates who were executed in 2000 was 13 per cent fewer than in 1999. In 2004, forty-five prisoners had been executed by October, with fourteen cases pending, most executions taking place in Texas. The total since 1977 was 930.

Supporters of the death penalty stress its deterrent force, its punishment role and its revenge element. A Gallup poll in May 2001 found that 65 per cent of respondents were for the death penalty and 27 per cent were against. If called upon to choose, 52 per cent would support the death penalty for murder and

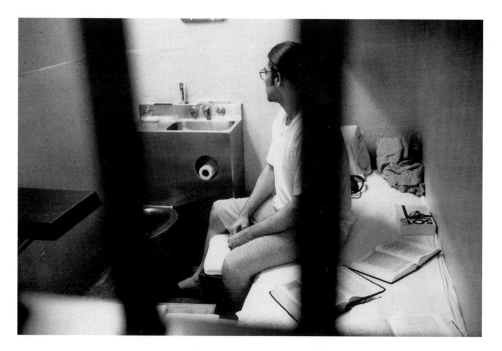

**PLATE 8.4** Prisoner on death row, Angola State Prison, Louisiana, 2000. The prisoner is held in a special wing of a prison prior to execution, in some cases for many years, awaiting the results of appeals against conviction and the death penalty.
(*Diana Walker/Time Pix/Rex Features*)

43 per cent would opt for life-imprisonment. Some 51 per cent thought that the death penalty is applied fairly and 41 per cent did not. These figures appeared to represent a decrease in support for the death penalty, possibly because of proven miscarriages of justice (discovered through DNA-testing or faulty investigations and trials). Opponents of capital punishment maintain that it is unconstitutional as a cruel and unusual punishment and does not serve as a deterrent.

But another Gallup poll in June 2004 reflected not only the uncertainty surrounding aspects of the death penalty, but also an underlying hard-line approach to punishment. About half of the respondents chose the death penalty as an appropriate punishment while just under half opted for life-imprisonment without the possibility of parole (early conditional release from prison). Significantly, when the respondents were not presented with life-imprisonment as an alternative, about seven in ten supported the death penalty. Furthermore, most Americans believed the death penalty is applied fairly, and about half said that it is not imposed often enough. A majority believed that it is not a deterrent to murder, but this perception did not greatly affect support for execution. Other opinion polls, according to PollingReport, suggest that there is still a strong support for the death penalty if no other alternatives are available and a belief that it is applied fairly, even though it is realized that some innocent people suffer. The only exceptions to the death-penalty solution appear to be those convicted people who are juveniles, mentally ill or mentally retarded. But a slight majority also feel that there should be a halt to all executions while the issue and its implications are studied in greater depth.

## *Prisons*

Although overall crime has decreased, the US has a higher percentage of its population behind bars than any other country and spends billions of dollars a year on its prisons. In 2003, there were slightly over 2 million inmates, over half of whom were convicted of violent offences. Texas, Florida and California had the most prisoners and (together with Illinois) the highest incidence of crime.

Many prisons tend to be old and do not serve as positive examples of rehabilitation. Prison policies are challenged by reformers advocating improved welfare systems, better education and drug-treatment programmes, with prevention, rather than punishment and detention, being the goals.

American administrations, in response to public concern about crime, have favoured the following:

- the death penalty,
- putting more police on the streets,
- building more prisons,
- allowing some prisons to be run by private firms,
- stressing punishment above rehabilitation,

- reducing parole,
- giving longer and tougher sentences for serious crimes and
- imposing immediate custodial sentences on criminals who repeat serious crimes ('three strikes and you're out').

The decrease in recent overall crime figures has been partly attributed to these factors, as well as to a relatively healthy economy, demographic changes (with an ageing population and declining numbers of fifteen to nineteen year olds), community policing and a policy of zero toleration of crime.

## Gun control

The Second Amendment guarantees to every citizen the right to bear arms: 'the right of the people to keep and bear arms shall not be infringed'. But its wording is ambiguous and refers to a time when the British tried to prevent colonists from raising an armed militia. Today, it is difficult to pass strong gun-control legislation, despite the fact that handguns are used in murders, rapes, robberies and assaults and the fact that there have been several mass and serial killings in recent years, including attacks in schools and shopping centres. Some 67 per cent of Americans own 200 million firearms of varying types, and 40 per cent have a gun in their home.

The National Rifle Association (NRA) and other lobbies against gun control (such as militia groups) vigorously oppose restrictions on the sale and use of firearms as a violation of the Constitution. Gallup and other polls in 2000 showed that 85 per cent of Americans wanted stricter or the same gun-control laws to curb crime. But 62 per cent opposed a complete ban on handguns and 36 per cent supported a ban. Some 45 per cent felt that protection of their persons and their homes is the main incentive behind gun-ownership although 51 per cent thought that this makes the home a more dangerous place to be.

Gun-control laws were in fact passed by Congress in 1993 and 1994. These included:

- the imposition of a five-day waiting period for the purchase of handguns to permit checks into the buyer's background,
- registration of all handguns,
- a ban on the sale of semi-automatic assault weapons,
- stronger penalties for gun offences and
- tighter licensing rules for gun-dealers.

However, these new laws were not excessively stringent, were for a trial period which has now ended (2004), could be circumvented, could be variously applied in different states and did not seriously challenge the 'right-to-guns' culture.

### Self-defence

The issue of gun control is connected to questions of self-defence, particularly at a time when some victim surveys suggest that 57 per cent of Americans have personally suffered from crime in one form or another and to greater and lesser extents. This finding is at variance with other polls which suggest a low personal experience of crime. But, historically, people's right to defend themselves, their families and their property has been a basic (and sometimes necessary) tradition in American life.

Despite the decline in the crime figures, there is still a lack of public confidence in the ability of the courts and legislators to cope with crime or to adequately and effectively protect individual citizens. People consequently feel that they must safeguard themselves in the face of criminals determined to commit criminal acts. Security has become a priority for many individuals, who devise ways to protect themselves and their homes from attacks, violence and burglaries. Some individuals, known as vigilantes, may deliberately break the law in order to defend themselves and receive public support and sympathy in many cases.

## Attitudes to the legal system

A Gallup poll in February 2004 in the run-up to the presidential election reported that, overall, crime did not appear as one of the top fourteen problems affecting the USA, although gun-control policy came in at number 12. Such findings were also echoed in other polls in 2004 marking a change from the 1980s and early 1990s when crime, violence and drug-usage had consistently appeared as leading worries and when overall crime figures were high.

Nevertheless, in an October 2003 Gallup poll, 60 per cent of respondents felt that there was more crime in the US than a year previously (25 per cent thought there was less). Some 17 per cent thought that the problem of crime was extremely serious, 37 per cent as very serious and 40 per cent as moderately serious. In terms of local-area crime, 33 per cent thought that it was moderately serious, 35 per cent as not too serious and 21 per cent not serious at all. When asked whether respondents were afraid to walk alone at night in their local area, 36 per cent replied 'Yes' and 65 per cent said 'No'. These findings indicate a difference between perceptions of national crime and personal experience in local neighbourhoods. Indeed, an ABC News poll in 2000 found that 82 per cent of respondents formed their opinion on national crime from news or media reporting rather than their own experience.

However, polls reveal that many Americans believe that crime and violence might directly affect their own lives and feel threatened by crime. They and their families feel safer at home and when walking in the neighbourhood after dark rather than at school or at a shopping mall at night. But fear of crime is probably greater than its actuality and a Pew Research Center poll in 2000 found that personal experience of theft and assault was very low.

Nevertheless, this research also found that Americans wish for strong responses to crime, with many feeling that the criminal-justice system was not tough enough. Crime could be combatted by having more job and community programmes for young people (63 per cent), longer jail sentences for those convicted of violent crimes (49 per cent), restrictions on the amount of violence shown on television and films (48 per cent), more police on the streets (46 per cent) and stricter gun-control laws (41 per cent).

Other polls showed large majorities had respect for and confidence in the police at local and state levels. On the other hand, a Harris poll in 2004 found that respondents had only a 10 per cent amount of great confidence/trust in law firms and (perhaps surprisingly) 29 per cent in the US Supreme Court. The criminal-justice system as a whole achieved only 10 per cent support in a 2003 CNN/*USA Today*/Gallup poll.

Attitudes to the criminal-justice system vary between liberals and conservatives. Conservatives are strong on law and order, feel that the rights of criminal suspects and defendants should be restricted, favour strong criminal penalties, harsh punishment and the death penalty and seek to overturn liberal legislation. Liberals are suspicious of the police and law-enforcement agencies, are against what they see as tough criminal legislation and penalties and favour extended civil rights for individuals.

Some critics argue that Americans often have irrational or contradictory attitudes to crime and violence and create a self-perpetuating image that the USA is a crime-ridden society. Such attitudes allegedly differ from those in other western countries. They suggest a belief that American crime is actually more violent and lawless than anywhere else. Many professionals and academics in the USA indeed seem to agree that America's fundamental problem is the cult of violence itself and feel that one way to reduce this is to restrict access to guns.

## Exercises

Explain and examine the significance of the following names and terms.

| | | |
|---|---|---|
| legalism | precedent | impeachment |
| common law | jurisdiction | civil law |
| judicial review | constitutionalism | US District Courts |
| legal aid | plea-bargaining | State Supreme Court |
| statutory law | ABA | adversary system |

continued

judiciary            Bill of Rights          contingency fees
Miranda              rights culture          pro-bono
litigation           commerce clause         jury

Write short essays on the following questions.

1.  Why is law such an important part of American life?

2.  Critically discuss the historical evolution of American law and the legal system.

3.  Examine the arguments for and against the death penalty and gun control.

4.  Attempt to explain attitudes to crime in the USA by analysing the polls in the text.

## Further reading

Abadinsky, H. (1995) *Law and Justice: An Introduction to the American Legal System* Chicago, Ill.: Nelson-Hall.

American Bar Association (latest edition) *Law and the Courts: a handbook of courtroom procedures* Chicago, Ill.: ABA Press.

Apple, J. G. and R. P. Deyling (1995) *A Primer on the Civil-Law System* Washington, DC: Federal Judicial Center.

Biskupic, J. and E. Witt (1997) *Guide to the US Supreme Court* Washington, DC: Congressional Quarterly Press.

Carp, R. A. and R. Stidham (1998) *Judicial Process in America* Washington, DC: Congressional Quarterly Press.

Fine, T. M. (1997) *American Legal Systems: a resource and reference guide* Cincinatti, Ohio: Anderson.

Stumpf, H. P. and J. H. Culver (1992) *The Politics of State Courts* New York: Longman Press.

Tushnet, M. V. (1999) *Taking the Constitution Away from the Courts* Princeton, NJ: Princeton University Press.

## Web site

Links to judicial branch/courts/crime statistics/civil rights: <http://usinfo.state.gov/usa/infousa>

# Chapter 9

# The economy

- Economic history
- American economic liberalism: theory and practice
- Social class and economic inequality
- The contemporary economy
- Industry and manufacturing
- Service industries
- Agriculture, forestry and fisheries
- Financial and industrial institutions
- Attitudes to the economic system
- *Exercises*
- *Further reading*
- *Web sites*

Historically, the US economy has been characterized by technological change and periods of recession, adaptation and steady (often rapid) growth. Agriculture was the main activity from colonial times to the mid-nineteenth century. It then quickly became more mechanized and efficient and used fewer workers. Industrial and manufacturing output had also increased greatly from the mid-nineteenth century. Such growth led to the USA becoming the world's richest country and its leading industrial nation by the early twentieth century.

Between 1945 and 1970, the USA achieved a large degree of self-sufficiency and an economic dominance, which resulted in American influence over the world economy. Since the 1970s, major changes have been the growth of service industries, a decline in traditional manufacturing industry, a relative weakening in the USA's position as other countries became more competitive and instability in some sectors such as trade and budget deficits. After 1970, globalization (interdependence of world trade and business) affected the US economy as it adapted to the changing order. Following a recession in the early 1990s, the economy grew strongly with increased output, low inflation and a drop in unemployment. But it slowed down again in 2000–1 and, although improving by 2004, it still experienced some problems.

## Economic history

US economic expansion from the nineteenth century can be explained by the country's size, substantial natural resources, commercial structures, population growth, the characteristics of its people, and the basic ideological principles that support its economic activity.

Prior to the colonial period, the indigenous Native-American inhabitants of North America had varied economies, ranging from nomadic food-gathering, fishing and hunting to settled agricultural communities. A similar basic economy was adopted by colonial Americans, who later developed more sophisticated agricultural systems based on small farms.

British settlers in the seventeenth century were often employed by British companies that had been granted trading charters by the English Crown, like the Virginia Company which established Jamestown in 1607. The colonies provided Britain with raw materials but were not supposed to compete in manufacturing exports with the mother country. This relationship collapsed when Britain tried to impose taxation and trade restrictions. After the War for Independence

(1776–83), the USA developed its own economic policies and markets. A greater variety of goods was produced by the eighteenth century as Americans expanded agriculture, farmed the prairies, increased their commercial interests and exported more products.

A belief in possibilities and personal advancement encouraged pragmatism, hard work and individual initiative. These qualities have been linked to religion (the Protestant work ethic) and the pioneer spirit of early settlers, whose survival lay in their own ingenuity. Many Americans today continue these values: retrain if unemployment occurs, create new jobs or businesses and move to fresh opportunities.

The USA in 1800 was still an agricultural society. Some 95 per cent of the people lived in rural areas and the economy was based largely on self-sufficiency. But nineteenth-century growth combined significant agricultural advances with expanding industrial and manufacturing bases. These were aided by government financial support and protectionism as well as by a transport revolution which established railway, canal and road infrastructures.

Agricultural productivity increased as small farmers made use of the trans-portation system, specialized in selected crops or animals, sold their products to a wider internal market and developed their export potential. But this growth led to overproduction and reduced prices. By the start of the twentieth century farmers were having difficulties.

Economic progress in the nineteenth century was also affected by the Civil War (1861–5) when twenty-three states of the industrializing north were opposed by eleven southern agricultural states on the issues of slavery and secession. A northern victory led to an emphasis on the nation's developing industrial base with great advances in the production of basic manufactured goods.

Between the Civil War and the First World War (1914–18), the USA rapidly industrialized and became an increasingly urban and (later) suburban country. Expansion was based on natural resources, iron production, and steam and electrical power. It was later helped by such technical advances and inventions as the internal combustion engine, the telegraph and telephone, radio, typewriters, assembly-line production and interchangeable-parts technology. Economies of scale in production and distribution led to the growth of large manufacturing units, and the export of manufactured goods now became more important than that of raw materials.

Economic activity was based on a commercial life free from restrictions. Business operated for profit in a 'market economy' where independent buyers and sellers determined the need for and price of goods. Few restrictions (like government intervention) were historically placed on business, and people were largely able to pursue their own economic interests. But this led to an unregulated capitalism as big business and the profit motive became central features of American life. The industrial progress was also accompanied by periodic slumps, unemployment and harsh job and living conditions for the expanding population (including African Americans from the south and European immigrants between 1890 and 1910).

The expanding economy resulted in the development of new products and the creation of corporations (large business companies) in most economic sectors. These based their production and competition policies on marketing, advertising, advanced technology, cheap products, rationalization of the work process, efficient management organization and good service. The growth of corporations enabled the USA to export many types of manufactured items abroad and consumer goods were spread throughout the domestic American market.

Larger corporations were formed through mergers and takeovers, leading to giant trusts and monopolies, which controlled competition. Trusts were identified with owners like Rockefeller in oil and Carnegie in steel, whose economic and political power influenced the whole economy. It was increasingly felt that government should regulate the trusts and monopolies, which were seen as anti-competitive.

Some anti-trust legislation (the 1890 Sherman Anti-Trust Law) had already been passed. But the trusts still controlled many large areas of production. President Theodore Roosevelt (1901–8) tried to regulate them by preventing restrictive deals between companies on products, prices, output levels and market shares, by limiting mergers that minimized competition and by improving employment conditions (such as an eight-hour working day). President Woodrow Wilson (1913–20) also attempted to check commercial markets. He passed a new anti-trust law, reduced protective tariffs against foreign competition and introduced reforms in agricultural and labour areas.

However, despite reforms, large corporations still had great power and the 1920s, 'the Roaring Twenties', was a period of instability and hardship for many people. Although low taxes promoted a rise in living standards, too much money was circulating in the economy and the consumption of services and goods increased. There was overproduction by factories and farms; overprotection of business against foreign competition through tariff barriers and financial speculation. The economy collapsed in October 1929 with the Wall Street Crash in the stock market. This marked the beginning of the worst economic depression in American history (the Great Depression).

Demands were made for more government regulation of business activity and for help to those who were suffering socially and economically. President Franklin D. Roosevelt (1933–45) argued that the depression was due to faults in the capitalist economy, tried to remedy the situation with his New Deal and was the first President to substantially intervene in the economy. New regulatory powers over the stock market were initiated by a Securities and Exchange Commission (SEC) and other commissions were created to supervise public utilities such as electricity. The unemployed were given jobs in public-works projects and financial help was granted to farmers who were suffering badly. A Social Security Act (1935) was the first major federal legislation to provide security against unemployment, job-related accidents and old age. These measures aimed to stabilize the economy, regulate commercial institutions, create internal demand for American products and prevent social and economic hardship.

The New Deal did not solve all social and economic problems. Consequently, governments since the 1930s have intervened to varying degrees in the economy by legislation, by using regulatory powers to influence commercial life or by controlled purchases from the private marketplace. But US governments are not generally opposed to business and have themselves invested in private sectors such as research, aerospace, development and defence. They aided economic growth in the nineteenth century, protected US industry, farmers and manufacturers against foreign competition by erecting tariff barriers, used public money to encourage private business and gave land to private interests to develop transport systems. The economy grew and competed successfully with European countries. Despite their embrace of free trade, US governments not only still protect the national economy internationally but also have problems in entering some overseas markets because of foreign trade barriers.

The economy grew after the Second World War (1939–45) and by the 1950s had achieved global dominance. Large corporations, such as Exxon, Wal-Mart, General Electric, Ford and General Motors, continue to influence American business. Some are multinational organizations owned by financial groups (rather than individuals) with diversified interests and plants worldwide, but there are many smaller corporations and businesses (three quarters of the corporate market) which create most jobs and can be very successful and influential.

Since the mid-twentieth century the US economy has experienced periods of high inflation, high unemployment, large trade gaps, government budget deficits, international competition and recessionary forces. However, it grew dramatically from 1994 with low inflation, low unemployment, stable prices, government budget surpluses, job creation and a vibrant stock market, before suffering a slowdown in the early 2000s. It recovered somewhat by 2004, but there are still weaknesses in areas such as unemployment, job creation, stock-market volatility, inadequate exports, excessive imports and variable GDP (Gross Domestic Product) growth.

The USA faces change and challenge in the twenty-first century because of varying economic cycles, recessionary threats, international competition and technological advances in computing, telecommunications and finance. It faces the risks and advantages of globalization, the growing economic strength of western Europe and potentially strong competitive economies in Asia (particularly China), Latin America and Africa.

**PLATE 9.1** General Electric turbine factory, Schenectady, NY. General Electric is one of the giant corporations in the US economy, producing electrical products and aircraft engines. It has been historically associated with media developments, such as television, and owns the National Broadcasting Company (NBC).

(*Ted Russell/Time Pix/Rex Features*)

# American economic liberalism: theory and practice

The founders of the USA stressed individual economic freedom. They were influenced by philosophers such as Adam Smith and felt that consumers and producers should pursue their own self-interest and profit-making activities in a market economy. The market (not central government) decides what to produce and what prices to charge for goods on the basis of demand and value. Ideally, greater competition and trade would result, society would benefit, the economy could produce what was needed, consumers could buy products at competitive prices and market forces would control the production and efficient distribution of goods.

Many areas of the economy, such as industry, health care, airlines, telephone systems, energy supplies and railways, are therefore in private rather than public or state ownership and US governments have historically been confined to a regulatory role in the economy. However, since the 1930s they have embraced more intervention by employing both anti-monopoly and deregulation measures (removal of restrictions to create freer markets) to promote competition in services and prices. They have broken up or deregulated airlines, railroads, trucking companies, telephone and telegraph systems, utilities and postal services. On the other hand, an attempt in 1998 by the Justice Department to split the software company Microsoft into two parts because of its alleged monopolistic behaviour was dismissed in 2001 by the US Court of Appeals.

Governments (particularly Democratic) and official bodies now intervene more actively in business. They exert influence through monetary and fiscal policy, such as interest rates (by the Federal Reserve System), and through subsidies and controls on prices, and as purchasers of goods and equipment, especially in the defence and aerospace industries. Regulation also includes safety standards for manufactured goods, labour, welfare and equal-employment reform, environmental protection, training schemes and pro-union legislation and improvements in working conditions (such as increases in the national minimum wage with the last rise in 1997 to $5.15 an hour). Such federal and state restrictions curb freedom of operation for employers and show the more intrusive role of contemporary government.

Economic restrictions are fiercely debated. Conservatives and corporations argue that there is too much regulation, bureaucracy and interference. Liberals generally support an interventionist role in economic matters. Americans have a distrust of 'big government', disagree about the appropriate role of government in the economy and are sceptical about the ability of government to solve many economic and social problems. But they also dislike the near-monopolistic nature of some 'big business', which may dominate consumer choice and give bad service and products. A Harris poll in January 2004 showed that only 12 per cent of respondents had a great deal of confidence in big business and major companies.

The USA therefore does not have an absolute 'free market' system. But Americans generally support free enterprise, individual initiative and the ability of a competitive market to deliver goods, services and resources nationwide.

Not all individuals can pursue economic success because of their differing circumstances and the influence of factors such as corporate power. A belief in individualism does not imply automatic success, although it is generally felt that achievement and material prosperity *may* result from personal hard work. There does not seem to be much envy directed at those who *do* succeed and few complain about 'the system' if they fail. There are no widespread pressures for alternative economic models. Debates are therefore concerned largely with how much government intervention and regulation and how much unrestricted corporate power there should be in the private enterprise system.

## Social class and economic inequality

The USA is often portrayed, and sees itself, as a classless and egalitarian society. But there have always been social and economic inequalities between Americans. These can constitute a class model divided into working, middle and upper classes based on job status, income, capital and birth. Nineteenth-century indus-trialization increased class and wealth gaps between industrialists, manufacturers, financiers and landowners on the one hand and workers on the other. It was argued that class divisions were a natural result of the freedom of competition.

In the twentieth century, workers were increasingly placed either in the white-collar service sector or the industrial blue-collar sector. It was felt that these groups fell outside European notions of the 'working class' and should more appropriately be seen as 'lower middle class'. However, many Americans were proud to see themselves as working class.

A mass-consumption society, a reduced manufacturing base and a rise in living standards have led to a decline in blue-collar workers, an increase in service-sector white-collar employees and a growth in professional and executive grades. Class distinctions have become less rigid, a middle-class ideology is now influential and a majority of Americans might consider themselves as middle class in terms of income and lifestyle. There is also a minority who have historically been classified as poor working class. Outside these groups are those people now described as an unemployable, alienated and often welfare-dependent under-class.

The USA is a very wealthy country and provides most of its people with one of the world's highest living standards. Median household income was $42,400 in 2003 (half of households received above this figure and half received less). But this figure represented a decline from previous years. The median annual earnings of full-time wage and salary workers was $31,720 in 2003. But median earnings of African Americans, Asians and Latinos trailed behind those of white workers, resulting in the former's relative income inequality.

Some 1 per cent of US households own 30.4 per cent of the nation's wealth, compared with 36.8 per cent for the next highest 9 per cent and 32.8 per cent for the remaining 90 per cent. The gap between rich and poor in the US is considerable. This inequality of income and wealth was seen in 2004 when 35.8 million Americans (12.5 per cent of the population) lived below the poverty lines of $18,660 for a family of four and $9,573 for a single person. This total has increased since 2002 and disproportionally features the African-American, Latino and Asian poor.

Arguably, such economic inequality is due to the actual increase in relative poverty, low wages for average female workers, some ethnic groups and the unskilled/semi-skilled, the existence of an under-class, the decline of trade unions and low tax rates for the wealthy. Tax cuts (which arguably benefit the affluent more than the poor), reduced welfare payments and an economic downturn may result in a society even more divided between the very rich and the very poor.

# The contemporary economy

## Taxation and federal budgets

Most of the US government's income (used for public spending) comes from income tax paid by individuals and social-security contributions paid by firms and workers. Corporate taxes (paid by companies on profits) and excise duties are a relatively small part of total federal receipts.

Americans pay less federal (or national) income tax than people in other western countries, but they also have to pay property tax, sales tax and state income tax, in addition to medical and dental costs. Tax increases to pay for government spending arouse opposition, especially from the middle class, and may determine election results. But tax cuts (as in 2001 and 2003 by the Bush administration) can affect provision of public services.

The median family with one income pays about 38 per cent of that income in various forms of tax. Those with higher incomes pay proportionally more taxes. The amount of tax Americans actually pay depends on tax cuts, on their ability to cope with complex tax forms and on their claims on a range of deductions, such as the interest on home mortgages (loans).

High government borrowing and spending in the 1980s and early 1990s resulted in large federal budget deficits (the gap between government income and expenditure). Budget deficits are seen as a sign of whether a government is out of control. Attempts to cut the deficit succeeded in the late 1990s and created budget surpluses. But surpluses began to fall in 2001 and the deficit grew again from the early 2000s.

## *Features of the contemporary economy*

The USA is the world's biggest economic power in terms of its GDP. This comprises the goods, services, capital and income which the country produces and in 2003 was $10.98 trillion, with a per capita GDP of $37,800. Some 2 per cent of GDP arises from agriculture, forestry and fishing, 18 per cent from industry and some 80 per cent from the service industries.

The GDP shows that the USA has a diversified economy. Its wealth reflects its abundant natural resources (coal, oil, gas, timber, hydroelectricity and minerals), agricultural output, industrial production and service-sector income. The USA produces 25 per cent of the world's agricultural products and manufactured goods (such as machinery, automotive components and vehicles, aircraft, chemicals and high-technology hardware). Traditional manufacturing industries have experienced setbacks and agriculture is under threat, while service sectors have expanded.

The USA is the world's biggest importer and exporter. This situation and the size of its economy mean that the USA is a crucial factor in global trade and business. But the US economy does not dominate as it did after the Second World War because of recurrent weaknesses and because the economies of other competing countries have grown strongly.

Internationally, the USA's balance of trade with other countries has been in deficit (importing more goods than it has exported) since 1980. In 2003, for example, exports amounted to $714.5 billion while imports were $1.26 trillion. These imports are in traditionally strong American areas such as petroleum, food and drink, machinery, iron and steel and consumer goods like television sets, cameras and computers which have suffered because of foreign competition. However, the deficit is helped to some extent by invisible exports such as financial services.

Globalization and international competition have forced the USA to become more interdependent with the economies of other countries and to reduce its protectionism. American investment capital and assets are an important element in the Canadian, Latin-American, European and Asian economies. But there is also considerable foreign investment and asset-holding in the US domestic economy.

US governments and corporations aim at a cooperative and stable international trading environment. The USA's main export partners are Canada, Mexico, Japan and Britain, while it imports primarily from Canada, Mexico, China, Japan and Germany. The USA finalized the GATT (General Agreement on Tariffs and Trade) talks in 1994, which aimed to promote freer and less protectionist world trade. US attempts to balance world trading-blocs led to the creation of the North American Free Trade Area (NAFTA) in 1994 with Canada and Mexico. This was enlarged to thirty-four countries in 2001 including Latin America and covering 800 million people. The USA is also concerned to stabilize its relationships with the European Union, China, Japan and the Pacific Rim countries, as well as improving the economies of Third World countries.

The US economy experienced difficulties from the 1970s until the early 1990s due partly to international factors (such as recession and competition) and partly to domestic conditions. US prices and costs (particularly in manufacturing) did not equal those of other competing countries, growth rates varied considerably, inflation (increase in the average level of consumer prices) fluctuated and unemployment grew. It was argued that the poor performance of the US economy was due to an emphasis on traditional manufacturing industry. The country had not adapted to a 'post-industrial age', in which high-technology and service industries were now a dominant part of GDP.

Critics maintained that the USA needed to modernize its factories, improve its products, reduce costs and prices, invest in services, high-technology industries and in specialist training, and that the government should promote industrial policies. Meanwhile, Republicans wanted lower taxes and less regulation of the economy. As in most countries, the relationship of industry and manufacturing to the service sector remains problematic.

The economy recovered and grew from 1994. Industry was restructured and productivity increased as a result of reductions in the workforce, advanced technology, freer trade and ruthless corporate management. Stable interest rates encouraged companies to invest and eased loan burdens. Unemployment and inflation fell. Smaller companies survived and 10 million new jobs were created. Prices and wages stabilized, productivity and growth improved, the dollar was strong and many people prospered in the mid- to late 1990s. However, much of

**TABLE 9.1** US inflation rate, 1982–2003.

| Year | % | Year | % |
|------|-----|------|-----|
| 1982 | 3.8 | 1993 | 2.7 |
| 1983 | 4.0 | 1994 | 2.7 |
| 1984 | 4.0 | 1995 | 2.5 |
| 1985 | 3.8 | 1996 | 3.3 |
| 1986 | 1.1 | 1997 | 1.7 |
| 1987 | 4.4 | 1998 | 1.6 |
| 1988 | 4.4 | 1999 | 2.7 |
| 1989 | 4.7 | 2000 | 3.4 |
| 1990 | 6.1 | 2001 | 1.6 |
| 1991 | 3.1 | 2002 | 2.4 |
| 1992 | 2.9 | 2003 | 1.2 |

*Source: US Bureau of Labor Statistics, 2004*

the economic growth was in the service sector, which, in some areas, often has low-paid, unskilled or semi-skilled and part-time jobs.

The early 2000s saw a slowdown as the USA headed for recession with growth and manufacturing weak and unemployment and inflation increasing. Consumer confidence slumped and the Federal Reserve in 2000–1 reduced interest rates to rectify the downturn. Moderate recovery took place in 2002 with the GDP growth rate rising to 2.4 per cent, although the stock market declined sharply, fuelled in part by dubious accounting practices in some major corporations. In 2003, growth in output and productivity, the recovery of the stock market and GDP growth at 3.1 per cent were promising signs, as was an inflation rate of 1.2 per cent. But in early 2004 job creation remained weak, jobs had been lost, interest rates rose and strong economic expansion was in doubt. Unemployment slowly continued to decline throughout October 2004, while growth fluctuated and inflation grew to 2.7 per cent. Long-term problems include inadequate investment in the economic infrastructure, sizeable trade and budget deficits and the stagnation or decline of family and individual incomes in the lower economic groups. Immediate problems affecting the economy in 2004 were high oil prices, a weak dollar, uncertainty on the stock exchange and rising interest rates.

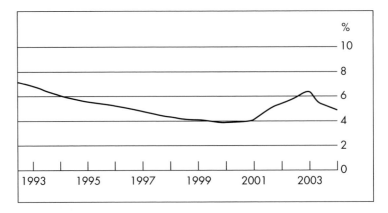

**FIGURE 9.1** US unemployment rate, 1992–2004.
*Source*: adapted from US Bureau of Labor Statistics, 2004

## The workforce

The workforce of 142 million (2003) is divided by occupation into managerial, professional and technical (31 per cent), sales and office (28.9 per cent), services (13.6 per cent), manufacturing, extraction, transportation and crafts (24.1 per cent) and farming, forestry and fishing (2.4 per cent). It has mobility and flexibility and is largely white collar. Not all workers gained from economic growth in the 1990s. The unemployment rate was 6.2 per cent in 2003 and incomes remained stagnant in 2004. The growth of technology has, for some critics, led to a 'two-tier labour market' in which those at the bottom lack the education and the professional and technical skills of those at the top. The former do not receive pay rises, health-insurance coverage and other benefits comparable to the latter. Since 1975, most of the gains in household income have been achieved by the top 20 per cent of households. Many less-skilled male workers in particular have experienced weak wage growth, job insecurity and falling living standards.

However, the economic impact of women (46 per cent of the workforce) as employees and employers has improved. More women now work and earn more. While the proportion of men with jobs has fallen, that of working women has risen. Male average earnings have fallen while those of women have grown. Although women's wages gained on men's for the first time in the 1980s, women's earnings as a percentage of men's earnings are still only 73 per cent.

Some 14 per cent of employed women work in executive, administrative and managerial positions (compared to 15 per cent of men), 18 per cent in a professional specialty (compared to 13.6 per cent of men), 40 per cent in technical, sales and administrative support (compared to 19.7 per cent of men), 17.4 per cent in service occupations (compared to 9.9 per cent of men), 2.1 per cent in production, craft and repair (compared to 18.6 per cent of men), 7.1 per cent as operators and labourers (compared to 19.3 per cent of men), and 1.1 per cent in farming, forestry and fishing (compared to 3.8 per cent of men).

Well-educated women have received the highest rewards, and the earnings of the top 5 per cent of working women have risen. Unskilled women have suffered, but less than unskilled men. This is because low-skilled men and women have different jobs, and because women work more often in the service sector.

The biggest gains have been for well-educated high-income women (particularly those married to high-income husbands) who continue working after marriage. However, fewer wives of lower-skilled men have joined the workforce and the wages of lower-skilled working wives have risen more slowly than those of better-educated women. Family income has thus risen at top levels and fallen at the bottom.

There has also been an increase in women business-owners. Their businesses are a growing and influential part of the corporate economy and are often small, home-operated and in the service or retail sector. But women-owned businesses in the manufacturing or construction sectors are growing and more women are attending business schools.

## Industry and manufacturing

Historically, manufacturing and industrial production has been a crucial factor in the US economy. Today, the sector is a leading global power, highly diversified and technologically advanced. It amounts to 18 per cent of US GDP. The most important areas are the manufacture of heavy transport and automotive

**PLATE 9.2** Hard-disk-drive manufacturing assembly, representative of the growth in high-technology industries in the USA.
(*Mark & Audrey Gibson/Rex Features*)

equipment (vehicles, aircraft and aerospace components), non-electrical goods, electrical machinery, food products, chemicals, steel, consumer goods, mining, oil, telecommunications, electronics and high-technology hardware.

The USA's traditional industrial and manufacturing heartland is the mid-west region of the Great Lakes, southern Michigan, northern Ohio and Pennsylvania around Pittsburgh. Growth and production here has fluctuated, declined in some areas or switched to high-technology industry, and other industrial regions have grown in the north-east, north-west and south-west (California). These specialize in high-technology and computer manufactures. Other fast-growing industrial regions are the south-east and Texas, where steel, chemical and high-technology industries have developed.

This industrial and manufacturing base is represented by corporations, such as General Motors (Detroit) and Ford (Michigan) in vehicles, Exxon (New York) in oil-refining, IBM (International Business Machines) (New York) in computers and General Electric (Connecticut) in electronics.

The industrial and manufacturing production growth rate has fluctuated in the 2000s and had a minus rate (–1 per cent) in 2003, but the USA is still the world's leading maker of industrial goods, and 14.5 million Americans are employed in manufacturing, although the number of blue-collar workers continues to decline.

# Service industries

Service industries have grown faster than other sectors since the 1950s and are now the most important economic sector, amounting to 80 per cent of GDP. This process is echoed in other industrialized countries and has encouraged discussion about 'post-industrial' societies.

Service industries vary in size from small firms to large corporations. They have developed nationwide, but particularly in the north-east. They include government services, business and health services, banking, finance consultancy, hotels, restaurants, leisure activities, trade, personal services and communications. Although more people are now employed in the service sector, many of them are in unskilled or semi-skilled and part-time positions and much of the sector tends to be manager-intensive rather than labour-intensive.

It is argued that the service sector is financed by and dependent upon the wealth and profits generated by technical advances in agriculture and manu-facturing. The open question perhaps is whether the service sector can sustain itself and grow at a time when the industrial sector may decline, or whether complementary and balancing sectors will develop.

# Agriculture, forestry and fisheries

Although US agriculture, forestry and fisheries have a large productivity, they contribute only some 2 per cent to the GDP.

## *Agriculture*

About 47 per cent of the US land area is farmland and is devoted to crops and livestock. The mid-west is an important agricultural region in the country, with corn (maize) and wheat as its main crops and largescale livestock and dairy farming in the upper mid-west states.

The south is a centre of traditional crops, like tobacco (the south-east and Kentucky) and corn and cotton (the south and south-west). Its economy has now diversified and expanded, so that Texas and Florida are the USA's main providers of cattle, sheep, cotton and rice. The west is an important region for cattle and wheat-farming in the Great Plains, fruit and vineyards in the Pacific states and livestock herds in the south-western and Rocky Mountain states.

The USA is the world's largest food producer and exporter and is largely self-sufficient in farm produce, although there are some imports. In 2002 only 6.2 million people lived on the 2.2 million farms and employment was about 2.5 per cent of the national workforce. Small subsistence farms have decreased, farm sizes have increased (agri-businesses) and labour has been reduced as competition, mechanization, technological advances and specialized farms have increased. High productivity has also resulted in surpluses and reduced prices.

Agricultural exports declined in the 1980s as other world markets expanded. Farmers had difficulties because of import restrictions by foreign countries and high dollar values. But free-trade GATT and World Trade Organisation (WTO) agreements on reduced tariff barriers have helped to stabilize the world position of American agriculture.

## Forestry

Forests cover a third of the USA, mostly in the west but also in the south and the north. About 80 per cent of the forests comprise softwoods and 20 per cent hardwoods; two-thirds produce wood items and timber commercially. Some 70 per cent of forests are privately owned, the federal government owns 20 per cent and state or local government supervises the rest. In recent years, the environmental aspect of forestry has grown, with an emphasis on ecosystem management and increased recreational and wildlife uses of the public forests.

## Fisheries

The USA ranked fifth in 2001 among world fishing nations in terms of its total catch of fish. Fishing fleets operate from ports on the Atlantic, the Pacific and the Gulf of Mexico, as well as on the Great Lakes. Alaska is the leading state and Louisiana has a large catch (chiefly shellfish), as do Texas and California. Massachusetts and Maine, important fishing centres since the colonial era, are major players in the fisheries industry. Their traditional fishing grounds (shared with the Atlantic provinces of Canada) are in danger of depletion.

## Environmental issues

Due to vehicle, industrial and domestic burning of fossil fuels, the USA is the world's largest producer of carbon dioxide. Air pollution results from this abuse, as does acid rain in the USA and Canada. Widespread water pollution is caused not only by the run-off of agricultural pesticides and fertilizers, but also from industrial waste. There are limited natural fresh-water resources in much of the western part of the country and a creeping desertification process has ensued. Despite signing some, but by no means all (for example, the Kyoto Climate Change Protocol), international environmental agreements, critics argue that the USA has not demonstrated a willingness to tackle domestic and international environmental concerns. Some public-opinion polls also suggest that the environment is not a prime concern for many Americans, despite a 2004 Gallup poll placing it in ninth place out of fourteen concerns.

# Financial and industrial institutions

American economic development, unlike that of other countries, was not accompanied by the creation of national financial institutions. Governments avoided centralizing the economic system until the twentieth century, and most financial and industrial institutions operated as private and local concerns.

## *Corporations and entrepreneurs*

The corporations of the nineteenth and early twentieth centuries owned by individuals like Henry Ford (automobiles), John D. Rockefeller (oil) and Andrew Carnegie (steel), and smaller corporations under personal or family proprietors, have decreased. Many businesses today tend to be owned by financial conglomerates or multinational companies, which invest in company shares for profit.

The actual running of the businesses is often done by professional accountants, executives or managers who may own only a small percentage of the corporation's stock or shares. The rise of an American executive and managerial culture was aided by the creation of business management schools which taught business techniques to their students.

Big corporations, like Exxon, Wal-Mart, General Motors, Ford, General Electric, Citigroup and IBM, now dominate American business and influence consumer patterns. Smaller corporations may be taken over by larger ones and large corporations expand through mergers in the pursuit of markets and profits.

Small companies and individual entrepreneurs account for three quarters of the corporate system and are an important part of the business world. They generate more new jobs than larger corporations, tend to be created by entrepreneurs and are often associated with the service sector. Some succeed and some (such as some dot.com companies in the late 1990s) fail.

The ethos of American business attracts people who are determined to succeed and who are prepared to work hard to achieve material success, careers and status. Workers had problems in the late 1980s and early 1990s under the pressures of domestic and international recession. Although the financial and business markets improved with the upturn in the economy from 1994, they again experienced difficulties in 2000–4.

## *Wall Street*

'Wall Street' is the financial centre of the USA, and is situated in lower and mid-town Manhattan, in New York City. It comprises business institutions, such as stockbrokers and financial companies (for example, Merrill Lynch), banks (such as Citicorp and Bank of America), insurance corporations, commodity exchanges (that deal in coffee, cotton, metal or corn, amongst others) and the New

York Stock Exchange (NYSE). These institutions deal with huge sums of money and control and invest much of Americans' capital. The performance of corporate America in 2000–4 left much to be desired with evidence of fraudulent behaviour, dubious accounting practices and incompetence.

Large corporations are dependent for their financing and prosperity upon stock exchanges on which stocks and shares in selected businesses are bought and sold. This system, as well as raising investment money, is an important indicator of businesses' financial standing. New York City's two stock exchanges (the NYSE and the American Stock Exchange) deal with the majority of stock sales and purchases in the USA. The computerized Nasdaq deals with hi-tech shares but does not have a trading floor as does the NYSE on Wall Street. The performance of the stock market in 2000–4 varied considerably and the outlook is uncertain since it is dependent on international factors, such as rising oil prices.

The NYSE (founded in 1792) comprises about 1,300 members who trade in stocks and bonds either for themselves or as agents for clients. It is a market for the buying and selling of stocks and bonds which are listed on the exchange's trading register, which are sold to the highest bidder throughout the day, the value of which can go up or down. A company must have a specified amount of stock and a minimum turnover of trade before it can be listed on the NYSE.

The NYSE is internationally known for its Dow Jones Average. This is a list which contains the prices of stocks and bonds in selected industrial and commercial companies on the exchange. It is adjusted throughout the working day and its movements are shown in points. The Dow Jones is influential and international financiers, investors and governments see it as an accurate indicator of the USA's economic health.

## The banking system

Americans have always been suspicious of banks. The 1929 Wall Street Crash, when banks closed and people lost their money, still affects people, and fears revive when the stock market performs badly as in 1987 and in 2001 following the 9/11 terrorist attacks on New York. Polls in 2004 found that only 19 per cent of respondents supported banks or were positive about them.

US law is supposed to regulate the banking system and curb any excessive growth of individual banks. There are about 12,000 different commercial banks in the USA, which provide personal and corporate financial services for clients.

**PLATE 9.3** (opposite) The New York Stock Exchange is the largest of the New York stock exchanges; the buying and selling of stocks and shares on its trading floor are hectic.
(*Sipa Press/Rex Features*)

Some banks are incorporated (or licensed) under national charter and are known as National Banks. Others are regulated under state charters. The banking system has been increasingly deregulated to allow other financial competitors, and banks have moved into new (and riskier) areas like securities trading, currency-dealing and insurance. There are also many non-bank institutions, such as personal credit groups and savings-and-loans associations.

It is argued that the banking system is not as closely regulated at federal and state level as it should be, particularly at a time when financial institutions are expanding and when fraud and bank-collapses still occur. Critics argue for more accountability and far more control and regulation over American financial markets.

## *Federal Reserve System*

The Federal Reserve System (created in 1913) is similar to central or national banks in other countries. Its banking framework comprises twelve Federal Reserve Districts throughout the USA, each with its individual Federal Reserve bank. The system is supervised in Washington by a Board of Governors, headed by an influential Chairman. The governors are appointed by the President and confirmed by the Senate. As independent appointees and custodians of the monetary system, they do not always agree with government economic policies. However, the US Treasury Department (the federal financial department) does generally work closely with the Federal Reserve. It can influence the financial markets by its supervision of the national debt and can adjust the amount of credit in the monetary sector by changing its deposits with the Federal Reserve banks.

The Federal Reserve sets the minimum financial reserves that must be held by commercial banks for them to operate, adjusts interest rates, controls the money supply in the economy, tries to reduce inflation, issues bank notes, implements US monetary policy and attempts to create a stable environment for corporate activity. Sixty per cent of commercial banks are members of the Federal Reserve and hold three quarters of bank deposits. It is argued that the success of the US economy since 1994 and its effective management in the downturn from 2000 have been due to the economic skills of the Federal Reserve rather than those of the politicians.

## *Trade/labour unions*

A union (the Knights of Labour) was formed in 1869 to organize workers and to press for better employment and social conditions. Further efforts to create labour organizations led in 1886 to the American Federation of Labour (AFL), which was a collection of independent craft unions.

More effective legal frameworks for worker representation and collective bargaining between employers and employees were established only in the 1930s, after strikes and struggles between union organizers, the police, government and employers. The Congress of Industrial Organizations (CIO), which was based on manufacturing industry, was formed in 1935. Although initially affected by conflicting loyalties among unions, the AFL and the CIO organized themselves on a wider industrial basis and in 1955 formed an umbrella institution, the AFL–CIO. A majority of unions and their members are now affiliated with the AFL–CIO.

American unionism is more associated with manufacturing industries and construction than white-collar jobs and the service sector. Unions have lost members and influence after being a powerful economic force from the 1930s to the 1950s. A minority of the labour force are now union members (13.2 per cent in 2002 compared with 35.5 per cent in 1945).

The decline in union membership stems from economic trends, such as the growth of service and high-technology industries in a post-industrial economy, foreign competition, economic recession, fewer manufacturing industries, increased automation and advanced equipment, less need for blue-collar workers and increased unemployment among union members. The failure of unions to protect the jobs of white- and blue-collar workers in the 1970s and 1980s also led to a drop in union influence. This allowed companies to restructure the labour market, sack full-time staff and employ cheap contract freelancers. The result was the creation of a two-tier workforce of skilled, highly paid staff and a poorly paid under-class with little industrial strength.

American unions have the right to strike, but this is restricted by cooling-off periods and compulsory arbitration in certain circumstances. Strike action can be unpopular and also counterproductive for union members who may lose their jobs as a result. After a period of forty-seven years when industrial action was low, the number of strikes increased in 1994 to forty-five stoppages but fell dramatically to nineteen in 2002.

Although US unions have achieved pay and insurance benefits for their members, many workers regard job security as more important since there are few redundancy payments by companies to employees, workers have little job security and minimum wages are low.

American unions are not highly organized, do not have the influence or political motivation of European labour, nor have they attracted a mass membership. There are several reasons for this situation. First, the political and economic power of employers and anti-union legislation by Congress (such as the Taft–Hartley Act of 1947) and states have minimized union impact. Second, the *laissez-faire* attitudes of the US economy and a belief in self-reliance and individualism encourage many workers to believe in the possibility of upward mobility and limits a united political identification with union activity. Third, many blue-collar workers look to the Republicans for economic answers. Fourth, the 'Red Scare' of the 1920s and anti-Communist agitation in the 1950s neutralized potential left-wing influences and the union membership tends to be at variance with the more politicized goals and ideology of union leaders. Fifth, corruption and scandals in the unions have alienated workers. Sixth, immigration to the US and the formation of ethnic groups have historically detracted from the solidarity of trade unionism. Seventh, there have been strong divisions between skilled and unskilled workers and between different craft unions. Workers have not been closely involved in corporate policy-making and some critics argue that unions have not consistently influenced the national economy in their favour.

However, there has been a slight increase in union membership among African and Asian Americans in recent years, and the AFL–CIO leadership is stronger. Shortages of both skilled and unskilled workers in prosperous times may also allow the unions to press more for wage increases and better conditions. Such developments could suffer from recessionary forces, cutbacks and rising unemployment.

## Attitudes to the economic system

A Gallup poll in February 2004, prior to the presidential election, showed that Americans felt that the economy (including unemployment and jobs) came second in the top fourteen problems facing the USA (although later polls suggested that it had climbed to first place). Taxes came sixth, the federal budget deficit was seventh and corporate corruption was placed tenth. These concerns reflected economic difficulties during 2000–4, following a period of prosperity and growth from 1994. Polls also revealed that many Americans, on an individual level, were reasonably optimistic about an economic upturn.

In terms of confidence in economic institutions, polls by Harris, CNN/USA Today/Gallup, Fox News and Bloomberg News in 2002–4 found that respondents had very low opinions of Wall Street (11–17 per cent support), organized labour (11–15 per cent), banks (19 per cent) and major business corporations and companies (6–13 per cent). Respondents in a 2004 Harris poll felt that big companies (83 per cent) and labour unions (48 per cent) had too much influence on government policy, while small businesses had very little. A *Newsweek* poll in March 2003 found that 70 per cent of respondents thought that the political system was so controlled by special and partisan interests that it could not respond to the country's real needs. A *Los Angeles Times* poll in 2003 found that large majorities had little trust in the executives of large corporations to do what was right and felt that cases of wrongdoing were widespread.

Dissatisfaction with the way government and politicians regulate the economy and big business is also significant, although somewhat contradictory. An ABC/*Washington Post* poll in 2002 found that 63 per cent of respondents felt that regulation was necessary to protect the public, although 30 per cent said that it did more harm than good. This scepticism reflects a continuing lack of trust by some in the government's handling of the economy.

Gallup polls in June/July 2001, at a time of serious recession in many economic sectors, had pointed to individual resilience and relative optimism. Seventy-seven per cent of respondents were not worried that they or their spouses might lose their jobs in the next twelve months, with 52 per cent considering it 'not at all likely'; 50 per cent were very satisfied and 39 per cent somewhat satisfied with their job or work; 26 per cent were very satisfied and 51 per cent somewhat satisfied with their financial situation. In a 2003 Harris Feel Good Index, 64 per cent felt good about their jobs and 59 per cent felt good about their future financial security.

In more specific job terms, the Gallup polls revealed that 65 per cent thought that enjoying a job was most important for them, 32 per cent considered being well paid as most important, 53 per cent preferred to increase their pay by doing their current job better rather than being promoted to a new job, 62 per cent preferred to work outside the home rather than staying at home to take care of house and family but only 13 per cent felt that both parents in a family should work full-time.

Some 57 per cent thought that women do not have equal opportunities with men in the USA and 50 per cent felt the same applied to racial minorities. In respondents' households, 40 per cent of men earn a lot more and 25 per cent a little more than women. Significantly, 67 per cent were in favour of the Bush Administration's tax cuts, although 66 per cent disliked or hated filling in their income-tax forms. A *Fox News*/Opinion Dynamics poll in May 2004 found that 51 per cent of respondents thought that federal taxes were 'too high' (44 per cent 'about right') and a Gallup poll showed that a large majority of respondents thought that upper-income people and corporations paid too little tax.

As a comment on American individualism and optimism, a 1995 *Time*/CNN poll found that 86 per cent agreed with the statement that 'People have to realize that they can only count on their own skills and abilities if they're going to win in this world'. A Gallup poll in June 2001 showed that 48 per cent of respondents were very satisfied and 38 per cent somewhat satisfied with the opportunities they have had to succeed in life.

These attitudes suggest that Americans feel that they have to stand on their own two feet, but that their optimism can be affected by the performance of the national economy and harsher economic conditions. Education, training and experience are seen as essential in obtaining those jobs which are available, and in progressing economically and socially.

# Exercises

Explain and examine the significance of the following names and terms.

| | | |
|---|---|---|
| AFL–CIO | Wall Street | entrepreneurs |
| Federal Reserve | NYSE | New Deal |
| Dow Jones Average | anti-trust laws | corporations |
| service industries | NAFTA | trade balance |
| budget deficit | GDP | deregulation |
| Rockefeller | Nasdaq | Roaring Twenties |

Write short essays on the following questions.

1. What is meant by the American 'free enterprise' economic system? Examine its advantages and disadvantages.

2. Comment critically on the present state of the US economy.

3. What do the opinion polls in this chapter tell us about people's attitudes to the economic system?

4. What are the strengths and weaknesses of the US trade-union movement?

## Further reading

Brenner, R. (2002) *The Boom and the Bubble: the US economy today* London: Verso.

Dethloff, H. C. (1997) *The United States and the Global Economy since 1945* New York: Harcourt Brace.

Heilbroner, R. and A. Singer (1999) *The Economic Transformation of America: 1600 to the present* New York: Harcourt Brace.

Stiglitz, J. (2002) *Globalization and its Discontents* New York: Norton.

## Web sites

**Economic statistics, income and poverty:**
<http://www.census.gov>
<http://www.bls.gov>
<http://www.bea.doc.gov>
<http://www.dol.gov>
<http://usinfo.state.gov>
<http://usinfo.state.gov/usa/infousa/trade/tradeovr.htm>
<http://usinfo.state.gov/products/pubs/oecon/htm>
<http://www.access.gpo.gov/su_docs/budget/index.html>

# Social services

This chapter examines those social services provided for individuals and groups by the private and public sectors in the USA. 'Social services' includes items such as health care, retirement pensions, unemployment payments, housing, disability allowances and welfare benefits. The latter are often associated with government or public help to the poor, but most social-services spending by both sectors is in fact on middle- and higher-income people rather than on the poor.

The existence and nature of such services differ from country to country. Their availability, as has happened in the USA, changes according to the attitudes of people and politicians. They are also conditioned by experiences with the actual workings of social institutions and the demands of social life.

Americans historically have believed in self-reliance and independence in social-service areas. These have been largely seen as personal matters and the responsibility of the family or individual rather than of state or federal institutions. The private-enterprise market is theoretically supposed to supply necessary services for which individuals should pay.

But, since at least the 1930s, there has been an awareness that some people (and not only the poor) are unable to provide for themselves because of their social and economic circumstances. Reformers have felt that the delivery of social help should be a national responsibility. The scope of many services has consequently changed and has been extended to new areas of social-security, welfare-assistance, health-care and housing needs.

However, these expanded provisions have not resulted in the USA becoming a welfare state on the model adopted by some European nations. It lacks a comprehensive range of centrally organized social and health-care services, which are financed by general taxation and which are available to all at the point of need, irrespective of income.

Americans therefore rely for the necessities of life on a mixture of federal- and state-funded government programmes (public sector), arrangements made by individuals themselves (private sector) and help given by voluntary organizations. Most services in the public and private sectors are paid for out of contributory systems, and benefits are gained by individuals who subscribe to particular programmes. Those unable to make such contributions receive help from non-contributory state and federal schemes, some of which are known as 'welfare', as well as from the voluntary services, which are dependent largely upon public donations. Many affluent Americans also receive direct and indirect benefits and services because of government subsidies or relief in areas such as education, home loans and tax breaks.

The contemporary combination of public and private social services has developed largely since the 1930s and results in a complex and diversified system. Some critics argue for a unified and national system which would be more responsive to social need. Others oppose such proposals, particularly in the welfare area. However, spending on social services by the public sector has increased since the 1960s and the country does provide limited assistance for some of its most needy inhabitants, such as people with disabilities, children and old people.

Americans generally still expect other people to stand on their own two feet by means of a job. A considerable number of unemployed and low-income individuals thus fall outside the social-service systems and are affected by poverty and need. Government policies since 1996 have restructured and restricted some welfare programmes, suggesting that the USA is moving further away from welfare-state models. Additionally, while the Bush (Jr.) administration has expanded old-age medical provision for prescription drugs, it has also advocated a partial privatization of the federal social-security system. Recent public opinion polls (2004) have indicated increased support for more and better public social-services programmes, such as universal health care.

## Social services history

Three hundred years ago, the USA was primarily a rural society in which most Americans worked in farming and in which there were few urban centres of any size. The essence of life for the majority was self-reliance in social, health, employment and housing needs.

Since then, the images of the independent farmer and frontiersman have conditioned American mythologies. Paradoxically, the societies of early agriculturalists and pioneers were also cooperative, with communal support and protection, as were many Native-American communities. Such contrasting images illustrate the tension in US life between individualism and communalism. They also affect how later Americans have responded to social services.

Industrialization and urbanization increased in the late-eighteenth and nineteenth centuries and brought misery to many people. Social help was still either largely private and individualistic or was provided by voluntary charities, such as the aid given by ethnic and religious groups to their members. However, some small assistance was also supplied by state and local governments. This mixture of services was conditioned by the tradition of self-reliance and self-help. There was (and still is) a distinction made in the USA between the 'deserving' poor who could be helped by existing resources and the 'undeserving' poor who were supposed to rectify their own conditions.

Most Americans were unwilling to let central institutions organize too many of society's affairs. They jealously protected their own independence and had a pride in coping and achieving by themselves. Politicians also avoided intervention in, and government spending on, social help. Consequently, no adequate national system of public social services developed in the late nineteenth and early twentieth centuries.

The system of self-reliance and fragmented aid could not cope with the economic collapse, large-scale unemployment, poverty and social problems caused by the Great Depression, which followed the 1929 stock-market crash. The existing resources of private, public and voluntary organizations proved insufficient in the 1930s when an estimated 40 per cent of the population lived in relative poverty.

The situation improved considerably with President Franklin D. Roosevelt's New Deal in the mid-1930s. Roosevelt was concerned to rectify faults in the economy and to provide frameworks for a measure of social protection. Social-security legislation was passed in 1935, which made benefits for workers and their families dependent on employment status and the payments that employees contributed during their working lives. The New Deal also provided jobs in public-sector works programmes for the unemployed and tried to improve the social and economic problems of African and Native Americans.

However, these programmes were not comprehensive and were directed towards people who were willing to work. Publicly financed non-contributory welfare was still unpopular in 1930s America, and there was antagonism towards those who would not work or help themselves. But two important federal welfare programmes, Aid to Families with Dependent Children (AFDC) and General Assistance (GA), were passed to help the needy, families, children and people with disabilities.

After the 1930s, reformers argued that such measures needed to be supplemented by further action. Federal, state and local governments became more involved in social services. Government thinking also changed as publicly funded programmes expanded considerably after the Second World War. Individuals and groups agitated for more assistance. War veterans, for example, were given federal medical, educational and housing benefits (the 'GI Bill of Rights'). A new culture of 'rights' to public social services became apparent. There was also a feeling in some quarters that the USA should be able to care for more of its citizens, particularly those who were in need.

Gradually, and on the basis of programmes such as the GI Bill, the federal government became more involved in providing public social services. However, such expansion was still piecemeal and was largely a response to need and public pressure, rather than a commitment to a consistent national policy. Social programmes were in fact developing under their own impetus and covered greater numbers of people.

From the 1960s to the early 1980s, more federal and state money was spent on public social services. President Lyndon Johnson (1963–8) introduced new programmes as part of his 'War on Poverty' and 'Great Society' campaigns, which were intended to alleviate need and suffering. For example, Medicare provided

**PLATE 10.1** Pictured at his desk in the White House in 1935, Franklin D. Roosevelt was a Democratic politician and US President from 1933 to 1945, the only one to have been elected four times. Popularly known as FDR, he was architect of the New Deal and leader during the Second World War.

(*Pix Inc./Time Pix/Rex Features*)

health care for the elderly, Medicaid supplied health services for the poor and a food-stamp programme gave coupons to the needy that were used to buy food in specified shops.

Johnson also introduced a range of other initiatives (such as 'Head Start') which attempted to attack poverty and unemployment through education, job training and regional-development programmes. Valuable though they were, these policies were not directed towards the establishment of an American welfare state. They were intended more as opportunities for those people who were prepared to work and to better themselves.

Nevertheless, the reforms formed a basis for future public social services, and agencies and departments were established to implement the new programmes. Increasingly in this expansive climate, some of the poor and needy came to regard non-contributory welfare and health care as a right and the number of claimants grew.

Public spending on social services increased through the 1970s and 1980s. There was also a move away from defence and military spending to expenditure on social programmes. Presidents after Johnson differed in their attitudes to social-service and welfare schemes. It also became difficult to persuade Congress to allocate public money to such services. Economic problems by 1980, such as rising inflation, curtailed new social legislation.

President Reagan (1981–8) tried to reduce the cost of welfare and public programmes during his administrations. He wanted Americans to be responsible for their own lives through self-help and to depend less on government aid. Despite such aims, the cost of social security, welfare schemes and unemployment compensation to the federal budget increased. Public social programmes had thus grown relatively rapidly. Republican administrations have not been keen to raise income taxes in order to pay for them, particularly welfare.

The Bush (Snr.) administration (1989–92) attempted to reduce social and public spending, but was forced to meet increased demand by tax rises. The Clinton administration (1992–2000) tried to introduce universal health care in 1993, financed mainly by individual and corporate contributions, which would cover all the population and improve the delivery of health services by controlling costs. However, this reform initiative collapsed, and instead there were demands from a Republican Congress for greater curbs in social-services spending.

Under pressure from Congress and from public opinion in 1996, Clinton changed US welfare policy by restructuring and cutting federal public spending on AFDC. Some saw this as an unravelling of New Deal programmes, returning the USA to the old mentality on social services and negatively affecting large numbers of people, such as families and children. Others argued that the welfare reforms moved the USA from a system of debilitating non-contributory benefit entitlement to one of personal responsibility.

There has been a devolution of welfare provision from federal authorities to the individual states since 1996–7. This means that there are different varieties of programmes (Temporary Assistance for Needy Families – TANF) and scales of help. Public money/federal grants have been directed by the states to training schemes, and more people have moved off welfare and into jobs and training. But economic downturns and a rise in unemployment produce increasing need and larger numbers of people living in defined poverty in 2004. Some individuals and families now have little recourse to help apart from charity.

Public-opinion polls suggest a popular demand for a universal health-care system financed out of increased taxation. But President George W. Bush (2000– ) has cut taxes and seems willing to privatize some areas of public social services to offset the costs of the system.

## The organization of contemporary social services

Some 30 per cent of payments for items such as health care, retirement, employ-ment protection and housing in the USA derive from the private sector. This means that individuals make arrangements for their own social needs, usually from insurance organizations which then pay for services when required. Companies and other bodies also use such private sources to insure their workers and members. The voluntary sector (charities, foundations and religious groups) is often included in the private sector. Its expenditure depends upon the donations (with some federal subsidies) that it receives to provide assistance for the needy and poor.

The public sector today amounts to some 70 per cent of all social-services and health-care payments. It comprises first, federal social-security benefits under a contribution system for all employed people and their families and, second, non-contributory welfare programmes, health services and housing organized by state and federal governments.

Social security, health care and welfare in the public sector now represent a very large budget item for American governments. An increasing elderly population is making added demands upon social security, however, and the quality of some public services varies from state to state. This is because of 'matching-funds' policies (whereby states have to equal federal grants), the varying wealth of individual states, their prioritization of programmes, differences in states' cost of living and the need to produce balanced budgets.

The main public-sector organization is by federal, state and local programmes. Budget responsibilities are allocated between Washington, DC and the states. At the federal level, public social services are administered through govern-ment programmes and different departments although the Department of Health and Human Services administers or supervises some of the schemes. Its estab-lishment as the Department of Health, Education and Welfare (HEW) in 1953 was a acknowledgement of responsibility for, and the importance of, social services. This federal organization can become uncoordinated due to the varied departments and responsibilities involved.

The state and local levels generally have the primary task of implementing and delivering their own public social services. These are also often divided between separate bodies. In some states, though, there are umbrella agencies that combine health, welfare and other related programmes.

# Public social services

Public social services can be divided into two parts. The first is the social-security system, to which workers contribute during their working lives and through which benefits are earned. The second includes people who receive assistance based on need. This is awarded according to means or income, but is not tied to contributions, and is generally known as 'welfare'.

Some citizens count on the existence of a welfare safety net based on public funds. Others debate its bureaucratic complexity, inefficiency, incompleteness, effects on the morals and initiative of welfare clients, abuse and cost. Public-sector services (particularly in health care, social security and welfare) are central issues in American politics.

## *Social-security benefits*

The Social Security Fund is a large and expanding part of public social services. It is administered from Washington and in 2002 its income amounted to $529,300 million. Social-security contributions produce 32 per cent of all federal income and social-security payments amount to 20 per cent of federal spending.

Social security originated in the 1935 Social Security Act. It is a social insurance programme and now covers three main areas: the Old Age, Survivors, Disability and Health Insurance programme (OASDHI), Medicare and Unemployment Compensation. Generally, employees and the self-employed contribute financially (some 7 per cent of earnings) to these programmes during their working lives. Employers also make contributions for their labour force. Workers (and their families) receive benefits as a result of these contributions. Benefits include pensions on retirement (usually at the age of sixty-five), which are relatively low at an average of $1,556 per month in 2003 for a married worker on average earnings, medical care for the elderly and disabled under Medicare, disability payments at an average of $837 per month in 2003, illness and accident provisions and unemployment payments.

The Department of Labor supervises the system of Unemployment Compensation, but each state administers its own programme. The majority of workers are covered, unemployment benefits last for between twenty-six and thirty-nine weeks; and the general compensation is about a quarter of the worker's earnings.

Since social security may not cover all the bills, provision for old age, illness and unemployment often has to include additional private resources for many Americans, such as savings, investments and insurance. Some employers and unions also provide further retirement-, unemployment-, health- and life-insurance services for employees, based on employer and (sometimes) worker contributions. There is concern that the Social Security Fund may be unable to finance its future obligations because greater numbers of workers are needed to support a growing elderly population. Suggestions have therefore been made that workers may use a percentage of their social-security contributions and invest the money as they wish. In effect, this amounts to a partial, if small, privatization of the social-security system.

## Welfare programmes

Public debate about poverty resulted in federal legislation from the 1960s. This provided financial help to the needy and poor, work, training and rehabilitation programmes, resources to house and feed the homeless and health care for the sick who lack financial provision. The cost of such programmes amounts to 6 per cent of the federal budget, but many people do not take up the public benefits to which they are entitled.

The cost of welfare programmes has been traditionally shared by federal, state and local governments. Generally, federal funds are distributed to the states, which should spend equal (or matching) amounts of money to the federal funds. Some northern states provide a lot of welfare help to their citizens and some southern states give relatively little. Each state devises and organizes its own programme. It defines, on the basis of a balanced budget, which families and individuals qualify for assistance in terms of needs.

Until 1996, the main federal welfare programmes, or non-contributory aid to the needy, consisted of Medicaid, AFDC and food stamps. There are other programmes under the GA scheme which provide income support, cash grants, aid for housing, school meals, Supplemental Security Income (SSI) for the elderly poor and help with other basic necessities.

Medicaid is a health scheme which started in 1956. It is operated by the individual states, is the largest direct federal aid programme for those under sixty-five and is paid for by national, state and county governments. It is supposed to provide essential health-care services for those who do not have private insurance or the financial ability to pay for medical treatment. In 2004 it catered for some 51 million people (21.2 per cent of children under eighteen, 6.3 per cent of people between eighteen and forty-four and 4.7 per cent of people between forty-five and sixty-four).

The second-largest programme of federal aid to the poor was (until 1996) AFDC. Payments to families (including single parents) with children were based on need, and the poverty-line (see below) was used as a guideline. AFDC payments varied between states, with southern states generally paying less than northern ones. By 1996, AFDC supported 15 million persons, of whom two-thirds were children.

Federal AFDC was abolished in 1996. Welfare responsibility was passed to the states, which receive partial federal block grants to run their own programmes, called Temporary Assistance for Needy Families (TANF). There is now a five-year lifetime limit on welfare benefits, which are not automatic, and most fit adults are required to work after two years on welfare.

As part of TANF schemes, 'Workfare' (work + [wel]fare) programmes require that welfare recipients, such as single parents, should be prepared to work (often in public-service jobs), take part in job-training schemes or attend educational courses. Care facilities are sometimes provided for families with small children, but these are often inadequate. Such programmes were intended to encourage recipients to move off welfare and into secure jobs. More people are now obliged to undertake workfare and training schemes as part of their state welfare entitlement. But some, single mothers in particular, who refuse workfare to stay at home with their children are losing welfare benefits and often end up in homeless shelters.

**PLATE 10.2** Woman participating in a workfare programme in Chicago, 1987. People accepted on to TANF welfare programmes must undergo training courses or obtain a job, usually in public-service employment.
(*Michael L. Abramson/Time Pix/Rex Features*)

The third programme derives from the 1964 Food Stamp Act. It provides food aid for eligible needy people and children, who lack an adequate diet. Recipients receive coupons or stamps which are used to buy food in approved shops at an average rate of one third of its normal price. Food stamps are now limited to a period of three months unless the recipients are working. The Department of Agriculture organizes the distribution of food and food stamps through state and local governments, and its cost in 2002 was $37,726 million.

This welfare system does provide a degree of assistance for the most needy, but people who are unemployed for long periods (and who have no other resources) may receive little help from the government. Employment is therefore a crucial factor for most Americans, from which stems their ability to provide for themselves. Without work, they can obtain little public assistance unless they fall into the welfare categories. The restructuring of AFDC benefits means in effect that after two years on welfare an individual must find a job. Hardship exemptions are available for the very poorest who cannot find work when the benefits end. Most people will be dependent on individual state welfare spending and on obtaining jobs which tend to be low-paid. Eighty per cent of those who had left welfare by 2000 did manage to find some kind of work, but recessionary economic effects from 2001 with growing unemployment have, among other factors, driven more people into poverty.

## The needy and the poverty line

In 2002, most welfare cases receiving TANF payments tended to be concentrated in a few states such as Georgia, Florida, California, Illinois, Indiana, Minnesota, Ohio, Michigan, Pennsylvania, New York, Texas, Utah and Washington DC. Welfare payments are made to people who do not have the resources to live at an appropriately decent minimum level. Eligibility is based on the 'official poverty level'. This is calculated annually (taking account of inflation) by the Federal Social Security Administration. It determines earned income levels below which a household is classified as 'poor'. Such income is equal to three times the cost of an adequate diet and depends on the number of people in a household. In 2004 it was $18,660 for a family of four and $9,573 for single people.

The number of people living in poverty fluctuates. In 2000, 31.1 million Americans (or 11.3 per cent of the population) were below the poverty line. But in 2003 the number had increased to 35.8 million (12.5 per cent of the population). Of these, 24.4 per cent were African Americans with a similar percentage of Latinos. This suggests that such groups are disproportionally represented among the poor in population terms. Children remain over-represented among the poor with a poverty rate of some 17.6 per cent of all children (or 13 million) in 2003. The number of poor people at any given time depends on the state of the national economy and can increase with a downturn and rising unemployment.

Poverty remains a reality for a sizeable minority of Americans. The poorest people tend to be concentrated in inner-city areas which suffer the greatest deprivation. But poverty is also a feature of rural regions. Most poor homes are those where householders have a low or no income. Sometimes these may be single mothers or fathers with young children, or homes where individuals may be pensioners, disabled or unemployed.

A crucial tax aid designed to lift the working poor with dependent children above the poverty line is the earned-income tax credit (EITC) established in 1975. Instead of facing higher taxes as their incomes increase, individuals with one dependent child (for example) can qualify for a tax credit up to a maximum wage. This means that they receive lump-sum payments or refunds from the Internal Revenue Service (IRS). More people would be in defined poverty without this aid, and the working poor are a vulnerable group.

Although fewer Americans are poor today than in the past, the debate on the 'poverty question' continues. Critics argue that the federal government should provide funds to eradicate poverty. Others feel that welfare programmes are expensive, inefficient and ineffective and do not give incentives to the poor to help themselves. It is maintained that an 'under-class' has developed that is dependent on welfare ('the dependency culture') and which includes disaffected people who may have opted out of national life. The 1996 limitation of federal welfare programmes may arguably break the cycle of permanent dependency, but its success assumes growth in the national economy and the creation of jobs.

## Single-parent families

Of the 58.3 million white American children under eighteen in 2002, 75 per cent lived with both parents, 18 per cent lived with their mother and 5 per cent with their father. Of the 11.6 million African-American children, 39 per cent lived with both parents, 48 per cent with their mother and 5 per cent with their father. Of the 12.8 million Latino children, 65 per cent lived with both parents, 25 per cent with their mother and 5 per cent with their father. A considerable (and disproportional) percentage of households were therefore headed by a single woman (divorced, widowed or single) and considerably fewer by a single man.

Such families are connected in the public mind with the needy, the poverty line, welfare and minority groups. But the number of these families has dropped by 8 per cent since 1996, possibly due to welfare restrictions, the effects of work-fare and increased marriage among recipients. In fact, some one-parent families do have incomes above the official poverty level and their children receive a minimum of welfare payments such as free school meals.

# Voluntary services

Given the level of poverty in the USA and the inability of federal and state governments to meet all the social requirements of the people, the existence of voluntary organizations which help those in need continues to be important. They are usually included in the private sector of social services, but they should strictly be seen as a complementary third sector to the private and public sectors.

There is a wide range of social services organized by local and national bodies, which help and campaign on behalf of the disadvantaged. Financial contributions (with tax breaks or relief) by Americans to such bodies and campaigns are generous and some 75 per cent of US households give money to them. Nationally, institutions like the Rockefeller and Ford foundations and other smaller bodies perform an important role in care research and in health and welfare programmes.

On a more grass-roots level, religious and other charitable voluntary organizations and unpaid volunteers are often crucial for people in local communities. They provide professional and non-professional aid, supply services for sick or elderly people, operate hospitals, care centres, clinics, retirement homes and shelters for the homeless; and visit old, disabled and needy people in the community. On these levels, they give what is often much-needed assistance and comfort. An estimated 50 per cent of Americans over eighteen (particularly retired persons) do volunteer work.

# Health care

Some Europeans feel that the American health-care system lacks a publicly funded and comprehensive national health service since federal funds pay for only 40 per cent of all health care. This aid covers some people of all income groups, but not all the population.

American critics (and popular opinion) also itemize the system's alleged limitations and present a diverse picture of medical provision. This suggests that available and adequate care depends upon the wealth, gender, residential and ethnic background of the patient. White males living in affluent neighbourhoods and some of the poor and elderly may be relatively well covered by private and public facilities respectively. But some people under sixty-five, those on average income, females generally, those from a non-white background and people who live in rural areas or inner-city locations may have difficulties in obtaining satisfactory health care.

American health services are divided between private and public sectors. Private hospitals, clinics and surgeries are in general well-equipped and efficient and run by a variety of commercial organizations or religious groups. Many of those in the public sector, financed by state and federal funds, tend to lack

**PLATE 10.3** A Franciscan nun cuts a girl's hair at St Raphael Social Service Centre, Hamilton, Ohio, 1995. This centre is typical of the voluntary services provided in the community by the churches and other groups. They are the most immediate for the needy.
(*Steve Liss/Time Pix/Rex Features*)

resources and adequate funding. While the USA has many high-quality medical facilities, gaining access to them is a problem for a substantial proportion of the population.

Most employees and their families (and the independently affluent) are normally insured for private health care through insurance schemes. These may be organized by employers and trade unions or individually against the cost of health treatment and loss of income if workers fall ill. Insurance premiums, which tend to be expensive, are made by deductions from wages and salaries or by individual contributions.

Generally, no one health-insurance policy covers all possible eventualities, and many individuals may have to subscribe to several policies in order to protect themselves adequately. Nevertheless, they may still themselves eventually have to pay for some treatment which is not covered by the insurance policies. Some 45 million Americans in 2003 (16 per cent of the population) had no health insurance cover either because they could not afford it or for other reasons (the third successive rise since 2000). But this annual figure is lower than the higher numbers of people who are without cover for shorter periods of time in any given year.

People's anxieties about illness are conditioned not only by relatively high insurance premiums, but also by the cost of treatment, which (especially for serious illness) is very expensive. There is some hostility towards the medical profession and drug companies whom the public often suspect of pushing up medical and drug costs for their own profit. Doctors, particularly those in the private sector, have high incomes and constitute an influential professional interest group. Many doctors and insurance companies have traditionally been opposed to public (or 'socialized') medicine in the USA. The Clinton administration's proposal for a universal health-care scheme in 1993 also failed to some extent because of opposition by employers and employees to high compulsory contributions to the programme.

In recent years, health-maintenance organizations (HMOs) or managed-care providers have expanded considerably and are the insurance providers for many Americans today. They offer savings plans and try to curb health costs by rationalizing and rationing treatment for patients, thus squeezing traditional insurance schemes and treatment offered by doctors. On one hand, they are very unpopular with patients and doctors who feel that adequate treatment is often limited by financial restraints. On the other, it is argued that HMOs have saved money, kept health care affordable and have sometimes improved upon previous medical standards.

In the public sector, health care is available to those who require it, but who lack the money and insurance to pay for the service. The federal non-contributory Medicaid programme gives federal grants to states for the free treatment of the poor and needy, blind and disabled people and dependent children. Because of matching-fund policies, the scope of Medicaid varies among states with some

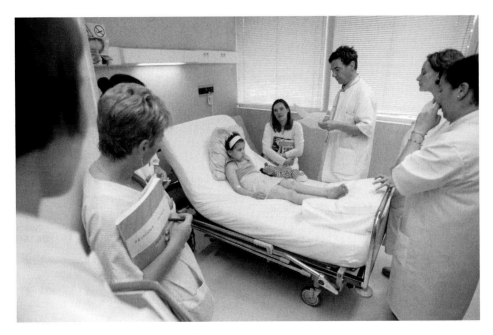

**PLATE 10.4** Day hospital ward rounds with doctors and interns (doctors under training).
(*Burger/Phanie/Rex Features*)

providing more aid than others, it covers only about 40 per cent of the poor
nationwide and the working poor are often outside the claims limits.

Nevertheless, state and local governments provide a range of public health
facilities for many categories of people from the poor to war veterans and the
armed forces. They operate or support hospitals, mental institutions, retirement
homes and maternity and child-health services. Public facilities may also be
supplemented by voluntary organizations, universities and other bodies, which
provide free health care for the local population. Ultimately, public health services
suffer from varying standards, inadequate coverage of the needy and differences
in the amount of money spent on them. This means that a majority of Americans
under sixty-five are dependent upon private medical-insurance schemes and the
private sector.

A second federal health programme, Medicare (formed in 1965), covers
much of the costs for the medical treatment of 37 million (2000) elderly (over
sixty-five) and disabled people and costs 8 per cent of federal spending. But this
is dependent upon social-security contributions during an employee's lifetime.
Additionally, because of the incomplete coverage of Medicare, many elderly
people may not be able to cover the full cost of some types of treatment, particularly the most expensive. They usually need additional private insurance
or savings for the balance of medical fees. The Bush (Jr.) administration has
provided aid to senior citizens for the purchase of prescription drugs. However,

few pensioners understand the system, it is alleged to be very costly and many old people and their doctors buy cheaper drugs from Canada.

In 2000, 13.5 per cent of GDP derived from US private and public health-care services. This GDP figure constitutes a major business sector and is larger than health-spending in other countries. But much of it is taken up by the incomes of the medical profession (with doctors having an average annual salary of $170,000), management or administrative costs and the expense of equipment and drugs.

It is argued that Americans are not receiving the full benefit of such expenditure, particularly when medical services can vary greatly. Compared with other countries, the USA spends more on health care but helps fewer people. In 2000, the World Health Organisation ranked the USA at thirty-seventh out of 191 countries for the quality of its health performance. It found that the top 10 per cent of Americans are the healthiest people in the world, a middle group receive a mediocre health deal, while the bottom 5–10 per cent have bad health services.

Developments in recent years have added to health-care costs. There have been more lawsuits for damages by patients against doctors and hospitals because of alleged inadequate or wrong treatment. Trial lawyers can profit considerably by fighting personal-injury lawsuits on a contingency fee basis. But the rise in such cases forces doctors to insure themselves against the risks of being sued. Medical care and vital decisions can be consequently influenced by these considerations. Drug companies also have to pay high compensation when medicines damage patients. Medicaid-spending has had to cope with the high health-care costs involved in treating AIDS (acquired immune deficiency syndrome), HIV (human immunodeficiency virus) patients and others with serious illnesses. Lawyers' fees, insurance policies and higher drug prices increase the overall cost of treatment which passes to the patient or insurer, while both the public and private sectors have to spend more to alleviate serious illness.

However, despite the alleged limitations of the American health-care system, life expectancy in 2004 was 74.6 years for men and 80.4 for women. Deaths from serious diseases and illnesses have in fact declined recently. These improvements are partly due to better diets, increased exercise and greater health awareness in the population, as well as better medical care and equipment. A Gallup poll in June 2001 reported that, despite growing problems with obesity at all ages, 54 per cent of respondents were very satisfied and 35 per cent were somewhat satisfied with their personal health.

# Housing

Homes are very important for many Americans and their families. They give a sense of material satisfaction, personal identification and individual lifestyle, around which family activities take place. The average American may also move home many times and home-ownership is very much associated with socio-economic mobility. A young family will move frequently in the early years from apartments to houses and up the housing market. There may be further moves from urban locations to the suburbs. Some people may restrict themselves to a particular area, but many Americans move large distances throughout the country.

Most Americans want to own their own homes, after usually renting in early adult years, and two-thirds prefer to live in suburban areas. Many achieve this ambition, and home-ownership (houses or apartments) is very high at 68 per cent of the housing market (117 million housing units in 2003). But some people do not succeed. Mobility is influenced by poverty, deprivation and unemployment. The housing market in the USA is consequently divided between the private sector for those who are able to buy or rent and the public sector for those who require assistance in obtaining low-rent property.

Some two-thirds of the housing units in the private sector are 'single-family dwellings', often of a detached type and usually having front and back yards or gardens. Other people live in apartments (whether purchased or rented) and the rest occupy a variety of different housing units.

Private houses and apartments are in general reasonably priced across a broad band, although they are subject to price fluctuations in the housing market. They are usually of good standard and comfortable, with many amenities. Most owners borrow money (a mortgage) which is secured by the value of their house and income in order to pay for them. In 2003, the median house cost $182,100 and had an average mortgage of 5.39 per cent. This entailed a monthly repayment on the mortgage of $817, or 18.3 per cent of average family income. House prices rose faster than incomes in the 1980s, but the housing market then suffered from the economic recession of the early 1990s. Since then, prices have increased again.

Public-sector housing in the USA is meant to provide for the minority of Americans who are unable to buy property or to afford high-rent private accommodation. The provision of such housing has been historically conditioned by the bias towards private provision and self-reliance. Individuals have been expected to make their own housing arrangements, rather than expecting these to be a public responsibility.

The growth of urban slums and substandard housing in the nineteenth century, together with social misery and threats to public health, resulted in the creation in 1934 of the Federal Housing Administration. This department (now the Department of Housing and Urban Development) provided loans to organizations which were willing to build low-rent accommodation for needy people and those on low incomes. Local and state governments also built public housing and implemented stricter building codes, health codes and public-sanitation regulations to deal with slum conditions.

**PLATE 10.5**  Graffiti on shopfront in Harlem, New York City. Harlem has long been a deprived inner-city African-American neighbourhood with slum dwellings and high levels of deprivation. (*Corbis*)

Attempts to create more low-cost public housing with federal funds in the cities and other areas (which were relatively successful in the 1960s and 1970s) have been frequently opposed by property-owners and sometimes by state and local governments. Federal financial aid has also been reduced. Although racial and religious discrimination in renting such housing has been curtailed, it still exists, often in veiled forms. While many states and cities have implemented fair-housing laws and fair-housing commissions, a large number of low-income people and minority groups in urban centres live in barely habitable housing and entry to low-cost housing for those who are unemployed or on welfare is restricted. Recently, there have been moves to make greater use of inner-city land and to replace inferior buildings with low-cost housing. Bad housing conditions are also experienced by people living in small towns and rural communities.

A Gallup poll in June 2001 found that 58 per cent of correspondents were very satisfied and 30 per cent were somewhat satisfied with their communities as places to live. Sixty-three per cent were very satisfied and 30 per cent were somewhat satisfied with their current housing.

## *The homeless*

Local, state or federal governments in the USA, as in many other countries, have failed to provide sufficient amounts of low-cost rented accommodation for low-income groups, and the federal government reduced subsidies for such housing from the 1980s. Since the number of poor Americans fluctuated in the 1980s and 1990s, the situation has resulted in homeless people throughout the nation, particularly African Americans. Estimates of their numbers, and the way they are calculated at particular times, vary, ranging from unofficial figures of up to three million and official figures from the Department of Housing and Urban Development of about half a million.

Voluntary organizations attempt to help the homeless by providing shelter and food for limited periods. Most of the funding for these bodies comes from private donations, although some finance is also provided by local and city governments. Federal government finance for the homeless continues to be relatively small.

## Attitudes to social services

At the beginning of the twentieth century, an estimated 50–60 per cent of the US population lived in relative poverty. Such statistics were later based on defined figures for poverty which decreased to 22 per cent in 1959 and to 11 per cent in 1973. It increased again in the 1980s and early 1990s, decreased to 11.3 per cent (or 31.1 million people) in 2000, but increased in 2003 to 12.5 per cent (35.8 million people).

While many Americans today are successful, independent and provide for themselves, relative poverty and need still exist. OECD figures (2003) suggest that income inequality between the richest and the poorest people in the USA is one of the largest in the world. Greater demands are made upon social institutions as the population has grown, people are living longer, the elderly require more health care, society has become more complex and individuals are affected to varying degrees by changing economic circumstances and a fluctuating job market. If privatization is not increased, it is inevitable that social-services costs will continue to rise in real terms and that the USA will contain individuals who must be provided for at public expense by a social safety net. Critics argue that the USA is politically unwilling to take on the kind of social responsibility and commitment for the whole community that this situation supposedly requires.

Polls on the causes of poverty have historically shown that one-third of Americans feel that people are poor or become poor due to their own lack of effort, one-third think that people are poor because of circumstances beyond their control and one-third believe that poverty stems from a mixture of both reasons.

The debate in the USA about the problems of the needy and poor is divided between traditional notions of self-reliance and the question of whether society should do much more in this field. It may appear that Americans lean too far in favour of individuals providing for themselves and do not give enough thought for those in need. A common expression in this context is 'The Lord helps those who help themselves'.

The virtues of self-reliance are often stressed by people who are already able to provide for themselves. Americans can sometimes be uncharitable to those citizens who are less successful or fortunate and can be unsympathetic to their position. Many feel that welfare has detracted from traditional virtues of responsibility, thrift and hard work and has contributed to a dependency culture.

Until the 1960s dependency upon welfare was widely perceived to be shameful and shaming.

The social services debate is not only about the poor and needy. It also questions whether the USA should adopt a nationally organized European-type 'welfare state', which provides comprehensive social and medical schemes for all funded out of general taxation. Historically, the biases against a centralized system have been considerable and the influence of private-enterprise economics and vested interests is felt in the social-services sector. The provision of a national system depends on political will, public acceptance and the organization and extent of services.

Traditionally, there has been a scepticism about centralized public services. Polls have shown that a majority of Americans thought that the federal government already controlled too much of people's daily lives. Only a minority felt that there should be government responsibility for *all* social services such as health care, housing, pensions and unemployment. These responses were far below those in European countries. There had been an unwillingness to contribute to national plans and a preference for personal decisions in how to spend one's money.

Nevertheless, American public social services have expanded since the 1930s in the face of opposition. They have been relatively successful, absolute poverty has declined, living standards have risen, greater public expectations have been created and social institutions have developed. The debate on what is possible and desirable continues as social services (both public and private) and individuals come under pressure and it is feared that present arrangements for Social Security, Medicare and other sectors may be unable to cope.

A Gallup poll in February 2004 reported that, of the top fourteen problems facing the country, health care ranked fifth with 82 per cent. A 2004 Harris poll showed that only 32 per cent of respondents had a great deal of confidence in the medical system while a 2003 CNN/*USA Today*/Gallup poll registered 19 per cent. Although another 2004 poll by the same organizations on honesty and ethical standards gave HMO managers only 9 per cent 'very high' ratings, nurses achieved 83 per cent support and doctors 68 per cent. A 2003 *ABC News/ Washington Post* poll asked respondents whether they thought health-care coverage should be provided for all, even if this meant raising taxes. Eighty per cent replied 'yes'. Such results were also echoed in other polls collated by Polling Report.com.

The Medicare system was changed in 2003 to allow senior citizens over sixty-five to receive help in paying for medical expenses and particularly prescription drugs, which can be very expensive. Opinions vary on this reform with respondents to a CNN/*USA Today*/Gallup poll in 2004 opposing it (35 per cent) because of cost and others favouring it (41 per cent), with 24 per cent having 'no opinion'. A majority felt that the changes will have little effect on the problem of making Medicare financially secure for the future, and a significant number thought that they would hurt the system. Although a majority in most polls is willing to pay higher taxes for a better and reformed health-care system (including Medicare), there are inconsistent opinions about how this improvement should be implemented.

Nevertheless, significant majorities in all polls are dissatisfied with the quality of US health care, feel that it has major problems, would prefer a universal health-care system and maintain that health-care coverage for all Americans is the responsibility of the federal government. In recent years, when polls ask how well respondents could cover the cost of medical care if their family was affected by major illness, 40 per cent say that they could cope easily, 44 per cent with difficulty and 14 per cent not at all. The cost of prescription drugs is the greatest concern.

The social-security system gives benefits such as pensions based on workers' contributions during their working lives. But a *CBS News/New York Times* poll in 2002 found that 55 per cent of respondents thought that the system would not have the money available to provide the benefits they expect on retirement. Suggestions have been made that workers should be able to divert up to 5 per cent of their social security to private investments in a partial privatization of the federal system. Sixty-seven per cent of respondents in a *Fox News*/Opinion Dynamics poll in January 2004 agreed with this and majorities were recorded in other polls. But the suggestion that workers should work until seventy before collecting full social-security benefits (such as pensions and Medicare) was opposed by a large majority. The problems of social security, such as raising enough money to pay for a bigger old-age-pensioner population, are considerable and a source of current debate. There also appear to be contradictions between the desire for universal health care paid out of taxation or compulsory contributions and the approval shown to partial privatization of social security.

# Exercises

Explain and examine the significance of the following names and terms.

| | | |
|---|---|---|
| welfare | AFDC/TANF | one-parent families |
| Medicaid | workfare | War on Poverty |
| medical lawsuits | poverty level | unemployment compensation |
| OASDI | food stamps | GI Bill of Rights |
| Medicare | self-reliance | non-contributory benefits |
| New Deal | mortgage | social security |
| homeless | HEW | EITC |

Write short essays on the following questions.

1. Critically discuss the provision for health care in the USA. Should there be a national health service providing free care for all?

2. Examine the American division between public and private sectors of health, social provision and housing.

3. Examine the results of public-opinion polls in this chapter and assess the attitudes of Americans to social services.

# Further reading

Alcock, P. and G. Craig (2001) *International Social Policy: welfare regimes in the developed world* London: Macmillan/Palgrave.

Gilens, M. (1999) *Why Americans Hate Welfare* Chicago, Ill.: University of Chicago Press.

Patterson, J. T. (1981) *America's Struggle Against Poverty, 1900–1980* Cambridge, Mass.: Harvard University Press.

Peterson, P. (1999) *Gray Dawn: how the coming age wave will transform America – and the world* New York: Random House.

Skocpol, T. (1995) *Social Policy in the United States* Princeton, NJ: Princeton University Press.

# Web sites

**Social services:** <http://usinfo.state.gov/usa/infousa>

**Medicine:** <http://www.medicare.gov>

**Homelessness and links:** <http://womenshousing.org>

# Chapter 11

# Education

# American attitudes to education: high expectations

Since the colonial period, Americans have expected a great deal from their educational institutions. Just teaching the usual subjects has rarely satisfied demands on the schools. Americans have also wanted learning to serve other social institutions, ideals and goals.

Such expectations invite disappointment and controversy. Combined with the circumstances of the country's history, they have also led to a very distinctive educational system. With its fusion of church and state, Puritan New England aimed at religious doctrination, making even learning the alphabet a series of theological lessons, though maxims of 'good sense' for getting on in the world also received attention. American optimism shines through in much later pedagogy. The founding fathers hoped schooling would discover natural merit in citizens and nurture an elite to defend the republic from tyranny. People on the frontier dreamed education would be the 'great leveller', a compensator for their alleged inferiority to coastal society and a guarantee of democratic equality.

Well into the twentieth century, schoolbooks fairly glow with faith in the possibility of endless self-improvement for boys dedicated to American ideals. The schools taught girls to play a supportive role, African Americans to know their place, Native Americans to be civilized and immigrants to be American workers. Until recently, only a few private institutions and schools outside the mainstream provided correctives to this hierarchy. Since the mid-1950s, civil-rights movements (starting with African Americans' demands for educational equality) have made schools a centre of contention over which traditions and ideals, what order in society and what means of reaching those goals Americans should support.

At the beginning of the twenty-first century, Gallup Organization Polls gave a reasonably clear list of the traditional and newer attitudes and goals the public has regarding the nation's schools. As in the past, the public was not satisfied with public education. In surveys, over half the public felt that private or church-related parochial schools were superior to the public school system, and would send their children to private schools if cost were not an issue.

By small margins the public favoured President George W. Bush's approval of government vouchers to cover the cost of sending children to private schools if parents found local public schools inadequate. Thoughout the 1990s attempts to establish national standards for knowledge in specific subjects was also a focus of efforts to improve the schools. In the early 2000s most people polled supported such standards. Large majorities also supported using yearly standardized tests to measure students' progress and the quality of schools, another approach President George W. Bush's No Child Left Behind Act put in practice. But people thought the best means of improving the schools were paying teachers better, using more federal money for schools (but letting local districts decide how to use it), using standardized tests and allowing voucher plans – in that order. The public further indicated that it highly approved of re-introducing the prayers and general religious content that were common in US schools before the 1970s. This mixture of ideas, some commonly advocated by self-identified conservatives and others usually expected from those who call themselves liberals, seemed characteristic of the evenly divided climate of opinion about political issues, including the schools, at the time.

Educational institutions become the bearers of each age's values. In part because expectations and the rate of change remain high in the USA, education is a focus of intense debate.

# American educational history

## *The colonial period*

Local control over education developed early in America and remains characteristic of its educational institutions. During the colonial period, the British authorities did not provide money for education, so the first schools varied according to the interest local settlers had in education. The common view was that parents were responsible for children's education. In the southern colonies, schooling often came from a private tutor, if the family could afford one. Each town tried to build a school in colonial New England and Pennsylvania.

The colonists expected the schools to teach religion, and a skill in reading was highly valued because it allowed people to read the Bible. Puritan Massachusetts founded the first American public school under a law entitled the 'Old Deluder Satan Act'. Reading, writing and arithmetic (the so-called three 'R's') were the core subjects and, through them, pupils prepared for local religious, economic and political life.

Higher education also began early in the colonial period. In 1636 Harvard College was founded, only six years after the Puritan migration to America began. By the Revolutionary War, nine colleges prepared a small elite of men for the ministry and leadership in public life. Although these colleges encouraged religious toleration, rivalry among them was evident, in part because all but two (Columbia and the University of Pennsylvania) represented one of the major Protestant denominations. At this point, church and state were not separated, and essentially private institutions of higher education regularly received public funding.

Building a society along the frontier also motivated the early development of schools. Because they were few and the wilderness vast, the settlers discovered that law, order and social tradition broke down unless people cooperated to establish the basic institutions of society. Thus, 'school-raisings' became as much a standard a part of cooperative community building as house- or barn-raisings.

## Before the Civil War

None the less, only five of the thirteen original states included provisions for public schools in the constitutions they wrote during the War for Independence (1776–81). In 1830, none offered statewide, free public education. Support for common schools was strong, however. Thomas Jefferson and other founding fathers insisted that universal public education was essential to produce the informed citizenry on which a democracy depended. In the 1780s the federal government passed laws providing for education and land for schools in the future states of the Great Lakes region.

Jefferson envisioned replacing Europe's aristocracy of birth with a school-bred *meritocracy* of talent. In the 1830s, President Andrew Jackson's Democratic Party opposed that ideal as elitist, and supported public schools as an equalizer that would give every man a chance to rise in society. Around the same time, reformers in the north-east, such as Horace Mann, publicized the notion that public schools could reduce the growing crime, poverty and vice of the cities by helping to assimilate their growing immigrant population. Towards those ends, Mann led a movement to lengthen the school year, add 'practical' subjects, raise teachers' salaries and provide professional teacher-training.

By the Civil War, all states accepted the principle of tax-supported, free elementary schools. Every state had such schools in some places, but most teachers were poorly trained, and the quality of the schools was considerably lower in the south and west. Most children went to school sporadically or not at all. In the north only one out of six white children attended public school in 1860. In the south, the figure was one out of seven, and it was illegal to give slaves schooling.

At the time, public opinion rejected the idea of mandatory school attendance, mainly because most people believed parents, rather than governments, should be responsible for education. Moreover, most parents needed their children's work or wages to make ends meet. Public secondary education was available at some 300 'free academies' across the nation, for those who could spare their children's contributions to the family economy.

As the states abolished established religions after the revolution, church and state became separate. Only gradually, however, did Protestant instruction disappear from public schools. In the north and mid-west, immigrant groups began to establish parochial (private, church-related) elementary and secondary schools in the 1840s to preserve their ethnic heritage and avoid pressures to assimilate in public schools.

The pattern of higher education was transformed before 1865. The Supreme Court distinguished between public and private colleges in 1819 and freed private institutions of higher learning from state control. Thereafter hundreds of private experiments in higher education appeared, even though public funding dropped to very low levels. During the Civil War, the Morrill Act (or Land Grant College Act) set a revolutionary precedent by laying the foundation for the state university. The beginning of the federal government's involvement in public higher education, the Act gave each state huge land areas for higher education. The result was dozens of land-grant colleges, which developed into state universities. Equally important, it promoted the higher education of larger numbers of students and called for college-level courses in agriculture, technical and industrial subjects, in order to attract students from the working classes. The first colleges to admit African Americans and women also opened before the Civil War.

## Immigration, assimilation and segregation, 1865–1945

The rapid pace of urbanization, industrialization and immigration brought a turning point in American education after 1865. In the popular print media, the immigrant slum child became the symbol of the dangers of these processes, and the public schools were asked to remedy the situation.

Assimilation through the schools seemed increasingly necessary as immigrants from southern and eastern Europe and several Asian nations arrived in large numbers. The schools were expected to Americanize these exotic newcomers by teaching them English, the principles of American democracy and the skills needed for the workplace. As important, the schools would get immigrant children out of unhealthy tenement housing, off the streets, out of factories and away from gangs. To accomplish these goals, compulsory school attendance laws were soon adopted in the states. By 1880 almost three quarters of school-aged children were in school.

These laws also applied to racial minorities. After the Civil War, the federal government's Freedmen's Bureau and other northern organizations founded many schools in the south for the former slaves. But whether African, Asian, or Native American, minority students everywhere were placed in separate schools. In 1896 the Supreme Court's *Plessy* v. *Ferguson* ruling gave legal backing to the segregation that already existed.

Politicians quickly put children in school, but they did not as quickly appropriate money for hiring more teachers and erecting new buildings. Overcrowded, poorly maintained schools and staff shortages were typical of American public schools between the 1880s and 1920s. Opening teaching to women (often the daughters of immigrants) provided the new teachers, and 'normal schools' to train them grew rapidly in number.

Around 1900, public-school teaching was not considered a profession. The average annual salary for teachers was lower than that of an unskilled worker, and many teachers had no more than a high-school education themselves. Yet real progress was made in teacher preparation in the decades after compulsory attendance laws were passed. States set standards for teaching licences, which increasingly included a college degree with courses in pedagogy. After the 1920s, 'school marms' and 'schoolkeepers' were members of a profession called 'educators'. Salaries for teachers, however, remained low, and the profession was regarded as one of the least prestigious.

In the same period, reformers assigned the schools new priorities and duties. John Dewey and others held that curricula and teaching methods had to be changed. Instead of moralistic piety and rote memorization, the schools had to give pupils practical skills suited to their environment and the habit of discovering knowledge for themselves. 'Learning by doing', personal growth, and child-centred rather than subject-centred teaching became the goal.

Public schools were to become community centres and the means of social progress. About this time, progressive education introduced physical education, music and fine arts, and vocational subjects (training in skilled occupations) as electives (optional courses). These educators also developed the after-school extra-curricular activities, such as team sports, that became a typical side of American education. In 1917, the federal government offered financial support to any public secondary school that emphasized vocational education. Some immigrant parents criticized progressive education because they felt less demanding electives took time away from academic subjects. They also objected to the frequent assumption that immigrant children did not need academic studies, since they would not go on to higher education.

After 1865, private church-related colleges, often founded by European immigrant groups, rapidly increased in number, especially in the mid-west. Co-educational higher education (colleges open to both men and women) became the norm there during the Civil War, when fee-paying women were necessary to replace the men who joined the Union armies. Co-education continued to spread, and by the 1920s almost half of American college students were women. Further east, however, the so-called Ivy League universities (Harvard and other prestigious schools from the colonial period) remained men's institutions, and hence, benefactors established separate women's colleges in that region. Racial segregation extended to higher education during this period, when colleges for African Americans, such as Howard University and the Hampton Institute, were founded in the south after the war. In 1890 a new Morrill Act provided the region with land for African-American public colleges that emphasized manual and industrial education.

After 1900, graduate and professional schools became more common. Advanced degree programmes began to transform some well-established universities into research institutions, and engineering schools, business colleges, law and medical schools were founded in growing numbers. For all but a small elite, however, a college degree seemed a luxury. Even in 1940, less than two of ten college-age people attended institutions of higher learning. Instead, as parents less often had farms, handicrafts or family businesses to pass on, they secured their children's future through further education at vocational, office, secretarial or management schools.

## The Second World War and the Cold War

The Second World War was a watershed in American higher education. To ease the return of war veterans to civilian life, Congress passed the Servicemen's Readjustment Act (the so-called 'G.I. Bill') in 1944. Under the Act, the federal government paid tuition and living costs for veterans in higher education and directly funded the expansion of study programmes for the first time. Within two years, half the people in college were veterans, many of them from working-class families with little education. More students graduated than ever before, and the typical student ceased to be a member of the upper middle or upper classes. By 1971, when the programme ended, nearly 2.5 million veterans had benefited from its provisions. Higher education in the USA had become mass education and was regarded as a right rather than a privilege.

The launching of the Soviet satellite *Sputnik* in 1957 spurred another increase in the federal government's role in public education. Now the schools were enlisted in the Cold War and called on to meet the challenge of Soviet technology. The National Defense Education Act (1958) provided federal money for research and university programmes in science and technology, as well as loans to college students. The legislation also alotted federal funds for teaching science, mathematics and foreign languages in high schools.

After 1958, federal money was targeted for college-level foreign-language teaching, the equipping of language laboratories, and eventually for the humanities in general. In the 1950s, state after state required teachers to sign 'loyalty oaths' to the USA, and Senator Joseph McCarthy (among others) attacked the universities as hotbeds of communism. Education became a patriotic obligation as well as a right.

## Race and school desegregation

The Supreme Court's *Brown* decision struck down the principle of separate-but-equal educational facilities for the races in 1954. One year later the Court ruled that public-school districts all over the nation had to present plans for achieving 'racial balance' in their schools. Federal school policy began to show a profound change in national priorities.

For almost twenty years, from 1955 to 1974, the court tried to desegregate America's public schools. It settled on bussing as the most effective way to integrate the schools. Until very recently, one universal rule in America was that pupils attended the school closest to their homes. Since African Americans and whites live in different residential sections of US cities, they attend different school districts. Residential segregation produces segregated schools. Therefore, the Supreme Court decided to 'bus' students to other districts until 'racial balance' in all city schools resulted.

In city after city across the nation, parents, school authorities and politicians of both races protested and resisted, but the Court held firm, with the result that whites fled to the suburbs in greater numbers and the small percentage who could afford to sent their children to private schools. Federal authorities decided that bussing plans could produce integrated schools only if they included the 'lily-white' suburban schools around major cities. After such plans began transporting white pupils into city schools, the public outcry grew louder. By 1974, the nation's mood had become strongly anti-bussing, and when asked to decide whether a city-and-suburbs bussing plan was constitutional, the Supreme Court backed down, saying no tradition in American public education was more deeply rooted than the local control of schools. Thus bussing stopped being effective for school desegregation.

The trend towards increasing integration of the races in the school slowed, and by the late 1980s the trend had reversed. *Re*segregation of the schools began. By 2003, over 40 per cent of the schools were mostly or entirely African American. An even larger percentage were 'racially segregated' if the definition includes schools that were predominantly Latino, Asian and African American. Most of these schools were located in the north, west, or south-west, because the court integrated southern schools first and did not support bussing between the suburbs and inner-cities of the north after 1974. Not only the end of bussing, but the continued 'white flight' (now to the outer suburbs) and decades of high immigration of mostly non-white, poor Latinos and Asian Americans contributed to the growing resegregation of the schools.

## *Affirmative action and the schools*

Starting in the 1960s, the federal authorities fought the effects of prejudice and the related problem of poverty through involvement in educational programmes. In 1963, Congress began providing money for college and university buildings. In 1964, it decided that federal funding was available only to educational institutions that proved they did not discriminate on the basis of race, religion or national origin. The Higher Education Act of 1965 helped minority and 'disadvantaged' students get college loans. State and federal grants to poorer public schools generally came in two ways. First, laws made the income levels in local districts the basis for distributing public funds. 'Low-income' areas qualified for extra grants and special programmes to attract good teachers. Second, governments more than tripled their contribution to the general budgets of cities with social and educational problems.

In general, federal government policy aimed to implement the principle of affirmative action that President Lyndon Johnson expressed in his commencement speech at Howard University in 1965:

> You do not take a person who for years has been hobbled by chains and liberate him, bring him up to the starting line of a race, and then say, 'You are free to compete with all the others', and still justly believe that you have been completely fair.

Affirmative-action programmes to improve women's and minority groups' access to education proliferated during the early 1970s. On the primary and secondary levels of public education, affirmative action first led to a redesigning of teaching programmes and textbooks. Discriminatory references to women and minorities were replaced with even-handed treatments, or more often, with 'positive role models' and examples of how women and minorities contributed to American history and culture. History and literature books, especially, changed as a result of this effort.

The hiring of staff on all levels was also affected because governments required educational institutions to become equal-opportunity employers. That meant hiring more teachers from minority groups at elementary and secondary schools and more women professors at universities and colleges. By law, educational institutions must encourage minority group members to apply for teaching positions. They must be sought out and interviewed or the school might lose government funding. Finding qualified women and minority-group members for positions became somewhat easier after the 1970s because of affirmative-action plans for teacher-training programmes and the increased number of students from these groups who completed university degrees.

Two affirmative-action programmes were designed to help 'disadvantaged' pupils succeed in primary and secondary schools. Head Start provides pre-school tutoring to children in educationally deprived families to help them begin formal schooling at the same level as those in more fortunate families. Upward Bound supplies remedial teaching, private tutoring and work–study programmes for older children. While Upward Bound has suffered repeated funding reductions, Head Start is considered a success and received additional congressional appropriations until very recently. It benefits close to a million children today.

Affirmative-action programmes in education provoked a number of US Supreme Court decisions. These did not call for the end of affirmative action, but changed the methods used to put it into effect. The best-known court cases in this area involved complaints from white males denied admission to university programmes, in their opinion, because female and minority-group applicants were given preferential treatment. In the *Bakke* decision (1977), for example, the Supreme Court ruled that it is unconstitutional to increase the number of students from racial minorities in university programmes by setting numerical quotas. In the 1990s voters ended California's and Texas's affirmative-action programmes by supporting propositions at elections to eliminate them. Early in the next decade the Supreme Court ruling in cases involving the University of Michigan more strictly limited admissions policies that favoured minorities in the interest of recruiting a diverse student body at institutions of higher learning.

## Accumulated expectations, disappointments and newer trends

In the early 1980s, Diane Ravitch, a well-known authority on US schools, listed the accumulated expectations Americans had for their educational institutions. It was hoped that education would:

- reduce social inequality;
- improve the economy and economic opportunity for individuals;
- spread the capacity for personal fulfilment;
- civilize and uplift the nation's cultural life;
- raise the level of and participation in its political life;
- lessen alienation, distrust and prejudice by increasing the contact among racial and socio-economic groups.

Perhaps understandably, a mood of disappointment with educational institutions has been evident in the USA since then because most of the social dilemmas the schools were supposed to solve remain serious problems. Bussing was largely abandoned, racial separation grew and the controversial effects of affirmative action led to the curtailing of those programmes. In the late 1990s the public added yet other expectation to its list, expressing support for more public money, national standards, religious values, testing and vouchers to raise the quality of the schools.

# Elementary and secondary schools

Local control over schools became traditional during the colonial period. The Constitution makes no mention of education, which reserves power over education to the states or people, according to the Tenth Amendment. All fifty state constitutions have quite specific provisions about education. Generally, these clauses (and state education laws) define the state's role and delegate primary responsibility for schools to local governments. As these are created by the states, their powers over education can be altered by the states.

Local authorities set up independent school districts, whose elected local boards of education make most decisions regarding public elementary and secondary schools. Generally, the districts organize their schools into kinder-gartens for five year olds, elementary schools for six to twelve year olds, middle schools (or junior highs) for pupils from thirteen to fifteen and high schools for students between sixteen and eighteen years old. The overall structure of educa-tion has several variants progressing from kindergarten through to doctoral degrees. See Figure 11.1 for a diagram of the most common of these. In the 2003–4 school year there were some 15,500 school districts with a total enrolment of over 48 million pupils.

Only when specific powers given to the federal government in the Constitution are involved, such as the protection of rights guaranteed in the Bill of Rights, do the federal authorities get directly involved in educational issues. In practice, the federal government seldom interfered with local schools to protect civil rights until the 1950s. The national government has also provided land for school sites, funds for special-educational projects and has influenced local school policy by making federal grants for education dependent on following non-discriminatory practices.

The federal government's involvement in education remains quite limited. Its administrative agency for overseeing and formulating educational policies was formed late and is still understaffed compared to that in other developed countries. Not until the early 1950s did Congress set up a federal Office of Education in the

**PLATE 11.1** Kindergarten play.
(*Janine Wiedel*)

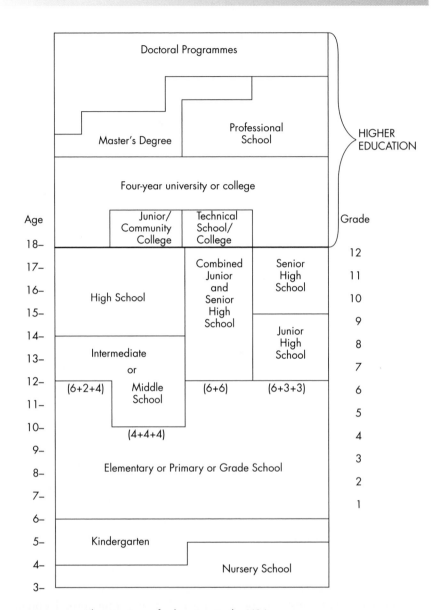

**FIGURE 11.1** The structure of education in the USA.

Department of Health, Education and Welfare. A separate Department of Education was not established until 1979. Ronald Reagan received considerable support then, when he promised to eliminate the department if he was elected. Even today the federal government provides on average only about 7 per cent of the funding for public primary and secondary schools.

Until the 1950s almost all state governments limited their involvement in education to two areas: establishing public state universities and setting general guidelines for public primary and secondary education. A state board of education, appointed by the Governor, formulated the guidelines, and the state's agency or department of education was to see that they were carried out in local districts.

The state Board of Education commonly sets only general minimum standards. It determines the number of days in the school year, the procedures for licensing teachers and administrators, the school-leaving age (usually sixteen), the 'core curriculum' that pupils must complete at each level of school and minimum requirements for academic progress at different grade levels. To graduate from secondary school, for example, students must pass a core curriculum that usually includes four years of courses in English, three in social studies and two in mathematics and science.

These common requirements serve several purposes. By establishing a degree of uniformity among diverse school districts, they allow educational leaders to keep the schools in line with standards in other states and developments in pedagogy. Hence, the core curriculum also facilitates the evaluation of individual schools and makes it easier for pupils to move from one district or state to another and gain admission to colleges and universities around the nation.

## Current trends in public school reform

In recent decades, state boards have increasingly implemented testing programmes to make individual districts more accountable for reaching a certain level of academic achievement at specified points in pupils' schooling. The same tests are often used in many states, and the results for districts and states are publicly available. The state board and parents are therefore better able to judge the relative success of the local schools in meeting educational goals. During the 1980s and 1990s, growing numbers of state boards won approval for statewide tests to measure teachers' mastery of core subjects and educational methods.

These trends and all the points on the public's agenda in the 1990s (outlined above) were included in the Bush administration's education-reform package. The No Child Left Behind Act it guided through Congress in 2001–2 appropriated more federal money for public education than any such legislation in decades. The Act, moreover, involves an unprecedented degree of top–down federal intrusion into state and local control over public schools. It requires the formulation of national and state standards of achievement in core curriculum subjects, greatly increased use of standardized testing of pupils and teachers to hold individual schools accountable to these standards, and a system of sanctions against public schools that do not meet annual targets for improvement. These include vouchers for sending pupils to other schools, including private religious institutions.

## *Localism and public education*

There are three important kinds of localism encouraged by the delegation of state authority to local school districts. Financial localism generally refers to the delegation of responsibility for funding schools to local districts. In the final decades of the twentieth century, state spending on education increased by as much as 70 per cent, and federal contributions to public schools grew significantly as well. Yet, local real-estate taxes still raise around 43 per cent of local school budgets. (The average school district receives this portion of its budget locally, half its funds from the state and the rest of its financial resources from the federal government.) In other words, local money still makes a very significant difference for public schools.

Forty-three per cent in a rich district with valuable homes and businesses represents the resources for better teaching salaries, buildings and equipment than those in most other districts. In the smaller school budget of a poor district, 43 per cent represents less money, and that has a proportional effect on resources for its schools. Each district is free to decide how high it wants to set property taxes for education. But even when poor districts approve higher tax rates to those of wealthy districts, they raise less money for schools because local property has so little value. Thus, financial localism (in combination with the causes of the great economic differences between school districts) is still the reason for wide variations in the quality of American public schools.

State plans to redistribute local property taxes aim to reduce the educational inequality resulting from financial localism. Redistribution plans collect the real-estate taxes in the state and place them in a fund for public education. This money is then distributed to even out the differences in school budgets across the state. Such plans can bring drastic changes in the school budgets of both rich and poor districts. Generally, they have taken money for education from suburbs and given it to inner-city areas. Hence, there has been less money for schools dominated by white pupils and more for schools with many Latinos and African and Asian Americans.

As expected, redistribution plans have met opposition. Some suburban groups have tried to preserve the advantages of their schools through private donations or special local education taxes. At least one state (New Jersey) responded by ruling that any increase in the school budgets of richer districts would result in an automatic equal increase in the budgets of poorer districts. State courts in several parts of the nation have demanded redistribution programmes.

Increased state contributions to local school budgets and redistribution plans have given state boards of education greater leverage in enforcing state-wide standards. However, state authorities often show a reluctance to use their power. Like the public they serve, they still believe that in a democracy, education should not be imparted by central authorities, but designed by the people in the governments closest to them. Such thinking and the opposition of suburban voters have limited the effects of redistribution plans. The result is that the money spent per pupil in predominantly white suburban schools is commonly two to three times that spent in racially mixed city schools. American traditions of financial localism in education remain strong.

Political localism is chiefly exercised through the members of the local board of education. They have more power over the schools than members of the state board do and are nearly always elected. Anyone who lives in the district can be a candidate for the board. The majority of those elected are parents, teachers and local business people. It is also common to elect a student to the board. The school system's chief administrator is usually an ex-officio member of the board with no vote but great informal influence over decisions. While some boards have difficulty reaching agreement because members represent opposing political views, often the board as a whole reflects the district's predominant conservative or liberal political attitudes.

The local board is powerful because it makes a range of important decisions. It determines the size and content of the school budget and controls the hiring and firing of teachers and administrators. The choice of subjects, programmes and educational goals beyond the state minimums is the board's, as is the definition of school disciplinary rules and routines. It must approve the selection of library and textbooks, and it has the final word on how educational facilities should be designed, constructed and maintained. Local boards make decisions on whether the district should apply to the state or federal government for aid under specific programmes. The boards that are most resourceful in applying for these funds get more help. In practice, that means districts with well-educated populations (and usually higher incomes) often succeed in getting more money from the state and federal governments.

Another important source of political localism is the PTSA (the Parent–Teacher–Student Association). The PTSA is a voluntary organization whose officers are elected by the members. It has no legal authority to make school policy, but its discussions often frame the issues debated and decided by the school board. Moreover, people who have been active in the PSTA are often the local residents who get elected to the board.

The third kind of localism in American education, social localism, refers to the distinctiveness of districts' educational priorities and goals that results from differences in their populations' social attitudes. These attitudes generally reflect the local population's dominant socio-economic class and mix of occupations, religions, races and ethnic groups. It can be argued that social localism produces differences in the public schools that are quite as significant as those caused by differences in districts' ability to pay for schooling. School-board members and PTSA leaders, who may or may not be representative of the local population, cannot afford to ignore these attitudes and the population characteristics from which they spring.

Social localism is significant because local boards make important policy decisions. It has led to public schools emphasizing agricultural methods, industrial arts, commercial studies, or college-level 'advanced placement' courses. It has inspired religious, white supremacist and assimilationist policies in some districts, and opposing policies in others.

Extreme examples of social localism have resulted in replacing evolutionary theory with the biblical story of creation in science courses, removing literary classics from school libraries, sex-education lessons and the presentation of alternative lifestyles and sexual orientations in elementary schools, a district policy of teaching that American society is the world's greatest and decisions to refuse the children of illegal immigrants public schooling. Many such extreme social policies are struck down by judicial rulings or changed after public reactions.

The goal of Americanizing immigrant children has been discarded. Today, after the civil-rights movements of the 1960s and 1970s, support for equal educational opportunity and pluralism (the belief in allowing several alternatives) is standard in the rhetoric (though not as often in the practices) of most American school districts. In fact, equal opportunity today means that both state and federal governments sometimes deem it necessary to intervene in the affairs of local school districts to ensure that minority students are given an education fitted to their special needs and problems. Pluralism produces even more various public schools as some local districts tailor their curricula to suit African as well as Latino and Asian immigrant children and add ethnic-studies courses and bilingual education programmes.

Pluralism in the public schools has also meant debate over the core curriculum. Led by scholars in college education departments who question the traditional content of required subjects, districts, states and even the federal government have tried to redefine common standards and the canon (accepted principle content) of subjects in recent decades.

Committees of recognized experts in many fields have met (sometimes for years) to develop national standards for subjects and a national curriculum. In the USA, however, that can only consist of suggested guidelines. The recently enacted No Child Left Behind Act, for example, offers national models for appropriate standards in core subjects at different grade levels, but it bows to the states' constitutional authority over education by leaving it to them to define each state's legal variant of the Act's rules. States still control educational programmes. The standards adopted in many districts and states to meet the general guidelines of the new law have caused publishers to redesign basic textbooks in most core subjects for all school levels.

## *Private elementary and secondary schools*

Pluralism means not only permitting great variety in the public schools but also allowing a wide variety of private schools. About 13 per cent of the school-age population attends one of the nation's more than 27,000 private schools. Private educational institutions show even more variety than the public schools. Four out of five are parochial schools (run by religious groups). By far the largest number of these are Catholic institutions, but fundamentalist sects, a range of other Protestant denominations, orthodox Jews, as well as Islamic and Asian religious groups also run parochial schools.

Non-sectarian private schools have a weak religious allegiance or are entirely secular. They are quite diverse but frequently promise a high standard of academic excellence, adherence to a particular theory of education, the ability to instill discipline and maturity, or some combination of these qualities. The Montessori schools offer a specific method of learning. Elite college-preparatory boarding schools (so-called 'prep schools') have exceptionally well-qualified faculties whose goal is to help the children of the wealthy gain admission to prestigious universities like those in the Ivy League, and to eventually take their place in the country's upper class. A variety of military academies specialize in dealing with 'problem children' whose parents can afford to reform their habits by subjecting them to the rigours of a regimented life away from home.

Private schools depend heavily on endowments (private donations), invest-ments and income from fee-paying students to meet their expenses. Public funding amounts to less than 10 per cent of their budgets. Until very recently, the courts limited the public funding available to parochial schools to programmes that benefit school pupils in general, rather than particular institutions. Thus, all children can receive government aid for some medical services, nutrition supplements and transportation to school.

A recent development is that in some areas parents can receive grants (or government vouchers) to pay for tuition at private schools. Especially in the inner cities, where private schools have a better record than nearby public schools, states have for some time operated voucher plans. The No Child Left Behind Act now makes this a possibility anywhere a local school repeatedly fails to meet annual improvement goals.

Some private educational institutions offer financial aid to attract students from a variety of social backgrounds, while others follow a restrictive admissions policy to maintain a more homogeneous student body. Exclusivity has always been an important attraction of many private schools. Bussing programmes to end segregation contributed to increased enrolment at all-white private insti-tutions. The Supreme Court's ban on group prayers and religious instruction in general in the public schools has caused others to turn to private education. Dissatisfaction with the public schools' academic standards, lax discipline, drug abuse or crime has convinced yet other parents to pay for private education. These problems are certainly more avoidable in private schools, since the expulsion of pupils who cause them is much simpler for private institutions.

# Higher education

High-school graduates enter higher education through a process of mutual selection in a system that is decentralized, diverse and competitive. Colleges and universities select a student body according to criteria set by the individual institution rather than by a central authority. The federal government has only an indirect influence on these standards through equal educational-opportunity programmes, civil-rights laws and constitutional rights. State approval is necessary for institutions of higher learning to operate and grant degrees, but once that is gained, state involvement is usually minimal.

This large degree of institutional independence has encouraged grass-roots experiments and innovations in higher education. The resulting diversity is enormous. The public sector includes the national military academies, fifty state university systems and hundreds of local technical or 'specialty' schools, community colleges, and city universities. In the private sector there are thousands of institutions, ranging from specialty schools to small church-related colleges to major universities with separate undergraduate, graduate and professional schools.

Thus entrance criteria reflect the particular character of the institution and the competition it faces from institutions of a similar sort. High-school graduates try to gain admission to a school that suits their individual needs. Students' requirements also vary greatly because the population is so heterogeneous, and secondary schools so different in type and quality.

In such a system, devices are needed to help institutions and students make informed choices in the selection process. There is no battery of nationally designed and evaluated examinations that pupils must pass to receive a high-school diploma. That fact and the great variation in the programmes and quality of US secondary schools make evaluating applicants' academic achievement difficult for colleges. To provide a basis for comparing pupils' skills, private agencies have developed competitive college-entrance examinations that are given all over the country on the same day. Almost all colleges and universities require applicants to take the best known of these, the Scholastic Achievement Test (SAT), and many prestigious schools also require pupils to submit their scores on other national tests.

In addition, institutions have admissions departments that visit and evaluate secondary schools, interview applicants and review pupils' application forms. Secondary schools have guidance departments with counsellors that evaluate colleges and universities for students and recommend programmes suited to their abilities and test scores. Regional organizations called accrediting bodies monitor the quality of secondary schools and institutions of higher education.

A closer look at some of these institutions of higher learning illustrates the choices students have. Post-secondary technical or 'specialty' schools offer training for specific occupations, such as accounting, computer-programming, laboratory work or business management. These institutions have become particularly numerous since the Second World War because of rapid changes in technology. Today, a few specialty schools are as prestigious as well-known universities.

Community colleges give courses covering the usual requirements for the first two years of college, at little or no cost to local residents. After that, students may graduate with an associate in arts (AA degree) or transfer into the third year of a full college or university programme and continue toward a bachelor of arts or science (BA or BSc degree). Community colleges are run by local authorities and offer many shorter certificate programmes suited to the occupational needs of a local area. As a result, many of their students are mature adults who study part-time.

Community colleges first appeared in the 1930s but did not become commonplace until around 1970. One of the more important recent developments in American higher education, community colleges fulfil a number of public expectations. They give reality to the consensus view that a basic college-level education should be available to the general population virtually free of charge. They satisfy the nation's commitment to 'life-long learning', the belief that retraining and continuing education are vital to the individual's and the nation's international competitiveness. Finally, they reflect public opinion that favours local control of education. Community colleges have opened the possibility of almost unlimited local control over courses of study and have also proved particularly adept at organizing cooperative programmes with local businesses and trade unions.

Although a clear majority of colleges and universities in the USA are private, four-fifths of high-school graduates choose public institutions. One important reason for this situation is that tuition (the cost of instruction) at city and state universities is often a small fraction of the fee charged at a private institution. Location also reduces the cost. City or state residents pay much lower tuition rates than students who come from other places. Public systems have purposely built campuses in many parts of the city or state so that students can live at home while they study.

Public systems also attract more students because some have open admissions policies and many have minimal acceptance requirements for area residents. The majority of secondary-school graduates who have average grades can thus avoid rejection in the intense competition for acceptance at more selective schools. Most of those are private, but city and state systems also have an enormous range of standards and programmes. Most states operate two university systems, one of them usually more oriented to applied studies and the other to academic work leading to research and the more prestigious professions. Many outlying 'branch' campuses of public universities are much like community colleges, but some concentrate on excellence through advanced courses in a limited number of fields. State university systems usually have a main campus that maintains higher overall standards. The best of these, the Berkeley campus of the University of California and the Madison campus of the University of Wisconsin, for example, have reputations that equal those of such elite private universities as Harvard, Yale, Princeton and Stanford.

Private higher education in the USA is typical of American pluralism. The private sector that educates a fifth of university-level students in the USA is large compared to that in other Western nations. Yet private institutions could expand their size greatly if they wished. On average, private colleges and universities accept only one in ten applicants.

There is no single or simple reason for this restrictive admissions policy. Inability to pay school costs is rarely the main reason for turning down an applicant. Good private institutions have little difficulty finding enough fee-paying students. Stipends, scholarships, low-interest loans, part-time work–study programmes or a combination of these are made available to people the institution wants. Private colleges and universities recruit as much as a third of their students among well-qualified poor, minority and foreign groups. Even the most prestigious institutions offer some of these recruits extra help (so-called remedial courses) as a form of affirmative action, because they believe in helping promising students in economic difficulty and think that studying with people of varied backgrounds is a vital part of a good education.

The reasons most private institutions have for remaining relatively small are related to their concept of a quality education. A few concentrate on high academic standards as their single definition of quality. Many more combine that goal with the ideal of a special community of learning. The ideal of community is often served by requiring students to live on campus and by having relatively few students per teacher to encourage the close contacts between students and faculty. A sense of community is also often established by bringing together staff and students who share a religious or ethnic background or socio-political orientation. Most American racial, nationality and religious groups have founded at least one private college or university.

Some institutions are common to both public and private higher education. The four-year liberal arts college, which about two-thirds of American students attend, is the most important of these. One of several units in a university or an independent organization, its purpose is to provide basic courses in a broad range of humanities and sciences. Liberal arts students usually do not specialize until their third year. That 'major', the capstone of their undergraduate education, is a requirement for the BA or B.Sc. degree.

A primary goal of the liberal arts college is making its graduates so-called 'well-rounded' individuals (generally well-informed and cultured people). By requiring a core curriculum, these colleges help maintain a common culture in the USA. Until around 1980 few questioned this canon of study and research, which aimed to expose students to the fundamental values of American and Western culture. Since then, the definition of the canon has conflicted with the ideal of pluralism.

**PLATE 11.2** Harvard University, founded in 1636 and the oldest of the universities in the 'Ivy League'.
(*Charles Sykes/Rex Features*)

Debate over the canon became so intense in the academy and educated public that Americans speak of the 'culture wars'. Nothing less than a redefinition of American identity or realizing cultural equality has been attempted. By the latter 1990s, many scholars had successfully argued that the canon of many subjects must be widened to include work of women and the non-Western cultures of many Americans. Debate continues, but the core curriculum is already much changed.

A liberal-arts degree is required before students can enter graduate schools. These may be professional schools, such as law or medical schools, or advanced liberal-arts schools that offer masters degrees (the MA or M.Sc.) and doctorates (the Ph.D.). To be admitted to graduate schools, students must normally take a competitive examination, either an entrance test for the professional school or graduate record exams (GREs) in liberal arts subjects. A hallmark of the best universities, America's high-quality graduate schools are internationally famous centres of research and magnets for well-qualified students from abroad.

Higher education in the USA is a competitive struggle. Over 60 per cent of high-school graduates (some 12 million people) entered colleges or universities each year in the 1990s, but only half of these students completed a degree. City and state universities normally 'weed out' one third to one half of the freshman class through tough introductory courses and exams that must be passed if a student is to stay enrolled. All American institutions of higher education use the system called continuous evaluation. It requires students to take mid-term and end-of-term examinations, write essays and term papers and complete additional tasks the instructor chooses to give. Course grades result from a weighted average of the student's marks on these assignments. A minimum overall grade average is necessary to continue one's studies.

## Recent problems and policy debates

'State of the nation' evaluations have become a regular part of public debate about American education. Presidential candidates, federal commissions and the US Secretary of Education, associations of the states, organizations of educators and private foundations regularly identify problems and suggest policy changes.

Concern over the quality of schooling at all levels has been the common theme in expert reports and public-opinion polls in recent decades. Efforts at reform have stabilized falling test scores on national public-school tests and college-entrance examinations but have not raised them significantly. Average achievement levels in language skills, mathematics and science have remained lower in the USA than in many other developed nations, according to comparative studies of secondary pupils, which also showed that American students spent less time doing homework.

The causes of unsatisfactory quality in public education have caused much debate. Some commentators on elementary and secondary schools claim that only the achievement levels of inner-city districts are a problem and that their poor results skewed the national averages. There was agreement, however, that continued 'white flight' to the suburbs and private schools produced increased racial segregation and inadequate funding in urban areas. Others thought the problem of quality was nearly universal in the public schools.

Polls in 2003 showed that the public linked lowered quality most to inadequate financial support, lack of discipline in the classroom and overcrowding, or to schools that were too large to allow students to develop a sense of shared community. The lack of well-qualified teachers or low pay scales for educators came much farther down on the public's list of concerns. In the wake of school shootings at the beginning of the twenty-first century, the schools continue to prioritize dealing with the causes of violence, such as problems at home, the availability of guns, violence and the attention given school shootings in the media, teasing and bullying, and the loss of a sense of community that results from how often American families move home.

Expert analyses of the causes of decline of school quality focus on curriculum changes. Some critics assert that students neglect basic skills because they are allowed to choose too many excessively vocational or undemanding electives. Such criticisms provoke heated responses, especially when they are linked with allegations that pluralism, the introduction of women's or non-Western 'multi-cultural' components, has weakened the core curriculum in schools. Revision of the academic canon is ongoing, as many institutions adjust their sense of the essential, learn to function according to newly required state standards under the No Child Left Behind Act, and implement stricter standards to meet yearly improvement targets.

Proposals for policy changes in public elementary and secondary schools show the conflicting opinions about decentralization. In Gallup polls, large majorities support requiring local schools to follow a central standardized national curriculum and to conform to national achievement standards. The same polls reveal strong support for school choice programmes, which often involve further decentralization. School choice allows families, rather than school authorities, to select the schools their children attend. Choice programmes began with the decentralizing of school districts by giving individual schools the autonomy to design their own curricula. The first autonomous public schools were so-called magnet schools in inner cities. These institutions were allowed to specialize in particular subject areas (such as the fine arts or science) and were given the funds and staff that, it was hoped, would bring voluntary desegregation by attracting students from other districts.

By 2000 magnet schools had multiplied, especially in large urban school systems, and school choice programmes now aim to maintain high standards by putting these schools in competition with each other. In increasingly large areas, universal choice completely breaks the connection between a place of residence and the public school a pupil attends. The No Child Left Behind Act institutionalized school choice by allowing parents to choose another school if the one nearest their home failed to reach state standards for improvement.

School choice advocates say the increased number of high-quality pro-grammes made available through choice gives students more chances to develop their abilities and point to reductions in racial segregation. Opponents argue that school choice relegates most staff and pupils to institutions that are weaker than ever before because they lack leadership and positive role models. They also criticize the concentration of the best faculty and pupils in magnet schools as an elitist approach that contradicts the ideals of American democracy. In 2004 well over a million children in the USA were being taught at home because their parents had decided to opt out of institutional schooling altogether.

# Exercises

Explain and examine the significance of the following names and terms.

| | | |
|---|---|---|
| No Child Left Behind Act | meritocracy | Horace Mann |
| Morrill Act | compulsory school attendance laws | John Dewey |
| progressive education | coeducational education | G.I. Bill |
| *Sputnik* | bussing | affirmative action |
| financial localism | political localism | programmes |
| independent school districts | state board of education | state redistribution plans |
| social localism | pluralism | parochial schools |
| community college | state university | private higher education |
| liberal arts college | graduate school | admissions policy |
| continuous evaluation | school choice programmes | magnet schools |

Write short essays on the following questions.

1. What do you view as major developments in the historical evolution of American education? Defend your views.

2. Debate the advantages and disadvantages of localism in public elementary and secondary education, keeping in mind the limits that have been put on local control.

3. Describe the private sector in American education. Is it good public policy for the USA to support alternatives to public schooling?

4. Discuss the issues of current debate in American education. Why are these questions important or difficult in the USA?

5. How can entering American higher education be described as a process of mutual selection in a system that is decentralized, diverse and competitive? Discuss the pros and cons of such a system.

## Further reading

Department of Education (2003) *Digest of Education Statistics* Washington, DC: DOE.

Gitlin, T. (1995) *The Twilight of Common Dreams: why America is wracked by culture wars* New York: Holt.

Kozol, J. (1991) *Savage Inequalities: children in America's schools* New York: HarperCollins.

Sowell, T. (1993) *Inside American Education: the decline, the deception, the dogmas* New York: Macmillan.

# Web sites

The National Center for Education Statistics (NCES): <http://www.nces.ed.gov>
The National Education Association (NEA): <http://www.nea.org>
<http://www.gallup.com/poll/indicators/education.asp>
<http://www.ed.gov>
<http://wwww.ed.gov/index.html>
<http://www.dese.state.mo.us.index.html>
<http://exchanges.state.gov>
<http://washingtonpost.com/wp-dyn/education>

# Chapter 12

# The media

- Media history
- Freedom of the media
- The contemporary print media
- The contemporary broadcasting media
- Attitudes to the media
- *Exercises*
- *Further reading*
- *Web sites*

The term 'media' may include any form of communication by which people are informed and entertained. In the USA, it refers generally to the print media (newspapers, books and magazines), the broadcasting media (television and radio) and electronic media such as the Internet (with 159 million users in 2002). Some of these forms are now also profitable parts of the film, video and computer industries as multimedia corporations have been established.

The media have evolved from simple methods of production and distribution to their present sophisticated technologies. They provide communications systems which convey words, images and messages to a mass audience, offer a diversity of consumer choice, cover homes and businesses, are an inevitable part of daily life and are powerful, influential and controversial.

Americans are very aware of and considerably conditioned by the media. The average full-time worker is exposed at home and at work to various forms of the media for some nine hours a day. Polls suggest, for example, that Americans receive 65 per cent of their news from television, 21 per cent from newspapers, 9 per cent from radio and 2 per cent from the Internet. Most is obtained from local television stations and newspapers and, to a lesser extent, from radio and national television and newspapers. There is also concern about, and resistance to, the media's dominant and pervasive roles. Government has frequently tried to muzzle the media (to little real effect) and pressure groups attempt to promote reform of media outlets.

The media may influence public opinion and partially shape attitudes by deciding what is newsworthy. Radio and television, for example, have minimized cultural and regional differences across the USA, but they have also reflected social diversity as they search for new markets. Access to power may be gained through media sources, which politicians use to influence voters. Political life and national and international events have thus become more immediate for Americans. But the mass of information and images may also confuse and desensitize audiences, leading some to reject the media.

Although non-commercial media exist, most US newspapers, magazines, publishers and radio and television stations are privately owned. They are businesses operating for profit and are closely tied to commerce, advertising and sponsorship. Companies use the media to encourage consumers to purchase their products through national and local advertising. The media rank as the country's third largest industry in terms of advertising revenue (2002). Critics oppose the alleged negative influence of advertising on media organizations, such as television.

However, consumer opinion also influences the media and conditions their agendas. They must respond to the public's wishes for a varied range of entertainment, information and news, if they are to be profitable. The ratings system for radio and television (statistics on audience approval) and print-media circulation figures are important determinants of success or failure.

Developments in mass communications and entertainment, such as computer technology, CDs, video and DVD, cable and satellite television, the Internet and printing advances have expanded the scope of the media society and helped to shape the country's cultural life. The growth of media outlets has widened this market, reduced the dominance of traditional formats, appealed to more diverse segments of the population and increased participation by viewers, readers and listeners. The availability of American television series, books, periodicals, satellite news programmes (such as CNN) and online newspapers abroad has also internationalized the US media's influence.

# Media history

Books and newspapers were the first media to emerge in early American history due to a public need for news, education and information. Book production increased when a printing press was set up in 1638 in Cambridge, Massachusetts. But presses and the print media were controlled politically by the British colonial authorities through a licensing system. Although the first newspaper, Benjamin Harris' *Publick Occurrences Both Foreign and Domestick*, was published in Boston in 1690, it was banned because it did not have a licence.

## The eighteenth century

Newspapers developed quickly in the eighteenth century. They gained influence and readership as they fought against licensing control and responded to political events and the demands of a growing population. The first, relatively comprehensive newspaper, the Franklins' *New England Courant*, was published in Boston in 1721. Papers then became a unifying force in the fight for independence from the British and communicated news of east-coast revolt to western settlers. After independence, court decisions bolstered freedom of speech and of the press.

Magazines were the last print media to emerge, expanded more slowly than newspapers and were partly influenced by middle-class wishes for entertainment. Andrew Bradford's *American Magazine* was the first magazine, appearing shortly before Benjamin Franklin's *General Magazine* (January 1741).

As the population grew and expanded westwards, the social role of the print media was emphasized. Presses and printshops were established by settlers, who published books of local laws, newspapers and magazines. After the War for Independence, newspapers declined in quality for a time. They became abusive and biased propaganda tools of political parties with vehement editorials in support of special causes and political programmes. Nevertheless, by 1800 there were some twenty daily papers and about a thousand weeklies in local areas, which increasingly made greater attempts at objectivity in order to gain and retain readers.

Newspapers had also gained the protection of the First Amendment of the Bill of Rights in 1791, which guaranteed freedom of the press. Americans were aware that some papers had supported them against the British before and during the War for Independence. They were determined that Congress should not have the power to infringe press freedom. This crucial development formed the basis of 'prior restraint' (the doctrine that the authorities cannot muzzle the press before publication).

## The nineteenth century

By the mid-nineteenth century, the print media became even more influential as social and cultural forces. There was an increase in literacy rates and an expansion of schools and libraries that created a mass market of readers. High-speed presses were manufactured to satisfy the market demand for news, entertainment, education and information. New magazines and newspapers emerged after 1825 and the market for novels, textbooks and general books increased as publishers organized the book industry into its modern structure.

There was a strong demand for novels, which sold in large numbers, and many were written by women. Novelists were aided by the introduction of paperback books in 1842. This development is still influential today, because paperbacks are an essential part of publishing firms' structure and are relatively cheap purchases for consumers. They began as supplements to newspapers and were later printed by orthodox book publishers.

Newspapers became a cheap and genuine mass medium and rapidly increased in number. They were mostly owned and edited by powerful and influential individuals who were personally involved in their papers. They introduced new publishing methods and forms of communication. James Gordon Bennett founded the first modern American newspaper, the New York *Herald*, in 1835. He employed reporters to gather news, appointed the first foreign correspondents, developed a Washington press corps and delivered the news before his competitors by using the telegraph and fast transportation.

Bennett was followed by Horace Greeley with his New York *Tribune* (1841), whose editorial page was very influential nationwide, and by Henry Raymond, who published the New York *Times* (1851). These and other owners improved news-gathering methods and developed innovative newspaper structures.

By the end of the nineteenth century, Joseph Pulitzer and William Randolph Hearst, with the *World* (1887) and the *Journal* (1895) respectively, dominated US newspapers. They were fierce rivals in a struggle for bigger circulation figures, produced papers which mixed sensational news reporting ('yellow journalism') with social crusading and introduced Sunday papers and the comic strip. A significant development occurred when E. W. Scripps founded the first newspaper chain (a collectivist structure under one ownership) from 1889. This trend became important in the twentieth century.

Newspapers (about 2,226 dailies by 1900) and other print media were now established as the primary means of communication for the population and had very large readerships. But journalism also became big business for some news organizations, which focused less on social crusading and more on maximizing profits.

## The twentieth century

Personal newspaper-ownership continued in the early twentieth century, although the total number of daily newspapers declined from their high point in the nineteenth century. Joseph Patterson printed the New York *Daily News* in 1919 (the first modern tabloid) and Robert R. McCormick published the *Chicago Tribune* from 1910.

Owners and editors realized that objective reporting rather than the earlier tendency to bias attracted more readers. Newspapers also became more conservative because advertising, on which they now depended financially, replaced circulation figures as the main source of income. Advertisers first aimed at a middle-class market, but later divided the population into other class and income groups. Different types of newspapers appeared, which reflected varied lifestyles, social status, education, political ideologies and consumption levels. Most newspapers were still concentrated in local areas and cities and were owned by individuals or companies. But economic pressures by the middle of the twentieth century forced many owners to sell their papers or join large chains which then dominated the media business.

Magazines and newspapers were similar in form and content and often embarked on crusading investigative journalism, which President Theodore Roosevelt called 'muckraking' (exposing scandal and corruption). Investigative reporting had previously been largely political. But it now also included criticisms of the general social system and attempted to gain public support for specific campaigns. Such investigative journalism became a feature of the print industries and was to spread to radio and television later in the twentieth century.

The print media were challenged first by Hollywood's silent films and later by sound motion pictures, which became the dominant entertainment sources of the 1920s and 1930s and an alternative attraction for audiences. These media forms also had to compete with radio broadcasting in the 1920s. Radio provided a new national and world perspective for many Americans. It unified country and city, minimized rural isolation, contributed greatly to cultural standardization and continues to be significant for news and entertainment.

Commercial television was introduced at the New York World's Fair in 1939, but the Second World War hindered its progress. After the war television began to dominate the other broadcast and print media. Its immediate information service affected the news function of newspapers, and its entertainment role challenged magazines, books and films. The other media coped with this and later competition (such as the Internet). Today, the US media are relatively decentralized with a large number of newspapers, magazines, radio and television stations and Internet web sites, although most are owned by multimedia conglomerates.

## Freedom of the media

The First Amendment to the Constitution states that Congress shall not make any law that abridges freedom of speech or of the press. This freedom from government control and censorship has been vigorously defended over the years. It has also enabled the press to serve as a watchdog over official actions, executive abuses and violations of individual rights.

All the media today (not only the press) claim equal treatment under the First Amendment and there is no overt government censorship of content or form. But freedom from prior restraint is not absolute. The Supreme Court has indicated that injunctions preventing publication could be granted if material clearly jeopardized national security and other exceptions have occurred in areas such as school newspapers. There are also licensing and anti-monopolistic regulations by the Federal Communications Commission (FCC), which make the broadcasting media less free than the print media. It is additionally argued that while the media appear to be constitutionally free, they are in fact subject to and conditioned by advertising, concentrated ownership patterns, economic pressures and consumer opinion.

Respondents to an *ABC News Nightline* poll in January 2003 felt that the right to a free press is essential/very important (38/49 per cent) and 59 per cent thought that the government should not have the right to control what information the news media can report. But, in a war-time situation, 60 per cent argued that the priority was the government's ability to keep military secrets, rather than a free press (34 per cent), 56 per cent thought that the news media should support the government (rather than questioning it) and 66 per cent felt that the government should have the right to prohibit the news media from reporting sensitive military information.

The media, in following their claimed constitutional rights and independence, have often pursued a confrontational or adversarial line towards public authorities and individuals. They have published official secrets, revealed classified documents and exposed corrupt practices, unethical behaviour and injustices in American life. This has led to tension between the media and public authorities.

For example, the *Washington Post* and the *New York Times* published the 'Pentagon Papers' in 1971. These were classified US Defense papers containing details of the American role in the Vietnam War. After appeals by the government, the Supreme Court ruled that the newspapers had a constitutional right to publish the information. The *Washington Post* also investigated and disclosed the Watergate scandal (resulting in the resignation of President Nixon). The media revealed the facts of the My Lai massacre in Vietnam and the Iran–Contra affair. Contemporary investigations continue into the activities of politicians, institutions and public figures (like the Clintons' Whitewater business dealings in the 1980s–1990s).

The question of the media's role, influence and power is controversial and debatable. Critics argue that the media have become too powerful and influential and that their freedom should be curtailed. The news media are accused of bias, distorted journalism, invasion of privacy, manipulating events, irresponsibility and of actively trying to shape public opinion by setting particular agendas. Actions for libel and obscenity, contempt-of-court charges to force the identification of journalists' sources and injunctions may be used against the media. These can protect individuals, organizations and the authorities in certain circumstances and arguably prevent absolute free expression by the media.

There is a close (for some critics unhealthy) bond between public authorities and the media. Each needs and uses the other to mutual advantage and gains access to sources and opinion-forming roles. The latest example is the practice of 'embedding' reporters with military units in the 2003 Iraq war. This connection may be unhealthily symbiotic and limiting for the media, rather than adversarial.

The mainstream US press has historically tended to ignore the private lives of its leaders. But this relationship has changed somewhat as tabloid newspapers, twenty-four-hour TV-news channels, talk-radio stations and Internet sites probe deeper into both the private and official lives of public figures. It is argued that such people have chosen their role and should be investigated, particularly if their private actions affect their public duties. The Internet (which is virtually uncontrollable by the government) and talk radio in particular have expanded opportunities for news, commentary, scandal-mongering and disclosure of classified information, some of which can be extreme. Some critics feel that a wide dissemination of information is healthier and more democratic than suppression and censorship.

## The contemporary print media

### The press (newspapers)

In 2003, some 1,457 daily newspapers (mornings and evenings during the week) were published in the USA, with a circulation of 55 million. This represented a decrease in the number of newspapers and circulation figures from 2002. But the 913 Sunday papers remained stable although circulation dropped to 58.8 million. In addition there are about 7,000 weekly, semi-weekly and monthly local newspapers.

Newspapers cater for different readerships. Some are characterized as 'quality' or 'serious' papers and have in-depth international and national news and feature coverage. Others are 'popular' or 'tabloid' publications, which emphasize crime, sports, comic pages, sex and scandal. However, critics argue that the majority of US papers have pretensions to quality and seriousness rather than sensational presentation.

It is often argued that the USA does not have a national press (centred in one city) or newspapers which are available in all parts of the country on the same morning. This is due partly to the nation's size and different time zones, but also because of a concern with local issues and identity. The one newspaper which is aimed at a national readership and regional distribution by means of satellite technology is the top-selling *USA Today*, which first appeared in 1984. It has brief articles rather than longer stories and a popular style.

However, almost all American papers are now available in online and updated format on the Internet. The national influence of some large quality metropolitan newspapers, such as the *New York Times*, the *Washington Post*, the

**TABLE 12.1** Average circulation of main daily newspapers, 2002.

| Newspaper | Description | Circulation |
|---|---|---|
| USA Today | popular | 2,136,068 |
| Wall Street Journal | quality | 1,800,607 |
| New York Times | quality | 1,113,000 |
| Los Angeles Times | quality | 925,135 |
| Washington Post | quality | 746,724 |
| (New York) Daily News | popular | 715,070 |
| Chicago Tribune | quality | 679,327 |
| (New York) Post | popular | 590,061 |
| (Long Island) Newsday | quality | 578,809 |
| (Houston) Chronicle | quality | 552,052 |
| San Francisco Chronicle | quality | 512,129 |
| (Dallas) Morning News | quality | 505,724 |
| (Chicago) Sun-Times | quality | 479,584 |
| (Boston) Globe | quality | 467,745 |

Source: Editor and Publisher International Yearbook, 2002

*Los Angeles Times* and the *Wall Street Journal*, together with *USA Today*, is considerable. These newspapers, and others such as the *Christian Science Monitor*, the (Baltimore) *Sun*, the *St Louis Dispatch* and the *Milwaukee Journal*, have international reputations.

Newspapers have experienced fundamental changes and developments in recent decades and have been forced to adapt to changed markets in order to survive. There has been a decline in the sales of most papers since the mass circulation years of the early twentieth century due to news competition from television and radio. The number of newspapers has also decreased because of mergers, conversions and closures. Readers have developed new media habits and circulation battles between different print formats (such as magazine supplements) have increased. But smaller dailies and weeklies have increased in number and circulation in local areas.

Newspaper decline has been accompanied by a reduction in competition and a lack of variety in publications. The number of cities with competing newspapers has been reduced and many cities have a single daily paper. Ownership is now held by a few publishers or corporations (media conglomerates) and 75 per cent of daily papers are now owned by newspaper chains.

Concentrated ownership of newspapers by large groups supposedly results in economies of size, efficiency and rationalization and gives greater profitability. But it also causes monopolistic conditions, a similarity in content and format and raises questions about objectivity and accuracy. While some quality papers are in fact local monopolies, it is argued that a greater diversity of newspapers would result in the counterbalancing of potential error and bias.

Newspapers have experienced significant technological changes in recent years, such as automated composing-rooms and the use of computer and electronic technology to process news. Some news is still gathered by individual reporters, but most newspapers, radio networks and television companies worldwide now obtain their news directly from two US-based news agencies: Associated Press (AP) and United Press International (UPI). They are independently owned and collect national and international news items which are sold to newspapers and other media sources. This means that a few news sources dominate in the US market, which results in comparatively homogeneous international and national news.

The big American papers themselves still provide a large number of their own news stories and sell copyrighted news and features to international and smaller national papers. This allows the wide dissemination of news throughout the USA and contributes to the influence of the larger papers. Similarly, the articles of independent syndicated columnists appear simultaneously in many newspapers. The stories in the big papers often influence local newspapers and television news programmes in their choice of newsworthy items.

It is argued that, following competition from television, newspapers generally have become more responsible, make their news columns as fair and accurate as possible, attempt to be objective in their reports and try to separate news from opinion (which is usually confined to political- and policy-influenced editorial pages).

Competition with television has led to new emphases in newspapers, particularly in investigative journalism. Although small local newspapers concentrate largely on local news, they may also be involved in wider issues (such as pollution) and have revealed cases of political corruption. It is the large city papers that are most active in investigative journalism and that have the resources for in-depth coverage. However, it is important not to overemphasize the amount of investigative reporting carried out by the US media. Few journalists engage in such work and many rely on common sources rather than their own independent investigations.

Investigative journalists argue that they are promoting important social change with their exposures, maintain that they perform a necessary democratic service and see themselves as servants of the public rather than officialdom. As in the past, some critics are opposed to investigative reporting, arguing that it constitutes a serious invasion of privacy in many cases and gives newspapers too much political influence.

## *Magazines and periodicals*

Some 11,000 magazines and periodicals are published in the USA at varying times from weekly and monthly to quarterly and half-yearly. They cater for most tastes and interests. Some have small and others large circulations. About 90 magazines sell over one million copies each issue and a smaller number have huge circulations. Some of these have international editions or are translated into other languages. Only six magazine companies account for half the total magazine revenue, indicating a high conglomerate concentration and influence. The best-selling (specialist) magazines deal with retirement (*Modern Maturity* and *NRTA/ AARP Bulletin*) and have sales of over 20 million. The list in Table 12.2 refers to generalist and specialist popular magazines covering television information, reading, travel and women's interests, many of which have experienced declining circulation since 1999.

Mass-circulation magazines declined from the 1950s because they had to compete for advertising and sales with television and newspapers. Rising costs of production and paper led to smaller formats and fewer magazines. Publications like *Life*, the *Saturday Evening Post* and *Look* did not survive as weeklies. A shift to specialization in specific areas has occurred, as magazines try to establish market positions, although sales of many magazines continue to drop.

However, general magazines (such as *Reader's Digest*) are an important element of American cultural life. They were originally designed for entertainment purposes, but they could also be influential in social and political areas. Today, general magazines are mainly informational and are concerned with very

**TABLE 12.2** Main general magazines: average circulation, 2002.

| Magazine | Circulation |
| --- | --- |
| Reader's Digest (general interest) | 11,944,898 |
| TV Guide (specialist) | 9,061,639 |
| Better Homes and Gardens (specialist) | 7,607,832 |
| National Geographic (specialist) | 6,657,424 |
| Good Housekeeping (women's interest) | 4,690,508 |
| Family Circle (women's interest) | 4,601,708 |
| Woman's Day (women's interest) | 4,239,930 |

Source: Audit Bureau of Circulations, 2002

varied aspects of social life. They are aimed at readers in specific age, interest or economic groups.

The more specialist magazines are targeted at people with particular professional occupations and interests and serve as an important means of communication among them. In fact, the majority of all magazines and periodicals are 'trade' or specialist publications. They cover business, professional, technical, industrial, scientific and scholarly areas.

US news magazines are very successful when compared with those of other countries in this field. *Time* (4,109,962 in 2002), *Newsweek* (3,125,151) and *US News and World Report* (2,032,286) dominate the news-magazine market. They sell well in the USA, although circulation has declined since 1999, have international and Internet editions and sell some of their news material to publications worldwide.

Some influential periodicals specialize in coverage of educational, political and cultural topics, such as *The Atlantic Monthly, Harvard Educational Review, Saturday Review,* the *New Republic, National Review, Scientific American, Foreign Affairs, Smithsonian* and the *New Yorker.* These, together with other specialist professional journals, supply the more serious end of the magazine market, and some of their material is reprinted internationally.

The leisure or hobby end of the magazine market is catered for by magazines which deal with sports, popular pastimes, motoring, fashion and leisure activities. Some, such as *Cosmopolitan* (3,021,720 in 2002) and *Vogue* (1,257,787) also sell internationally.

## Book publishing

There was concern in the twentieth century that radio, film and television might reduce the appeal of reading and book sales. But book purchases did increase and the US led the world in the number of books read per head of population. However, a National Endowment for the Arts survey in 2004 found that there had been a decline of 10 per cent in literary readers (to include popular and classical) from 1982–2002, which suggested that reading was at risk in the USA.

Historically, US schools generally have encouraged reading and a love of books, public libraries have actively sponsored book-usage in local communities nationwide and there are no restrictive laws which control book-selling and prices. There is an open market in new and used books, which are widely sold in a variety of sales outlets, such as supermarkets, in addition to standard book shops.

American books cover a comprehensive range from fiction to technical works. They have become an important leisure, as well as an educational and professional, activity. There are 2,500 major book publishers in the USA, with about six conglomerates accounting for more than half of total book revenues. They publish hard cover and paperback books and differ in size and variety of publications. Many thousands of new books are published each year and a large export trade has contributed to the worldwide influence of American books, especially in the scientific and technological fields.

About a quarter of the publishing structure deals with books intended for a general audience, such as fiction, bestsellers, biography, art books and children's books. Three quarters of the publishing business is divided among text-books, reference works, subscription book clubs and scientific and technical publications.

## The contemporary broadcasting media

The broadcasting system (radio and television stations) is characterized by its diversity and division into commercial and non-commercial sectors. The commercial sector is largely financed by money from businesses that pay to advertise goods or services before, during and after programmes, or by subscriptions from cable and satellite users. Advertising is a large and profitable industry and its connection with the media is controversial because of its influence. The non-commercial sector, like the Public Broadcasting Service (PBS), is largely non-profit-making, educational or cultural in nature and is run by organizations such as colleges and universities. Even though it is funded by individual subscriptions, corporate sponsorship and grants from foundations, private bodies, educational sources and the government, it has to survive on limited budgets. Although public television does not carry advertising, its credits to corporate sponsors do look like the format of television commercials.

All radio and television stations must be licensed to broadcast by the Federal Communications Commission (FCC). This is an independent federal agency, financed by Congress, whose members are appointed by the President. It controls the stations by granting limited-period licences to applicants and has a supervisory and regulatory role. The FCC does not control the actual reception of broadcast programmes through the air. This means that there are no licence fees in the USA for owning equipment such as television sets. Broadcast reception is freely available in most cases, except for cable and decoded satellite services.

There is no direct government censorship of broadcasting content, but the FCC, with its licensing power, does regulate media-ownership by ensuring that there are no monopolies and that a variety of services, programmes and frequencies are provided throughout the country. Its 'fairness doctrine' also requires stations to give equal time to opposing views, and commercial stations must show free 'public-service' announcements, such as Red Cross blood drives and Alcoholics Anonymous programmes.

## Television

Television is the dominant and most controversial national medium. In 2003 some 98 per cent of American homes had at least one television set of which the majority were colour and which might have been watched for an average 4.3 hours a day. Surveys suggest that television is the most important source of news for most Americans. It can be influential in forming opinions and consumer choice and may be potentially capable of affecting the outcome of political elections.

The Federal Communications Act of 1934 established local television stations as the bodies legally responsible for all their output, no matter where their programmes originated. There are about 1,200 television stations in the USA, which vary in size and have separate identities and characteristics. Some 280 are non-commercial and 920 are commercial stations.

Most commercial television stations are affiliated with and receive many programmes from the current Big Four private national television networks, which buy most of their programmes from independent production companies. The Big Four are the American Broadcasting Company (ABC, established in 1943), the National Broadcasting Company (NBC, established in 1926), the Columbia Broadcasting Service (CBS, established in 1928) and Fox Broadcasting Company (established in 1986).

The networks compete against each other to attract the highest audience ratings and advertising revenue. Thus, most of the programmes that most people watch follow the same formats nationwide and similar programmes are shown at the same time during prime time (7.30 p.m. to 11 p.m.). This structure had traditionally given the three older networks (ABC, NBC and CBS) great influence. Until the 1980s, they dominated American television, having a combined share of 90 per cent of the total television audience.

In addition to their entertainment role, the networks have news-gathering organizations in the USA and worldwide. They broadcast nationwide news and current-affairs programmes throughout the week, such as CBS's *Sixty Minutes*

**TABLE 12.3** Favourite prime-time commercial TV programmes, 2002–3.

| Rank | Title | Genre |
|------|-------|-------|
| 1 | CSI | crime and forensics |
| 2 | Friends | sitcom |
| 3 | Joe Millionaire | reality game show |
| 4 | ER | hospital series |
| 5 | American Idol | pop competition |
| 6 | Survivor (Thailand) | reality adventure game show |
| 7 | Everybody Loves Raymond | sitcom |
| 8 | Survivor (Amazon) | reality adventure game show |
| 9 | Law and Order | crime |
| 10 | NFL Monday Night Football | sports |
| 11 | CSI: Miami | crime and forensics |
| 12 | Will and Grace | sitcom |

Source: Nielsen Media Research, 2002–3

and NBC's *Meet the Press*. Local commercial television stations also have news teams, reporters and film crews to provide local news programmes, but may be parochial and limited in scope.

However, the largest television network (in terms of the numbers of its stations) and an alternative to commercial television is the advertising-free PBS. This system was created in 1967 by the Public Broadcasting Act and has about 280 stations sharing programmes. The recent growth of these television stations has been considerable, although they have a much smaller audience than commercial television. The high quality of their news, entertainment and educational programmes (such as the children's programmes, imported drama series and films) have attracted selective audiences.

## Independent, cable and satellite television

Since the 1980s, the power of the original Big Three networks has declined because of competition. New challenges came from independent television stations that were originally unaffiliated with the networks and that broadcast syndicated programming, comprising mostly repeats of earlier network series. They have built larger audiences nationwide by expanding the quality and range of their services and by using broadcast technology and cable and satellite facilities.

Cable stations originally provided television programmes to subscribers in communities which could not receive air broadcasts because of geographical limitations. There are now many different types of schemes, systems and programmes. Cable companies transmit cable and other network, affiliated, independent and public television services. There were 9,947 cable-television systems in the USA in 2002, and the number of households with basic cable facilities was 68.9 million in 2002 (or 68 per cent of those households with television sets). The top cable networks in 2003 were TBS Superstation, ESPN (sports), C-SPAN and the Discovery Channel.

Cable companies charge a fee to subscribers for the cable service and are financed through this revenue and advertising. Viewers may pay additional sums for specialist channels and special live broadcasts. There has been a big increase in religious cable stations and ethnic cable channels nationwide with networks for African, Latino, Jewish, Chinese, Japanese, Portuguese, Greek, Hindi and Korean interests.

Satellite television also threatened the dominance of the original Big Three networks. It initially offered programmes to rural populations who could not receive cable systems. It gives those people who have a satellite dish and pay subscriptions a wide range of television channels.

**PLATE 12.1** CNN reporting of the Gulf War, 1991. Coalition action (Operation Desert Storm) to free Kuwait from Iraqi occupation was covered by CNN reporters in Baghdad, where they worked under Iraqi censorship.

A further threat to the Big Three supremacy was the home-video market, with videos for sale or rent. By 2003 there was at least one video-cassette recorder (VCR) in 91 per cent of those American homes which had television sets. Video is now itself being challenged by increasingly huge sales of Digital Versatile Disks (DVDs).

Traditional network television has thus faced competition to retain its audience as viewers have changed to other services. Cable, satellite and independent television stations are attractive because they offer many different channels and a range of alternative choices. In 2002, household-viewing shares were 39 per cent for the Big Four networks, 3 per cent for public television, 11 per cent for independent and satellite stations, 49 per cent for basic cable and 6 per cent for pay cable.

## Attitudes to commercial television

US commercial television programmes have a mixed reputation in the USA and abroad. A variety of opinions and criticisms have been levelled by consumers and public officials.

Commercial television has been attacked for its bias towards commercial and mass-entertainment programmes ('reality' series, talk shows, soap operas and quiz games) which sell advertised goods and services. Advertising companies and station-owners may also interfere in programme content in the pursuit of profit. Some consumers criticize such programming, which is aimed at the lower end of the television market, and argue that companies should develop quality educational and news programmes. News broadcasting is also controversial because it can either appear to trivialize events by its reporting techniques or try to affect public opinion by the biases in its news coverage.

Commercial television is attacked for its portrayal of gratuitous violence and for the alleged impact of violence and explicit sex upon both children and adults. The debate over possible links between violence and sex on television and its occurrence in society continues, although such programmes are not now shown in the early evening and 'v-chip' technology allows parents to censor children's viewing.

There is a considerable amount of citizen involvement in other television-related issues, such as groups campaigning for better quality children's television and others that attack the alleged explicit language and immorality on television. Minorities and women are also concerned with television programmes and object to the representation of ethnic and gender stereotypes.

Commercial television (and the advertising companies) are often sensitive to such criticisms, since it can affect their profits. It is argued that objections have made commercial television into a more conservative institution, and there are indications that advertisers and owners may be paying more attention to the public's wishes.

Nevertheless, attitudes to American commercial television are not solely a list of complaints and negative comments. Not all of it is of poor quality. Some situation-comedy series are professionally made and are popular worldwide. Television can also perform essential educational and informative functions, with high-quality documentaries and in-depth news presentations. It provides live coverage of important events, occurring both domestically and worldwide. It has the capacity to closely examine politicians and their policies, so that viewers may make up their own minds about a range of issues. Politicians and advertisers are also very aware of television's power and influence, and this may help to moderate their behaviour.

## Radio

Radio had a revolutionary impact following its commercial introduction to the USA in the 1920s. It (and its immediate news function) helped to unify the population of the cities and the countryside, increased the national and world awareness of Americans and informed them about the events of the Second World War. Radio was overtaken by television in the 1940s and has had to develop new markets and emphases to survive. It has become divided into formats and specialities that are directed at specific consumer markets and this has increased the diversity of radio offerings. Some 89 per cent of American homes have a set, and radio is still popular and important, particularly on the local level, for its news, participatory (talk radio) and entertainment roles.

There is no one national radio station in the USA. Instead, cities and local areas have several independent stations and all are regulated by the FCC which grants them operating licences. They have different approaches: small-town stations carry local news and community interest items, as well as national and international news derived from larger stations; big cities are served by a large number of local stations and have many different formats.

There were 11,000 radio stations nationwide in 2003, most of which were commercial organizations. Commercial radio-ownership is concentrated in the hands of a relatively few conglomerates. Commercial stations obtain their funding mainly from the advertising on their programmes which are purchased from many different sources, although they do also make their own programmes. The public radio stations are generally owned and operated by educational institutions and religious groups, with a similar high reputation as PBS for their documentaries, news and debates. The National Public Radio network (NPR) is an umbrella organization of most non-commercial radio stations.

Diversity of choice is the key element of radio in the USA and many stations provide twenty-four-hour services to satisfy their customers. Most commercial radio stations are organized around and follow a specific format, which is designed to attract particular audiences. Permission from the FCC is necessary if a station wishes to change its format.

Some stations consequently provide music programmes (mixed or specialist) such as country and western, popular music, rock and roll, light classics, classical music and jazz. Others concentrate on news, studio interviews and discussions, talk shows and interviews, phone-ins (audience participation by telephone) and religious programmes. Stations with a talk format account for 10 per cent of stations and the number of listeners and active participants has increased considerably. Some stations broadcast only news for twenty-four hours a day, while most others provide five-minute summaries hourly or half-hourly. Others offer a variety or mixture of the above. In 2003, the primary format of top commercial radio stations were country and western, news and talk, religion, oldies, Spanish, adult contemporary, contemporary Christian and Top Forty.

## Attitudes to the media

The media themselves decide what are newsworthy political and public issues on which to concentrate. This choice often reflects an organization's views, editorial policy and individual journalists' personal opinions, although the media insist that they try to be objective, present all sides of a case and use self-censorship in order to avoid overt bias.

Attitudes to bias (or partiality) in the US media are revealing. A Pew Research Center poll in 2000 found that 57 per cent of respondents thought that members of the news media often let their political preferences influence the way they report the news, while 32 per cent believed that this happened 'sometimes'. A Gallup poll in September 2003 reported that 45 per cent of respondents thought that the news media was too liberal, 14 per cent thought it too conservative, while 39 per cent felt that political balance was 'about right'. A survey by the Roper Organization in 1984 found that 41 per cent of respondents thought that the media were biased against specific sections of society. Very different groups, such as business executives, workers, liberals and conservatives, all nevertheless thought that the media were against their own organizations and interests. Such even-handed findings, which might indicate that the media in fact are doing a neutral job, point to the difficulties in assessing media bias.

Some American research has suggested that there is a clear positive bias towards established institutions and values in the US media, although (perhaps surprisingly) not much partiality for particular political candidates and political policies.

It is argued that there is therefore a general media bias or scepticism aimed at all politicians and policies. The tendency is towards negativism rather than positivism and this produces an unfortunate undercurrent in reporting. Television is seen as more critical than newspapers and magazines, and the national media are more critical than local media.

The commercial bias of the media (except for PBS) is more obvious for critics and the public. Most media are private businesses and must sell subscriptions and advertising in order to make a profit and survive. Larger audiences (or numbers of readers) create greater advertising revenue and may result in the media printing or broadcasting what advertisers want.

On the other hand, the media must give the public what *it* wants in order to retain audiences. The media as a whole (but particularly television) can become entertainment rather than information or education and can employ emphases, such as human-interest stories, conflict, action, melodrama, the visual and the superficial. Such emphases may lead to a lack of quality, particularly of news, and may detract from the media's information role.

In summing up a complex situation Welch et al. suggested that:

> The media have to be responsive to the people to make a profit. They present the news they think the people want. Because they believe the majority desire entertainment, or at least diversion, rather than education, they structure the news towards this end. According to a number of studies, they correctly assess their consumers. For the majority who want entertainment, network television provides it. For the minority who want education, the better newspapers and magazines provide it. Public radio, with its hour-and-a-half nightly newscast [. . .] and public television, with its hour nightly newscast [. . .] also provide quality coverage. The media offer something for everyone.
>
> (1995: 244)

In terms of the news media and their influence, a Harris poll in February 2004 reported that only 17 per cent of respondents had a great deal of confidence in television news and 15 per cent in the press. A CNN/*USA Today*/Gallup poll in June 2003 showed that only 16 per cent of respondents had a great deal of confidence in television news (19 per cent 'quite a lot' and 47 per cent 'some'), while only 11 per cent had a great deal of confidence in newspapers (22 per cent 'quite a lot' and 49 per cent 'some').

A Council for Excellence in Government poll in June 1999 examined the media's more general role in American society and found that respondents thought that the media was second only to special-interest groups in being most responsible for what was wrong in government. A Gallup poll in February 1999 reported that 48 per cent of respondents thought that the media were out of touch with average Americans and 50 per cent believed they were in touch. In July 2002, the Pew Research Center asked respondents whether they thought that news organizations got the facts straight or whether their stories and reports were often inaccurate. Only 35 per cent felt that organizations got the facts straight and 56 per cent considered that stories and reports were often inaccurate. Some 58 per cent thought that the news media got in the way of society solving its problems and 31 per cent thought that the media helped society. Fifty-nine per cent felt that media criticism kept political leaders from doing wrong, and

49 per cent believed that criticizing the military helped to keep the nation prepared for any potential emergency.

Other polls reveal that many consumers feel that a laissez-faire attitude to the media is inadequate. They believe that current efforts to control violent entertainment are not enough and that media portrayals of violence are causes of real-life violence. A Gallup poll in February 2004 found that for viewers watching major television networks the following bothered them the most: violence (61 per cent), sexual content (58 per cent), profanity or swear words (58 per cent) and homosexuality (52 per cent). Some 75 per cent felt that the entertainment industry (films, television and music) needs to make serious efforts to significantly reduce the amount of sex and violence portrayed. When watching made-for-TV films or series on the networks, a 2000 Gallup poll reported that 52 per cent were shocked by something they saw and 45 per cent were not. Although aware of v-chip technology, 96 per cent did not use it. Similar reactions were expressed about negative racial and gender stereotypes. All these objections were voiced about films, videos, music, the Internet and television and reflected concerns about what audiences (particularly children) see and hear. Respondents favoured government legislation to restrict such depictions.

# Exercises

Explain and examine the significance of the following names and terms.

| | | |
|---|---|---|
| yellow journalism | William Randolph Hearst | ratings |
| muck-raking | newspaper chains | networks |
| *New England Courant* | advertising | formats |
| conglomerates | *Washington Post* | Watergate |
| syndication | cable television | PBS |
| FCC | bias | UPI |
| v-chip | ESPN | injunction |

Write short essays on the following questions.

1. Should the freedom of the American media be curtailed?

2. Analyse the contemporary significance of American newspapers in terms of their historical development.

3. Discuss the structure and influence of US television.

4. Examine the American media in terms of the public opinion polls in this chapter.

# Further reading

Barnhurst, K. G. and J. Nerone (2001) *The Form of News* London: Routledge.

Dautrich, K. and T. H. Hartley (1999) *How the News Media Fail American Voters: causes, consequences and remedies* New York: Columbia University Press.

Fallows, J. (1996) *Breaking the News: how the media undermine American democracy* New York: Pantheon Books.

Fuller, J. (1996) *News Values: ideas for an information age* Chicago, Ill.: University of Chicago Press.

Garry, P. M. (1994) *Scrambling for Protection: the new media and the First Amendment* Pittsburgh, Pa.: Pittsburgh Press.

Krimsky, G. A. and J. M. Hamilton (1996) *Hold the Press: the inside story on newspapers* Baton Rouge, La.: Louisiana State University Press.

Teeter, D. and D. R. Le Duc (1995) *Law of Mass Communications: freedom and control of print and broadcast media* Westbury, NY: Foundation Press.

Welch, S., J. Gruhl, M. Steinman, J. Comer, M. M. Ambrosius and S. Rigdon (1995) *Understanding American Government* St Paul, Minn.: West.

# Web sites

<http://usinfo.state.gov/usa/infousa>
<http://usinfo.state.gov/usa/infousa/media/media.htm>
<http://usinfo.state.gov/usa/infousa/media/mediaovr.htm>
<http://www.gallup.com/poll/indicators/indmedia.asp>
<http://usinfo.state.gov/usa/infousa/media/broadcast.htm>
FCC: <http://www.fcc.gov>
PBS: <http://www.pbs:org/insidepbs>
The *Washington Post*: <http://www.washingtonpost.com>
The *New York Times*: <http://www.nytimes.com>
CNN: <http://www.cnn.com>
*Time*: <http://pathfinder.com/time/magazine/magazine.html>
*USA Today*: <http://www.usatoday.com>

# Chapter 13

# Religion

- Religious history
- Contemporary US religion
- Church, state and politics
- Religion and education
- Attitudes to religion
- *Exercises*
- *Further reading*
- *Web sites*

Many Western countries have experienced modern declines in religious observance and increased secularization. These developments have been variously attributed to the effects of industrialization, consumerism, materialism, individualism and expanded education. However, despite such general images, the American people appear to be very religious.

The extent of this religiosity is difficult to determine since the US Bureau of the Census is not allowed, by law, to ask questions on religious identity. Evidence is therefore gathered from surveys, public-opinion polls and church sources, not all of which provide full or accurate information. Some public-opinion polls, for example, report that 65 per cent of Americans are formal members of religious denominations, while others find that 90 per cent have a nominal religious identification. A majority of people say they are very interested in spiritual matters and that religion is important in their lives. They also feel that the influence of religion is decreasing and that beliefs are increasingly treated as arbitrary and unimportant.

As in other countries, formal membership of, or nominal identification with, religious denominations is not always translated into active observance, and religious commitment varies significantly across the USA. Polls suggest that 41 per cent of Americans have gone to a religious service in the last week, and 60 per cent say that they attend on a weekly or monthly basis. Southerners appear to be the best attenders, followed by mid-westerners, easterners and westerners. Religious observation may sometimes be more socially directed than devout. Religious beliefs may also exist outside formal denominational identity and involve a disillusionment with present conditions and a vague unstructured striving for self-definition.

Nevertheless religion, in whatever form, does play a role in the USA. It is illustrated in the large variety of religious groups which reflect personal, communal and ethnic identities for citizens, in its influence on national institutions and morality and in the country's history.

## Religious history

The contemporary diversity of US religious life derives from Native-American religions, colonial history and the waves of later immigrants into the country. The historical development of religious practices needs therefore to be emphasized in order to appreciate the present.

This history is characterized by certain features. First, there is a distinctive religious pluralism (many different faiths) in the USA. Second, religious activity with evangelical (conversion or salvation-based) and fundamentalist characteristics has been an important feature at various times. Third, these features have often created conflict within faiths, between religions and for the larger society. Fourth, there has historically been an emphasis on the social aspects of religion and welfare provision by the churches. Fifth, religion has been closely linked to a belief in democracy and freedom. Sixth, religious identities and membership of churches have often been connected with social class and ethnicity. Seventh, there is a constitutional emphasis on separating religion from the state.

Throughout American history, all or some of these features have been reflected in periodic religious movements (known as awakenings or revivals), which have varied in intensity and scope: religious activism, missionary work, utopian ideals and an interest in ecumenism (cooperation between different faiths). There has also been religious discrimination and intolerance, periods when American religiosity has been very low and increasing secularism.

## *The colonial period*

Colonial settlement resulted in many religious denominations. Some colonists practised faiths that were based on different types of established European Christianity. Dissenters from such traditions wished to create communities where they could practise their own religions without persecution and create an ideal 'city upon a hill'. Religion on these levels was central to, and influenced people's daily and commercial lives.

Most early colonists were Christian Protestants whose faiths influenced future US society. There were, however, conflicts between denominations. For example, in the early seventeenth century, Virginia's population largely comprised members of the established Anglican Church of England. The Anglican Church taxed Dissenters who settled in the colony, Quakers were banned and Baptist ministers were arrested. Paradoxically, French Huguenots, German Protestants and Scots-Irish Presbyterians were allowed their own congregations.

Meanwhile, two groups of Calvinist settlers (later called Congregationalists) had arrived in New England who were different from the established Virginia Anglicans. The first group (Pilgrims) came to Plymouth, Massachusetts in 1620 from England and Holland to found their own church. They were separatists who had left the Church of England because they disapproved of its doctrines and because they had suffered persecution. The second larger group arrived in Massachusetts Bay in 1630 and were Puritans who wanted to purify the Church of England.

Neither group was religiously tolerant. They expelled Church of England members and initially confined membership of their congregations to people who had personally experienced conversion. They believed that God had chosen or predestined specific individuals to achieve salvation. Hard work was a means of pleasing God, and any resulting prosperity was a sign that He regarded them favourably. It is argued that this Puritan (Protestant) work ethic is a conditioning factor in a general American ambition to succeed materially in life.

Religious diversity was most obvious in the middle colonies. These were settled by Protestant groups such as Welsh and Dutch Calvinists, Scottish Presbyterians, Swedish and German Lutherans, Baptists and English Quakers. Protestants and Roman Catholics established themselves in Maryland (formed originally as a haven for Catholics), with religious toleration for all Christians. Puritan pressure during the English Civil War resulted in toleration for Roman Catholics becoming limited and it ended in 1692.

The first Catholics to arrive in America in the sixteenth century, outside the original thirteen colonies, were missionaries from Spain, Portugal and France. They established churches and missions in the south and west of the country in present-day Texas, California, Florida and New Mexico.

A few European Jewish traders also settled in the English colonies, despite an official ban on Jewish immigration. Newport, Rhode Island, became the main colonial centre of Jewish life, with other groups in New York, Charleston and Philadelphia.

Most of the original thirteen colonies had an official established church (and therefore a link between church and state) from colonial times until the War for Independence. The Anglican Church represented Virginia, Maryland, the Carolinas, Georgia and parts of New York, and the Congregational Church was established in New England. Other groups, such as the Presbyterians, Lutherans and Baptists, did not become the established church in any colony.

## The eighteenth century

There was a change of emphasis in the eighteenth century. Although some (if by no means all) early colonists had been motivated by religious beliefs, the majority of immigrants now travelled to the USA for material advancement, free land or commercial adventure. There was a decline in religious influence and observation, and it is estimated that in 1750 only 17 per cent of the population formally belonged to a religious group. However, many people might still have retained nominal adherence to a traditional faith.

Immigrants continued to arrive in the eighteenth century, often with distinct religious identifications such as Scots-Irish Presbyterians from northern Ireland. Some of these settled in New York and New England, where they shifted the Congregational (Puritan) church towards Presbyterianism. Others went to New Jersey, Pennsylvania and western Virginia. German Lutherans continued to immigrate and Jews arrived from Germany and Poland, but the main emphasis was still on Protestant Christian denominations.

**PLATE 13.1** St John's Episcopal Church is the oldest church in Richmond, Virginia. It held the Second Virginia Convention, 1775, which discussed taking up arms against Britain. (*Corbis*)

Two events significantly affected colonial communities in the eighteenth century and produced more active religiosity, at least for a time: first, the Great Awakening (religious revival) and second, the American War for Independence. The Great Awakening affected the colonies in the 1730s and 1740s and was the forerunner of modern evangelical activities. It was an emotional reaction to the formalistic and unappealing nature of most religious practices. It began in Massachusetts among the Congregationalists and spread along the east coast from Maine to Georgia and along the western frontier to include Presbyterians, Methodists and Baptists.

Revivalist (or evangelical) preachers tried to convert people to their religions by stressing the need for repentance and rebirth and a personal experience of salvation. The Great Awakening created friction, and churches were split as ministers and congregations either supported the revivalists or opposed their emotionalism and conversion practices. The radicalism of the Great Awakening partly influenced revolutionary sentiment and the coming War for Independence.

The War for Independence from Britain was a time of conflict for American religion with divided loyalties among the churches. Scots-Irish Presbyterians,

Lutherans, Baptists and Congregationalists were mainly on the American side of the struggle, while the Methodists remained neutral. Some Anglicans supported the British and others the American cause, as did Catholics in Pennsylvania and Maryland. Pacifist religious bodies, such as the Moravians, Quakers and Mennonites, were often persecuted during the war because of their beliefs.

The Methodist and Baptist churches recovered quickly after the war, but the Anglican church lost much prestige due to its ties with England. Attempts to retrieve its position failed and the creation of a new American Protestant Episcopal Church in its stead proved necessary.

However, despite the Great Awakening and the War for Independence, religiosity at the end of the eighteenth century was weak and most Americans were not active church members. The Great Awakening had not had a lasting or deep effect, the new Episcopal Church was largely inactive and other religious groups had become either austere and intellectual or had departed from their original religious doctrines. Protestant Christianity appeared to be declining with the abolition of most established churches after the War for Independence.

## The nineteenth century

Religious groups recovered in the nineteenth century as further revivals occurred, the population expanded westwards, immigration increased, missionary activities grew and the churches involved themselves in social concerns as a result of industrialization and economic growth. However, the Civil War (1861–5) was a testing time for American religion.

A second Great Awakening came at the beginning of the century on the east coast and spread westwards along the frontier. It sometimes led to superficial emotionalism and divisions within the churches, but it also increased the number of evangelical groups, such as the Baptists, Presbyterians and Methodists. This growth influenced future religious development and the creation of modern evangelical and fundamentalist movements. A further influence, if restricted largely to literary intellectuals, was Transcendentalism, which stressed the individual and nature as a reaction to traditional Puritanism.

Religious groups were increasingly subject to conflict within themselves and with other churches, especially between 1830 and 1860. This resulted in theological quarrels, division of churches and formation of many sects. For example, attempts to unite the Congregationalists and Presbyterians ended in separation. There was tension between the High (east coast) and Low (frontier) Church wings of the Episcopal Church. Splits occurred among the Lutherans, but the arrival of conservative German immigrants after 1830 prevented the liberal wing from dominating the church. Norwegian and Swedish Lutheran immigrants from 1840 also supported the conservative wing.

New religious movements or sects, with very different beliefs, were formed as a reaction to traditional faiths in the nineteenth century, such as Spiritualism,

Millerism (Seventh-Day Adventism), Mormonism, Perfectionism and Shakerism. Many other religious groups, often with a strong social emphasis, were also established from the 1850s.

Meanwhile, the Roman Catholic Church was greatly strengthened by Irish, French and German immigration from 1830 and by immigrants from eastern and southern Europe (such as Italy) later in the century. The church, after earlier internal conflict, was eventually controlled by its hierarchy of bishops. It proved attractive to the new immigrants, and Irish settlers in particular were to influence the church in future years. Catholic newcomers suffered considerable prejudice and hostility from the dominant Protestant groups.

Indeed, some of the more extreme Protestants attempted to maintain strict Puritan traditions and to oppose the influence of Roman Catholic immigration. For example, the Woman's Christian Temperance Union (1874) tried to stop the use of alcohol and campaigned to maintain the Puritan sabbath.

Between 1840 and 1880 the Jewish population expanded from 15,000 to 225,000 because of repression and persecution in Germany and central Europe. Some Jews were Orthodox, but many became members of the new Reform movement. This adapted traditional practices to modern conditions and helped Jews to assimilate more easily to American life. Jews experienced anti-Semitism and discrimination in society, particularly from Protestants.

Despite religious tensions and the emergence of new sects, a more liberal spirit developed during the nineteenth century. Churches became involved in education and created schools and colleges with religious identifications. From 1820 increasing immigration promoted new outlooks and activities among the churches. Influential inner-city missions were formed on the east coast that addressed the new problems (poverty and unemployment) of a wealthier and bigger population. Critics argue that these mission movements and their activism, rather than the two Great Awakenings, saved American Christianity and increased religiosity.

Slavery and the Civil War were divisive threats to religion. The anti-slavery position was based on biblical, humanitarian and democratic impulses, but there were conflicting interpretations of slavery from both anti- and pro-slavery camps. Some churches, like the Episcopal Church, tried to be neutral, while others were divided. Post-war America experienced religious uncertainty and inaction as churches tried to recover from the effects of the war and society sought to accommodate the abolition of slavery morally and practically.

After 1880 US wealth increased substantially, due to industrialization and a booming economy. Divisions grew between rich and poor, and there was much social misery and inequality. There were conflicts between employees and employers, leading to strikes, unemployment and industrial unrest. The churches responded to these problems. Some emphasized social and moral commitment, supported the workers and provided for their social and economic needs, and many clergy played an active role in the community. This social concern is still a feature of contemporary religious groups in the USA.

## The twentieth century

Religious variety in the USA increased at the end of the nineteenth century and during the twentieth century as large numbers of immigrants arrived from central, eastern and southern Europe, Latin America and Asia.

On the whole, this strengthened the Roman Catholic Church, but the new arrivals also included Asian religions, such as Hinduism, Sikhism and Islam, as well as considerable numbers of Jewish immigrants fleeing persecution in Europe. Eastern Orthodox churches were also established by Greek, Russian, Armenian and Syrian immigrants. Such groups concentrated in bigger cities and some retained their own languages in religious and daily life. This produced tight-knit communities with strong ethnic identities, but it also distanced them from many Americans. The result was often intolerance (based upon ignorance and Protestant dominance) directed against the new arrivals.

Critics have argued that a diversity of religions led to competing pressures in US life in the twentieth century between pluralism and ecumenism (closer relations between faiths), social action and spiritual renewal and secularism and religious growth.

Religious pluralism can indicate vitality and toleration of different religions, but it may also be divisive as denominations quarrel with each other. The dominant Protestant majority in early US history promoted basic national characteristics, but it often treated Roman Catholic, Jewish and other immigrants with suspicion and hostility. This situation slowly changed in the early twentieth century and considerably since the 1950s, due to immigration, population growth in ethnic communities, improved social attitudes and a decrease in the Protestant majority. Three major faiths (Protestant, Catholic and Jewish) then shared American religious life with many other churches, groups and sects.

The pluralistic and somewhat divisive nature of US religion has been offset by ecumenical movements among different faiths, which have become more tolerant and cooperative. Traditional churches divided by historical disputes, like Congregationalists, Lutherans, Presbyterians and Methodists, became closer. Cooperation has occurred at local and national levels between Protestants, Catholics, Jews and Orthodox groups with the creation of ecumenical organizations. For example, the Anti-Defamation League (1913) and the National Conference of Christians and Jews (1928) reduced anti-Semitic tension in the early twentieth century. There was also a growing assimilation of immigrant groups into the larger society as old-world languages diminished and 'national' churches and synods merged. Internationally, American Protestants helped to found the World Council of Churches in 1948, and ecumenism was treated positively by the Second Vatican Council (1962–5), which encouraged Catholics to be more open to other religions and modern developments.

By the 1970s, ecumenism declined. This was due to a concern that individual church beliefs might become weaker through cooperation and to an increasing conservatism that caused divisions in some church groups. Nevertheless, Protestants, Catholics and Jews have become less divided, and anti-Catholicism and anti-Semitism are not as virulent or as widespread as they once were. Catholics and Jews have achieved greater status and recognition in American life, and religions such as Islam, Buddhism and Hinduism have been accepted. The emphasis has turned to coexistence with many faiths, rather than ecumenism.

There are areas of tension that are reflected in opposed views of social action and spiritual renewal. Social action stresses religion's public role and follows American traditions of liberal theology and social commitment. Some churches have campaigned for social change, provided welfare services and have debated social problems and moral concerns such as starvation, racial inequality, poverty, refugees, the Vietnam War, industrial relations, abortion, same-sex relationships and educational issues. This liberal social position has often necessitated new theological interpretations of belief and practice.

Some evangelical and fundamentalist groups within Protestantism emphasize spiritual renewal and reflect a desire among many Americans for more personal religious commitment and simple faith. Such movements are founded on a close reading of and literal interpretation of the Bible. They are traditional and orthodox in a strict maintenance of their beliefs, stress the importance of personal salvation, are suspicious of social action and oppose liberalizing trends. Their emphasis on fundamental beliefs and fellowship has led them to reject not only evolutionary theories (Darwinism) in favour of creationism (the literal Bible story), but also new interpretations of the Bible and what they consider to be corrupt forms of modern life. Many Protestant churches in the early twentieth century, and especially since the 1960s, consequently experienced a series of battles between liberals, modernists, evangelicals and fundamentalists.

Some fundamentalists left their churches to form new groups where they could practise their beliefs. Others have joined evangelical Christian churches. These, and fundamentalism, are connected to earlier traditions of revivalism with their evangelical espousal of the Christian gospel, conversion, emotional experiences and personal salvation through admission of one's sins. Evangelical Christian groups have become a powerful force in the USA in recent decades, have attracted much media and popular attention and have grown strongly. Some of these churches may collapse because of lack of support or because of scandals, and it is significant that Americans may change frequently from one church or denomination to another.

The terms 'evangelical', 'conservative', 'the Christian Right' and 'fundamentalist' tend to be used interchangeably and somewhat loosely. 'Fundamentalist' can be applied to Protestant and any other religious groups with absolutist beliefs. 'Evangelical' is often applied to many Christian denominations with very varied titles, but which are mostly based on the doctrine of salvation and converting people to their beliefs in a 'born-again' experience. They believe in the Bible as the authoritative word of God and in a personal relationship with

Christ. Their anti-modern, anti-secular conservative message is based on moral values, the role of the family and education. They provide simple certainties for many Americans and stress individual responsibility and commitment.

Evangelical ministers and fundamentalist movements use television and radio to spread their message and have become very skilful in their use of the media. They own or control some 1,300 radio or television stations. The preachers can become very popular celebrities, and their media performances attract large audiences and advertising revenues, with the result that religious broadcasting has become very profitable. After a fall in popularity and influence in the late 1980s, the evangelical churches recovered strongly from the mid-1990s and now have a powerful political voice on the right.

Spiritual renewal has also led people to join a wide variety of sects, cults and churches. Common to them all is an attempt to create a sense of belonging through close emotional fellowship. The more extreme groups, such as the Moonies and some guru-led organizations, have aroused hostility among many Americans. Their techniques of recruitment, alleged brainwashing of members and religious fanaticism are heavily criticized.

Some Americans, in the search for personal spiritual growth, ethnic identity and answers to modern problems, have joined or converted to eastern religions

**PLATE 13.2** Mosque, Michigan. Mosques have been built in areas of concentrated Muslim settlement throughout the USA.
*(Sipa Press/Rex Features)*

such as Islam (including the African-American Nation of Islam), Hinduism and Buddhism. Others seek religious satisfaction in a wide range of alternative beliefs such as the occult, Native-American religions, astrology and witchcraft.

It is argued that the emergence of so many religious and pseudo-religious groups and the possible diffusion of national identity in this amorphous situation have led concerned Americans to embrace a 'civil religion' centred on US political traditions. It is a mixture of religion, morality and nationalism which emphasizes symbols, emblems and traditions, such as the national motto ('In God We Trust') and the pledge of allegiance to the flag ('One Nation Under God'). 'Civil religion' supposedly overarches the varieties of belief and gives the USA a moral character and sacred mission. Although this may be a source of national integration, it can also be divisive, and its contemporary influence, while formerly evident in the public-school system, is debatable.

There has also been an increased secularism in twentieth-century US life which has conflicted with religious growth. Personal decisions are made without recourse to religious teachings or interpretations. Secularism has particularly affected education. Some private schools and colleges had previously been created by churches as a way of promoting religious belief, but in the twentieth century public schools were increasingly secularized by state authorities. A more relaxed and informal American society, with increased leisure and entertainment opportunities, has also contributed to the growth of secularization.

Despite the overall trend towards secularism, more Americans were involved with religious groups and activities in the mid-twentieth century. This coincided with greater interest in religion after the Second World War. Since then, there has been decline in some churches and growth in others.

## Contemporary US religion

US religion underwent significant changes after the post-war revival. The influence and membership of mainstream Protestant and traditional denominations declined in the liberal social climate of the 1960s and 1970s. Increasing pluralism led to new religious groups such as fundamentalist and evangelical churches (which attract large numbers of members), various sects, cults and eastern religions such as Islam, Hinduism and Buddhism.

Despite these changes, the large majority of religious Americans today are still within the so-called Judaeo-Christian tradition and some eight in ten Americans in polls identify their religious preference as Christian. US religion consequently consists of three main faiths in terms of their history, numbers and influence: Protestantism, Catholicism and Judaism.

In trying to assess how many Americans belong to the various religious denominations, it is important to realize that many respondents to public-opinion polls and surveys are nominal and preferential rather than active adherents.

Thus, a May 2004 Gallup poll showed that respondents identified their religious affiliations or preferences as Protestant (50 per cent), Roman Catholic (23 per cent), Jewish (2 per cent), Mormon (1 per cent) and Orthodox (1 per cent), while other non-specific forms of Christianity amounted to 9 per cent. A specific element (presumably including Islam, Hinduism and Buddhism) amounted to 3 per cent, and 9 per cent of respondents had no affiliation or preference. Younger people between eighteen and twenty-nine years of age are more likely than older people to have no religious preference and are also less likely to be Protestants.

## *Protestants*

Protestantism is the largest and most diverse of the American faiths. Although a majority of Americans might consider themselves as 'Protestants', they are divided into at least 220 different churches and sects, with conservative, mainstream and liberal outlooks. There is thus no one umbrella denomination for all Protestants. Each church is independent, supports itself financially, employs its own ministers, constructs its own buildings and follows its own beliefs and practices.

The Presbyterian (263,238 million members in 2003), Lutheran (8.2 million), Episcopal (2.3 million), Reformed churches (1.9 million) and small Congregational churches constitute mainstream Protestantism from early US history. The large memberships of the Baptist churches (30 million) and Methodists (12.3 million) are now considered part of this mainstream Protestant grouping (despite their evangelical history). The largest, mainly white, Protestant denomination is the Southern Baptist Convention (16.1 million), while the largest African-American Protestant denomination is the National Baptist Convention (5 million).

Protestantism is divided between mainstream churches and fundamentalist or evangelical churches with conservative beliefs. Mainstream churches also have different emphases. The more traditional ones tend to have somewhat liberal theological and social attitudes, are composed largely of middle- or upper-class people and have formal worship and service patterns. Other churches, like the Southern Baptists, may consist of lower-income groups and encourage emotional responses to religion, such as 'born-again' conversions.

While mainstream Protestant churches have lost members since the 1970s, evangelical or fundamentalist Protestant churches, such as the Seventh-Day Adventists, the Church of the Nazarene and the Assemblies of God, have increased their membership. They offer absolutist moral instruction and traditional values and appeal to those Americans who want moral direction and certainty. The mainstream Protestant churches have responded by retreating somewhat from their earlier 'liberalism' in order to attract members, although the American Episcopal Church is currently in conflict with the worldwide Anglican Communion because of its consecration of an openly gay bishop.

## Roman Catholics

Although there was large Catholic immigration into the USA in the nineteenth and twentieth centuries, society was still mainly Protestant in religion and national attitudes.

The Roman Catholic Church today is the second largest religion after Protestantism, but the biggest in terms of a single denomination. It had about 19,496 churches and 65.3 million members in 2003 and has a predominantly white membership. Its membership, whether practising or not, has increased in recent years because of Latino population growth and immigration and Asian immigration.

Catholicism was historically confined to ethnic groups such as the Irish, Polish, Italians and Germans in the big cities and was initially largely working class. This urban concentration enabled Catholics to achieve considerable political power at the local, if not the national, level. After the Second World War, Catholics greatly improved their educational standards, income and class status, and many affluent Catholics moved to the suburbs. The church built more churches and schools for its growing population, although parochial schools have now declined in number and influence.

The movement of Catholics from tightly knit urban communities to the suburbs has arguably meant a consequent loss of Catholic identity. Catholics are now more eager and willing, after years of discrimination against them, to mix with non-Catholics socially. Hostility towards Catholics has largely disappeared as was illustrated by the election of Catholic John F. Kennedy as President in 1960. American Catholics are also influential in international campaigns and domestic social projects and tend to be more ecumenically minded today than they have been in the past.

Religious and social change has created internal tensions within the Catholic community. Members are not as active in church activities as they were, and attendance at weekly mass has declined. The church is divided between liberals and conservatives with opposed opinions on birth control, abortion, the celibacy of priests, gay and lesbian relationships and the question of potential women priests. These concerns have provoked clashes with conservative Vatican views. A serious development in recent years has been evidence of Catholic priests sexually abusing young people and the alleged cover-up of such behaviour by the Catholic leadership. This has resulted in horrified criticism within the church and by outsiders and a resulting lack of trust.

## The Jewish community

Jews historically have settled mainly on the east coast in the big cities. After immigration, their religious practices changed somewhat and now range from traditional Orthodox to moderate Conservative and liberal Reform groups. Most

**PLATE 13.3** Service at St Gertrude's Roman Catholic Church, Chicago, Illinois. Roman Catholic congregations are widespread throughout the USA.
(*Steve Liss/Time Pix/Rex Features*)

groups have been concerned to preserve their Jewish heritage and traditions. As the Jewish population grew, they established Hebrew schools and contributed to Jewish charities. The creation of the state of Israel in 1948 was an additional focus for Jewish identity. Although anti-Semitism increased in the early twentieth century, this has now been reduced because of changing social attitudes, ecumenism and sympathy for Jewish suffering in the Second World War. Jews have assimilated into American society and are more accepted than they once were. They have also become more liberal and secularized with increased intermarriage (nearly a third) between Jews and non-Jews, leading to fears about the collapse of the religious community. There were an estimated 4.1 million religious Jews in 2003, divided into the main Reform, Conservative and Orthodox traditions. But a significant number of other ethnic Jews (1.1 million) are secular or non-religious or have become members of a faith other than Judaism.

## Other religious groups

There are other significant US religious groups in addition to the three main faiths, such as Buddhism (estimated 2–3 million in 2003), Hinduism (1.3 million), Islam (5–6 million) and Sikhism (250,000). It is argued that Islam today is a fourth major faith in the USA which, combined with other Asian religions, has a growing representative importance.

# Church, state and politics

Church and state in the USA are supposedly separate. The First Amendment of the Bill of Rights (1791) states that 'Congress shall make no law respecting an establishment of religion, or prohibiting the free exercise thereof'. This prohibits the establishment of a national church or state-supported religion or the promoting of religion and protects individuals' right to practise their own faiths. The First Amendment applies only to the federal government, not to the states. The Fourteenth Amendment (1868) has therefore been interpreted to mean that the states must also protect rights of religion guaranteed by law.

Religion, or the lack of it, is a private matter and Americans have long fought for the liberty to organize their own lives. A CNN/*USA Today*/Gallup poll in 2003 found that 54 per cent of respondents thought that the promoting of a religion by the government or in schools always harms the rights of those people who do not belong to that religion. This finding seems to indicate that only a bare majority are in favour of the principle of non-promotion. Indeed, a *Newsweek* poll in 2002 reported that 54 per cent of respondents felt that, in terms of the separation of church and state, the government should not avoid promoting religion in any way.

There were established churches before the War for Independence and Massachusetts had an official church into the 1830s, but eventually all churches were separated from the state and government. There are no church taxes, the churches are not supposed to receive any direct state or federal support, there are no legal or official religious holidays and no political party is affiliated to a particular denomination. Any attempt to impose legislation in these areas would be regarded as violating the Constitution.

Religious groups are therefore independent organizations and are self-supporting. They depend upon their members' financial contributions for their existence and payment of expenses. Americans' donations to their churches are very generous with 45 per cent of all charitable donations going to religion. Fundamentalist and evangelical churches attract the greatest amounts. Local religious buildings and their congregations are the strengths and centres of US religion. They also provide social, cultural and community activities, supply relief services for the poor and needy and engage in missionary work domestically and overseas.

As society has become more complex and government more pervasive, church and state have sometimes interfered with each other. States in the past restricted freedom of religion by prohibiting Catholics and Jews from voting or holding public office. The law has also indirectly interfered with those minority religions which require special working practices, such as Mormons and Seventh-Day Adventists. In such cases, however, the Supreme Court and Congress have often invalidated limitations by permitting exceptions to the general rule. The Supreme Court has also restricted adherents' free practice of religion if their behaviour is against the public interest. The Bush administration has arguably blurred the distinction by its espousal of faith-based social services and federal funding of religious groups in this area. The division between church and state is not absolute, and both Congress and the Supreme Court have sometimes reached decisions which appear to contradict the First Amendment. It is argued that the inconsistencies between civic duty and individual conscience are incapable of resolution and result from the tensions within the First Amendment itself.

Although religion is supposed to be a private matter, public and private life are not inseparable. Given the prevalence and diversity of denominations in American life, it is perhaps inevitable that religion and its moral concerns should influence public and political debates on issues such as abortion, the death penalty, same-sex marriage and armed conflicts.

A religious sensibility is also reflected in national symbols and emblems such as the US seal, the currency and the pledge of allegiance to the American flag. US Presidents have often belonged to a religious group and politicians frequently refer to God and the Bible in their speeches. US Presidents swear the inaugural oath of office on the Bible, sessions of Congress commence with prayers and both Houses of Congress have official chaplains. It is sometimes difficult therefore to draw a distinct line between government and religion in the USA.

Formal religion generally has little real influence in national political matters or institutions beyond rhetorical expressions. Politicians are conscious of the constitutional position and its restrictions upon government action, as well as the restraints of religious tolerance. However, personal beliefs and values may affect the way in which some individuals react to political issues and how they actually vote in elections. There has, for example, been a recent increase in the number of evangelicals and Catholics who vote Republican.

A source of national debate about religion and politics has revolved around the role of evangelical groups and their leaders. Many of them are very visible, actively propagate their beliefs and attempt to influence public opinion, social institutions and political processes. They do not restrict themselves to moral and religious matters, but are involved in and campaign on political issues such as anti-abortion legislation and the restoration of prayers in public schools. The evangelical right, sometimes known as 'the moral majority' or the 'Christian coalition/right' (because of its absolutism and stress upon alleged American values), has supported conservative politicians in election campaigns, and some of its leaders have also attempted to gain political office.

Opinions about the role of religion in politics and social issues remain somewhat confused. A Pew Research Center poll in 2004 reported that 51 per cent of respondents thought that churches should be able to express political and social views, while 44 per cent believed that they should not. But 65 per cent considered that churches should not express support for any one candidate in a political election over another, while 25 per cent thought they should. Yet a

CNN/*USA Today*/Gallup poll in 2003 showed that 90 per cent of respondents approved of the words 'In God We Trust' on all US coins. These words have not been invalidated by the Supreme Court.

# Religion and education

Administrative and financial organization of public schools is carried out by local communities, and school boards composed of elected citizens oversee the schools in their area. They establish school policy and often decide what is to be taught. It is at this level that battles between fundamentalists and modernizers over the school curriculum have been fought, such as the debates over school prayers and the teaching of evolution and creationism. Religious education is supposed to be neutral. The constitutional separation of church from state means that public schools can teach about religion, but they cannot promote it.

Nevertheless, it is argued that in practice most public schools were for a long time active proponents of Protestant Christianity, by means of the morning prayer and other activities. This reflected a historical Protestant dominance in US society. It was felt that such an emphasis was no longer valid when Judaism and Catholicism were recognized as two of the three great American religions after the Second World War.

In 1962–3, the Supreme Court reflected this new fact of religious and social life. It ruled that laws requiring the reciting of the Lord's Prayer, Bible verses or prayers in public schools were unconstitutional because they violated the principle of separation between church and state by fostering or promoting religion. In 1984 the US Senate rejected two constitutional amendments that would permit prayers in public schools. Such decisions have thus banned prayers in public schools, although the practice does continue, particularly in the rural south. Moreover, the reciting of a non-denominational prayer is widely supported by a large majority of Americans (78 per cent in a 2003 *USA Today*/Gallup/CNN poll).

In 2001 the Supreme Court ruled that religious groups must be allowed to meet for religious activities in public schools after class hours. Court rulings have also allowed state-university property to be used by students for religious purposes as long as that property can also be used by others for other purposes. In 1992 the Supreme Court banned clergy from offering prayers at graduation ceremonies in public schools. These cases distinguish between state recognition of religion by the participation of officials at public ceremonies and the participation of students in voluntary religious activities on state property.

It is argued that public schools continue to imbue schoolchildren with patriotic attitudes by means of civil religion, like the oath of allegiance to the flag (with its phrase 'One Nation, Under God'). However, the Supreme Court ruled in 1942 that no child should be obliged to take part in the flag salute.

On the other hand, the private sector of education accounts for 15 per cent of student enrolment. Some private schools are still run by churches or religious groups at both primary and secondary levels, with Catholic parochial schools being in the majority (40 per cent). Such schools are often intended to supply religious orientation and education. Some other private schools, particularly those founded in the 1970s and 1980s, have no religious identification.

The question of whether private schools (church-supported or not) should receive public money is vigorously debated and the private sector generally receives no funding from federal or state governments. Rising costs resulted in Congress granting parochial schools free lunches, transportation, textbooks and health and social services in 1965, but the Supreme Court has struck down most other forms of aid. Two 1985 decisions prohibited public-school teachers from teaching courses in private religious schools with public funds.

## Attitudes to religion

American attitudes to religion and religious belief, as demonstrated in public-opinion polls, tend to be very positive. A Gallup public-opinion poll in May 2004 reported that 55 per cent of Americans felt that religion was very important in their lives and 29 per cent thought it fairly important. These figures indicate that 84 per cent of people considered that religion was personally significant for them, irrespective of whether or not they might be practising members of a denomination. Earlier polls have suggested that between 57 and 61 per cent of respondents considered themselves as religious. Americans thought they were less religious than in the 1950s and 1960s, that religion was more important to older than younger Americans and more important to women than men. Some 60 per cent of respondents in a March 2003 Gallup poll believed that religion could answer all or most of today's problems, slightly down on previous findings, but 26 per cent thought that religion was old-fashioned and out of date.

In a May 2004 Gallup poll, 26 per cent had 'a great deal', 27 per cent 'quite a lot' and 28 per cent 'some' confidence in the churches and organized religion. This marks an increase in confidence since 2002. A November 2003 Gallup/*USA Today* poll also reported very high to high (56 per cent) ratings for the honesty and ethical standards of the clergy (despite sex scandals in the Roman Catholic Church).

The mixture of personal beliefs among Americans may be seen in Table 13.1. Here, traditional sources of religious belief are much in evidence, while alternative belief systems gain some support. Such varied findings have been consistent over recent years, as has belief in the efficacy of prayer and direct experience of God.

Substantial numbers of Americans in a Gallup 2001 poll doubted scientific evolution (without God) as the explanation for the origin of human beings. Biblical creationism was regarded favourably by 45 per cent of the public, 37 per

**TABLE 13.1** American personal beliefs, 2003.

|  | Believe (%) | Don't believe (%) | Not sure (%) |
|---|---|---|---|
| God | 92 | 5 | 3 |
| Heaven | 85 | 10 | 5 |
| miracles | 82 | 14 | 4 |
| angels | 78 | 15 | 7 |
| Hell | 74 | 20 | 6 |
| the Devil | 71 | 24 | 5 |
| unidentified flying objects (UFOs) | 34 | 55 | 11 |
| ghosts | 34 | 60 | 6 |
| astrology | 29 | 64 | 7 |
| reincarnation | 25 | 62 | 13 |
| witches | 24 | 69 | 7 |

Source: Fox News/Opinion Dynamics poll, September 2003

cent believed in God-guided evolution and only 12 per cent accepted evolution without the guidance of God.

In terms of education, 68 per cent favoured teaching creationism together with evolution in public schools, 40 per cent favoured teaching only creationism, but this was opposed by 55 per cent. The use of school property after hours for student religious meetings was favoured by 72 per cent (26 per cent opposed), 80 per cent believed that students should be allowed to recite a spoken prayer at school graduations, 66 per cent thought spoken prayer should be allowed in the classroom (opposed by 34 per cent) and 62 per cent felt that religion had too little presence in public schools. A majority of Americans also favoured retaining 'One Nation, Under God' in the pledge of allegiance.

A *Fox News*/Opinion Dynamics poll in September 2003 reported that 69 per cent of respondents thought that religion played too small a role in most people's lives today. Closely connected to religion, other polls over time have suggested that a large majority of respondents do not think that the ethical and moral standards of Americans today are as high as they should be, that morals were one of the top problems facing the country and that they thought that the country's moral and cultural values had changed for the worse since the 1960s because the USA has become too permissive. These findings suggest the tensions between American reality and aspiration.

# Exercises

Explain and examine the significance of the following names and terms.

| | | |
|---|---|---|
| secularization | Protestantism | evangelicalism |
| civil religion | pluralism | school prayers |
| Puritans | fundamentalism | Congregationalists |
| Episcopal Church | social action | sectarianism |
| ecumenism | Great Awakenings | denomination |
| creationism | evolution | Fourteenth Amendment |

Write short essays on the following questions.

1. How is the diversity of contemporary denominations reflected in, and due to, American religious history?

2. Describe and examine the ways in which American religion has been characterized by division and conflict.

3. Analyse the growth and present position of one of America's main faiths: Protestantism, Catholicism or Judaism.

4. Examine the public-opinion poll findings in the text and evaluate whether they are contradictory or significant for US religious life.

## Further reading

Abrams, E. (1997) *Faith or Fear: how Jews can survive in a Christian America* New York: Free Press.

Ahlstrom, S. (1972) *A Religious History of the American People* New Haven, Conn.: Yale University Press.

Corbett, M. and J. M. Corbett (1999) *Politics and Religion in the United States* New York: Garland.

Fowler, R. B. and A. D. Hertzke (1995) *Religion and Politics in America: faith, culture and strategic choices* Boulder, Col.: Westview.

Haddad, R. T. and A. T. Lummis (1987) *Islamic Values in the United States* Oxford: Oxford University Press.

Jocks, C. (2001) *Native American Religions* London: Routledge.

Olmstead, C. E. (1960) *History of Religion in the United States* Englewood Cliffs, NJ: Prentice-Hall.

*The World Almanac and Book of Facts, 2004*, New York: World Almanac Books.

Wuthnow, R. (1988) *The Restructuring of American Religion* Princeton, NJ: Princeton University Press.

# Web sites

<http://usinfo.state.gov/usa/infousa/facts/factover/homepage.htm>
<http://www.usia.gov/journals/journals.htm>
<http://bsuvc.bsu.edu/~00amcorbett/relpol.htm>
<http://www.religiousmovements.org>
<http://religiousmovements.lib.virginia.edu/profile/profiles.htm>
<http://www.dallasnews.com/religion>

# Chapter 14

# The arts, sports and leisure

- The arts
- Sports
- Leisure
- *Exercises*
- *Further reading*
- *Web sites*

The diversity of contemporary US society is reflected in how Americans organize their artistic, sporting and leisure lives. These features reveal very different cultural habits at all social levels, represent the amateur and the professional, are present in the private and public spheres and are divided between participatory/active and spectator/observer activities. Some have also varied in popularity over a 300-year-old history or been superceded by new cultural developments.

There are also differences between popular, elite and folklorist cultures, although these are not fixed. For example, what was previously elite has often become more widespread, some folk music, such as the rural blues, has been popularized and urbanized and sports over time have been democratized. All these forms to varying degrees are dependent upon private finance and donations, sponsorship and advertising, attendance fees and an economic production system which responds to demand and the search for profit. There is also a degree of state and federal funding such as the National Endowment for the Arts (NEA).

These cultures often derive from mixed origins. There are American aspects in some sports, music, painting and modern dance, which convey a distinctive national identity. However, some, like baseball, country and western music and the musical, arguably partly derive from non-American sources. 'Ethnic' and folklorist expressions, such as slave and settler traditions, Latino music and dance, Jewish and Chinese theatre, Native-American crafts and Asian cinema, reflect their culture of origin rather than a purely American identification.

All have helped to create not only American cultural identities but also an American-oriented internationalized mass culture. This 'cultural imperialism' is resented in some countries which seek to preserve their own artistic inheritance. Critics also attack what they see as the US mass market pandering to the lowest common denominator of taste and quality. Americans have produced entertainment to which many people worldwide respond positively, both for its initial inventiveness and strangeness and its later incorporation into a global culture. American influences and a mass market do not necessarily imply that customers are passive victims of alleged cultural imperialism and inferior products.

A general American work ethic, competitive ethos, ambition and drive for success and achievement also embrace sporting, leisure and artistic pursuits. These are taken very seriously (some might say too seriously) on both professional and amateur levels. Those Americans who play sports, either professionally or on an amateur basis, often do so because they are concerned to win, as well as to achieve the large amounts of money available in many of the professional games.

Even holiday and leisure activities for some may have a competitive edge and a deliberately planned and goal-oriented context.

Alleged American values, such as self-improvement and self-definition, may also be echoed by those people who go to concerts and the theatre or who pursue other artistic activities. They indulge in these not only for fashionable reasons, but often because they genuinely feel that the arts are self-improving and that so-called elite culture is an admirable and positive thing in itself. Many Americans also exercise, take part in keep-fit classes and diet, at least initially, to improve themselves by become healthier and fitter in body and mind, although these activities can sometimes become faddish crazes.

Not everyone is a fitness fanatic, a culture vulture, professionally ambitious or obsessed with goals. Many people are spectators rather than active participants, whether of sports, concerts or as visitors of museums. Relatively high figures for television-viewing and the dubious quality of many entertainment programmes suggest that the USA has its fair share of passive viewers and those who are not concerned with high culture, self-improvement or achievement. However, even simplistic television quiz games may have a vicariously competitive thrill to them and mindless entertainment can be a relaxing escape from competitive daily life and work.

Sporting, leisure and artistic activities are important for many people and central to their lives. This is reflected in the large amounts of money spent by Americans on attendance fees, sports equipment, training, musical instruments, electronic equipment and cultural or recreational buildings. A huge advertising expenditure is also devoted to them, mainly through newspapers and television. 'Entertainment' (broadly defined) regularly comes near the top of total advertising fees after cars and retailing services. Research in 2000 by the National Endowment for the Arts (NEA) showed that while personal spending on the performing arts, movie theatres, spectator sports and books has increased, it is falling as a proportion of total recreation expenditure. The purchase of computers, videos, DVDs, electronic games and software however makes up an increasing share of spending, which suggests that more people are following arts, sport and leisure activities through technology, often in the home, and that some activities like reading are declining in relative terms.

American history in sports and the arts has its darker side. Discrimination has been widespread, so that African Americans, Native Americans, Jews and women, among other minorities, have experienced considerable racism, discrimination and exclusion. This applied not only to performers, but also to spectators who were segregated and to sports which were divided on colour and ethnic lines. In the early twentieth century, there was a gulf between America's divided society and its democratic ideals, which placed civil rights on the public agenda in an attempt to widen access to cultural activity.

While overt racism and discrimination have been reduced, they still influence contemporary pursuits. Stereotyping exists so that, for example, African

Americans find it difficult to advance in professional tennis and golf, which still have white upper-class images. Those individuals such as the Williams sisters in tennis and Tiger Woods in golf who do succeed are held up as role models. The impact of women in a range of sports also increased considerably in the late twentieth century. It should also be emphasized that the first, partial breakthrough of minorities and women into the wider US society frequently came initially through sports and the arts.

## The arts

The development of the arts (both elite and popular) in the USA has been influenced both by European traditions (partly brought to America by European immigrants) and the development of a distinctive domestic culture. Historically, there has been a tension between the two traditions, with many Americans believing in the allegedly superior artistic forms of Europe. European sophistication was placed against domestic originality. Over time, the tension has decreased and the two now both coexist and intermix.

The USA today is still, often stereotypically, perceived as a society in which low-quality television, sports, film and other forms of popular or mass entertainment take precedence over the more 'highbrow' arts. Europeans, in particular, have traditionally regarded America as lacking what they would term a sophisticated 'high culture'.

However, statistics suggest that more Americans than previously, of all ages and social groups are proportionally attending dance performances, classical or symphonic concerts, music recitals and opera as well as visiting a varied range of quality museums. These activities indicate a wider and more acceptable cultural profile for the 'elite' arts now than in the past. Artistic activity has developed from the 1960s and there has been increased participation by amateur and professional individuals and groups in the arts across a wide range of painting, music, modern dance, theatre, ballet and film. The media, particularly television networks and PSB, have helped to establish an interest in and support for the arts through their promotion, sponsorship and coverage of cultural events.

The NEA reported in 2002 (on the basis of a survey of public participation in the arts) that, counting all art forms and types of participation, 76 per cent of American adults (157 million people) made the arts part of their lives and experienced the arts in some form. Almost one-third of adults had been to at least one jazz, classical music, opera, musical, play or ballet performance during 2002, not including elementary or high-school performances. Attendances at most of these events had remained steady since 1992, with a big increase for musicals or musical plays. About one quarter of adults had visited an art museum or art gallery in 2002, nearly two thirds attended a range of arts and cultural events, visited historic sites, fairs and festivals or read literature, four in ten reported performing or creating art themselves, over half (a decline since 1992) watched or listened to the arts on television, radio, recorded media or the Internet and 5 per cent attended an active arts-related educational class, of which weaving, photography, pottery, painting and drawing, creative writing, choirs, opera, jazz, dance/ballet, classical music and acting led in popularity.

The number of arts-related companies or organizations has also increased since the 1960s. For example, in 2003 there were some sixty-three opera companies with annual budgets of $1 million or over, seventy-seven symphony orchestras with annual budgets in excess of $1.6 million and 100 outstanding and well-financed ballet and dance companies. Many of these have world reputations and international conductors, directors and soloists. Increasing numbers of cultural buildings are being built throughout the USA, with lavish styles and facilities.

Some of these activities are probably still associated with traditional notions of 'high culture'. On the other hand, many people are following other more popular art forms, such as film and theatre. It seems as though increasing numbers (particularly the young) are returning to these and other cultural pursuits (including electronic forms) in preference to television, which has arguably become the province of older viewers.

This cultural development is being carried out with some direct financial support for the arts from federal or state governments. Although their role in supporting, financing and sponsoring the arts increased significantly from 1970, funding and involvement decreased in the 1990s. A federal independent agency, the NEA was created in 1965 and encourages and develops artistic ventures by bringing them to all Americans in all areas of the country and by providing a lead in arts education. It receives considerable federal funding and distributes this to the arts, particularly at state and local levels. In its support role, the NEA is the country's largest annual funder of the arts. Although much of the money goes to administrative costs, specific activities such as music, media arts, museums, theatre, arts in education, dance, opera, visual arts and literature benefit from NEA aid.

The arts in the USA have traditionally depended for their survival and promotion upon their commercial status and on admission fees in order to make a profit. However, the private financial contributions of individuals, philanthropic foundations (such as Ford and Rockefeller) and commercial corporations are also important for artistic funding. There is tax relief or deductions (tax breaks) on donations to the arts from individuals and companies.

In addition to some art forms which may be inspired and influenced by the European and classical traditions, American artists (painters, sculptors, musicians, dancers and film-makers) have developed distinctive forms of expression as the national cultural scene has expanded and evolved. Innovation, experiment, variety and reactions to earlier styles have been characteristic of this progress, and have resulted in a variety of arts, which have had a substantial effect on America's cultural life. The work of American artists has become famous overseas and cities like New York, Chicago and San Francisco have become international centres of artistic excellence.

American painters and artists in the nineteenth and early twentieth century were influenced by traditional European styles. They continued, as some do today, the established realist and naturalist traditions, but often adapted these to specific American themes, locations and subject matter.

After the Second World War, new American painters arrived on the traditional scene with revolutionary and distinctively American concepts, such as cityscapes and gritty urban lifestyles. Modernist, cubist and abstract influences then arrived from Europe, from which developed an American abstract expressionism. This was initially begun by New York artists such as Jackson Pollock, Willem de Kooning and Mark Rothko in the 1940s, who rejected established painting styles and subject matter and organized their work around instinctual use of colour, space and texture. These painters attracted international attention and New York became increasingly a centre of renown in the art world.

Succeeding generations reacted in their turn to abstract expressionism and moved on to new styles. Painters in the late 1950s and 1960s such as Robert Rauschenberg and Jasper Johns concentrated on collage-type painting and used a variety of ordinary objects to produce works of mixed media. Other innovators, such as Andy Warhol and Roy Lichtenstein, introduced 'pop art'. This genre used everyday items of the consumer society and popular culture to reflect and comment on what the artist saw as distinctive features of modern America. By this process, the ordinary became iconic.

American painters and sculptors continue to experiment with a wide range of styles and materials and have created a number of exotically named artistic movements, such as 'op art', graffiti art and performance art. Their distinguishing features have been change, reaction, variety, new techniques and a refusal to be restricted to specific philosophies, styles, schools or media. They gather their inspiration from many sources and influences. The very definition and existence of art is often ironically challenged in their 'postmodernist' work.

Interesting as some of these visual art styles have been, perhaps a more influential expression of US artistic distinctiveness has been in music. In previous centuries American classical music was influenced by European traditions, standards and styles. The breakthrough to a distinctive American voice came with George Gershwin and Aaron Copland in the early twentieth century, who incorporated domestic forms (such as African American influences, jazz and folk songs) into European standards. This mixture of old and new styles continued through the century. There was also an impetus to make classical music more accessible to greater numbers of people as combined programmes of mainstream and new music were introduced by orchestra directors and conductors.

The more accessible and commercial forms of American music historically have been mainstream popular, ragtime, blues, jazz, the musical, country and western and rock and roll, which have often tended to mix with and influence each other over time. They have been domestic American successes, but many have also been exported and have greatly affected world culture.

Mainstream popular music with a distinctive American voice was largely initiated by Stephen Foster in the early nineteenth century. He combined European styles with African-American rhythms and themes to produce classic American songs. By the end of the nineteenth century, popular music had become commercially successful, and production was centred on New York City. A succession of songwriters like Irving Berlin and Cole Porter created American standards, which have survived to the present day.

A succession of popular singers and performers have been associated with this mainstream category. A Reuters International/Zogby poll of April 1999 found that respondents thought that Barbra Streisand was the best female singer of the twentieth century and Frank Sinatra was the best male singer.

African American composers also wrote and performed popular music in the late nineteenth and early twentieth century. Ragtime was an African-American music that was popularized by Scott Joplin and derived partly from the rural blues tradition of often melancholy and fatalistic folk songs and church music which reflected the lives of poor African Americans. Bessie Smith was an early and popular exponent of the blues style and mixed the rural tradition with urban themes.

The blues also inspired jazz at the end of the nineteenth century. It is argued that this is America's most original and native music form. It was first played by African-American musicians in the south, derives mainly from African influences and southern slave culture, combines elements of ragtime, slave songs and brass bands and is a fluid, improvised and rhythmic form of music. Traditionally, New Orleans has been the city of jazz, but it later spread to other parts of the country. Jazz reached the height of its popularity in the 1930s and 1940s. It was then incorporated into big-band music and popularized by artists and band leaders like Louis Armstrong and Duke Ellington.

Reflecting an American capacity for experiment, jazz developed an alternative cooler sound from the 1950s. It also influenced music such as pop, rock and roll and American musicals. Today, jazz is popular in the USA and overseas, although it has lost its mass audience appeal, and the best jazz is supposedly provided in New York, Chicago and Los Angeles, rather than the south.

American country and western music has become very popular in the USA and worldwide. Like jazz, it also originated in the American south and was based on the folk-song traditions of early Scottish, Irish and English colonial settlers. It developed into modern country music in the 1920s and is played on the guitar, banjo or fiddle. Its typically mournful or melancholic lyrics dealt with love and poverty and reflected the disadvantaged rural life of poor whites in the south-east and Appalachia, although modern country music deals with more contemporary concerns. Country music has expanded beyond its origins, but Nashville, Tennessee, is still regarded as its home.

American folk music also has a worldwide attraction. It originally had a working-class, underprivileged and rural emphasis, hailed from North Carolina and West Virginia, and was mainly based on Scottish, Irish and English folk ballads. It later took on American themes through figures such as Woody Guthrie. In the 1960s, it developed a wider and more commercial appeal through singers such as Judy Collins, Bob Dylan and Joan Baez who also introduced social and political comment into their texts. Dylan then moved from acoustic to electric guitar and blended folk with rock. Other folk music became heavily commercialized.

Rock and roll developed in the 1950s as another distinctively American form. Many of its practitioners, such as Elvis Presley and later Jimi Hendrix, Janis Joplin and Bruce Springsteen, combined the traditions of African-American rhythm and blues and country and western. It became a popular form of music with young Americans and others worldwide and was associated with a succession of rock idols. Its sound, rhythm and style dominate the popular music scene and have influenced other forms of pop music, whether in imitation or reaction. Rock and roll has become very commercialized in recent decades. It was initially centred on live concert performances in huge stadiums or open venues, but these have decreased and rock generally has become confined to studio production and the issue of videos, compact discs (CDs) and DVDs. Interestingly, touring and live shows have been taken over by foreign musicians. In terms of the all-time North American tour lists (1985–2002), artists from Europe hold places in the top seven spots, with music acts such as the Rolling Stones, U2, Pink Floyd and Paul McCartney.

An *ABC News* poll in August 2002 found that respondents thought that Elvis Presley was the greatest rock and roll star of all time, well in front of other candidates such as Jimi Hendrix, John Lennon, Mick Jagger and Bruce Springsteen. Some 91 per cent thought that Presley had had a lasting impact on American culture and 85 per cent thought that this impact was positive. An *NBC News/Wall Street Journal* poll in April 2002 found that 41 per cent of respondents considered that rock music has had a positive impact on American society, culture and values, while 34 per cent thought that its impact has been negative.

Popular offshoots of these musical traditions, whether in reaction or modification, are found in a wide range of contemporary music such as rap and hip-hop; urban-influenced styles which can include R&B, blues, dance, disco, funk, fusion, Motown and soul; reggae with its Caribbean origins; gospel, hymn, Christian, inspirational, spiritual and religious songs; ethnic musical expression; standards; Big Band; Swing; Latin; mood and easy listening genres; electronic; and instrumental.

The modern musical is of American origin (although some critics trace it to Italian models and the English music hall/ pantomime tradition) and developed in the early twentieth century. Its combination of acting, music and dancing was often allied to escapist plots and exotic shows in glossy theatres. Some later musicals became more serious and socially aware, but the early entertainment emphasis continued. The musical had recently fallen on hard times and has had to compete with successful foreign imports, particularly from Britain that are indebted to the original American format. But the American version of the musical is now proving more popular than the British.

Americans spend billions of dollars on music. According to sales figures collected by the Recording Industry Association of America (2002), rock accounted for 24.7 per cent, rap/hip-hop (13.8 per cent), R&B/urban (11.2 per cent), country (10.7 per cent), pop (9 per cent), religious (6.7 per cent), jazz (3.2 per cent), classical (3.1 per cent), soundtracks (1.1 per cent), oldies (0.9 per cent), New Age (0.5 per cent), children's (0.4 per cent) and other forms (8.1 per cent).

These statistics illustrate catholic tastes. They include the traditional but also the appeal of popular, urban-based and 'ethnic' music, and indicate the importance of a youth culture in the USA. The music business is very lucrative and profitable for the record companies. The consumer culture has commercialized native forms and American music has capitalized on its worldwide attraction and sales. Americans also attend live music shows and concerts and each form of music has its own musicians, clubs and followers.

Modern dance developed as a new distinctively American art form in the early twentieth century. Isadora Duncan, one of its first exponents, based her dances on Greek classical art and was more successful in Europe than America. Her followers, such as Martha Graham in New York, combined modern dance with developments in American music and ethnic life. They rejected the formal restrictions of classical ballet and improvised expressive, random dance movements. Modern (and contemporary) dance in America has developed very successfully and has incorporated different elements like African-American music, video, back-projection, films and African dance movements.

The film industry and Hollywood have been most influential on American culture, domestically and internationally. The film industry started on the east coast, but later moved to Los Angeles, and Hollywood became the centre of American film-making. In the early twentieth century, the motion picture (first silent, then with sound) was the most popular and dominant art form. In the 1940s, the Hollywood production studios were releasing some 400 films annually, seen by 90 million people each week.

Hollywood has always been an entertainment business concerned with selling a product. Its films were originally designed for American audiences and it has reflected American culture by its handling of themes such as the family, romance, individualism, heroism, female roles, children and patriotism. These have been used in different film genres in different periods and have reflected changing social conditions in the USA. Film-makers also strove for financial profits by making film with mass appeal and repeated successful formulas such as westerns, gangster films, comedies and musicals. The system also produced classic films, whose appeal has endured.

**TABLE 14.1** The best movies ever made, 1998.

| Rank | Title | % |
|------|-------|---|
| 1 | Gone With the Wind | 27 |
| 2 | The Wizard of OZ | 11 |
| 3 | Schindler's List | 9 |
| 4 | The Godfather | 8 |
| 5 | Star Wars | 8 |
| 6 | It's a Wonderful Life | 8 |
| 7 | Casablanca | 6 |
| 8 | The Bridge on the River Kwai | 4 |
| 9 | Citizen Kane | 4 |
| 10 | Lawrence of Arabia | 2 |
| 11 | Singin' In the Rain | 2 |
| 12 | The Graduate | 1 |
| 13 | On the Waterfront | 1 |

Source: Gallup/CNN/USA Today, June 1998

During the decades of Hollywood's golden age in the early to mid-twentieth century, films, movie stars and movie theatres were glittering and grandiose. The film industry sold a package in which the cinema-goer was a consumer and the star was a commodity with a lifestyle and image specifically devised for public consumption and approval. Other merchandized items, such as fan clubs, were tied into this package and sold to the mass audience. A Gallup/CNN/*USA Today* poll in June 1998 asked respondents to comment on a list of the best movies ever made, as selected by the American Film Institute. The poll showed a mixture of early and later favourites (see Table 14.1) and reflected similar findings in later polls.

The film industry and the star system have changed over the years (although the celebrity cult continues). They have had to adapt to changing moral, social, economic and industrial climates. The original studio structure altered as a result of a series of mergers. The major companies were effectively taken over by financiers in the 1930s and eight companies (Paramount, MGM, Warner Brothers, RKO, Twentieth Century-Fox, Universal, Columbia and United Artists) were formed. After a prosperous period during the Second World War, the industry was split up by anti-monopolistic legislation. In 2004, Hollywood's last major independent studio, Metro-Goldwyn-Mayer (MGM), negotiated a partner-sale with Japan's Sony Corporation. MGM was formed in 1924 after a merger with other studios and produced classics such as *Ben Hur*, *Gone with the Wind* and *The Wizard of Oz*.

Classical Hollywood of the early twentieth century, with its powerful studios and business tycoons, was largely finished. Fewer more expensive films were made and independent production companies increased. Hollywood was moving away from the studio system and its large-scale productions to a culture of accountants and cost considerations. The post-war period saw the making of increasingly different varieties and genres of film and Disney, for example, became an important source of full-length films. Disney is now a very large entertainment group after its 1995 merger with the ABC television network and has continued to develop its theme parks worldwide.

The increasing influence of television forced the film industry to redefine itself in order to keep its market share of leisure activities. The number of television sets in the USA has grown hugely from the early 1950s. Cinema audiences declined and were halved by 1953. Hollywood responded by making films for teenagers (a rapidly increasing consumer market) and western television series such as *Gunsmoke* and *Cheyenne*. It also introduced some short-lived innovations like Cinerama (wide-screen projection) and 3-D (three-dimensional) films.

Gradually from the 1970s and 1980s Hollywood studios were taken over by conglomerates with diverse business interests such as Gulf and Western, and there was increased competition from independent film-production companies. As new technologies such as video developed, media companies and film studios were increasingly owned by multimedia conglomerates such as Time Warner Inc. Time Warner merged with the Turner Broadcasting System (which owns the CNN cable-television news channel) in 1995 and with America Online in 2000 to become the world's largest media and entertainment group.

Hollywood has therefore changed considerably as the film, media and entertainment industries have developed. It is a multimedia corporate business system, as well as a film industry, with many commercial tie-ins. Production costs have become crucial, and it is difficult to find finance to embark on new film ideas. The audience has also changed. Young people in particular still go to the cinema both out of interest and for social reasons, but older people tend to watch television films and series, videos or DVDs in the home. Some 98 per cent of American households had at least one television set in 2003, 91 per cent had VCRs, 43 per cent CD-players and 70 per cent received basic cable services (48 per cent premium cable).

Television series such as *Friends*, *Seinfeld* and *Frasier*, soap operas such as *Dynasty* and *Dallas* or comedy sitcoms such as *Will and Grace* or *Everybody Loves Raymond*, have become an important staple diet of the film-production industry and studios rent their feature films (often specifically made for television) to television networks. Big films with huge budgets and expensive stars are still being made, although more are being filmed on locations outside Hollywood and California, such as New York and Texas as well as abroad, in an effort to cut rising costs at a time of declining cinema audiences and to search for new markets and ideas. However, the USA remains the largest producer of films for a world

**PLATE 14.1** Halle Berry winning the Best Actress award (the first African American to do so) at the Oscar ceremony in Hollywood for her role in *Monster's Ball*, 2002. (*Sipa Press/Rex Features*)

audience, some of which succeed while others fail. American themes are still examined in films, but Hollywood is now both an American institution and part of international popular culture.

In terms of judging the best movie actors of the twentieth century, respondents to a Reuters/Zogby International poll in March 1999 thought that John Wayne came first in the male category, followed by James Stewart, Paul Newman, Tom Hanks, Harrison Ford, Clark Gable, Mel Gibson and Robert De Niro. In the female category, Katharine Hepburn came first, followed by Meryl Streep, Bette Davis, Elizabeth Taylor, Julia Roberts, Meg Ryan, Demi Moore and Audrey Hepburn. These lists reveal a balance between old and contemporary Hollywood.

Although the golden age is past, film is still an entertainment medium with huge domestic and international appeal. Instructional films are also being made by the film industry and can be used in business, industry, advertising and training programmes. Hollywood and the film industry have consequently had to adapt to changing ownership structures and different social tastes and audiences in order to remain profitable and to develop new markets. In the scramble for entertainment profits based on established themes and successful formulae, many of Hollywood's commercial films are heavily criticized within the USA for their concentration on violence, sexual explicitness and gratuitous action. An Associated Press Poll in June 1999 found that respondents thought that the biggest problems with movies today were 'too much violence' (32 per cent), 'tickets cost too much' (30 per cent), 'not as good as they used to be' (17 per cent) and 'too much sex' (13 per cent).

# Sports

Sport in the USA was until the mid-twentieth century relatively isolated from national and international events. It had a provincial and minority image, although it did provide many Americans with team identification and some respite from the pressures of everyday life. Sport has now become a microcosm of national life and reflects the national condition. Issues such as international competition, global prestige, drug abuse, sex discrimination, labour–management relations, the power of television and advertising, racism, gambling and corruption have all been associated at various times with both amateur and professional sport. The billions of dollars spent on contemporary sport and its buildings can also reflect adversely on local communities that might have prioritized their spending on other areas of social life.

US sports are taken very seriously by some people and are large commercial businesses for others. On some levels, many Americans are obsessively involved with winning and money, but others may still see sport as a wholesome and positive means of enriching their lives, are highly involved in their sports as participants and spectators and are dedicated to the success of their particular teams.

American sports divide into the professional and amateur ranks. Professionally, the most popular and favourite spectator-oriented sports have traditionally been National Football League (NFL) games (with their Super Bowl finals), major league (National and American) baseball (with its World Series), basketball, National (Ice) Hockey League, horse-racing and greyhound-racing. The football season begins in early autumn, basketball is an indoor winter sport and baseball is played in spring and summer, although there is now some overlap. Some sports have moved up or down in popularity and baseball in particular has declined in its support. A Harris poll in October 2004 suggested that the nation's favourite sports were professional football (at 30 per cent), baseball (15 per cent), college football (11 per cent), men's professional basketball (7 per cent), automobile racing (7 per cent), men's college basketball (6 per cent), men's golf (4 per cent) and hockey (4 per cent).

In terms of a possible national representative quality, it is argued that baseball and American football are uniquely American in their combination of baseball's individualism and football's teamwork ethos. Baseball (in spite of the popularity statistics above) is said to be the nation's premier sport since most Americans have supposedly played it from childhood onwards, whether as the full game, Little League baseball or the softball variant (mainly for women). Baseball allegedly originated in the USA before the Civil War as rounders. This is a traditional English children's game played on the street, or in any open space, where the ball is thrown underarm to the hitter and has similarities with softball. It is also maintained that baseball is more democratic than football and basketball since it can be played by people of average height and weight.

An interesting feature of the American sports scene is that since few other countries play baseball, basketball and American football on a professional and large-scale level, competition in them is largely restricted to the USA and there is no international opposition as such. However, although these games are seen as distinctively American sports, they are increasingly being played in other countries.

In terms of other sports, a significant development in April 1996 was the inaugural match in Major League Soccer (MLS), which marked America's latest attempt to introduce a professional soccer league. Earlier attempts had failed, but it was hoped that the 1994 World Cup held in the USA would generate new enthusiasm. It is suggested that the growth of soccer has been America's silent sporting revolution. There are now 20 million registered soccer players in the country and surveys indicate that more than 50 million Americans are 'soccer literate'. Although soccer has long been played on college and university campuses, it is now proving to be popular with corporate sponsors, Latinos, women (40 per cent of all registered players, with the US women's team winning the World Cup in 1999) and affluent households (50 per cent of soccer fans are from households with an income over $60,000). It also rivals the traditional place of Little League baseball as the sport of young suburban families, although it will probably not overtake American football in popularity.

**PLATE 14.2** Goose Tatum of the Harlem Globetrotters basketball team, holding off an opponent in 1946. The technically skilled Globetrotters toured the world in the 1950s and 1960s and their exhibition games became very attractive, commercialized events.
(*Hank Walker/Time Pix/Rex Features*)

Although some professional and college sports such as football, ice hockey and boxing are tough action games, American sports do not suffer the same amount of spectator violence as some other countries' sports. Events such as baseball and football can still be family outings. They have a carnival atmosphere and a large element of show business, including cheerleaders who orchestrate the crowds and marching bands that provide additional entertainment.

There is extensive media coverage of sports by both newspapers and television, which reflects the popularity and commercial standing of sports in the USA. Sports programmes are an integral part of televison and radio programming and attract large audience figures as the networks and other stations fight for market share. Some cable stations (such as ESPN, the Entertainment and Sports Programming Network) are devoted exclusively to sports events, report for some twenty-four hours a day and attract very large audiences. The various media forms, particularly television, have not only created a profitable, audience-based industry, but have made sport accessible for many more people, who are unable either to attend or to afford live events.

The media popularization of sports has also been accompanied by increasing commercialization. The television networks and cable stations compete to obtain financially rewarding contracts from the professional sports bodies which allow the stations to televise their sports events. Advertisers are attracted by the mass audiences and pay the television stations to advertise mainly male-oriented products on their sports programmes. Advertisers benefit from the resulting sales of their products and the sports bodies receive fees and funding from their broadcasting rights contracts. Some, such as the NFL, receive much of their revenue from the networks and cable companies.

Professional baseball, basketball and football are both sports and big business in which team-owners virtually control the players and realize their assets, investments and profits as players are bought and sold. In the case of baseball, the rules have been changed to allow players greater freedom and they (and other professionals) now earn huge salaries. Disputes between the players' union and owners have sometimes halted baseball seasons and fans have become more dissatisfied with baseball and other professional sports because of strikes, high ticket prices and the big business ethos.

The commercialization of American professional sports can affect an athlete's career. Success and financial rewards are connected not only to the person's ability and competitive skills, but also to the marketability of the athlete, who must have agents to act on his or her behalf, take part in publicity campaigns, endorse and promote products such as sportswear and attract sponsorship by corporate advertisers.

There is a tendency in American sports to an almost obsessive competitiveness. As they have become more profit-oriented, success has become paramount and the importance of winning for participants and owners at all levels assumes considerable dimensions. Critics feel that this attitude has detracted from the traditional spirit of teamwork and playing games for fun.

**PLATE 14.3** Crowd at an American National Football League match. The New York Giants originated in New York City but now play their home games in the Giants Stadium at the Meadowland Sports Complex, East Rutherfood, NJ.
(*John Powell/Rex Features*)

An increased commercialization of college sports has also taken place. Schools and colleges provide a variety of sports activities as well as practice and match facilities for their students. These are highly organized and competitive and generally receive substantial local publicity and support. The sports include American football, basketball, baseball, tennis, wrestling, gymnastics, athletics (or track and field), soccer, swimming, volleyball, fencing and golf.

Outstanding high-school athletes may receive scholarships to enable them to go on to college or university, where sports are an essential part of the educational programme. College sports, which are still supposed to be amateur, have become increasingly competitive and commercialized. College sports teams contribute much finance (through television rights and ticket sales) to, as well as publicity for, their individual institutions and are given considerable local community support. Football and basketball are the most financially rewarding college sports and the top college teams can attract large amounts of money. The emphasis on recruiting top high-school athletes can affect the college's academic reputation, because college sports stars have traditionally been recruited solely to play their sport, to earn profits for the college and possibly to move on to the higher professional ranks, rather than to learn and gain an academic education.

The apparent popularity of professional and amateur sports would seem to suggest that a large majority of Americans are avid and committed sports fans with a tribal affection for certain games and teams. A Gallup poll in January 2001 asked respondents whether they would describe themselves as sports fans or not. A majority of 58 per cent said they would and 48 per cent said they would not. The 'yes' response marked a drop of 4 per cent since 2000 and does not represent overwhelming interest.

Polls also reveal interesting attitudes to individual sports. CNN/*USA Today*/Gallup polls in 2002 and 2003 asked respondents whether they were fans of specific professional games, with the following 'yes' results:

- baseball 36 per cent;
- football 50 per cent;
- basketball 33 per cent;
- ice hockey 24 per cent;
- golf 27 per cent;
- tennis 19 per cent;
- auto-racing 31 per cent; and
- wrestling 12 per cent.

College sports also seem to be slipping in popularity, with 39 per cent of respondents being fans of college football ('no', 53 per cent) and even lower percentages who followed college basketball and baseball.

All these figures seem to suggest significant changes in Americans' attitudes to organized sport, particularly at the professional level. Fans have become disillusioned with strikes, high ticket prices, drug abuse, gambling scandals, excessive salaries of players, the behaviour of club-owners and an apparent disrespect for fans by both owners and players. Many would prefer to watch college games rather than the professional code.

## Leisure

A Harris poll in October 2003 found that adult respondents spent forty-nine median hours per week at work (paid work, keeping house and going to school or college) and had nineteen median hours per week available for leisure activities. These figures represent a slight increase in work and a slight decrease in leisure time over recent years but still conflict with a general view that Americans are spending more time at work with less time for leisure. They do in fact indicate a relative balance between the two areas.

Participatory leisure pursuits in the USA can involve different individual (and sometimes institutionalized) physical and sporting activities. A range of more passive pastimes such as reading, television-watching and attendance at cultural events may include social and artistic activities which require some active participation.

Participation in physical activities is varied. Interest in these areas increased from the 1960s and coincided with the new popularity of health fads, dieting and exercise. In part, this was a reaction to research studies which showed that Americans smoked too many cigarettes and were becoming increasingly over-weight and sedentary in their lifestyles. Fitness was promoted by the medical profession and the government, which allied physical strength and fitness to national power and vitality. Running (jogging), aerobic exercises and dancing, racquetball (an American form of squash played in a four-walled court by two or four people using a short-handed racket), swimming, bicycling, tennis, golf, skiing and fast-paced walking were encouraged and gained acceptance and popularity. It became fashionable for people of all ages and both sexes to exercise, to take part in some form of sport, to be physically fit and to place an emphasis on nutrition and diet.

A government survey in 2003 found that 32 per cent of Americans said that they engaged in regular leisure-time activities of moderate or vigorous intensity such as walking, running, biking or playing basketball. But a large percentage are not active either at work or leisure. Another government report in 2001 rated the most popular sports or exercise-related participatory activities among the population (see Table 14.2).

Some Americans can be fanatical and obsessive about fitness and health. They buy the latest expensive training equipment, clothes, books and videos on the subject and feel that fitness is glamorous and connected to a general American ideal of healthy, young and lean bodies. Joggers and runners are a frequent sight in the streets, aerobic exercises and weight-training are popular with both men and women, health clubs have multiplied and there are numerous public and private institutions which provide facilities for those who want to keep fit or play sports. Some of these are provided free by local communities or by commercial businesses for their employees. Others are private clubs for those who can afford to pay for their services.

Commercial business has taken advantage of these developments and has provided a wide range of stylish sporting clothes and equipment, reaping large profits. Book publishers, magazines and television programmes dealing with health and fitness concerns have also fed the market. Health companies produce a wide range of supposedly beneficial products, as do food and beverage businesses. Affluent Americans spend substantial sums of money to achieve a slim and fit effect. Some go to extreme and even dangerous limits to produce individual fitness. Even those who cannot afford high prices for equipment and clothes nevertheless indulge in exercise. It is easy to put a basketball ring on the garage door or telegraph pole, or to run in the streets or countryside.

In spite of all the facilities, individual good intentions and television procla-mations about diets and exercise, it is claimed that 55 per cent of adult Americans

**TABLE 14.2** Exercise-related activities, 2001.

| Rank | Activity | % |
|------|----------|---|
| 1 | Walking | 33 |
| 2 | Swimming | 24 |
| 3 | Camping | 20 |
| 4 | Gym | 19 |
| 5 | Cycling | 17 |
| 6 | Ten-pin bowling | 16 |
| 7 | Billiards | 13 |
| 8 | Basketball | 12 |
| 9 | Hiking | 11 |
| 10 | Golf | 10 |
| 11 | Aerobic exercising | 11 |
| 12 | Running/jogging | 9 |
| 13 | Hunting with firearms | 7 |
| 14 | Baseball | 7 |
| 15 | Back-packing | 6 |
| 16 | Softball | 6 |
| 17 | Soccer | 5 |

Source: US Bureau of the Census 2001

Note: Some people take part in more than one activity.

(or 120 million of all ages) are overweight and 23 per cent are obese, with women more likely to be obese than men. These figures contrast with the 1970s when only a quarter of the country's adult population was officially regarded as overweight.

It is argued that the explanations for this situation are that Americans are eating more of the wrong food and are exercising less. Polls and the Centre for Disease Prevention and Control reveal that between 80 and 90 per cent of Americans consider themselves to be overweight, unfit and lacking in exercise: one in four admits to being completely sedentary, another 40 per cent rarely exercises, 22 per cent of them smoke, 20 per cent suffer from high cholesterol and 80 per cent say that their efforts to improve their fitness and diet do not last long. This situation is made worse by fast-food eating among many Americans, a lack of home-made food, employment stress, sedentary lifestyles and the overeating of fatty food. However, Americans are more tolerant of overweight people than previously and no longer equate this with unattractiveness.

Americans have a wide range of leisure pursuits other than exercise-related activities, some of which have a surprising prominence. Television-viewing (including arts programmes), attending arts activities, socializing in and outside the home, reading, home improvements, film-going, gardening, visits to theme and arts parks, volunteer and charity work and computer use have appeared regularly at the top of opinion polls. A poll in July 2003 that asked respondents which were their two or three favourite leisure-time activities gave the results contained in Table 14.3.

This list is significant for its variety as well as for indicating some changes from previous polls. The place of reading is interesting and impressive with an increased lead over television-watching in recent years. There are some 1.8 million books in print at present, which represents 1.5 million more than fifty years ago and 175,000 new titles are published every year. Although actual book sales are declining in terms of total leisure expenditure, a minority of Americans may spend more than $60 a year on books, a larger number spend between $48 and $60, while a slight majority spend less than $48. The highest-spending areas are California, the north-east coast and Alaska.

A Gallup poll in 1998 also showed the hold that books and libraries have traditionally had on the American public. Sixty-four per cent of respondents had visited a library in the previous year, which was a 13 per cent increase on earlier years. Two thirds of Americans have a library card and one in ten visited a library twenty-five times or more in the previous year. Eighty-one per cent of the respondents said that they visited libraries to take out books. In an age of competing electronic information nine out of ten expected libraries and books to exist in the future.

**TABLE 14.3** Leisure-time activities, 2003.

| Rank | Activity | % |
|------|----------|---|
| 1 | Reading | 24 |
| 2 | Spending time with family/children | 17 |
| 3 | Watching television | 17 |
| 4 | Fishing | 9 |
| 5 | Going to movies | 7 |
| 6 | Socializing with friends/neighbours | 7 |
| 7 | Playing team sports | 6 |
| 8 | Exercise (aerobics, weights) | 6 |
| 9 | Gardening | 6 |
| 10 | Church/church activities | 5 |
| 11 | Watching sporting events | 5 |
| 12 | Computer activities | 5 |
| 13 | Eating out | 5 |

Source: The Harris Poll, October 2003
Note: Some peole take part in more than one activity.

But an NEA survey presented in July 2004 on the basis of census material from 2002 suggested that reading was at risk in the USA and documented an overall decline of 10 per cent in literary readers from 1982 to 2002, which represented a loss of 20 million potential readers. According to the survey, the rate of decline is increasing and had nearly tripled in the decade from 1994 to 2004. The term 'literature' was defined to include popular genres as well as contemporary and classic literary fiction but excluded, among other categories, biography and history.

The decline was common to all demographic groups of Americans, but was greatest in the eighteen to twenty-four group. The survey suggested that if the decline continued, literary reading as a leisure activity will virtually disappear within fifty years and argued that American culture was at risk. The electronic media are instead becoming the dominant influence in young people's worlds and there are allegations about 'dumbing down' in the schools.

More precise readings of the NEA and census statistics show that while the total number of readers has fallen, their actual numbers today remain relatively high. The number of Americans who read fiction, poetry or plays is 46.7 per cent, more than those (35 per cent) who attended a sports event in 2002. Some 55 per cent of these readers are women and 38 per cent are men. Americans also read books outside of, but including, the NEA's definition of 'literature'. Of these, a 'light' reader reads one to five books a year, 'frequent' readers twelve to forty-nine and 'avid readers' more than fifty.

# Exercises

Explain and examine the significance of the following terms.

| | | |
|---|---|---|
| Hollywood | modern dance | tax breaks |
| baseball | ragtime | *Dallas* |
| 'pop art' | banjo | college football |
| aerobics | racquetball | bowling |
| softball | fads | abstract expressionism |
| NEA | the musical | rounders |

Write short essays on the following questions.

1. To what extent are some sports and films uniquely American?

2. Discuss the role of advertising and television in American sports, arts and leisure.

3. Critically examine the opinion polls on the arts, sports and leisure. What do these indicate about the diversity of American society?

# Further reading

Balio, T. (1990) *Hollywood in the Age of Television* Cambridge, Mass.: Unwin Hyman.

Cullen, J. (ed.) (2001) *Popular Culture in American History* Oxford: Blackwell.

Davies, R. O. (1994) *America's Obsession: sports and society since 1945* New York: Harcourt Brace.

Schatz, T. (1981) *Hollywood Genres: formulas, filmmaking, and the studio system* New York: Random House.

Schlosser, E. (2002) *Fast Food Nation* New York: Perennial.

# Web sites

<http://usinfo.state.gov/usa/infousa/arts/arts.htm>

<http://usinfo.state.gov/journals/itsv/0698/ijse/ijse0698.htm>

The National Gallery of Art: <http://www.nga.gov>

The National Football League: <http://www.nfl.com>

The National Hockey League: <http://www.nhl.com>

The National Archives: <http://www.nara.gov/education>

The National Endowment for the Arts: <www.arts.gov and arts.endow.gov>

# Appendices

## Declaration of Independence in Congress, 4 July 1776

### *The unanimous declaration of the thirteen United States of America*

When, in the course of human events, it becomes necessary for one people to dissolve the political bonds which have connected them with another, and to assume, among the powers of the earth, the separate and equal station to which the laws of nature and of nature's God entitle them, a decent respect to the Opinions of mankind requires that they should declare the causes which impel them to the separation.

We hold these truths to be self-evident: That all men are created equal; that they are endowed by their Creator with certain unalienable rights; that among these are life, liberty and the pursuit of happiness; that, to secure these rights, governments are instituted among men, deriving their just powers from the con-sent of the governed; that whenever any form of government becomes destructive of these ends, it is the right of the people to alter or to abolish it, and to institute new government, laying its foundation on such principles, and organize its powers in such form, as to them shall seem most likely to effect their safety and happiness. Prudence, indeed, will dictate that government long established should not be changed for light and transient causes; and accordingly all experience hath shown that mankind are more disposed to suffer, while evils are sufferable, than to right themselves by abolishing the forms to which they are accustomed. But when a long train of abuses and usurpation, pursuing invariably the same object, evinces a design to reduce them under absolute despotism, it is their right, it is their duty, to throw off such government, and to provide new guards for their future security. Such has been the patient sufferage of these colonies; and such is now the necessity which constrains them to alter their former systems of government. The history of the present King of Great Britain is history of repeated injuries and usurpations, all having in direct object the establishment of an absolute tyranny over these states. To prove this, let facts be submitted to a candid world.

He has refused his assent to laws, the most wholesome and necessary for the public good.

He has forbidden his governors to pass laws of immediate and pressing importance, unless suspended in their operation till his assent should be obtained; and, when so suspended, he has utterly neglected to attend to them.

He has refused to pass other laws for the accommodation of large districts of people, unless those people would relinquish the right of representation in the legislature, a right inestimable to them, and formidable to tyrants only.

He has called together legislative bodies at places unusual, uncomfortable, and distant from the depository of their public records, for the sole purpose of fatiguing them into compliance with his measures.

He has dissolved representative houses repeatedly, for opposing, with manly firmness, his invasions on the rights of the people.

He has refused for a long time, after such dissolutions, to cause others to be elected; whereby the legislative powers, incapable of annihilation, have returned to the people at large for their exercise; the state remaining, in the meantime, exposed to all the dangers of invasions from without and convulsions within.

He has endeavoured to prevent the population of these states; for that purpose obstructing the laws for naturalization of foreigners; refusing to pass others to encourage their migration hither, and raising the conditions of new appropriations of lands.

He has obstructed the administration of justice, by refusing his assent to laws for establishing judiciary powers.

He has made judges dependent on his will alone, for the tenure of their offices, and the amount and payment of their salaries.

He has erected a multitude of new offices, and sent hither swarms of officers to harass our people and eat out their substance.

He has kept among us, in times of peace, standing armies without the consent of our legislatures.

He has affected to render the military independent of, and superior to, the civil power.

He has combined with others to subject us to a jurisdiction foreign to our constitution, and unacknowledged by our laws, giving his assent to their acts of pretended legislation:

For quartering large bodies of armed troops among us;

For protecting them, by a mock trial, from punishment for any murders which they should commit on the inhabitants of these states;

For cutting off our trade with all parts of the world;

For imposing taxes on us without our consent;

For depriving us, in many cases, of the benefits of trial by jury;

For transporting us beyond seas, to be tried for pretended offences;

For abolishing the free system of English laws in a neighbouring province, establishing therein an arbitrary government, and enlarging its boundaries, so as to render it at once an example and fit instrument for introducing the same absolute rule into these colonies;

For taking away our charters, abolishing our most valuable laws, and altering fundamentally the forms of our governments;

For suspending our legislatures, and declaring themselves invested with power to legislate for us in all cases whatsoever.

He has abdicated government here, by declaring us out of his protection and waging war against us.

He has plundered our seas, ravaged our coasts, burned our towns, and destroyed the lives of our people.

He is at this time transporting large armies of foreign mercenaries to complete the works of death, desolation, and tyranny already begun with the circumstances of cruelty and perfidy scarcely paralleled in the most barbarous ages, and totally unworthy the head of a civilized nation.

He has constrained our fellow-citizens, taken captive on the high seas, to bear arms against their country, to become the executioners of their friends and brethren, or to fall themselves by their hands.

He has excited domestic insurrection among us; and has endeavoured to bring on the inhabitants of our frontiers the merciless Indian savages, whose known rule of warfare is an undistinguished destruction of all ages, sexes, and conditions.

In every stage of these oppressions we have petitioned for redress in the most humble terms; our repeated petitions have been answered only by repeated injury. A prince, whose character is thus marked by every act which may define a tyrant, is unfit to be the ruler of a free people.

Nor have we been wanting in our attentions to our British brethren. We have warned them, from time to time, of attempts by their legislature to extend a unwarrantable jurisdiction over us. We have reminded them of the circumstances of our emigration and settlement here. We have appealed to their native justice and magnanimity; and we have conjured them, by the ties of our common kindred, to disavow these usurpations, which would inevitably interrupt our connections and correspondence. They, too, have been deaf to the voice of justice and of consanguinity. We must, therefore, acquiesce in the necessity which denounces our separation, and hold them, as we hold the rest of mankind, enemies in war, in peace friends.

We, therefore, the representatives of the United States of America, in General Congress assembled, appealing to the Supreme Judge of the world for the rectitude of our intentions, do, in the name and by the authority of the good people of these colonies, solemnly publish and declare, that these United Colonies are, and of right ought to be, FREE AND INDEPENDENT STATES; that they are absolved from all allegiance to the British Crown, and that all political connection between them and the state of Great Britain is, and ought to be, totally dissolved; and that, as free and independent states, they have full power to levy war, conclude peace, contract alliances, establish commerce, and do all other acts and things which independent states may of right do. And for the support of this declaration, with a firm reliance on the protection of Divine Providence, we mutually pledge to each other our lives, our fortunes, and our sacred honour.

*John Hancock and
fifty-five others*

## Constitution of the United States of America and Amendments

(Passages no longer in effect are printed in italic type.) Brief identifications of the content of provisions are underlined in parentheses.

### PREAMBLE (The people establish the Constitution)

We the people of the United States, in order to form a more perfect union, establish justice, insure domestic tranquillity, provide for the common defense, promote the general welfare, and secure the blessings of liberty to ourselves and our posterity, do ordain and establish this Constitution for the United States of America.

### ARTICLE I (Congress, the legislative branch)

**Section 1**  All legislative powers herein granted shall be vested in a Congress of the United States, which shall consist of a Senate and a House of Representatives. (Bicameralism)

**Section 2**  The House of Representatives shall be composed of members chosen every second year by the people of the several States, and the electors in each State shall have the qualifications requisite for electors of the most numerous branch of the State Legislature. (Qualifications for voters)

No person shall be a Representative who shall not have attained to the age of twenty-five years, and been seven years a citizen of the United States, and who shall not, when elected, be an inhabitant of that State in which he shall be chosen. (Qualifications for members)

Representative and direct taxes shall be apportioned among the several States which may be included within this Union, according to their respective numbers, *which shall be determined by adding to the whole number of free persons, including those bound to service for a term of years and excluding Indians not taxed, three-fifths of all other persons.* The actual enumeration shall be within three years after the first meeting of the Congress of the United States, and within every subsequent term of ten years, in such manners as they shall by law direct. The number of Representatives shall not exceed one for every thirty thousand, but each State shall have at least one Representative; *and until such enumeration shall be made, the State of New Hampshire shall be entitled to choose three, Massachusetts eight, Rhode Island and Providence Plantations one, Connecticut five, New York six, New Jersey four, Pennsylvania eight, Delaware one, Maryland six, Virginia ten, North Carolina five, South Carolina five, and Georgia three.* (Apportionment according to the census)

When vacancies happen in the representation from any State, the Executive authority thereof shall issue writs of election to fill such vacancies.

The House of Representatives shall choose their Speaker and other officers; and shall have the sole power of impeachment. (Impeachment)

**Section 3** The Senate of the United States shall be composed of two Senators from each State, *chosen by the legislature thereof,* for six years; each Senator shall have one vote.

*Immediately after they shall be assembled in consequence of the first election, they shall be divided as equally as may be into three classes. The seats of the Senators of the first class shall be vacated at the expiration of the second year, of the second class at the expiration of the fourth year, and of the third class at the expiration of the sixth year,* so that one-third may be chosen every second year; *and if vacancies happen by resignation or otherwise, during the recess of the legislature of any State, the Executive thereof may make temporary appointments until the next meeting of the legislature, which shall then fill such vacancies.* (Staggered Senate elections)

No person shall be a Senator who shall not have attained to the age thirty years, and been nine years a citizen of the United States, and who shall not, when elected, be an inhabitant of that State for which he shall be chosen. (Qualifications)

The Vice-President of the United States shall be President of the Senate, but shall have no vote, unless they be equally divided.

The Senate shall choose their other officers, and also a President *pro tempore*, in the absence of the Vice-President or when he shall exercise the office of President of the United States. (President pro tempore)

The Senate shall have the sole power to try all impeachments. When sitting for that purpose, they shall be on oath or affirmation. When the President of the United States is tried, the Chief Justice shall preside; and no person shall be convicted without the concurrence of two-thirds of the members present. (Impeachment)

Judgement in cases of impeachment shall not extend further than to removal from the office, and disqualification to hold and enjoy any office of honour, trust or profit under the United States; but the party convicted shall nevertheless be liable to indictment, trial, judgement and punishment, according to law. (Judgement regulations in cases of impeachment)

**Section 4** The times, places and manner of holding elections for Senators and Representatives shall be prescribed in each State by the legislature thereof; but the Congress may at any time by law make or alter such regulations, except as to the places of choosing Senators. (<u>Rules for Congressional elections</u>)

The Congress shall assemble at least once in every year, and such meeting *shall be on the first Monday in December, unless they shall by law appoint a different day.*

**Section 5** Each house shall be the judge of the elections, returns and qualifications of its own members, and a majority of each shall constitute a quorum to do business; but a smaller number may adjourn from day to day, and may be authorized to compel attendance of absent members, in such manner, and under such penalties, as each house may provide. (<u>Qualifications</u>)

Each house may determine the rules of its proceedings, punish its members for disorderly behaviour, and with the concurrence of two-thirds, expel a member. (<u>Expulsion</u>)

Each house shall keep a journal of its proceedings, and from time to time publish the same, excepting such parts as may in their judgement require secrecy; and the yeas and nays of the members of either house on any question shall, at the desire of one-fifth of those present, be entered on the journal. (<u>Required congressional record</u>)

Neither house, during the session of Congress, shall, without the consent of the other, adjourn for more than three days, nor to any other place than that in which the two houses shall be sitting. (<u>Adjournment regulations</u>)

**Section 6** The Senators and Representatives shall receive a compensation for their services, to be ascertained by law and paid out of the treasury of the United States. They shall in all cases except treason, felony and breach of the peace, be privileged from arrest during their attendance at the session of their respective houses, and in going to and returning from the same; and for any speech or debate in either house, they shall not be questioned in any other place. (<u>Pay and immunity</u>)

No Senator or Representative shall, during the time for which he was elected, be appointed to any civil office under the authority of the United States, which shall have been created, or emoluments whereof shall have been increased, during such time; and no person holding any office under the United States shall be a member of either house during his continuance in office. (<u>Limitation related to civil officers</u>)

**Section 7** All bills for raising revenue shall originate in the House of Representatives; but the Senate may propose or concur with amendments as on other bills. (<u>The right to tax</u>)

Every bill which shall have passed the House of Representatives and the Senate, shall, before it becomes a law, be presented to the President of the United

States; if he approve he shall sign it, but if not he shall return it with objections to that house in which it originated, who shall enter the objections at large on their journal, and proceed to reconsider it. If after such reconsideration two-thirds of that house shall agree to pass the bill, it shall be sent, together with the objections, to the other house, by which it shall likewise be reconsidered, and, if approved by two-thirds of that house, it shall become a law. But in all such cases the vote of both houses shall be determined by yeas and nays, and the names of the persons voting for and against the bill shall be entered on the journal of each house respectively. If any bill shall not be returned by the President within ten days (Sundays excepted) after it shall have been presented to him, the same shall be a law, in like manner as if he had signed it, unless Congress by their adjournment prevent its return, in which case it shall not be a law. (Procedure of bills, veto power of the President)

Every order, resolution, or vote to which the concurrence of the Senate and House of Representatives may be necessary (except on a question of adjournment) shall be presented to the President of the United States; and before the same shall take effect, shall be approved by him, or being disapproved by him, shall be repassed by two-thirds of the Senate and House of Representatives, according to the rules and limitations prescribed in the case of a bill. (Presidential approval)

**Section 8**  (Enumerated [specified] powers of Congress)

The Congress shall have power

To lay and collect taxes, duties, imposts, and excises, to pay the debts and provide for the common defense and general welfare of the United States; but all duties, imposts and excises shall be uniform throughout the United States;

To borrow money on the credit of the United States;

To regulate commerce with foreign nations, and among the several States, and with the Indian tribes;

To establish an uniform rule of naturalization, and uniform laws on the subject of bankruptcies throughout the United States;

To coin money, regulate the value thereof, and of foreign coin, and fix the standard of weights and measures;

To provide for the punishment of counterfeiting the securities and current coin of the United States;

To establish post offices and post roads;

To promote the progress of science and useful arts by securing for limited times to authors and inventors the exclusive right to their respective writings and discoveries;

To constitute tribunals inferior to the Supreme Court;

To define and punish piracies and felonies committed on the high seas and offences against the law of nations;

To declare war, grant letters of marque and reprisal, and make rules concerning captures on land and water;

To raise and support armies, but no appropriation of money to that shall be for a longer term than two years;

To provide and maintain a navy;

To make rules for the government and regulation of the land and naval forces;

To provide for calling forth the militia to execute the laws of the Union, supress insurrections, and repel invasions;

To provide for organizing, arming, and disciplining the militia, and for governing such part of them as may be employed in the service of the United States, reserving to the States respectively the appointment of the officers, and the authority of training the militia according to the discipline prescribed by Congress;

To exercise exclusive legislation in all cases whatsoever, over such district (not exceeding ten miles square) as may, by cession of particular States, and the acceptance of Congress, become the seat of government of the United States, and to exercise like authority over all places purchased by the consent of the legislature of the State, in which the same shall be, for erection of forts, magazines, arsenals, dock-yards, and other needful buildings; – and

To make all laws which shall be necessary and proper for carrying into execution the foregoing powers, and all other powers vested by this Constitution in the government of the United States, or in any department or officer thereof. (The 'necessary and proper' clause, implied powers of Congress)

**Section 9** *The migration or importation of such persons as any of the States now existing shall think proper to admit shall not be prohibited by the Congress prior to the year 1808; but a tax or duty may be imposed on such importation, not exceeding 10 dollars for each person.* (Slave import and limited powers)

The privilege of the writ of habeas corpus shall not be suspended, unless when in cases of rebellion or invasion the public safety may require it. (Habeas corpus)

No bill of attainder or *ex post facto* shall be passed.

No capitation, or other direct, tax shall be laid, unless in proportion to the census or enumeration herein before directed to be taken.

No tax or duty shall be laid on articles exported from any State.

No preference shall be given by any regulation of commerce or revenue to the ports of one State over those of another; nor shall vessels bound to, or from, one State, be obliged to enter, clear, or pay duties in another.

No money shall be drawn from the treasury, but in consequence of appropriations made by law; and a regular statement and account of the receipts and expenditures of all public money shall be published from time to time.

No title or nobility shall be granted by the United States; and no person holding any office of profit or trust under them, shall, without consent of the Congress, accept of any present, emolument, office, or title, of any kind whatever, from any king, prince, or foreign state.

**Section 10**  No State shall enter into any treaty, alliance, or confederation; grant letters of marque and reprisal; coin money; emit bills of credit; make anything but gold and silver coin a tender in payment of debts; pass any bill of attainder, *ex post facto* law, or law impairing the obligation of contracts, or grant any title of nobility. (Restrictions on powers of the states)

No State shall, without the consent of Congress, lay any imposts or duties on imports or exports, except what may be absolutely necessary for executing its inspection laws; and the net produce of all duties and imposts, laid by any State on imports and exports, shall be for the use of the treasury of the United States; and all such laws shall be subject to the revision and control of the Congress.

No State shall, without the consent of Congress, lay any duty of tonnage, keep troops or ships of war in time of peace, enter into any agreement or compact with another State, or with a foreign power, or engage in war, unless actually invaded, or in such imminent danger as will not admit of delay.

## ARTICLE II  (The President, the executive branch)

**Section 1**  The executive power shall be vested in a President of the United States. He shall hold his office during the term of four years, and, together with the Vice-President, chosen for the same term, be elected as follows:

Each State shall appoint, in such manner as the legislature thereof may direct, a number of electors, equal to the whole number of Senators and Representatives to which the State may be entitled in the Congress; but no Senator or Representative, or person holding an office of trust or profit under the United States, shall be appointed an elector.

*The electors shall meet in their respective States, and vote by ballot for two persons, of whom one at least shall not be an inhabitant of the same State with themselves. And they shall make a list of all the persons voted for, and of the number of votes for each; which list they shall sign and certify, and transmit sealed to the seat of government of the United States, directed to the President of the Senate. The President of the Senate shall, in the presence of the Senate and House of Representatives, open all the certificates, and the votes shall be counted. The person having the greatest number of votes shall be President, if such number be a majority of the whole number of electors appointed; and if there be more than one who have such majority, and have an equal number of votes, then the House of Representatives shall immediately choose by ballot one of them for President; and if no person have a majority, then from the five highest on the list said house shall in like manner choose the President. But in choosing the President the votes shall be taken by States, the representation from each State having one vote; a quorum for this purpose shall consist of member or members from two-thirds of the States, and a majority of all the States shall be necessary to a choice. In every case, after the choice of the President, the person having the greatest number of votes of the electors shall be the Vice-President. But if there should remain two or more who have equal votes, the Senate shall choose from them by ballot the Vice-President.* (Electors)

The Congress may determine the time of choosing the electors and the day on which they shall give their votes; which day shall be the same throughout the United States.

No person except a natural-born citizen, *or a citizen of the United States at the time of the adoption of this Constitution*, shall be eligible to the office of President, neither shall any person be eligible to that office who shall not have attained to the age of thirty-five years, and been fourteen years a resident within the United States. (<u>Qualifications for President</u>)

In case of the removal of the President from office or of his death, resignation, or inability to discharge the powers and duties of the said office, the same shall devolve on the Vice-President, and the Congress may by law provide for the case of removal, death, resignation, or inability, both of the President and Vice-President, declaring what officer shall then act as President, and such officer shall act accordingly, until the disability be removed, or a President shall be elected. (<u>Presidential succession</u>)

The President shall, at stated times, receive for his services a compensation, which shall neither be increased nor diminished during the period for which he shall have been elected, and he shall not receive within that period any other emolument from the United States, or any of them. (<u>Presidential compensation</u>)

Before he enter on the execution of his office, he shall take the following oath or affirmation:- 'I do solemnly swear (or affirm) that I will faithfully execute the office of the President for the United States, and will to the best of my ability preserve, protect and defend the Constitution of the United States.' (<u>Presidential oath of office</u>)

**Section 2** The President shall be commander-in-chief of the army and navy of the United States, and of the militia of the several States, when called into the actual service of the United States; he may require the opinion, in writing, of the principal officer in each of the executive departments, upon any subject relating to the duties of their respective offices, and he shall have power to grant reprieves and pardons for offences against the United States, except in cases of impeachment. (<u>Powers of President</u>)

He shall have power, by and with the advice and consent of the Senate, to make treaties, provided two-thirds of the Senators present concur; and he shall nominate, and by and with the advice and consent of the Senate, shall appoint ambassadors, other public ministers and consuls, judges of the Supreme Court, and all other officers of the United States, whose appointments are not herein otherwise provided for, and which shall be established by law; but Congress may by law vest the appointment of such inferior officers, as they think proper, in the President alone, in the courts of law, or in the heads of departments.

The President shall have the power to fill up all vacancies that may happen during the recess of the Senate, by granting commissions which shall expire at the end of their next session.

**Section 3** The President shall from time to time give to the Congress information of the state of the Union, and recommend to their consideration such measures as he shall judge necessary and expedient; he may, on extraordinary occasions, convene both houses, or either of them, and in case of disagreement between them, with respect to the time of adjournment, he may adjourn them to such time as he shall think proper; he shall receive ambassadors and other public ministers; he shall take care that the laws be faithfully executed, and shall commission all the officers of the United States. (State of the Union message)

**Section 4** The President, the Vice-President and the civil officers of the United States shall be removed from office on impeachment for, and or convictions of, treason, bribery, or other high crimes and misdemeanours. (Impeachment)

### ARTICLE III (The Supreme Court, the judiciary branch)

**Section 1** The judicial power of the United States shall be vested in one Supreme Court, and in such inferior courts as the Congress may from time to time ordain and establish. The judges, both of the Supreme and inferior courts, shall hold their offices during good behaviour, and shall, at stated times, receive for their services a compensation which shall not be diminished during their continuance in office.

**Section 2** The judicial power shall extend to all cases, in law and equity, arising under this Constitution, the laws of the United States, and treaties made, or which shall be made, under their authority; to all cases affecting ambassadors, other public ministers and consuls; to all cases of admiralty and maritime jurisdiction; to controversies to which the United States shall be a party; to controversies between two or more States; *between a State and citizen of another State*; between citizens of different States; between citizens of the same State claiming land under grants of different States, and between a State, or the citizens thereof, and foreign states, citizens or subjects. (Jurisdiction)

In all cases affecting ambassadors, other public ministers and consuls, and those in which a State shall be party, the Supreme Court shall have original jurisdiction. In all the other cases before mentioned, the Supreme Court shall have appellate jurisdiction, both as to law and fact, with such exceptions, and under such regulations, as the Congress shall make.

The trial of all crimes, except in cases of impeachment, shall be by jury; and such trial shall be held in the State where said crimes shall have been committed; but when not committed within any State, the trial shall be at such place or places as the Congress may by law have directed. (Jury trial)

**Section 3** Treason against the United States shall consist only in levying war against them, or in adhering to their enemies, giving them aid and comfort. No person shall be convicted of treason unless on the testimony of two witnesses to the same overt act, or on confession in open court.

The Congress shall have power to declare the punishment of treason, but no attainder of treason shall work corruption of blood, or forfeiture except during the life of the person attainted.

### *ARTICLE IV* (The states)

**Section 1** Full faith and credit shall be given in each State to the public acts, records, and judicial proceedings of every other State. And the Congress may by general laws prescribe the manner in which such acts, records, and proceedings shall be proved, and the effect thereof.

**Section 2** The citizens of each State shall be entitled to all privileges and immunities of citizens in the several States.

A person charged in any State with treason, felony, or other crime, who shall flee from justice, and be found in another State, shall on demand of the executive authority of the State from which he fled, be delivered up, to be removed to the State having jurisdiction of the crime. (Privileges)

*No person held to serve or labour in one State, under the laws thereof, escaping into another, shall, in consequence of any law or regulation therein, be discharged from such service or labour, but shall be delivered up on claim of the party to whom such service or labour may be due.* (Fugitive slaves)

**Section 3** New States may be admitted by the Congress into this Union; but no new State shall be formed or erected within the jurisdiction of any other State; nor any State be formed by the junction of two or more States, or parts of States, without the consent of the legislatures of the States concerned as well as of the Congress. (New states)

The Congress shall have power to dispose of and make all needful rules and regulations respecting the territory or other property belonging to the United States; and nothing in this Constitution shall be so construed as to prejudice any claims of the United States, or of any particular State.

**Section 4** The United States shall guarantee to every State in this Union a republican form of government, and shall protect each of them against invasion; and on application of the legislature, or of the executive (when the legislature cannot be convened), against domestic violence. (Promises to states)

### *ARTICLE V* (Amendments)

The Congress, whenever two-thirds of both houses shall deem it necessary, shall propose amendments to this Constitution, or, on the application of the legislatures

of two-thirds of the several States, shall call a convention for proposing amendments, which, in either case, shall be valid to all intents and purposes, as part of
this Constitution, when ratified by the legislatures of three-fourths of the several
States, or by conventions in three-fourths thereof, as the one or the other mode
of ratification may be proposed by the Congress; provided *that no amendments
which may be made prior to the year one thousand eight hundred and eight shall in
any manner affect the first and fourth clauses in the ninth section of the first article;*
and that no State, without its consent, shall be deprived of its equal suffrage in
the Senate. (Ratification)

### *ARTICLE VI* (Effects of Constitution)

All debts contracted and engagements entered into, before the adoption of this
Constitution, shall be as valid against the United States under this Constitution,
as under the Confederation.

This Constitution, and the laws of the United States which shall be made
in pursuance thereof; and all treaties made, or which shall be made, under
the authority of the United States, shall be the supreme law of the land; and the
judges in every State shall be bound thereby, anything in the Constitution or laws
of any State to the contrary notwithstanding. (Supremacy clause)

The Senators and Representatives before mentioned, and the members
of the several State legislatures, and all executive and judicial officers, both of the
United States and of the several States, shall be bound by oath or affirmation
to support this Constitution; but no religious test shall ever be required as a
qualification to any office or public trust under the United States. (No religious
test)

### *ARTICLE VII* (Ratification)

The ratification of the conventions of nine States shall be sufficient for the
establishment of this Constitution between the States so ratifying the same.

Done in Convention by the unanimous consent of the States present, the
seventeenth day of September in the year of our Lord one thousand seven hundred
and eighty-seven and of the Independence of the United States of America the
twelfth. In witness whereof we have hereunto subscribed our names.

*George Washington and thirty-seven others.*

# The Bill of Rights (The first ten Amendments)

*AMENDMENT I (1791)* (Basic freedoms; separation of church and state)

Congress shall make no law respecting an establishment of religion, or prohibiting the free exercise thereof; or abridging the freedom of speech, or of the press; or the right of the people peaceably to assemble, and to petition the government for a redress of grievances.

*AMENDMENT II (1791)* (The right to bear arms)

A well-regulated militia being necessary to the security of a free State, the right of the people to keep and bear arms shall not be infringed.

*AMENDMENT III (1791)* (Quartering of soldiers)

No soldier shall, in time of peace, be quartered in any house without the consent of the owner, nor in time of war, but in a manner to be prescribed by law.

*AMENDMENT IV (1791)* (Search and seizure)

The right of the people to be secure in their persons, houses, papers, and effects, against unreasonable searches and seizures, shall not be violated, and no warrants shall issue but upon probable cause, supported by oath or affirmation, and particularly described, the place to be searched, and the persons or things to be seized.

*AMENDMENT V (1791)* (Rights in court cases)

No person shall be held to answer for a capital, or otherwise infamous crime, unless on a presentment or indictment of a grand jury, except in cases arising in the land or naval forces, or in the militia, when in actual service in time of war or public danger; nor shall any person be subject for the same offence to be twice put in jeopardy of life or limb; nor shall be compelled in any criminal case to be a witness against himself, nor be deprived of life, liberty, or property, without due process of law; nor shall private property be taken for public use without just compensation.

*AMENDMENT VI (1791)* (Rights of the accused)

In all criminal prosecutions, the accused shall enjoy the right to a speedy and public trial, by an impartial jury of the State and district wherein the crime shall have been committed, which district shall have been previously ascertained by law, and to be informed of the nature and cause of the accusation; to be confronted with the witnesses against him; to have compulsory process for obtaining witnesses in his favour, and to have the assistance of counsel for his defence.

## AMENDMENT VII (1791)  (The right to a trial by jury)

In suits at common law, where the value in controversy shall exceed twenty dollars, the right of trial by jury shall be preserved, and no fact tried by a jury shall be otherwise reexamined in any court of the United States, than according to the rules of the common law.

## AMENDMENT VIII (1791)  (Bail; cruel and unusual punishment)

Excessive bail shall not be required, nor excessive fines imposed, nor cruel and unusual punishment inflicted.

## AMENDMENT IX (1791)  (Rights retained by the people)

The enumeration in the Constitution, of certain rights, shall not be construed to deny or disparage others retained by the people.

## AMENDMENT X (1791)  (Reserved powers)

The powers not delegated to the United States by the Constitution, nor prohibited by it to the States, are reserved to the States respectively, or to the people.

## LATER AMENDMENTS

## AMENDMENT XI (1798)  (Law suits against states)

The judicial power of the United States shall not be construed to extend to any suit in law or equity, commenced or prosecuted against one of the United States by a citizen of another State, or by citizens or subjects of any foreign state.

## AMENDMENT XII (1804)  (Electoral votes)

The electors shall meet in their respective States, and vote by ballot for President and Vice-President, one of whom, at least, shall not be an inhabitant of the same State with themselves; they shall name in their ballots the person voted for as President, and in distinct ballots the person voted for as Vice-President, and they shall make distinct lists of all persons voted for as President, and of all persons voted for as Vice-President, and of the number of votes for each, which lists they shall sign and certify, and transmit sealed to the seat of government of the United States, directed to the President of the Senate; – the President of the Senate shall, in the presence of the Senate and House of Representatives, open all the certificates and the votes shall then be counted; – the person having the greatest number of votes for President shall be the President if such number be a majority of the whole number of electors appointed, and if no person have a majority, then from the persons having the highest numbers not exceeding three on the list of those voted for as President, the House of Representatives shall choose immediately, by ballot, the President. But in choosing the President, the votes shall be taken by States, the representation from each State having one vote; a quorum for this purpose shall consist of a member or members from two-thirds of the States, and a majority of all the States shall be necessary to a choice. And if the House of Representatives shall not choose a President whenever the right of choice shall devolve upon them, before *the fourth day of March* next following, then the Vice-President shall act as President, as in the case of death or other constitutional disability of the President.

The person having the greatest number of votes as Vice-President shall be the Vice-President, if such number be a majority of the whole number of electors appointed; and if no person have a majority, then from the two highest numbers on the list the Senate shall choose the Vice-President; a quorum for the purpose shall consist of two-thirds of the whole number of Senators, and a majority of the whole number shall be necessary to a choice. But no person constitutionally ineligible to the office of President shall be eligible to that of Vice-President of the United States.

## AMENDMENT XIII (1865) (Abolition of slavery)

**Section 1** Neither slavery nor involuntary servitude, except as a punishment for crime whereof the party shall have been duly convicted, shall exist within the United States, or any place subject to their jurisdiction.

**Section 2** Congress shall have the power to enforce this article by appropriate legislation.

## AMENDMENT XIV (1868) (Citizenship for former slaves; due process and equal protection clauses)

**Section 1** All persons born or naturalized in the United States, and subject to the jurisdiction thereof, are citizens of the United States and of the State wherein they reside. No State shall make or enforce any law which shall abridge the privileges or immunities of citizens of the United States; nor shall any State deprive any person of life, liberty, or property, without due process of law; nor deny to any person within its jurisdiction the equal protection of the laws.

**Section 2** Representatives shall be appointed among the several States according to their respective numbers, counting the whole number of persons in each State, excluding Indians not taxed. But when the right to vote at any election for the choice of Electors for President and Vice-President of the United States, Representatives in Congress, the executive and judicial officers of a State, or the members of the legislature thereof, is denied to any of the male inhabitants of such State, being twenty-one years of age and citizens of the United States, or in any way abridged, except for participation in rebellion, or other crime, the basis of representation therein shall be reduced in the proportion which the number of such male citizens shall bear to the whole number of male citizens twenty-one years of age in such State. (Apportionment)

**Section 3**  No person shall be a Senator or Representative in Congress, or Elector of President and Vice-President, or hold any office, civil or military, under the United States, or under any State, who, having previously taken an oath, as a member of Congress, or as an officer of the United States, or as a member of any State legislature, or as an executive or judicial officer of any State, to support the Constitution of the United States, shall have engaged in insurrection or rebellion against the same, or given aid or comfort to the enemies thereof. Congress may, by a vote of two-thirds of each house, remove such disability.

**Section 4**  The validity of the public debt of the United States, authorized by law, including debts incurred for payment of pensions and bounties for services in suppressing insurrection or rebellion, shall not be questioned. But neither the United States nor any State shall assume or pay any debt or obligation incurred in aid of insurrection or rebellion against the United States, or any claim for the loss of emancipation of any slave; but all such debts, obligations, and claims shall be held illegal and void.

**Section 5**  The Congress shall have power to enforce, by appropriate legislature, the provisions of this article.

## AMENDMENT XV (1870)  (Voting rights for freed male slaves)

**Section 1**  The right of citizens of the United States to vote shall not be denied or abridged by the United States or by any State on account of race, colour, or previous condition of servitude.

**Section 2**  The Congress shall have power to enforce this article by appropriate legislature.

## AMENDMENT XVI (1913)  (Federal income tax)

The Congress shall have power to lay and collect taxes on incomes, from whatever source derived, without apportionment among the several States, and without regard to any census or enumeration.

### AMENDMENT XVII (1913) (The direct election of Senators)

**Section 1** The Senate of the United States shall be composed of two Senators from each State, elected by the people thereof, for six years; and each Senator shall have one vote. The electors in each State shall have the qualifications requisite for electors of (voters for) the most numerous branch of the State legislatures.

**Section 2** When vacancies happen in the representation of any State in the Senate, the executive authority of such State shall issue writs of election to fill such vacancies: Provided, that the legislature of any State may empower the executive thereof to make temporary appointments until the people fill vacancies by election as the legislature may direct.

**Section 3** This amendment shall not be so construed as to affect the election or term of any Senator chosen before it becomes valid as part of the Constitution.

### AMENDMENT XVIII (1919, repealed 1933) (Prohibition)

**Section 1** *After one year from the ratification of this article the manufacture, sale, or transportation of intoxicating liquors within, the importation thereof into, or the exportation thereof from the United States, and all territory subject to the jurisdiction thereof, for beverage purposes, is hereby prohibited.*

**Section 2** *The Congress and the several States shall have concurrent power to enforce this article by appropriate legislation.*

**Section 3** *This article shall be inoperative unless it shall have been ratified as an amendment to the Constitution by the legislatures of the several States, as provided by the Constitution, within seven years from the date of the submission thereof to the States by the Congress.*

### AMENDMENT XIX (1920) (Voting rights for women)

**Section 1** The right of citizens of the United States to vote shall not be denied or abridged by the United States or by any State on account of sex.

**Section 2** The Congress shall have the power to enforce this article by appropriate legislation.

### AMENDMENT XX (1933) (The President's term of office)

**Section 1** The terms of the President and the Vice-President shall end at noon on the 20th day of January, and the terms of Senators and Representatives at noon on the 3rd day of January, of the year in which such terms would have ended if this article had not been ratified; and the terms of their successors shall then begin.

(The start of sessions of Congress)

**Section 2** The Congress shall assemble at least once in every year, and such meeting shall begin at noon on the 3rd day of January, unless they shall by law appoint a different day.

(Presidential succession)

**Section 3** If, at the time fixed for the beginning of the term of the President, the President-elect shall have died, the Vice-President-elect shall become President. If a President shall not have been chosen before the time fixed for the beginning of his term, or if the President-elect shall have failed to qualify, then the Vice-President-elect shall act as President until a President shall have qualified; and the Congress may by law provide for the case wherein neither a President-elect nor a Vice-President-elect shall have qualified, declaring who shall then act as President, or the manner in which one who is to act shall be selected, and such persons shall act accordingly until a President or Vice-President shall have qualified.

**Section 4** The Congress may by law provide for the case of the death of any of the persons from whom the House of Representatives may choose a President whenever the right of choice shall have devolved upon them, and for the case of the death of any of the persons from whom the Senate may choose a Vice-President whenever the right of choice shall have devolved upon them.

**Section 5** Sections 1 and 2 shall take effect on the 15th day of October following the ratification of this article.

**Section 6** This article shall be inoperative unless it shall have been ratified as an amendment to the Constitution by the legislatures of three-quarters of the several States within seven years from the date of its submission.

## AMENDMENT XXI (1933) (Repeal of prohibition)

**Section 1** The eighteenth article of amendment to the Constitution of the United States is hereby repealed.

**Section 2** The transportation or importation into any State, Territory, or Possession of the United States for delivery or use therein of intoxicating liquors, in violation of the laws thereof, is hereby prohibited.

**Section 3**  This article shall be inoperative unless it shall have been ratified as an amendment to the Constitution by conventions in the several States, as provided in the Constitution, within seven years from the date of submission thereof to the States by the Congress.

### AMENDMENT XXII (1951)  (Term limits for the President, 2 terms or 10 years)

**Section 1**  No person shall be elected to the office of President more than twice, and no person who has held the office of President, or acted as President, for more than two years of a term to which some other person was elected President shall be elected to the office of President more than once. But this article shall not apply to any person holding the office of President when this article was proposed by the Congress, and shall not prevent any person who may be holding the office of President, or acting as President, during the term within which this article becomes operative from holding the office of President or acting as President during the remainder of such term.

**Section 2**  This article shall be inoperative unless it shall have been ratified as an amendment to the Constitution by the legislatures of three-quarters of the several States within seven years from the date of its submission to the States by the Congress.

### AMENDMENT XXIII (1961)  (Electoral College votes for the District of Columbia)

**Section 1**  The District constituting the seat of Government of the United States shall appoint in such manner as the Congress may direct:
    A number of electors of President and Vice-President equal to the whole number of Senators and Representatives in Congress to which the District would be entitled if it were a State, but in no event more than the least populous State; they shall be in addition to those appointed by the States, but they shall be considered for the purposes of the election of President and Vice-President, to be electors appointed by a State; and they shall meet in the District and perform such duties as provided by the twelfth article of amendment.

**Section 2**  The Congress shall have the power to enforce this article by appropriate legislation.

### AMENDMENT XXIV (1964)  (Prohibition of poll taxes)

**Section 1**  The right of citizens of the United States to vote in any primary or other election for President or Vice-President, for electors for President or Vice-President, or for Senator or Representative in Congress, shall not be denied or abridged by the United States or any State by reason of failure to pay any poll tax or other tax.

**Section 2** The Congress shall have the power to enforce this article by appropriate legislation.

### AMENDMENT XXV (1967) (Presidential succession)

**Section 1** In the case of the removal of the President from office or of his death or resignation, the Vice-President shall become President.

**Section 2** Whenever there is a vacancy in the office of the Vice-President, the President shall nominate a Vice-President who shall take office upon confirmation by a majority vote of both Houses of Congress.

**Section 3** Whenever the President transmits to the President *pro tempore* of the Senate and the Speaker of the House of Representatives his written declaration that he is unable to discharge the powers and duties of this office, and until he transmits to them a written declaration to the contrary, such powers and duties shall be discharged by the Vice-President as Acting President.

**Section 4** Whenever the Vice-President and a majority of either the principal officers of the executive departments or of such other body as Congress may by law provide, transmit to the President *pro tempore* of the Senate and the Speaker of the House of Representatives their written declaration that the President is unable to discharge the powers and duties of his office, the Vice-President shall immediately assume the powers and duties of the office as Acting President.

Thereafter, when the President transmits to the President *pro tempore* of the Senate and the Speaker of the House of Representatives his written declaration that no inability exists, he shall resume the powers and duties of his office unless the Vice-President and a majority of either the principal officers of the executive department(s) or of such other body as Congress may by law provide, transmit within four days to the President *pro tempore* of the Senate and the Speaker of the House of Representatives their written declaration that the President is unable to discharge the powers and duties of his office. Thereupon Congress shall decide the issue, assembling within forty-eight hours for that purpose if not in session. If the Congress, within twenty-one days after receipt of the latter written declaration, or, if Congress is not in session, within twenty-one days after Congress is required to assemble, determines by two-thirds vote of both Houses that the President is unable to discharge the powers and duties of his office, the Vice-President shall continue to discharge the same as Acting President; otherwise, the President shall resume the powers and duties of his office.

### AMENDMENT XXVI (1971)  (Voting rights for young people)

**Section 1** The right of citizens of the United States, who are eighteen years of age or older, to vote shall not be denied or abridged by the United States or by any State on account of age.

**Section 2** The Congress shall have the power to enforce this article by appropriate legislation.

### AMENDMENT XXVII (1992)  (Timing of congressional pay raises)

No law varying the compensation for the service of Senators and Representatives shall take effect until an election of Representatives shall have intervened.

# Index